Vermont
AN EXPLORER'S GUIDE

Vermont

AN EXPLORER'S GUIDE

Christina Tree & Peter Jennison

The Countryman Press
Woodstock, Vermont

Note to the reader: none of the entries included in any volume of the Explorer's Guide Series have been paid for.

Library of Congress Cataloging-in-Publication Data

Tree, Christina.
  Vermont, an explorer's guide / Christina Tree and Peter Jennison.
—3rd ed.
    p. cm.
  Includes index.
  ISBN 0-88150-110-7 (pbk.) : $14.95
  1. Vermont—Description and travel—1981—Guide books.
I. Jennison, Peter S.   II. Title.
F47.3.T73 1988
917.43'0443—dc19   87-32083
                                                                    CIP

Maps by Richard Widhu

Cover design by Frank Lieberman

Cover photograph by Winston Pote
Back cover photograph of Basin Harbor, courtesy of the Vermont Travel Division

The publisher gratefully acknowledges the efforts of those intrepid folks who helped to steer this Explorer's Guide over the rough spots: Roy Kaufman (Capital City Press), Ann Aspell and Anne Davis, Andrea Chesman and Richard Ruane (Little Chicago Editorial Services), Ron Doucette, Kelly Kingsbury and Arvilla Young (NK Graphics), Rebecca Davison and Susan Mesner (Kailyard Associates). And a somewhat grudging word of thanks to the 3M Company, manufacturer of Post-it® Note Pads.

Printed in the United States of America

Contents

Introduction: "Contrary Country"

Welcome to Vermont, the Switzerland of North America (as Lord Bryce, the British ambassador and historian called it in 1909), and to this third edition of the most comprehensive guide to its assets and charms, hidden and obvious. It is intended for Vermont residents, as well as visitors. No other portrait of the state gathers so much practical information between two covers.

The book divides Vermont into areas, whose boundaries usually coincide with those of the local chambers of commerce. Each section begins with a verbal snapshot of the surroundings and historical vignettes, followed by words of guidance, getting around, things to see and do, and descriptions of just about every legal form of recreation—skiing, horseback riding, sailing, hiking, swimming, canoeing, golf, or whatever else is handy. Then come capsule descriptions, with prices, of places to stay, representing some 90 percent of the lodgings in a given area, followed by suggestions for dining or eating out, selective shopping hints, entertainment and special events.

In the two previous editions of this book, we hadn't thought it becoming to mention that none of our entries has been paid for. But, time and again as we crisscrossed the state checking out inns for this edition, we were asked, "How much will it cost me to be listed?" When we replied, "nothing," we often heard, "You've made my day—getting anything that helps your business for free these days is a real treat." Or, "We paid $250 to be mentioned in one bed and breakfast guide and no one even bothered to stop by and see what we're like."

(Please note two things: the prices cited in the book are those available at press time in late 1987 and may have escalated somewhat since then; and that many of the inns described here automatically add a 10 or 15 percent service charge to their bills, as well as the 6 percent state rooms and meals tax.)

Vermont's popularity as a summer resort for the city-weary means that you might want to look outside the prime attractions of Manchester, Woodstock and Stowe (unless you haven't ever visited them) and seek out the less-traveled areas like the verdant lower

Champlain valley, the pristine hill villages, the Islands, and, of course, the Northeast Kingdom.

Every Green Mountain village offers something of interest: an unusual small inn, antique or craft shop, cheese maker, gourmet restaurant, or simply vistas of such breathtaking beauty that they demand mention. And Vermont is full of surprises. No matter how many trips a visitor makes, the unexpected is always around the corner: a spectacular view, a splendid house or barn, even a cluster of tarpaper shacks in a hollow of appalling poverty within two miles of a posh summer or winter playground for the affluent.

Today's visitor is more likely than not to be welcomed by ex-visitors. Innkeepers, shopkeepers and craftspeople tend to be here by choice rather than birth: 38.8 percent of the state's population of 512,000 came "from away." This post-World War II stage of Vermont's colorful history is as worthy of note as its 14 years as an independent republic.

The years of sovereignty, between 1777–1791, stamped Vermont with the indelible "contrary country" brand, to borrow a phrase of the late Ralph Nading Hill. Some contemporary Vermonters, surveying the murky horizons of the 1990s, mutter conspiratorially about secession. But when basically conservative Vermonters voted in nearly 200 town meetings in 1982 for a bilateral nuclear arms freeze, they were not just being ornery. They acted traditionally, in the spirit that animated Ethan Allen's Rabelaisian Green Mountain Boys, who wrested independence from the grip of Hampshiremen and 'Yorkers as well as from "The Cruel Minestereal Tools of George ye 3d"; and in the abolitionist fervor that impelled Vermonters to flock to the colors in record numbers when President Lincoln called for troops to preserve the Union. They voted their consciences with much the same zeal when, in both World Wars, the legislature declared war on Germany, in effect, before the United States did; and with the prescience that prompted Vermont to lead the nation in the enactment of protective land-use laws.

The portrait of the legendary Vermont Yankee—frugal, wary, taciturn, sardonically humorous—has faded somewhat in today's homogenized, shopping-center culture. The Vermonter has made some concessions to the microchip age, but as Ralph Nading Hill, the Vermont historian, wrote in *Yankee Kingdom*, "his individuality has not yet been eroded away. And the character of the countryside that Bernard DeVoto said is every American's second home remains largely the same. The valley towns, white and serene, seem to have become a universal symbol of nostalgia—of belonging somewhere, even to those who have seen only pictures of them reproduced on

In Memory of William French,
Son to Mr Nathaniel French; Who
Was Shot at Westminster. March $\bar{y}$ 13th,
1775, by the hands of Cruel Ministereal tools
of Georg $\bar{y}$ 3d; in the Corthouse, at a 11 a Clock
at Night; in the 22d year of his Age.

Here William French his Body lies.
For Murder his Blood for Vengance cries.
King Georg the third his Tory crew
tha with a bawl his head Shot threw.
For Liberty and his Countrys Good.
he Lost his Life his Dearest blood.

Headstone in the Westminster burying ground

calendars. The reason is, perhaps, that the people of a rootless age find something admirable about a slice of hillcountry that has resisted being made over into the latest fashionable image."

A principal reason for this sense of permanence is that, prudently, Vermonters have not torn down the past; rather, abandoned farm houses have been restored, and in a score of towns, adaptive preservation techniques have been thoughtfully used to convert obsolete woolen mills into enclosed markets. The former State Penitentiary in Windsor, once the oldest in the country still in use, has been transformed into low-income housing units. The post-war infusion of light industry, moreover, has been carefully sited in ways that leave the surrounding landscape mostly undisturbed.

As the flatland author, born in Hawaii and raised in New York City, Chris Tree defends her expertise about Vermont. Her infatuation with the state began in college. "The college was in Massachusetts, but one of my classmates was a native Vermonter whose father ran a general store and whose mother knows the name of every flower, bird and mushroom. I jumped at her invitation to come 'home' or to 'camp' and have since spent far more time in Vermont than my friend. As a travel writer for *The Boston Globe*, I have spent nineteen years writing newspaper stories about Vermont towns, inns, ski areas and people. I interviewed John Kenneth Galbraith about Newfane, Pearl Buck on Danby. I rode the Vermont Bicentennial Train, froze a toe on one of the first inn-to-inn ski treks, camped on the Long Trail and in state parks, paddled a canoe down the Connecticut, slid over Lake Champlain on an ice boat, and soared over the Mad River Valley in a glider. I have also tramped through the woods collecting sap, ridden many miles with Vermont Transit, led a foliage tour, collided with a tractor, and broken down in a variety of spots ranging from Stowe's Main Street to the village of Marshfield—'Can't fix it here. No way for you to get out of here. No place to stay either.'

"Of all my experiences, the most prized has been getting to know Vermonters, something which I find increasingly difficult in resort areas, and one reason why I frequently head for the rolling farm country on the high plateaus east of the Green Mountains in central Vermont and in the Northeast Kingdom. The other reason is that rental cottages or 'camps' are far cheaper off the beaten path, a consideration when you travel as a family of five. Which isn't to say that we don't enjoy Stowe, Woodstock, the Mad River Valley and Southern Vermont. My excuse for remaining a flatlander is an embarrassment of riches in both senses: aside from lacking the funds to move, we simply cannot decide which part of Vermont to move to."

Peter Jennison, the "born again" Vermonter, returned to his native heath in 1971, because, like many latter-day immigrants, he was tired of working in New York City and being held hostage by the New Haven Railroad. When he is asked "How long have you lived in Vermont?" he is apt to reply, "Since 1769," thinking of the miller, John Saxe, who settled in Highgate. Indeed, he is the fifth generation to have been born in the same room in the family's former Swanton dairy farm. Since returning to Vermont, he has founded a publishing company ("necessity being the mother of ingenuity"), edited and published the *1976–77 Vermont Bicentennial Guide*, and served on several town boards. "I haven't done half the things Chris has," he admits, "but in over fifty years I have almost qualified to join the 251 Club—whose numbers aspire to visit every town and gore—and I've seen how the state has been transformed from an almost wholly agrarian society to a far more sophisticated place to live, a land of infinite variety where people still mind their own business. We have freedom *and* unity—the state motto."

Peter added a quotation from Charles T. Morrissey's *Vermont: A History*: ". . . the entire state is a reminder of the American past, a remnant from the agrarian culture which once we were. It is understandable why Americans come here from other states in search of the mystic chords of memories, and why some want to build a fence around Vermont in order to preserve it as a specimen of Americana, a national park of the Yankee spirit which infused our national psyche."

The authors wish to thank the staffs of the Vermont Travel Division (especially the late Bill Braum) and of local chambers of commerce for their assistance in providing information for the book, and express their boundless gratitude, individually and collectively, to all of their Countryman Press colleagues, particularly Gordon Pine and Louis Wilder, for their encouragement, support and patience. They are very grateful to Reed Cherington, of Brownington, who helped research and expand the coverage of the Northeast Kingdom.

Christina Tree
Peter S. Jennison

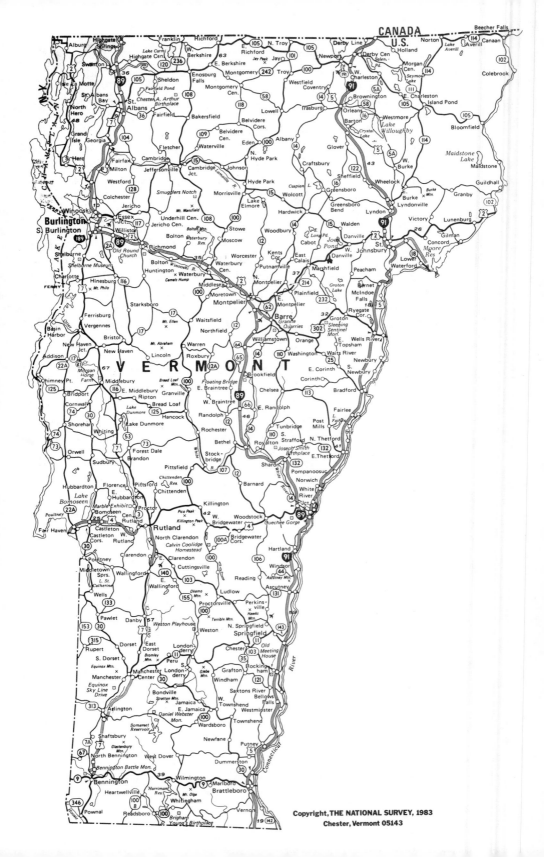

Copyright, THE NATIONAL SURVEY, 1983
Chester, Vermont 05143

What's Where in Vermont

AGRICULTURAL FAIRS "Vermont Agricultural Fairs and Field Days," a pamphlet available from the Vermont Department of Agriculture, Montpelier, lists the major events, beginning with the **Vermont Maple Festival** in St. Albans in April, and filling every weekend in July, August, and September. The most famous are the **Champlain Valley Exposition,** Winooski, around Labor Day; **Orleans County Fair** in Barton (five days) and the **Bondville Fair** (two days), both in late August; the **Vermont State Fair** in Rutland (nine days, the biggest); and the **World's Fair** in Tunbridge (four days, the most colorful of all).

AIR SERVICE **Business Express** (Delta Connection), Burlington to Boston: 1-800-221-1212.

Continental connects Burlington with most major US cities: 1-800-525-1280.

Eastern Express connects Burlington, Rutland, Lebanon and Keene, New Hampshire (serving much of Southern Vermont and the Connecticut River Valley) with Boston: 1-800-327-8376.

Piedmont and **Piedmont Commuter** connects Burlington with most US points: 1-800-251-5720/348-7833.

United Airlines connects Burlington with most US points via Chicago; 1-800-241-6522.

US Air connects Burlington with most East Coast destinations: 1-800-428-4322.

AMTRAK Regretably, as of the time of this writing, AMTRAK service in Vermont has been suspended. Necessary track repairs for passenger safety and peace of mind are slated to begin sometime in 1988, and we hope in a future edition to be able to report that the "Montrealer" is running once more. Stay tuned. Meanwhile, passengers from points south may detrain in Springfield, Massachusetts and use "AMBUS, connecting motor coach service" for the train's former stops (see chart). For further information call 1-800-872-7245. There is also **New York to Montreal** service up the New York shore of Lake Champlain with ferry connections to the Vermont shore, the most practical of these being at Port Kent, with frequent summer ferry service to Burlington.

ANTIQUARIAN BOOKSELLERS "Old Books in the Green Mountain State," a listing of the 40 or more current members of the Vermont Antiquarian Booksellers Asso-

AMBUS Stops	Arrives (Going North)	Arrives (Going South)
Springfield (MA)	3:55 PM	2:54 PM
Northhampton (MA)	4:30	1:45
Brattleboro	5:20	1:05
Bellows Falls	5:50	12:40
White River Jct.	6:35	11:25 AM
Montpelier	8:25	10:15
Waterbury	8:45	9:55
Burlington	9:15	9:25

ciation, is available from the secretary of VABA: Michael Dunn, PO Box 436, Newport 03855.

The best known of these dealers is **Tuttle Antiquarian Books,** a part of the Rutland/Tokyo publishing house specializing in genealogies and local histories, with 20,000 books to browse through. The most unusual browsers' haven is the **Haunted Mansion Bookshop** in Cuttingsville. The VABA has an annual fair at the Woodstock Inn the first or second Sunday of August.

ANTIQUING   A pamphlet guide, "Antiquing in Vermont," listing more than 120 members of the Vermont Antiques Dealers' Association is available by sending a self-addressed #10 envelope to Barbara Mills, Route 5, Hartland, VT 05048. Major concentrations of dealers can be found in **Bennington, Brandon, Burlington, Middlebury, Manchester,** and **Woodstock.**

APPLES   During fall harvest season there is a demand not only for bushel baskets already filled with apples but also for empty baskets and the chance to climb a ladder and fill it with MacIntosh, Red Delicious, or others among the many varieties of apples grown in Vermont—primarily in the **Champlain Valley** and in the **Lower Connecticut River Valley** between Springfield and Putney. Detailed listings can be found under descriptions of these areas and by requesting the "Vermont Apples" pamphlet from Vermont Department of Agriculture, 116 State Street, State Office Building, Montpelier, VT 05602.

AREA CODE   The area code for all of Vermont is 802, the reason why we have omitted listing it at all within the text.

ART GALLERIES   Vermont's principal collections of art (painting, sculpture, and decorative arts) are found in the **Bennington Museum** (works by Grandma Moses), the **Robert Hull Fleming Museum** at the University of Vermont, Burlington; the **Christian A. Johnson Memorial Gallery** at Middlebury College; the **Athenaeum** in St. Johnsbury; the **Shelburne Museum** in Shelburne; the **Chaffee Art Gallery,** Rutland; the **Southern Vermont Art Center,** Manchester; the **Thomas Waterman Wood Art Gallery,** Montpelier; the **Dana House,** Woodstock (John Taylor Arms); and in such private galleries as the **Peel Gallery of Fine Art** in Danby, **Gallery Two** in Woodstock, the **Tontine Gallery** in East Barnard, and **North Star** in Grafton. Galleries are also listed in "300 Things to See and Do in Vermont," issued by the Preservation Trust of Vermont, and available free from the State Travel Division.

AUCTIONS   Most major upcoming auctions are announced in the Thursday edition of the Vermont newspapers, with a listing of items that will be up for bid. Auctions may be scheduled at any time, however, during summer months, advertised primarily on local bulletin boards and in shop windows. Among well-known auctioneers and auction houses: William Dupras of Randolph Center; Butch Sutherland, Woodstock; C. W. Gray of East Thetford, every Monday night, year-round (livestock); Arthur Hicks, Hick's Commission Sales, Morrisville.

BALLOONING   Inquire at the Stoweflake Resort, in Stowe (253-7355). The State's major ballooning events are the **Lake Champlain Balloon Festival** held in early June, and the **Annual Balloon Festival** in Quechee, in late June.

BARNS   Many barns along the highways and byways have distinctive touches, such as ornate Victorian cupolas, and still more are connected to farmhouses in the "extended" architectural style as shelter for the farmer's trips before dawn in deep snow.

Just a dozen round barns survive in Vermont, all built between 1899 and World War I. The concept of the round barn is thought to have originated with the Shakers in Hancock, Massachusetts, where the original stone barn, built in 1824, is now the centerpiece of a museum. The Vermont survivors include: the **Moore barn** in East Barnet; the **Hastings barn** in Waterford; the **Metcalf barn** (Robillard

Flats) in Irasburg; the **Parker barn** in Grand Isle, converted into a housing center for the elderly; two barns in Coventry; the **Powers barn** in Lowell; the **Parker barn** in North Troy; one in Enosburg Falls; **Southwick's** in East Calais; and the **Joslin round barn** Waitsfield. Note that the name ascribed to each barn belongs to the builder rather than to present owners. Round barn addicts should check at local general stores for location and secure permission to photograph the structures.

Among other Vermont barns open to the public are the vast five-story, 416-foot-long **Norman-style Farm Barn,** and the impressive stable and carriage house at **Shelburne Farms** in Shelburne. The round barn once in Passumpsic has been moved to the Shelburne Museum.

BED & BREAKFAST B & Bs are listed under their respective locations in this book and new ones appear each month, replacing the old guest house (which serves no meals at all) in towns and the "farm house vacation" (which traditionally serves all three meals) in the country. The B & Bs that we have inspected range from working farms to historic mansions, from $25 to $125 per room.

BICYCLING Vermont is considered *the* state in which to go bicycle touring. It's estimated that in 1987 some 15,000 pedal pushers, representing a wide span in ages (but not counting camp groups) and biking abilities, joined organized tours through Vermont. **Vermont Bicycle Touring** (better known as VBT) introduced the whole notion of guided bike tours for adults back in 1971. Its founder, John Freidin, is the author of *25 Bicycle Tours in Vermont* (Backcountry Publications), the bible of independent bicyclists. Now owned by Bill Perry, VBT (Box 711, Bristol 05443) offers a choice of more than 50 different tours (varying lengths) on more than 350 days, spring through fall. At latest count there were 9 cycle touring groups based in Vermont, most furnishing equipment, guides, a support van (the "sag wag"), and lodging at country inns. **Vermont Country Cyclers** (Box 145, Loomis Hill Road,

Waterbury Center 05677) is the other big operator and features elegant lodging. **Bike Vermont** (PO Box 75, Grafton 05146, and Box 207, Woodstock 05091, headed by Bob McElwain, features smaller groups than the other two. In the past few years touring options have been increased by companies like **Vermont Mountain Bike Tours** (Tom Yennerell, PO Box 526, Pittsfield 05762), **Back Road** CRAFTSBURY Common 05827), **New England Bicycle Tours** (John McKeon, PO Box 26, Randolph 05060) and **Outdoor Tours Unlimited** (Bryan Liss, Maple Corner, PO Box 97, Calais 05648) feature wide-tire, sturdy-framed mountain bikes, ideal for exploring dirt roads. There are also two outfits—**Bicycling Inn to Inn** (c/o Churchill House Inn, RD 3, Brandon 05733) and **Cycle Inn Vermont** (c/o Okemo Inn, RFD 1, Box 133, Ludlow 05149)—composed of innkeepers whose establishments are a comfortable bike ride from each other. Participants are largely on their own but rental equipment is available and baggage is transferred from inn to inn.

We should note that there are eight **American Youth Hostels** in Vermont offering spartan lodging and facilities for making your own meals (see *Hostels*). Stowe's bike path and rental mountain bikes make it an ideal place to sample the sport.

BIRDING A handy booklet "Check List for Birds of Vermont" is available from either the Green Mountain Audubon Society, Box 33, Burlington 05401, or Vermont Fish & Game, Montpelier 05602. Outstanding birding areas include the **Missisquoi National Wildlife Refuge** in Swanton and the 4,970-acre **Victory Basin** east of St. Johnsbury. The 230-acre **Green Mountain Audubon Nature Center** in Huntington (434-3068) is open year-round Tuesday–Friday, 9–5 and weekends 1–4.

The **Vermont Institute of Natural Science** (457-2779), Woodstock 05091, sponsors bird walks in all parts of the state, frequently led by Walter G. Ellison, author of "A Guide to Bird Finding In Vermont," available from VINS at $5.95 and $1.50 mailing charge per copy.

BOATING The pamphlet "Vermont Vacation Guide," available from the Vermont Travel Division (see *Information*) includes an annually updated list of boat (motor, sail, and canoe) rentals. Also see *Canoeing, Cruises,* and *White Water.* The Official State Map (also see *Information*) notes public boat launch areas. A booklet "Laws and Regulations Governing the Use and Registration of Motorboats" is available from the Vermont Department of Public Safety, Marine Division, Montpelier 05602.

BOOKS For a complete bibliography, write for the "**Books about Vermont**" catalogue, from the Vermont Historical Society, 109 State Street, Montpelier 05602. In addition to the books we mention in specific fields or on particular subjects, here are some of the most useful current titles: *The Vermont Atlas and Gazetteer,* compiled and published by David De-Lorme and Company, Freeport, Maine; *Vermont: A History* by Charles Morrissey (W. W. Norton); *Vermont Place Names: Footprints in History* by Esther Swift (Stephen Greene Press); *Lake Champlain: Key to Liberty* by Ralph Nading Hill (Countryman/Backcountry); "**Contrary Country**" by Ralph Nading Hill (Shelburne Museum); and the three gorgeously illustrated albums put out by *Vermont Life Vermont, a Special World, Vermont For Every Season,* and *The Vermont Experience; Vermonters* by Fox and Tinney (Countryman Press). For children, *Vermont, The State with the Storybook Past* by Cora Cheney (New England Press) is the best. Keith Jennison's classic collections of Vermont humor, like *Yup . . . Nope & Other Vermont Dialogues* (Countryman Press) are in most bookstores and many gift shops. A basic reference directory is *The Vermont Year Book,* published annually by the National Survey, Chester.

BOOKSTORES There are good general bookstores in Barre, Bennington, Brattleboro, Bridgewater, Burlington, Chester, Essex Junction, Hardwick, Londonderry, Lyndonville, Manchester, Middlebury, Montpelier, Morrisville, Newport, Randolph, Rutland, St. Albans, Shelburne,

South Burlington, Springfield, Stowe, Waitsfield, Winooski, and Woodstock. Several of them with special significance, like **Johnny Appleseed, Bear Pond, Northshire,** and the **Vermont Bookshop** are mentioned in the text under Selective Shopping in their respective towns. The most complete stock of Vermontiana is on sale in the **Vermont Historical Society Shop** in Montpelier.

BUS SERVICE Vermont Transit. For a current timetable contact Vermont Transit Co., Inc. (864-6811 or 1-800-451-3292), 135 St. Paul Street, Burlington 05401. The major routes are: (1) up the western side of the State from New York City and Albany via Bennington, Rutland, and Burlington to Montreal; (2) from Boston via White River Junction and Burlington to Montreal; (3) Boston to Burlington via Rutland: (4) Quebec to New York City with connections to Boston via Newport and St. Johnsbury. Read the timetable carefully and you will find most corners of the state of Vermont—and a number elsewhere in northern New England—are served. Children under 12 years travel half price; one child under five can travel free. Vermont Transit Tours, geared to Vermont residents who want out for a day (to Boston's Quincy Market) or weekend (to New York City or Montreal) or more than two weeks (Florida and other points south) are described in newsletters available from the Burlington office.

CAMPS, for children. There are 55 summer camps for boys and girls in the state; for a listing contact the Vermont Camping Association, PO Box 133, Fairlee 05045.

CAMPGROUNDS Private. A listing of the 90 private campgrounds that belong to the Vermont Association of Private Campground Owners and Operators (VAPCOO) can be found on the state map; a brochure detailing the locations, facilities, services, and numbers of sites at each is available from Lake Dunmore Kampersville, PO Box 214, Middlebury 05753.
    State Campgrounds. Thirty-six fine campgrounds are maintained by the Department of Forests, Parks and Recreation

(244-8711) in state parks in nearly every corner of Vermont. They offer more than 2,000 campsites, many with lean-to shelters, none with hook-ups. There are two classes of parks: Class A, which have beaches and swimming, and Class B, which do not. From May through September reservations may be made by phone, provided it is followed by full payment, or by payment with the reservation form in the Vermont State Parks brochure, available from the Department of Forests, Parks and Recreation, Montpelier 05602. Anytime after January 3, a campsite can be reserved for six days to two weeks by writing to the park ranger listed in the brochure. Reservations for less than six days cannot be accepted before June 1.

The State Parks brochure describes each park, also gives details on group camping sites. Vermont State Park campsites are all screened by trees from neighboring sites, and are well-maintained; many parks have organized programs: hikes, campfire sings, films and lectures. Most parks are relatively uncrowded, especially midweek when the only sites likely to be filled are in Branbury, Stillwater, Groton Forest, and Lake St. Catherine. On hot weekends in July and August the following parks are also apt to be crowded: Branbury, Burton Island, Kill Kare, Crystal Lake, Lake St. Catherine, Sand Bar, Shaftsbury, and Silver Lake. We have provided details, including phone numbers, for each park as it appears within the text. A listing can also be found on the state map. A separate pamphlet, "Guide to Primitive Camping on State Lands," is available from the Department of Forests, Parks and Recreation.

Green Mountain National Forest Campgrounds. Within the 300,000-acre preserve, 94 fine, well-developed campsites are offered. They are available on a first-come, first-serve basis for a maximum 14-day period at a modest charge, posted at the entrance of each area. Camping is also permitted, without fee or prior permission, virtually anywhere on National Forest land. Before pitching your tent, however, we recommend that you visit one of the three district ranger of-fices, in Manchester Center, Middlebury, or Rochester, and inquire about proper places to camp. A free mini-map is available from the Green Mountain National Forest (775-2579), PO Box 519, Rutland 05701.

U. S. Army Corps of Engineers. The Department of the Army, New England Division, Corps of Engineers, has constructed two camping areas in Vermont. The Winhall Brook Camping Area at Ball Mountain Lake in Jamaica offers 108 campsites near flush toilets, showers and swimming, free on a first-come first-serve basis; for details contact the Basin Manager, Upper Connecticut River Basin Office, North Springfield Lake, 98 Reservoir Road, Springfield 05156. The Corps of Engineers also built the 30-site camping area of Quechee Gorge near the North Hartland Dam, now maintained by the State.

CANOEING   Organized canoe trips have increased dramatically in recent years. For details, contact:

Battenkill Canoe, Box 65, Route 313, West Arlington 05250 (day trips, inn-to-inn tours throughout the state); **Canoe Vermont,** c/o Mad River Canoe, PO Box 610, Waitsfield 05250 (on the Winooski, the Batten Kill, Otter Creek, and the Connecticut featuring lodging in inns, also "pole and pedal" tours); **Clearwater,** Route 100, Waitsfield 05673; **Canoe the Connecticut,** c/o Inwood Manor, East Barnet 05821; **The Mustard Seed,** Dam Road, Box 77, Chittenden 05737; **Outdoor Tours Unlimited,** Maple Corner, PO Box 97, Calais 05648; **Vermont Voyageur Expeditions,** Route 242, Montgomery Center 05471.

Helpful publications include: **AMC River Guide—New Hampshire/Vermont,** good for detailed information on canoeable rivers, available from the Appalachian Mountain Club, 5 Joy Street, Boston, MA 02108. "Summer Canoe Trips in Vermont," a one-page overview is free from the Vermont Department of Forest, Parks and Recreation, Waterbury 05676. "Vermont Guide to Fishing Map," free from Vermont Fish & Wildlife Department, Waterbury 05676 notes falls, rapids, boulder fields, dams and other potential dangers. *Canoe Camping Vermont & New*

Hampshire Rivers (Backcountry Publications) is a handy guide. "**Winooski River Canoe Guide**" is $2 from the Winooski Valley Park District, Ethan Allen Homestead, Burlington 05401. (Also see *White Water*.)

CANOE RENTALS   Rentals are available from the Canoe outfitters listed above and from the boat rental sources listed in the free "Vermont Vacation Guide" available from the Travel Division (see *Information*).

CHEESE   A century ago, almost every Vermont town had its cheese factory to which farmers brought their daily surplus milk. Just one of these factories survives, a picturesque three-story wooden building in Healdville: **Crowley Cheese**, the oldest, continually operated cheese factory in the country. The Crowley family began making cheese in this area in 1824 and occupied the factory until 1966, when retired educator Randolph Smith took over, perpetuating the old technique of kneading the curds by hand into popcorn-size pieces, thus producing a smoother, moister cheese than other cheddars. **Cabot Farmer's Co-op** in northern Vermont is a modern plant producing 12 million pounds of cheese a year, maintaining a slick visitors center with a video orientation, plant tour and gift shop. **Grafton Village Cheese Company** in Grafton had its beginning around 1890 and was resurrected by the Windham Foundation in 1966; visitors view the cheese-making from outside, through a picture window. **The Plymouth Cheese Corp.**, founded in 1890 by Col. John Coolidge, father of President Coolidge, is now operated by John Coolidge, son of the president. The factory shop is open (see Plymouth) year-round, producing an old-fashioned Vermont Granular Curd Cheese. At **Shelburne Farms** (open daily, year-round), near Burlington, Alec Webb makes cheddar from a single herd of Brown Swiss cows. In New Haven, **Orb Weaver Farm** produces a creamy, aged Colby-type cheese made in small batches, entirely by hand, (available in 2 lb wheels and one pound waxed wedges). In Swanton, **Lucille Farm Products,** a family-owned business, has been making mozzarella, provolone, ricotta and feta cheeses since 1938; in Richmond, **Richmond Cheese Company** also makes mozzarella and provolone; in Hinesburg, **International Cheese Company** produces a line of traditional cheeses; and in Enosburg Falls, **Franklin County Cheese Corp.** produces bakers' cheese and fresh cheesecake. Unfortunately, the state's two goat cheese producers—Vermont Butter & Cheese Co. and Guilford Cheese Company—do not sell from their doors.

CHILDREN (especially for) **Alpine Slides** delight children of all ages at Bromley (where there is also a **Mountain Rafting Ride**) as well as Pico and Stowe.

Alpine Lifts, which operate in summer, are also a way of hoisting small legs and feet to the top of some of Vermont's most spectacular summits. **Mt. Mansfield,** Vermont's highest peak is accessible via the Gondola. **Killington Peak,** second highest in the state, can be reached via chairlift on weekdays and by a 3½mile gondola ride on weekends. **Jay Peak,** commanding as dramatic a view as the others, is accessible on a smooth-riding tram.

Santa's Land in Putney is the only commercial attraction geared specifically to children.

The **Discovery Museum** in Essex Junction is a rewarding, hands-on experience; exhibits range from small animals and snakes through computers.

The **Shelburne Museum** has many exhibits that please youngsters, as does the **Fairbanks Planetarium and Museum,** St. Johnsbury, which is filled with stuffed animals, birds, and exhibits from near and far.

Skiing. Over the past few years, as ski areas have come to compete for family business, most ski resorts have developed special programs for children: see *For Children* under each ski area described in the text.

In summer some ski areas, notably Smugglers Notch and Bolton Valley, put on special programs for children, and at Killington, the Green Mountain Guild stages special children's productions. Also see *Farms* and *Railroad Excursions*.

Montpelier on the Move's "Fool's Fest"

CHRISTMAS TREES   A listing of Christmas tree growers, most of them cut-your-own places, is available from the Vermont Department of Agriculture, 116 State Street, Montpelier 05602.

COLLEGES   A brochure listing all the state's colleges, giving details of what is offered, is published by the Consortium of Vermont Colleges, available from the Vermont Travel Division (see *Information*).

COVERED BRIDGES   The State's 115 surviving covered bridges are marked on the official state map.

CRAFTS   More than 1,000 Vermonters make their living from craft work. There are also more than 100 retail craft outlets in the state, ranging from back kitchens to the two nonprofit **Vermont State Craft Centers,** one in Windsor (674-6729) and the other showcasing over 250 professionals, at Frog Hollow (388-4871), in Middlebury. Within this book we have described outstanding local craftspeople and crafts shops as they appear geographically. We have also included major crafts festivals. Among the most outstanding: in July, the **Woodstock Craftsmen's Fair; Burklyn Summer Fair of Vermont Arts & Crafts; The Killington Art Show; Art on the Mountain** at Haystack Ski Area in Wilmington; and the **Southern Vermont Craft Fair** in Manchester. In September: the **Stratton Arts Festival** (four weeks, until mid-October). In October, the **Mt. Snow Craft Fair,** and the **Fall Festival of Vermont Crafts** in Montpelier; and in November the **Burlington Craft Fair.**
    "Vermont Hand Crafters" a descriptive listing for the 280 members of this nonprofit organization is available from PO Box 9385, South Burlington 05403.

CRUISES   If you don't own a yacht there are still plenty of ways to get onto Vermont rivers and lakes. Possible excursions include the *Belle of Brattleboro* that sails up and down the Connecticut from Brattleboro; the *Spirit of Ethan Allen,* a paddle-wheeler-style excursion vessel based in Burlington; the *Mount Independence* from Whitehall; the schooner *Homer W.*

Dixon that sails Lake Champlain out of Burlington; *The Intrepid* from Malletts Bay; and both the *Mt. Mills* and the *Heather Sue* that sail on Lake Whitingham from Wilmington. For details check under respective locations in this book.

DINERS   Vermont will not disappoint diner buffs. Devotees will be cheered by the news that **Miss Bellows Falls Diner** was added to the Register of National Historic Places in 1983. Hearty meals of reasonable prices can be found at the **Miss Newport** (good coffee), East Main Street, Newport; at **Henry's Diner** (known for its Yankee pot roast, lobster roll, and generally good three squares), and at **The Oasis,** both on Bank Street, Burlington. The **Parkway Diner** at 1696 Williston Road, South Burlington is known for its Greek Salad, lobster roll, and Parkway Special: roast beef on pumpernickel roll. The **Lyndonville Diner** on Bond Street, Lyndonville, is admired for its pies (a breakfast special). **Blue Benn Diner,** 102 Hunt Street in Bennington, serves imaginative vegetarian as well as standard diner fare; both the **Green Mountain Diner,** Main Street in Barre, and the **Fairlee Diner,** North Main Street in Fairlee, are known for the best pies, soups, and generally good home-cooking in their areas. Add to these **Cindy's Diner** in St. Albans, **Don's Diner** in Bennington, **Jad's Family Diner** (try the turkey) in Brattleboro, and **Delaney's Country Girl Diner** in Chester.

EMERGENCIES   Emergency numbers are given on the inside cover of Vermont phone books. Within this book we have furnished the number of the medical facilities serving each area at the end of each chapter.

EVENTS   Almost every day of the year some special event is happening somewhere in Vermont. Usually it's something relatively small and friendly like a church supper, contra dance, community theatrical production, concert, or crafts fair. We have worked up our own *Calendar of Events* but would like to mention here that up-to-date, detailed listings of current events are available from the Vermont Travel Division, 134 State Street, Montpelier 05602. Check also in local weekly newspapers and area shopping guides.

FACTORY OUTLETS   Within the book, we have mentioned some, but not all of the factory outlets in the state of which we are aware. Our bias has been to favor distinctly made-in-Vermont products. Among our favorites: **Johnson Woolen Mills** (outstanding wool clothing for all ages) in Johnson; **Bennington Potters** (dinnerware, planters, etc.) in Bennington and Burlington; **Vermont Marble** in Proctor; **Weston Bowl Mill** in Weston; **Townshend Furniture** in Townshend; **Kennedy Bros.** (woodenware) in Vergennes; and **American Maple Products** in Newport. Vermont has its share of Dunham and Dexter shoe outlets.

"**Vermont Factory Outlets**" has been compiled by the Vermont Chamber of Commerce; it's available from the Vermont Travel Division, 134 State Street, Montpelier 05602.

FARMS   In 1987, Vermont had just 2,700 fulltime dairy farms (compared to 26,490 in 1945) and a scant 862,831 acres—out of the state's total 6 million acres—were being cultivated. Still, the farmhouse and barn are a symbol of Vermont to out-of-staters, and the highlight of a Vermont vacation for most children is a visit to the barn. A pamphlet guide to Vermont's "**Red Clover Trail**" lists the farms, orchards, and other agricultural operations that welcome visitors. Available from the Vermont Travel Division, 134 State Street, Montpelier 05602. Within this book, we have attempted to list farms that take in guests.

FARMERS' MARKETS   From mid-June to early October you can count on finding fresh vegetables, fruit, honey, and much more at farm prices in commercial centers throughout the state. Check the times and places in Burlington, Enosburg, Morrisville, Newport, St. Johnsbury, Fair Haven, Middlebury, Montpelier, Rutland, Brattleboro, Manchester, and Windsor. Current details about the farmers' markets are found in the "Vermont Vacation Guide"

and "Vermont Fruits & Vegetables" pamphlets; both are available from the Vermont Travel Division (see *Information*).

FARMSTANDS   The handy "Vermont Fruits & Vegetables" pamphlet contains descriptive listings of roadside stands as well as pick-your-own places, and farmers' markets. It's produced by the Vermont Department of Agriculture, 116 State Street, Montpelier 05602.

FERRIES   On Lake Champlain a number of car-carrying ferries ply back and forth between the Vermont and New York shores, offering splendid views of both the Green Mountains and the Adirondacks. The northernmost, the **Plattsburg Ferry,** crosses from Grand Isle, Vermont, on Route 314, (12 minutes). From Burlington the **Lake Champlain Ferries** (864-9804) cross to Port Kent, New York (1 hour). The **Essex Ferry** crosses from Route F-5 near Charlotte, Vermont, to Essex, New York (20 minutes). Check schedules for hours of operation and rates. All three of these are operated by the Lake Champlain Transportation Company, descendant of the line that was founded in 1828 and claims to be "the oldest steamboat company on earth." Near the southern end of the lake, the **Fort Ticonderoga Ferry** (897-7999) provides a scenic shortcut between Larrabees Point, Vermont, and Ticonderoga, New York. This small, car-carrying ferry makes the six-minute crossing continuously between 8 AM and 9 PM during the summer season and on a shorter schedule in spring and fall. Service runs from late April through the last Sunday in October. Officially, the "Fort Ti Ferry" has held the franchise from the New York and Vermont Legislatures since 1799, but records indicate the service was initiated by Lord Jeffery Amherst in 1757 for use of his soldiers in the campaigns against the French. Its boast is "serving people and their vehicles since Mozart was three years old."

FIDDLING   Vermont is the fiddling capital of the East. Fiddlers tend to include concert violinists, rural carpenters, farmers, and heavy equipment operators, who come from throughout the East to gather in beautiful natural settings. The season begins over the July 4 weekend with the **Annual Fiddler's Concert,** Kents Corner, Calais. They follow, in sequence; **Ryegate Fiddle Festival,** South Ryegate; **Cracker-barrel Fiddle Festival,** Newbury; **Burklyn Old-Time Fiddler's Contest** Burke Mountain Base Lodge, East Burke; **Annual Old-Time Fiddling Contest,** Chelsea; the **Certified State Championships,** Bellows Falls; and in late September, the **National Championship Fiddle Contest,** Barre. Fiddle Festivals tend to start around noon and end around dusk. The **Northeast Fiddling Association,** which publishes newsletters of all events, can be contacted at RFD 1, Stowe 05672.

FISHING   Almost every Vermont river and pond, certainly any body of water serious enough to call itself a lake, is stocked with fish. Brook trout are the most widely distributed game fish. Visitors age 15 and over, must have a three-day, 14-day, or a non-resident license good for a year, available at any town clerk's office, the local fish and game warden, or assorted commercial outlets. Since these sources may be closed or time-consuming to track down on weekends, it's wise to obtain the license in advance from the **Vermont Fish & Game Department,** Montpelier 05602; request an application form, ask also for a copy of "**Vermont Guide to Fishing,**" detailing every species of fish and where to find it on a map of the state's rivers and streams, ponds, and lakes. Boat access, fish hatcheries, and canoe routes are also noted. A list of contoured depth charts for more than 80 Vermont lakes and ponds is available from the **Vermont Department of Water Resources (Depth Charts),** Montpelier 05602; prices vary; minimun order is $1.

The State's most famous trout stream is the **Batten Kill** in the southwest, focus of a fly fishing school offered by the **Orvis Company** in Manchester Center, which has been in the business of making fishing rods and selling them to city people for more than a century (it also maintains an outstanding museum devoted to fly fishing). In Stowe, **REC Corp.** (253-7346) now

rivals Orvis as a producer of fly fishing equipment and has its own fly fishing school. Many inns, notably along Lake Champlain and in the Northeast Kingdom, offer tackle, boats, and advice on where to catch what. Land-locked salmon can be found in some northern lakes, and the Atlantic salmon has begun to return to the Connecticut River; other common species include bass, walleyes, northern pike, and perch.

Virtually every Vermont body of water has one or more fishing access areas, and they are used year-round. Ice anglers can legally take every species of fish (trout only in a limited number of designated waters) and can actually hook smelt and some varieties of whitefish that are hard to come by during warmer months; the **Great Benson Fishing Derby** held annually in mid-February on Lake Champlain draws thousands of contestants from throughout New England.

The **Lake Champlain International Derby,** based in Burlington (phone 862-7777 for details) is a big summer draw.

Northland Trout Tours (496-6572) offers guide service to fishing the Mad River, Dog River, and the Winooski.

Books to buy include the *Vermont Atlas and Gazetteer* (David DeLorme and Co., Falmouth, Maine), which offers town-by-town maps and gives details about fishing species and access; Frank Holan's *The Fisherman's Companion,* $5.95, (a handy guide to gear, bait, techniques, etc.) published by Alan C. Hood of Putney, distributed by Backcountry Publications of Woodstock; and *The Atlas of Vermont Trout Ponds,* $5.95, and *Vermont Trout Streams,* $9.95, both from Northern Cartographic Inc., (Box 133, Burlington 05402).

FOLIAGE   For very good reason, Vermont takes its foliage seriously. The Travel Division (see *Information*) maintains a foliage number and sends out weekly bulletins on color progress, which is always earlier than assumed by those of us who live south of Montpelier. Those in the know usually head for northern Vermont in late September, when the tiny villages of Victory and Granby stage their annual **Holiday in the Hills** over the weekend that coincides with peak color in their area; followed by a week of town-by-town festivities culminating in the **Northeast Kingdom Annual Fall Foliage Festival** (see St. Johnsbury Area). By the following weekend central Vermont is usually ablaze, but visitors should be sure to have a bed reserved before coming because organized bus tours converge on the state from throughout the United States, with a growing contingent each year from Canada and the rest of the world. By the Columbus Day weekend, when what seems like millions of Bostonians and New Yorkers make their annual leaf-peeking expedition, your odds of finding a bed are dim, unless you take advantage of those chambers of commerce (notably Middlebury, Woodstock, Manchester, and St. Johnsbury) that pride themselves on finding refuge in private homes for all comers. During peak color we recommend that you avoid Vermont's most heavily trafficked tourist routes, especially Route 9 between Bennington and Brattleboro; there is plenty of room on the back roads, especially those unsuited to buses. If possible, avoid roads entirely; this is ideal hiking season.

FORESTS AND PARKS   More than 300,000 Vermont acres are managed by the U.S. Forest Service. They are traversed by 512 miles of trails, including the Appalachian/ Long Trail that follows the ridgeline of the main range of the Green Mountains (see *Hiking*). The Forest harbors six wilderness areas. Use of off-road recreational vehicles is regulated. Information—printed as well as verbal—about hiking, camping, skiing, berry picking, and birdwatching is available from the ranger stations in Manchester Center, Middlebury, and Rochester. For details (request a free "minimap" and "Winter Recreation Map") write: Green Mountain National Forest, PO Box 519, Rutland 05701. Large color maps of either the northern or southern sections of the GMNF cost $1; detailed topographic maps of most sections are also available for $2. Also see *Campgrounds*.

The Department of Forest, Parks and Recreation (828-3375), Waterbury 05676 manages a total of 157,000 acres of land, offering opportunities for hunting, fishing, cross-country skiing, snowmobiling, primitive and supervised camping. The 40 exceptionally well-groomed state parks, including 35 camping and 35 day-use areas, are described in the invaluable "Vermont State Parks" brochure available from the Department.

The state forests are largely undeveloped for hiking: trails can be found in the Mt. Mansfield State Forest and in Willoughby State Forest (overlooking Willoughby Lake); many of the trails detailed in current guidebooks (see *Hiking*) traverse state forests; for current cross-country ski trail information contact the Vermont Travel Division, Montpelier.

GAPS, GULFS, AND GORGES Vermont's mountains were once much higher before they were pummeled some 100,000 years ago by a mile-high sheet of ice. Glacial forces contoured the landscape we recognize today, notching the mountains with a number of handy "gaps" through which men eventually built roads to get from one side of the mountain to the other. Gaps frequently offer superb views and access to ridge trails. This is true of the **Appalachian, Lincoln, Middlebury,** and **Brandon Gaps,** all on the Long Trail; and of the **Roxbury Gap** east of the Mad River Valley. Gaps at lower elevations are "gulfs," scenic passes that make ideal picnic sites: note **Granville Gulf** on Route 100, **Brookfield Gulf** on Route 12, and **Williamstown Gulf** on Route 14. The State's outstanding gorges include: 140-foot deep **Quechee Gorge,** which can be viewed from Route 4 east of Woodstock; **Brockway Mills Gorge** in Rockingham (off Route 103); **Cavendish Gorge,** Springfield; **Clarendon Gorge,** Shrewsbury (traversed by the Long Trail via footbridge); **Brewster River Gorge,** south of Jeffersonville off Route 108; and **Jay Branch Gorge** off Route 105.

GOLF   Golfers find Vermont's 52 courses are generally less crowded, less expensive and more scenic than other links. Roughly half are 18 holes and a half dozen are justly famed throughout the country. A full program of lodging, meals, and lessons is available at **Mount Snow, Killington,**

Stratton Mountain, and neighboring Haystack, Sugarbush, and Stowe. The Woodstock Inn, and others, also offer golf packages. The Manchester area boasts the greatest concentration of courses. A complete list of courses can be found on Vermont's Official State Map, and a descriptive list of golf courses is available from the Vermont Travel Division, 134 State Street, Montpelier 05602.

Vermont Golf Courses: A Player's Guide by Bob Labbance and David Cornwell is a useful new book that describes all 50 of the courses open to the public, including detailed course maps, yardages, fees, opening/closing dates, starting times, and more. The 144-page, trade paperback may be ordered from the New England Press, Box 575, Shelburne 05482, at $14.45 postpaid.

HERBS   Herb farms are a growing phenomena in rural Vermont; sources of live perennials and herbs; herbs dried into fanciful wreaths; sachets, potpourri or seasonings, distilled as scents. In our wanderings we have happened on: Meadowsweet Herb Farm, attached to a handsome farmhouse on a back road in Shrewsbury; Cambridge Herbary, the source of 88 different kinds of herbs raised and processed by Vermonter Sally Bevins west of Jeffersonville; Talbot's Herb and Perennial Farm in Hartland, east of Woodstock off Route 4; Rathdowney, 3 River Street, Bethel 05032.

HIKING   There are over 700 miles of hiking trails in Vermont—which is 162 miles long as the crow flies, but 264 miles as the hiker trudges, following the Long Trail up and down the spine of the Green Mountains. But few hikers are out to set distance records on the Long Trail. The path from the Massachusettts to the Canadian border, which was completed in 1931, has a way of slowing people down. It opens up eyes and lungs, and drains compulsiveness. Even diehard backpackers tend to linger on rocky outcrops, looking down on farms and steeples. A total of 98 sidetrails (175 miles) meander off to wilderness ponds or abandoned villages, mostly maintained, along with the Long Trail, by

the Green Mountain Club, founded in 1910, which also maintains 70 shelters, many of them staffed by caretakers during summer months. The Club's *Guide Book to the Long Trail* ($5.50 for members, $8.50 for nonmembers plus $1.25 for postage and handling) gives details on trails and shelters throughout the Long Trail system. It also publishes a *Day Hiker's Guide to Vermont* ($5 to members, $7.50 to nonmembers, plus $1.25 to mail) as well as smaller guides; "Day Hiking in Vermont," a pamphlet guide to 19 day hikes and "The Long Trail" brochure are free with SASE; contact the Green Mountain Club, PO Box 889, 43 State Street, Montpelier 05602. The Appalachian Trail Conference (PO Box 807, Harpers Ferry, West VA 25425 includes detailed descriptions of most Vermont trails in its *A Guide to New Hampshire and Vermont* ($15.90) and a wide assortment of trails are nicely detailed in *Fifty Hikes in Vermont* by Heather and Hugh Sadlier (Backcountry, $8.95). (Also see *Forests and Parks* and *Campgrounds.*) Note: on public land you may camp and build fires only at designated areas. On private land you must have the permission of the landowner to build a fire between April and November and, of course, you should seek permission to camp.

Backpackers who are hesitant to set out on their own can team up with Outdoor Tours Unlimited (Maple Corner, PO Box 97, Calais 05648), with Vermont Voyageur Expeditions (Montgomery Center 05471; 326-4789) or Earthwise Adventures for Women (RR 1, Box 155, Brookline 05345; 365-4412). Hikers who prefer solid beds and gourmet meals to sleeping bags and trail food can take advantage of treks available through Vermont Hiking Holidays (PO Box 845, Waitsfield 05673; 496-2219). Vermont Walking Tours features guided walks on back roads and wilderness paths in the Northeast Kingdom with food and basic lodging at The Craftsbury Center, Box 31, Craftsbury Common 05827; 586-7767. Two groups of inns have also offered support services (route planning, baggage transfers) as well as meals and lodging. Hike Inn to Inn is based at the Churchill House (RFD #3, Brandon 05733;

247-3300) and **Walking Inn Vermont** involves five inns between Ludlow and **HISTORIC HOUSES AND SITES** Vermont itself is close to being "living history." An outstanding free map/guide to **"300 Things to See and Do in Vermont"** has been published by the Preservation Trust of Vermont and is available from the Vermont Travel Division (see *Information*). Our personal pick of historic sites are the **Calvin Coolidge Birthplace** at Plymouth Village; **Brownington Village** in the Northeast Kingdom; and **Shelburne Farms** on Lake Champlain. Historic Places are listed on the official state map.

HORSEBACK RIDING   A list of riding stables, specifying trail and sleigh rides, is included in the free booklet, "Vermont Vacation Guide," available from the Vermont Travel Division (see *Information*). It's worth noting that **Cambridge Stables** in Cambridge (see text) offers overnight pack trips and that **West River Lodge & Stable** in Brookline offers inn-based trail rides and lessons. Also check under **Morgan, South Hero, Stowe, West Burke, Barre, South Woodstock, Waitsfield.**

HOSTELS   The seven hostels in Vermont are affiliated with **American Youth Hostels** (AYH), 1332 I Street NW, Suite 800, Washington, D.C. 20005 from which you can secure a handbook describing all U.S. facilities. Hostels are open to all travelers who are AYH members (membership costs adults $21, children $11, and families $31). Nonmembers may use hostels for an additional $2 per night. They supply simple lodging and cooking facilities and are geared to bicyclists and skiers. The Vermont hostels are in **Colchester, Rochester, Stowe** (open to students only in winter), **Warren, Waterbury Center, Woodford,** and **Craftsbury Common.** The AYH booklet comes free with membership. Hostelers are expected to carry their own sleeping sack and personal eating utensils, to reserve bunkspace ahead and to arrive between 5 and 8 PM; hostels customarily close between 10 AM and 5 PM; checkout is by 9:30 AM; alcohol is not permitted on the premises.

HUNTING   "Vermont Guide to Hunting," a free pamphlet lists and locates major wildlife management areas in the state and is available, along with a current, **"Digest of Fish & Wildlife Laws"** from the Vermont Fish and Game Department, Montpelier 05602. A non-resident small game hunting license costs $27, a regular hunting license is $55, a bow and arrow license (needed in addition to the regular hunting license) is $10 and a non-resident trapping license is $300; resident hunting and trapping licenses are both $7. **Deer season** begins 12 days before Thanksgiving and lasts for 16 days. **Bow and arrow season** also lasts 16 days beginning the second Saturday in October; **hare and rabbit season** extends from the last Saturday in September to the second Sunday in March; **gray squirrel** from the last Saturday in September to the last Thursday before regular deer season. **Partridge and ruffed grouse** may be shot between the last Saturday in September and December 31 with a limit of four daily, eight in possession. **Black bear** season is determined annually. Licenses may be secured from local town clerks, or wardens, also ahead of time by mail from the Fish and Game Department. In order to purchase a Vermont hunting or combination license, a person must show or submit a certificate proving he has satisfactorily completed a hunter safety course, or a previous hunting or combination license issued to him.

ICE CREAM   Vermont's quality milk is used to produce some outstanding ice cream as well as cheese. The big name is, of course, **Ben and Jerry's,** proud producers of what *Time* has billed "the best ice cream in the world." Their plant on Route 100 in Waterbury (featuring factory tours, free samples, real cows, and a gift shop full of reproductions in every conceivable shape) has quickly become one of the state's most popular tourist attractions. Other good Vermont ice creams include **Page's Ice Cream** in West Brattleboro, **Wilcox Brothers** in Manchester, and **Mountain Creamery** in Woodstock.

INFORMATION   In 1988, Vermont published four excellent, free aids to explore the state; (1) **Vermont's Official State Map** includes symbols locating covered bridges, golf courses and picnic spots, ski areas, recreation sites, and boat launch ramps. On the reverse side are descriptive listings of museums, galleries and historic places, fishing and hunting rules and license fees, state and private campgrounds, state liquor stores, and hospital emergency rooms. (2) "**Vermont Vacation Guide**," a 24-page booklet, is filled with details about where to find what. (3) A "**Vermont Events**" tabloid lists the myriad small happenings that spice any visit to the Green Mountain State, as well as year-round attractions, seasonal attractions, and information sources throughout the state. (4) The "**Four Season Vacation Rentals**" booklet (see rental cottages) gives up to date accommodation information. All four publications are available from the Vermont Travel Division (828-3236), 134 State Street, Montpelier 05602. The state maintains four pamphlet-filled *Welcome Centers:* at Fair Haven (265-4763), on Route 4A at the New York border; in Guilford (254-4593), on I-91 at the Massachusetts border; in Highgate Springs (868-7861), on I-89 at the Canadian border.

The state's free printed material can also be found at the **New England Vacation Center** (212-307-5780), 630 Fifth Avenue, New York City and at the **Vermont Information Center** (514-845-9840) in Montreal at 117 Ste. Catherine Street West, Suite 710. A handy piece of basic exploration equipment is available from the Vermont State Chamber of Commerce (223-3443), Box 37, Montpelier 05602: "**Vermont Traveler's Guidebook**" contains paid listings of lodging, restaurants, camping, shops, and attractions. The "**Vermont Craft Treasure Trails**" has paid listings of shops, antique stores, and art galleries. Within this book we have noted local chambers of commerce, town by town. In towns not served by a chamber, inquiries are welcomed by the town clerk.

First-time visitors may be puzzled by Vermont's Travel Information System of directional signs that replace billboards (banned since 1967, another Vermont "first"). Stylized symbols for Lodging, Food, Recreation, Antiques and Crafts, and Other Services are sited at intersections off major highways; at interstate rest areas; at incoming border Welcome Centers; and at other key points of travel interest. **Travel Information Plazas** should be consulted to get oriented to the system. They are indicated on the state map by: "Travel Information Plaza."

INNS   "**Vermont Country Inns**," a descriptive listing of more than 200 lodging places, is available from the Vermont Travel Division, 134 State Street, Montpelier 05602 (828-3236). We have described many inns in their respective towns quoting 1987–88 rates. These prices are, of course, subject to change and should not be regarded as gospel. Summer rates are generally lower than winter rates; weekly or ski-week rates run 10 to 20 percent less than the per diem price quoted. Many inns insist on MAP (Modified American Plan—breakfast and dinner) in winter but not in summer. Most resorts have American Plan—(three meals); and we have shown European Plan (EP: no meals) where applicable. Most add a 15 percent service charge and remember the 6 percent state tax on rooms and meals. It's prudent to check which, if any, credit cards are accepted. Many of the inns we have included are described in several inn guides, among which we like *The Guide to the Recommended Country Inns of New England* by Elizabeth Squier and Suzy Chapin (Globe/Pequot Press); "**Best Places to Stay in New England**" by Christina Tree and Bruce Shaw (Harvard Common). It should be noted that the inns that are included in these books tend to be those that pride themselves on their gourmet fare and restful ambiance; there are also many unsung inns with a more casual but welcoming atmosphere, usually a better bet with children. We have noted places in which children are unwelcome and have attempted to note the few places that accept pets.

For quick reference, note our "Index to Lodging."

LAKES   The state famed for green mountains and white villages also harbors more than 400 relatively blue lakes: big lakes like **Champlain** (150 miles long) and **Memphremagog** (boasting 88 miles of coastline but most of it in Canada), smaller lakes like **Morey, Dunmore, Willoughby, Bomoseen,** and **Seymour.** Lakes are particularly plentiful and people sparse in Vermont's **Northeast Kingdom.** A century ago there were many more lakeside hotels; today just a half dozen of these classic summer resorts survive; **Quimby Country** in Averill, **Highland Lodge** in Greensboro, the **Tyler Place** in Highgate Springs, the **Basin Harbor Club** near Vergennes, **Eagle's Nest Resort** and the **Lake Morey Club.** There are a half dozen smaller, informal inns on scattered lakes, but that's about it. Still, you can bed down very reasonably within sound and sight of Vermont waters either by renting a cottage (more than half of those listed in "Four Season Vacation Rentals," available from the Vermont Travel Division, are on lakes) or by taking advantage of **state park campsites** on Groton Lake, Island Pond, Maidstone Lake, Bomoseen, Lake Carmi, Elmore, Lake St. Catherine, and Silver Lake (in Barnard). On Lake Champlain there are a number of state campgrounds, including those on **Grand Isle** (accessible by car) and on Burton Island (accessible by public launch from St. Albans Bay). See *Campgrounds* for details about these and the free campsights on **Ball Mountain Lake** maintained by the Army Corp of Engineers. There is public boat access to virtually every Vermont pond and lake of any size. Boat launches are listed on the state map.

LIBRARIES The small village of **Brookfield** boasts the state's oldest, continuously operating public library, established in 1791. Most libraries that we mention here date, however, from that late nineteenth-century philanthropic era when Andrew Carnegie's largesse filtered down to places like **Swanton,** or when wealthy native sons were moved to donate splendidly ornate libraries to their home town. Notable examples are to be found in **Barre, Chester, Ludlow, Wilmington, Rutland, Newport, Woodstock, St. Johnsbury,** and **Brattleboro.**

Two of our favorite libraries lie within a short drive of each other, one on the common in **Craftsbury Common** and the second—a converted general store—in **East Craftsbury,** where there is a special back room for youngsters, with a ping pong table amid the books. Unfortunately, visitors may not check out books unless they happen to be staying within the community that the library serves. However, visitors are free to use Regional Libraries, open 8:30–5, Monday–Friday and 9–5 on Saturdays, closed on Saturdays in July and August. **Regional libraries** are located in **St. Johnsbury; Berlin,** near Barre; in **Georgia,** near St. Albans; **Dummerston,** near Brattleboro; and in **Rutland.**

For research, the **Vermont Historical Society Library** in Montpelier is a treasure trove of Vermontiana and genealogical resources, as is the Wilbur collection of the **Bailey-Howe Library** at the University of Vermont.

LLAMA TREKING Popular in the West, llama treking is a novelty in New England. The sure-footed, whimsical animals are great companions, following behind you and carrying your gear on the trail. This being Vermont, the llamas are simply enlisted to carry your gear between inns. For details contact **Country Inns Along the Trail,** The Churchill House Inn, RD 3, Brandon 05733; 247-3300. **Willoughby Lake Llama Farm** (525-4700) in Westmore also offers organized pack trips in summer months (see Newport Area Lake Country).

MAGAZINES *Vermont Life,* the popular and colorful quarterly published by the Agency of Development and Community Affairs and now edited by Tom Slayton, is an outstanding contemporary chronicle of Vermont's people and places, featuring distinguished photographers. Single issues cost $2.50; $9 a year, $23 for three years; 61 Elm Street, Montpelier 05602.

Vermont History, a quarterly scholarly journal, is published for members of the Vermont Historical Society, Montpelier.

Upper Valley is a glossy bimonthly published at $6 a year at 89 Main Street, West Lebanon, New Hampshire 03784.

The Prosper Publishing Company, Barnard 05031, publishes lively quarterlies, including *Woodstock Common* and similar magazines for Rutland and Stowe.

Vermont Business Magazine is a well-written, tabloid-sized monthly that provides investigative reportage, analysis and overview of the state's economic doings from politically conservative and entrepreneurially aggressive points of view. Subscriptions are $12 per year, $22 for 2 years; free to Vermont businesses and government agencies. Manning Publications, Inc., P.O. Box 6120, Brattleboro, VT 05301.

Vermont Woman is a Burlington-based monthly with a moderate feminist stance. The focus is on the social and particularly the political scene "for Vermont women of achievement." $15 per year from Vermont Woman Publications, 200 Main St., Suite 15, Burlington, VT 05401.

Southern Vermont, bimonthly, 58 Elliot Street, Brattleboro 05301, $9.95 per year.

MAPLE SUGARING   Vermont produces an average of 500,000 gallons of maple syrup each year, more than any other state. Nearly 2,000 maple growers tap an average of 1,000 trees each. One-fifth to one-quarter gallon of syrup is made per tap, boiling down 30 to 40 gallons of sap for each gallon of syrup. The process of tapping trees and boiling is stubbornly known as "sugaring" rather than syruping, because the end product for early settlers was sugar. Syrup was first made in the early nineteenth century, but flagged when imported cane sugar was easy to come by. The Civil War revived the maple sugar industry: Union supporters were urged to consume sugar made by free men and to plant more and more maples. The annual pamphlet listing of "**Maple Sugarhouses Open to Visitors**" indicates which producers sell sugar and maple cream along with syrup; many do, but the big product now is the "liquid sunshine" for which people have learned to pay a high price in recent years.

For our money, the only place to buy syrup is at a sugarhouse during the season. The trick is finding one in full steam.

Traditionally, sugaring season begins with Town Meeting (first Tuesday in March). The fact is, however, that sap runs only on those days when temperatures rise to 40 and 50 degrees during the day and drop down into the 20s at night. And when the sap runs it must be boiled down quickly. What you want to see is the boiling process: sap churning madly through the large, flat evaporating pan, darkening as you watch. You are enveloped in fragrant steam, listening to the rush of the sap, sampling the end result on snow or in tiny paper cups. Sugaring is Vermont's rite of spring.

The "Maple Sugarhouses Open to Visitors" pamphlet (available from the Vermont Travel Division, 134 State Street, Montpelier 05602) lists more than 100 maple producers, giving their phone numbers (be sure to phone before going to check if there is sugaring that day); and the method used for collecting sap—many farmers now use plastic pipeline that runs directly from tree to collecting tank, but there are still some oxen and horses out there, pulling the collecting tank around from tree to tree bucket. There are two big **Maple Festivals** each spring, the biggest one in **St. Albans,** a three-day happening that includes tours through the local sugarbush (usually the second weekend in April) and a late April celebration in **St. Johnsbury,** home of Maple Grove Maple Museum, "the world's largest maple candy factory." At **Maple Grove** (May 30–late October) and at **American Maple Products** (year-round) in Newport you can see a movie about maple production; the story of sugaring is also dramatized in the **New England Maple Museum** in Pittsford. We have listed maple producers in the areas in which they are most heavily concentrated.

MAPS   The Official State Map (see *Information*) is free and extremely helpful for general motoring in Vermont, but will not suffice for finding your way around on the webs of the dirt roads that connect some of the most beautiful corners of the state. Among our favorite places in which you can be guaranteed to get lost using the State Map: the high farming country between Albany, Craftsbury and West Glover; similar country between Chelsea and Wiliamstown; south from Plainfield to Orange; and between Plymouth and Healdville. There are many more. We strongly suggest securing a copy of *The Vermont Atlas and Gazetteer* (David DeLorme & Co., Falmouth, Maine) if you want to do any serious back road exploring, or *The Vermont Road Atlas and Guide* from Northern Cartographics, PO Box 133, Burlington 05402. We also suggest obtaining the free "**mini-map**" and "**Winter Recreation**" map available from the Green Mountain National Forest, PO Box 519, Rutland 05701.

MONEY Don't leave home without MasterCard or Visa, the two credit cards that are far more readily accepted in Vermont than American Express or personal checks. Each inn has its own policy about credit cards and checks; some accept cash only.

MOTORING   The Official State Map, updated annually (see *Maps*) comes free from local chamber of commerce information booths as well as state information centers (see *Information*). Motorists should bear in mind that gas stations can be infrequent in rural areas and often close early in the evening. **State highway rest areas** with pay phones and bathroom facilities, indicated on the State Map, are found on I-91 at Guilford (a Welcome Center) northbound; at Bradford, north and southbound; at Barnet, northbound; at Derby, southbound; and Coventry northbound. On I-89 there are rest areas at Sharon, north and southbound; and at Randolph, north and southbound. Note the work of Vermont sculptors commissioned for these rest areas by the Vermont Council on the Arts in cooperation with the Vermont Marble Company. In 1982, the Vermont stretch of I-89 was dedicated to honor veterans and casualties of the war in Vietnam.

Picnic sites with tables and benches are scattered along most major routes throughout the state; picnic tables are clearly marked on the state map.

AAA Emergency Road Service: 1-800-622-4755.

MOUNTAIN TOPS While Vermont can boast only seven peaks above 4,000 feet, there are 80 mountains that rise more than 3,000 feet and any number of spectacular views, six of them accessible in summer and foliage seasons to those who prefer riding to walking up mountains. **Mount Mansfield** at 4,343 feet, the state's highest summit, can be reached via Mountain Auto Road. This mid-nineteenth-century road brings you to the small Summit Station at 4,062 feet from which a half-mile Tundra Trail brings you to the actual summit. The Mt. Mansfield Gondola, a four-passenger enclosed lift hoists you from the ski area's main ski lodge up the Cliff House (serving light meals all day) from which a trail also heads up to the Chin. **Killington Peak,** Vermont's second highest peak at 4,241 feet, can be reached via another 3½-mile Gondola ride (operating weekends only): and by a 1¼-mile ride on a chairlift. Both lifts take you to a summit restaurant and a nature trail that even the small children can negotiate. **Jay Peak,** a 3,861-foot summit towering like a lone sentinel near the Canadian border, is accessible via a 60-passenger tram (daily except Tuesdays). Traveling east from Jay you come to 3,267-foot **Burke Mountain** with its 2½-mile Auto Road yielding a sweeping view of the Northeast Kingdom. A view of the Connecticut River Valley from the 3,144-foot summit of **Mt. Ascutney** can be reached by driving up the winding Toll Road in Ascutney State Park.

MUSEUMS A number of free publications, notably the Official State Map and the "300 Things to See and Do in Vermont" pamphlet, list museums, which vary from the immense **Shelburne Museum** with its 36 buildings, many housing priceless collections of Americana, plus assorted exhibits like a completely restored lake steamer and lighthouse, to the **American Precision Museum,** an 1846 brick mill that once produced rifles. They include a number of outstanding historical museums (our favorites are the **Sheldon Museum** in Middlebury, the **Old Stone House Museum** in Brownington, and the **Dana House** in Woodstock) and some collections that go beyond the purely historical: **Bennington Museum** (famed for its collection of Grandma Moses paintings as well as early American glass and relics from the Revolution), and the **Fairbanks Museum and Planetarium** in St. Johnsbury. The **Billings Farm and Museum** in Woodstock, shows off its Blue Ribbon dairy and has a fascinating, beautifully-mounted display of nineteenth-century farm life and tools.

MUSIC   The Green Mountains are filled with the sounds of music each summer. The internationally famous **Marlboro Music Festival** (254-8163), at Marlboro College, presents chamber music under the direction of Rudolf Serkin on weekends from early July through mid-August. The **Vermont Mozart Festival** is a series of 20 concerts performed at a variety of sites, ranging from beautiful barns at the University of Vermont and Shelburne Farms to a Lake Champlain ferry boat, including some striking classic and modern churches and a ski area base lodge (862-7352). Other concerts are presented at the **Summer Music School** in Adamant (229-9297), at the Town House in Hardwick by the **Craftsbury Chamber Players** (888-3158), and in Stowe, for a week in late July, the **Performing Arts Festival** (253-7321). In Putney, a series of three evening chamber music concerts each week are presented in the **Yellow Barn** (387-6637); other concert series are performed at the **Southern Vermont Arts Center** (Thursday and Sunday, 362-1405); the **Fine Arts Center,** Castleton College (468-4611, ext. 285); the **Dibden Auditorium,** Johnson College (635-2356); and at **Johnson Hall,** Middlebury College (388-2763). The **North Country Concert Association** (43 Main Street, Derby Line) performs at sites throughout the Northeast Kingdom lake area. The **Vermont Symphony Orchestra,** oldest of the state symphonies, figures in a number of the series noted above and also performs at a variety of locations ranging from Brattleboro's Living Mem-

orial Park and the State House Lawn to Wilson Castle, throughout the summer. In Weston, the **Kinhaven Music School** offers free concerts on summer weekends.

OPERA HOUSES   Northern New England opera houses are a turn-of-the-century phenomenon: theaters built as cultural centers for the surrounding area, stages on which lecturers, musicians and vaudeville acts, as well as opera singers performed. Many of these buildings have long since disappeared, but those that survive are worth noting. The **Hyde Park Opera House,** in Hyde Park, built in 1910 has been restored by the Lamoille County Players, who stage four annual shows— one play, two musicals, and an annual foliage season run of "The Sound of Music." The **Barre Opera House,** built in 1899, is an elegant, accoustically outstanding second-floor theater, which is the home of the Barre Players; productions are staged here year-round. In **Derby Line,** in the second-floor **Opera House** (a neoclassic structure that also houses the Haskell Free Library), the audience sits in Vermont watching a stage that is in Canada. The **Chandler Music Hall** in Randolph has been restored for varied uses.

PICK YOUR OWN   A list of orchards and berry farms open to the public can be secured from the Vermont Department of Agriculture, 116 State Street, State Office Building, Montpelier 05602. **Strawberry** season is mid- to late June. **Cherries, plums, raspberries,** and **blueberries** can be picked in July and August. **Apples** ripen by mid-September and can be picked through foliage season.

QUILTS   A revival of interest in this craft is especially strong in Vermont, where quilting supply and made-to-order stores salt the state. For information contact the **Green Mountain Quilters Guide,** c/o L. Leister, RD 2, Bethel 05032, which sponsers several shows a year. The **Vermont Quilt Festival** is held for three days in mid-July in Northfield, including exhibits of outstanding antique quilts, classes and lectures, vendors, and appraisals. The

Quilt Fest in Newport is held in July, and **The Friendship and Island Heritage Quilters Show** in South Hero is held in August.

Shops specializing in quilts and/or supplies can be found in Middlebury, Brattleboro, Randolph, Essex Junction, Newfane, South Hero, Rutland, Stowe, Waitsfield, Winooski, Weston, and Woodstock.

RAILROAD EXCURSIONS   Vermont's rail excursions are not in heavily touristed places. The **Green Mountain Flyer** runs between Bellows Falls on the Connecticut River and either Chester (13 miles) or Ludlow (another 14 miles), depending on how far you want to go. Named for the fastest train on the old Rutland Railroad, the excursion is run by the employee-owned Green Mountain Railroad, which also hauls talc, lumber, and limestone slurry between Bellows Falls and Rutland (see Bellows Falls for details). Based in Morrisville, 10 miles north of Stowe, there is also **Vermont Land Cruises,** offering 35-mile runs to Joe's Pond in summer and during foliage season, operated by the Lamoille Valley Railroad, another small freight line. During foliage season there are also the **St. J & L.C.** Railroad excursions, offered twice-weekly from St. Johnsbury to Greensboro Bend. The 57-mile round trip rides are sponsored by a nonprofit rail club. See Northeast Kingdom for details.

RENTAL COTTAGES AND CONDOMINIUMS "Four Season Vacation Rentals," an annual booklet available from the Travel Division (828-3236), Montpelier 05602, lists upwards of 200 properties, most of them either lakeside cottages or condominiums near ski areas, but also including a variety of housing, ranging from wooded summer camps by a stream to aristocratic brick mansions with priceless views. We have found this publication indispensable for exploring the state—as a family of five—at all seasons. Rentals average $350 per week, usually more in winter, less in summer; incredible bargains by any standard.

RESTAURANTS   Culinary standards are rising every day: one can lunch, simply and inexpensively nearly everywhere, and dine superbly in a score of places where the quality would rate three stars in Boston or New York, but is at least a third less expensive. Fixed price menus (prix fixe) have been so noted.

We were tempted to try to list here our "favorites" but the roster would be too long. Restaurants that appeal to us appear in the text in their respective areas. The range and variety are truly extraordinary. Note: a pamphlet "Vermont Guide to Smoke-Free Dining," listing restaurants with smoke-free sections, is available from the Vermont Lung Association (1-800-642-3288).

ROCKHOUNDING   "Rockhounding in Vermont," a good writeup of Vermont's rockhounding sites, special events, and the state's geological history, is available free from the Vermont Travel Division, Montpelier 05602 (828-3236). The most obvious sites are: **Rock of Ages Quarry and Exhibit** in Barre and the **Vermont Marble Company Exhibit** in Proctor (a film, free samples). Major exhibits of Vermont fossils, minerals, and rocks may be viewed at **Perkins Geology Hall,** University of Vermont, Burlington; the **Fairbanks Museum** in St. Johnsbury; and the **Melendy Mineral Museum,** South Londonderry (phone for an appointment). An annual **Rock Swap and Mineral Show** is held in early August, sponsored by the Burlington Gem and Mineral Club. Gold, incidentally, can be panned in a number of rivers notably Broad Brook in Plymouth; Rock River in Newfane and Dover; Williams River in Ludlow; Ottauquechee River in Bridgewater; White River in Stockbridge and Rochester; Mad River in Warren, Waitsfield, and Moretown; Little River in Stowe and Waterbury; and the Missisquoi in Lowell and Troy.

SHEEP   Sheep are multiplying quickly in Vermont, and may someday again outnumber cows, as they did in the mid-nineteenth century. Their modern appeal is primarily for their meat, but a number of farmers specialize in processing wool, notably the **Boutchers** in Whiting, and **Gisela Gminder** of Morrisville (who offers weaving lessons at her Stowe Wool and Feathers Shop). "**Vermont Sheep Plus,**" a descriptive listing of the members of the Vermont Sheep Breeders Association, is available from the Vermont Sheepbreeder's Association; check with the president, Don Mitchell RFD 2, Vergennes 05491 (545-2278). A number of colorful festivals are presently staged by and for sheep breeders, the oldest and biggest being the "**Sheep to Shawl**" **Festival** held at Burklyn in East Burke each May, involving teams of contestants who must card and spin fleece, then weave, knit or otherwise produce a shawl—all between 10 AM and 3:30 PM of a festive day in which lambs are also sold, sheared, and consumed (for lunch).

SHIPWRECKS Well-preserved nineteenth-century shipwrecks are open to the public (licensed divers) at three Underwater Historical Preserves in Lake Champlain near Burlington. *The Phoenix,* the second steamboat to ply Lake Champlain, burned to the waterline in 1819. *The General Butler,* an 88-foot schooner, fell victim to a winter gale in 1876. A coal barge, believed to be the *A.R. Nowes,* broke loose from a tug and sank in 1884. Contact Giovanna Peebles, state archaeologist; 828-3226

SIGHTSEEING TOURS In-state group tours by bus or van are available from an increasing number of establishments, among them: **Bromley Sun Lodge** (824-6941), Peru 05152; **Cascades/Green Mountain Tour Company** (422-3731), RR1, Box 53B, Killington 05751; **Central Vermont Chamber of Commerce** (229-5711), Box 336, Barre 05641; **Connecticut River Holidays** (463-3069),Box 467, Depot Square, Bellows Falls 05101; **Dostal's Resort Lodge & Green Mountain Tours** (824-6700), RD 1, Box 31, Magic Mountain, Londonderry 05148; **Killington and Pico Areas Association** (773-4181), Box 114, Killington 05751; **Matterhorn of Dover** (464-8011), Route 100, Box 208, West Dover 05356; **Mount Snow Vermont Tours & Vermont Vacation Tours** (464-2076), or 800-742-7669), Route 100, Box 571, West Dover

05356-7669; **Old Red Mill** (464-3700), Box 464, Wilmington 05363; **St. Johnsbury Chamber of Commerce** (748-3678), 30 Western Avenue, St. Johnsbury 05819; "**The Vermont Experience**" (767-4747), Route 100, Granville 05747; **Vermont Transit Tours** (862-9671 or 800-451-3292), 135 St. Paul Street, Burlington 05041; **Vermont with LaMont** (496-6535), Box 295, Waitsfield 05673; **Vermont Backroad Tours** (226-7910), Box 64, Carlton Road, Cavendish 05142.

SKIING, CROSS-COUNTRY Cross-country centers and tours are listed in a free book co-published by the Vermont Ski Areas Association and the Vermont Travel Division (see *Information*). We have included each commerical touring center as it appears geographically. Vermont's most extensive network of cross-country trails can now be found (moving south to north) in the Mt. Snow area (where a ridge trail connects Mount Snow and Haystack), in the Mad River/Sugarbush Valley, and at Stowe. Some of the best higher elevation trails in the state are found at Bolton Valley, also a good spot for telemarking lessons, and there is a wide choice of terrain in Woodstock and at Mountain Meadows near Killington, an area in which Mountain Top Inn offers snowmaking on much of its system. A number of centers are part of the Catamount Trail, on which skilled cross-country skiers have made their way from the Massachusetts to the Canadian border. For details contact the Catamount Trail Association, Box 897, Burlington 05402. Packaged inn-to-inn tours, with baggage transported for you, can be found in all parts of Vermont. For details contact the **Churchill House Inn,** Brandon; the **Colonial House,** Weston; the **Sugarbush Inn,** Warren; **North Wind Tours,** Waitsfield; **4 Season Touring** in Townshend (Box 132; 365-7937); **Outdoor Tours Unlimited** Box 97, Calais (229-4570); **Vermont Voyageur** in Montgomery; **Vermont Adventure Vacations** in Waitsfield (1-800-338-1056); the **Craftsbury Area Association** in Craftsbury Common (586-2514). Other guided tours are offered by **Nordic Adventures** in Rochester; **Konari Outfitters** in Vergennes (featuring ski or snowshow tours with sleds), RD 1, Box 441B, Vergennes (759-2100); **Plum Creek,** Box 771, Waitsfield (496-6886), **Search for Nature,** Box 424, Jericho (453-3983); and **Vermont Voyageur,** offering moutaineering and winter camping as well as inn-to-inn. Details, if not supplied here, are found in the book. For details about marked cross-country trails in state preserves contact the Department of Forests, Parks and Recreation (828-3375), Montpelier 05602, and for those within the Green Mountain National Forest, request the Winter Recreation map (see *Forests and Parks*). Other possibilities are described in *25 Ski Tours in the Green Mountains* by Daniel Ford (Backcountry Publications).

SKIING, DOWNHILL Since the 1930s, when America's commercial skiing began with a Model-T Ford engine pulling skiers up a hill in Woodstock, skiing has been a Vermont speciality. There are 19 ski areas in Vermont and all but one (Mad River Glen) belong to the Vermont Ski Area Association, which publishes a glossy winter guide in conjunction with the Vermont Travel Division (from whom it's available free; see *Information*). Unfortunately this guide includes no rates. Watch for the November ski section in major newspapers that compile these crucial data. In 1987–88 lift tickets range from $19 adult at **Maple Valley,** a 13-trail area on Route 30 in West Dummerston to $35 per adult at Killington, by far the largest ski resort (107 trails) in the East. Mount Snow, Vermont's second largest area (under the same ownership as Killington) charges $32; the lowest charge at a major mountain is Mad River Glen ($22 per adult), which also has the lowest percentage (15%) of snowmaking cover (still conditions are frequently excellent). Increasingly, over the past decade, a number of long-established Vermont ski areas have become self-contained resorts. Both Bolton Valley and Smugglers' Notch cater to families; Okemo, Stratton, and Sugarbush offer varied skiing and facilities, appealing to a full range of patrons. Ascutney and Pico are smaller but also offer slopeside condos and resort facilities. Though no longer Vermont's biggest, Stowe remains Ski Capital of the East

when it comes to the quantity and quality of inns, restaurants, and shops. Bear in mind that lodging, lifts, and lessons all cost far less by the week than weekend, especially during nonholiday stretches. We have described each ski area as it appears geographically. A 24-hour snow condition report for the State is available by phoning: 229-0531. (November–June).

SLEIGH RIDES A list of sleigh rides is available from the Vermont Travel Division (see *Information*).

SNOWMOBILING Some 1,800 miles of well-marked, groomed trails are laced together in a system maintained by the **Vermont Association of Snow Travelers.** VAST's corridor trails are up to eight feet wide, maintained by 200 local snowmobile clubs; for detailed maps and suggestions for routes and activities, contact the Vermont Association of Snow Travelers (229-0005), Box 839, Montpelier 05602. For information about guided tours and inn-to-inn snowmobile programs, contact the **Vermont Travel Division.** Vermont has a reciprocal registration agreement with New York, Maine, New Hampshire, and Quebec; otherwise registration is required to take advantage of trails within state parks.

SOARING Sugarbush Soaring (496-3730), Sugarbush Airport, Warren. The Mad River Valley is known as one of the prime spots in the East for riding thermal and ridge waves and the **Sugarbush Airport** is a well-established place to take glider lessons or rides, or to simply watch the planes come and go. The **Fall Wave Soaring Encampment** held in early October draws glider pilots from throughout the country. Gliders and airplane rides are also available at the **Morrisville/Stowe State Airport** (888-5150) and at **Post Mills Aviation** in Post Mills (333-9254), where soaring lessons are also a speciality along with simply seeing the Connecticut Valley from the air.

SPAS Vermont is the setting for a select few of the country's finest spas. The oldest of these is **New Life Spa,** directed by Jimmy LeSage at Stratton. Housed in a Tyrolean-style ski lodge, it offers full resort facilities (including summer tennis and golf, winter skiing) and a mix of sound nutritional advice and exercise. **The Village Spa** at the Green Mountain Inn in Stowe is a less-structured but equally potent blend of exercise (ranging from mountain biking to skiing), careful eating and pampering. **The Equinox** in Manchester Center is the state's newest and most expensive spa, adding medical diagnosis and a rich assortment of body treatments to the exercise and diet regime.

SUMMER SELF-IMPROVEMENT PROGRAMS Whether its improving your game of tennis or golf, learning to take pictures, to weave, cook, identify mushrooms, fish, bike, or simply to lose weight, there is a summer program for you somewhere in Vermont. See Tennis, Golf, Canoeing, and Fishing for lodging and lesson packages. Prestigious academic programs include the **Russian School** at Norwich University (Russian only is spoken in all social as well as class activities; both undergraduate and graduate courses are offered); **intensive language programs** at Middlebury College, and a **writers' program** at the college's Breadloaf summer campus. Senior citizens can take advantage of some outstanding courses offered at bargain prices that include lodging as part of the Elder Hostel program. The participating Vermont campuses are at Bennington College in Bennington; Castleton State College in Castleton; College of St. Joseph the Provider in Rutland; Green Mountain College in Poultney; Lyndon State College in Lyndonville; St. Johnsbury Academy; Southern Vermont College in Bennington; and the Craftsbury Center in Craftsbury Common. For details write to Elder Hostel, 80 Boylston Street, Boston, Massachusetts 02116. The state's oldest most respected **crafts program** is offered by Fletcher Farm Craft School, Ludlow 05149: off-loom weaving, creative needlework, quilting, pottery, raku and stained glass, plus meals and lodging (minimum age 18).

Vermont Studio School and Colony in Johnson is relatively new but already has a national reputation. Working artists come to renew their creative wellsprings or explore completely new directions during intensive sessions that feature guidance and criticism by some of the country's premier artists. For details phone: 635-7000.

Craftsbury Center in Craftsbury has summer programs for all ages in running and sculling and **Lyndon State** has a running camp.

SWIMMING On the Official State Map, you can pick out the **35 day-use areas** that offer swimming, most with changing facilities, maintained by the State Department of Forests, Parks & Recreation ($1 per adult, 50¢ per child). A similar facility is provided by the Green Mountain National Forest in **Peru,** and the U.S. Army Corps of Engineers has tidied corners of its dam projects for public use in **Townshend** and **North Springfield.** There are also public beaches on roughly one-third of Vermont's 400 lakes and ponds (but note that swimming is prohibited at designated "Fishing Access Areas"), and plenty on **Lake Champlain** (see Burlington, Charlotte, Colchester, Georgia, and Swanton). Add to these all the town recreation areas and myriad pools available to visitors, and you still haven't gone swimming Vermont-style—until you have sampled a Vermont swimming hole. These range from deep spots in the state's ubiquitous streams to 100-foot deep quarries (**Dorset Quarry** near Manchester, and **Chapman Quarry** in West Rutland are famous) and freezing pools between waterfalls (see the Mad River Valley). We have included some of our favorite swimming holes under *Swimming* in each section, but could not bring ourselves to share them all. Look for cars along the road on a hot day and ask in local general stores. You won't be disappointed.

TENNIS Vermont claims as many tennis courts per capita as any state in the union. These include town recreation facilities and sports centers as well as private facilities. Summer tennis programs, combining lessons, lodging and meals, are offered at **Bolton Valley, Killington,** the **Village at Smuggler's Notch,** at **Stratton** and at two **Sugarbush** resorts (Sugarbush Inn and the

Bridges). Check *Tennis* under entries for each area.

A description listing of Vermont tennis courts is included in the "Vermont Vacation Guide" available from the Vermont Travel Division, 134 State Street, Montpelier 05602. One of the world top tennis tournaments—the **Volvo International**—is held at Stratton Resort in August.

THEATER Vermont's two long-established summer theaters are both in the Manchester area: the **Dorset Playhouse** and the **Weston Playhouse**. The **Green Mountain Guild** presents a series of summer musicals at the **Killington Playhouse**. Other summer theater can be found in Castleton, in Waitsfield (the **Valley Players**) and Warren (**Phantom Theater**), and in Stowe (the **Stowe Playhouse** and the **Lamoille County Players** in Hyde Park). For a complete and current listing consult the Vermont Vacation Guide available free from the Vermont Travel Division (see *Information*).

TRAINS   See *AMTRAK*

WATERFALLS Those most accessible include: the falls at **Brewster River Gorge** in Jeffersonville; in **Bristol Memorial Forest Park,** Bristol; **Buttermilk Falls** (a popular swimming hole) in Ludlow; **Carver Falls** in West Haven (126 feet high); the falls in **Clarendon Gorge; Cow Meadows Ledges** in Newbury; **Duck Brook Cascades** in Bolton; the **East Putney Falls** and **Pot Holes; Glen Falls** in Fairlee; **Great Falls** of the Clyde River in Charleston; **Hamilton Falls** in Jamaica; **Little Otter Creek Falls** in Ferrisburg; **Middlebury Gorge; Moss Glen Falls** in Granville Notch; the seven falls on the **Huntington River** in Hanksville; **Shelburne Falls in Shelburne; Texas Falls** in Hancock, **Cadys Falls** in Morrisville; **Bingham Falls** in Stowe; and **Northfield Falls,** Northfield. We have spent some time looking without success for Big Falls in Troy (we gave up after learning that a few people had died there

in recent years), and could not penetrate the swampy ground around Moss Glen Falls in Stowe. Most of these sites can be located on the *Vermont Atlas and Gazetteer* maps (See *Books*).

WEATHER REPORTS   For current weather info in Vermont dial the following numbers. For **Northern Vermont**: 862-2375; **North Central**: 476-4101; **South**: 464-2111; and **South Central**: 773-8056.

WHITE WATER   During the spring, white water season beginning in mid-April, experienced canoeists and kayakers take advantage of white water stretches on the **White,** the **Lamoille, Clyde** and **West River,** among others. Thousands gather in Jamaica for races on the **West River** between the flood control dams.

For guided white water weekend and midweek trips in northern Vermont (for the novice and intermediate canoeists), contact **Vermont Voyageur Expeditions,** Montgomery Center 05471. **Vermont Whitewater** (649-2998), Box 800, Norwich 05055, open April–early May and the first weekend in October, offers guided white water rafting trips on the West River.

WILDFLOWERS Vermont boasts five times the natural flora growing in other Northeastern States, some 1,927 varieties, and in a few places this wealth has been gathered into compact spaces for viewing. In Charlotte, on Route 7, the **Vermont Wildflower Farm** invites you to stroll its six acres of pathways, fields, and woodlands in which species are labeled for the layman; open daily from mid-May through Christmas; free (425-3500). We must also mention the **Putney Nursery** in Putney, founded and nurtured by the late George Aiken, dean of Vermont politicians and author of the classic *Pioneering with Wildflowers* (Countryman Press); and the **Vermont Institute of Natural Science** in Woodstock, which offers fern walks on its own land and field trips for "bog-trotters."

Calendar of Events

Here is a roster of events that can be counted on each year. They appear, along with precise dates and phone numbers, in the "Vermont Events" brochure published by the Vermont Travel Division (see *Information*). They represent half the actual happenings that you will find publicized on the doors and windows of Vermont general stores. At the end of each section of this book, we have listed the main events for that area.

JANUARY Ski season, but relatively quiet period on the slopes, a time for frequent downhill races, for scheduled guided ski tours and for the week-long Okemo and Stowe Winter Carnivals. The village of Brookfield celebrates its Ice Harvest Festival on the final Saturday.

FEBRUARY Bringing the most dependable snow conditions and school vacations, this month is high ski season. It is the time for cross-country ski marathons—through the Middlebury Gap and around the town of Brattleboro—and for winter carnivals in Manchester, Middlebury, Springfield, Jay, Chester, Bennington, Strafford, Lyndonville, Newport, and Woodstock. On a weekend in late February, thousands of fishermen converge on the village of Benson for New England's biggest ice fishing derby.

MARCH Town Meeting, the first Tuesday of the month, often coincides with the start of maple sugaring season, a time when visitors are welcome to watch sap being "boiled off" in every corner of the state (see *Maple Sugaring*). Spring skiing is celebrated in a series of madcap races and other happenings that add up to "March Madness" at Sugarbush, "March-

fest" at Smugglers' Notch, "Spring Fever Weekend" at Mt. Snow, and "Spring Thing" at Bolton Valley.

APRIL Easter is hailed with sunrise services on the summits of Mt. Snow, Stowe, and Jay Peak, among others. Sugaring season culminates with the World's Biggest Maple Festival in St. Albans, and a few weeks later with the St. Johnsbury Maple Sugar Festival. April is also the time for white water canoe races and for white water rafting on the West River. It marks the opening of trout season, but is better known as Mud Season, a time to avoid dirt roads. Many inns close.

MAY May Day is celebrated with an annual slalom at Killington and with a white water canoe race on the Passumpsic in East Burke. In mid-May there is a Festival of Traditional Crafts at the Fairbanks Museum, St. Johnsbury, and an Arts Day, which fills both Chelsea greens with things crafted and old. At the late May Sheep & Wool Festival, at Burklyn Hall Barns in East Burke, contestants must turn a fleece into a wool shawl in a matter of hours. Late May marks the first chicken barbecues of the season and the Memorial Day opening of State Parks.

JUNE The Vermont Dairy Princess is crowned at the Vermont Dairy Festival, held in Enosburg Falls for two days in early June. Mid-June is the time for strawberry suppers in churches and granges throughout the state. The Annual Balloon Festival in Quechee attracts balloonists from throughout the East towards the end of the month. The Discover Jazz Festival in Burlington features free performances.

JULY AND AUGUST Vermont's short summer season begins formally with the July 4th weekend and ends on or before Labor Day. Ongoing events throughout this season include summer theater (see *Theater*), the Marlboro and the Vermont Mozart Festivals, and the baked bean suppers every Saturday night in Brownsville.

JULY July 4th weekend is the single most celebrated event in the state. Among the colorful places to be are Bristol (parade, fair, kiddie matinee); Calais (fiddlers' contest); Woodstock (road race, craft fair, fireworks); Jeffersonville (frog jumping and a lumberjack contest); Plymouth (events commemorating Calvin Coolidge's birth); Post Mills (a lobster bake at the airport); Saxtons River (where volunteer firemen play a unique form of water polo); Stowe (marathon, fireworks, barbecue); Brattleboro (parade and fireworks); East Corinth (auction and chicken barbecue); and a banjo contest in Newfane. On the following weekend, a big antique festival is held either in Dorset or Manchester. Mid-July is the time for a sugar-on-snow supper in Morgan, for dog shows in Woodstock and Stowe. In late July, there is the Slavic Festival at Norwich University, Northfield; the Vermont Quilt Festival, Northfield, is the largest show of its kind in the northeast; the Aquafest on Lake Memphremagog at Newport; and the Cracker Barrel Bazaar in Newbury (known for its Old Time Fiddling); not to mention Lamoille County Field Days, held at Morrisville or Johnson; the Antiques and Uniques Festival at Shelburne; and the Annual Swanton Festival and the Old Round Church Pilgrimage, in Richmond.

AUGUST More events are packed into August than into the rest of the year put together. Among the highlights: Old Rockingham Days (car rally, fireworks, dancing) at the Rockingham Meetinghouse; The Volvo International Tennis Tournament, at Stratton Mountain Resort; the week-long Art on the Mountain display of arts and crafts at Haystack Mountain; the Grace Cottage Hospital Fair Day (parade, auction, barbecue), held on Townshend's handsome green; and the Southern Vermont Craft Fair in Manchester. Antique and classic cars rally at Stowe; rockhounds meet in South Burlington for the Champlain Valley gem and mineral show; and horse lovers gather at the Morgan Horse Farm in Weybridge for Vermont Day. Bennington Battle Day is celebrated mid-month. Some of the state's most striking rural buildings—the Old Meetinghouse at Weathersfield, the Old Stone House in Brownington, and the Kent Tavern in Kents Corner—are the settings for special events. In a natural amphitheater, off in a field near Glover, thousands gather to view the Annual Domestic Resurrection Day circus, staged by the Bread and Puppet Theater. A different crowd attends the old-fashioned agricultural fairs held in New Haven, Fairfax, Barton, Lyndonville, and Wilmington. However, some of the best August events are the small-town chicken pie suppers, book sales, Old Home days, and crafts shows geared to residents but welcoming visitors.

SEPTEMBER The last days of summer are celebrated over Labor Day weekend with the Northfield Labor Day Weekend fest, featuring the largest parade in the state; a Fun Run and barbecue in Jeffersonville; the Vermont State Fair in Rutland; and the Champlain Valley Exposition in Winooski. Early September is also the time for a Wurstfest of German music, dancing and food at Stratton; and a Heritage Festival in Newfane. The colorful World's Fair attracts a wide following to Tunbridge, and Dowsers from throughout the world gather for a convention in Danville. Harvest Festivals are held in Bristol, Brookfield, and at Shelburne Farms; and apple picking begins throughout the state, especially Addison and Windham counties. Foliage generally peaks in Northern Vermont by the third weekend, a cause for Holiday in the Hills hosted by the tiny villages of Victory and Granby, followed by a week in which the towns of Walden, Cabot, Plainfield, Peacham, Barnet, and Groton each take their turn hosting visitors for a day with public breakfasts, lunches, dinners and special tours, adding up to the Northeast Kingdom Fall Foliage Festival. The National Traditional Old Time Fiddler's Contest is held on the final weekend in Barre, and the annual Banjo Contest in Craftsbury.

OCTOBER During the first two weeks, fall foilage reaches its peak color in southern Vermont, and leaf-peekers converge on this area from throughout the country. See *Foliage* for tips. Montpelier stages its Fall Festival of Vermont Crafts; Stowe and Jay both hold Octoberfests. Dover and Dummerston Center host Apple Pie Festivals. Bow and arrow season for deer begins the second Saturday.

NOVEMBER Wild game dinners are held in Tinmouth and Bradford. Deer season opens 12 days before Thanksgiving. Christmas bazaars are held in Waitsfield, St. Johnsbury, Brandon, Burlington, and Woodstock. Most ski areas gear up snowmaking equipment hoping for a white Thanksgiving.

DECEMBER Christmas bazaars can be found throughout the state, along with pick-your-own Christmas tree farms. Candlelight tours are held of Historic Hildene; Manchester Village and Woodstock hold special events. Innkeepers pray for snow to help fill their beds during Christmas vacation.

Southern Vermont

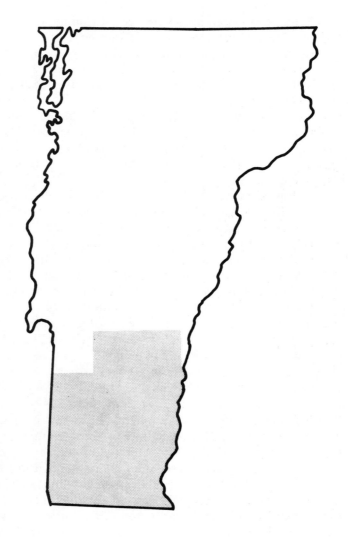

The Lower Connecticut and West River Valleys

The southeast corner of Windham County falls within the bailiwick of the Brattleboro Area Chamber of Commerce. This area includes the Connecticut River towns of Putney and Westminster, the West River towns of Newfane and Townshend, the Whetstone River town of Marlboro, and the beautiful backroaded hills between these valleys. All three rivers and, of course, the roads that follow them meet in Brattleboro—as do the residents of this area whenever they go to a supermarket, discount store or movie. But "Brat," as it is locally known, is so entirely different from the villages—and each of the villages from each other—that it is impossible to talk about them all at once. Permit us, therefore, to introduce them one by one.

Brattleboro is now a college town without a college—or so I was told by a fellow customer at the Common Ground, an unusual worker-owned restaurant on newly fancied Elliot Street. For the past decade this restaurant has served as a rallying point for the young people who have been moving into the surrounding hills. Many came here first as students at one of a half dozen nearby educational institutions and a few came for the music at Marlboro or one of the burgeoning music centers. Others come to study with the Experiment in International Living, a world-wide educational exchange organization that dates back to 1932 and has trained thousands of Peace Corps volunteers since the 1960s. Some newcomers have opened shops and restaurants, causing the old river town to take on a new look.

It's not the first time that Brattleboro has taken on a different personality. During its long history the state's largest town has shed many skins. The very site of Fort Dummer, built in 1724 just south of town, has been obliterated by the Vernon Dam. Gone too is the early nineteenth-century trading and resort town; no trace remains of the handsome Federal-style commercial buildings or the two elaborate hotels that attracted trainloads of customers who had come to take their water cures. The gingerbread station itself is gone, along with the wooden casino in Island Park and the fine

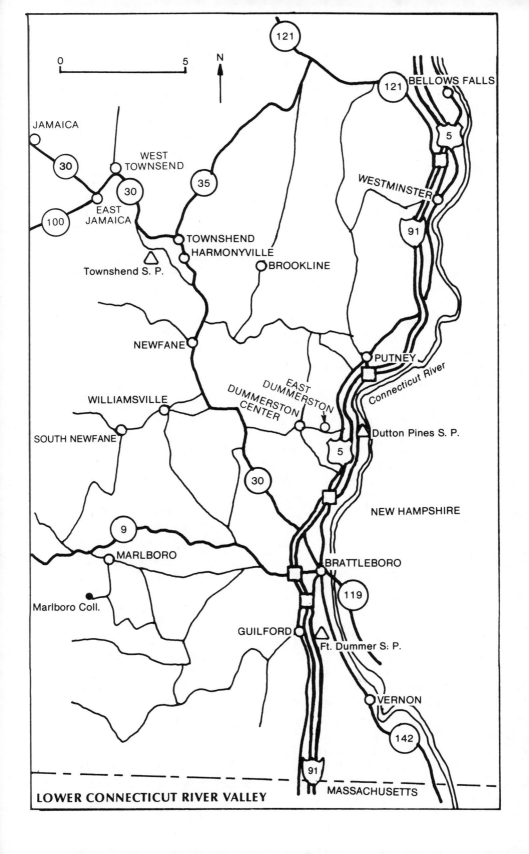

LOWER CONNECTICUT RIVER VALLEY

brick town hall, complete with gilded opera house. And the great slate-sided sheds up on Birge Street are the sole evidence that thousands of Estey organs were once made here.

Still, a motorist bogged down in the eternal Main Street bottleneck notices Brooks House, built splendidly in 1869 as an eighty-room hotel, now converted to housing, offices and shops. If you park, you will find that Elliot Street has been fitted out with new lights and specialty shops, and that the surviving rail station is now the Brattleboro Museum and Art Center, filled with historical and changing exhibits.

Brattleboro is actually full of pleasant surprises. For example, there are the beautiful grounds of the Brattleboro Retreat and the extensive sports facilities at Living Memorial Park. Live theater, music, and dance are presented without hoopla. The fanfare seems to be reserved for the annual winter carnival, begun eons ago by Fred Harris, who is also famed for founding the Dartmouth Winter Carnival and the U.S. Eastern Amateur Ski Association. The Carnival climaxes with a cross-country ski race, the granddaddy of all such "citizen races" currently held around the country.

VILLAGES   Newfane. A columned courthouse, matching Congregational Church, and town hall—all grouped on a handsome green—are framed by dignified white clapboard houses, including two of Vermont's most elegant inns.

When Windham County's court sessions began meeting in Newfane in 1787, the village was about the same size as it now: twenty houses and two hotels. But in 1787 the village was two miles up on Newfane Hill. Beams were unpegged and homes moved to the valley by ox-drawn sleighs in the winter of 1825.

Newfane inns have been famous for more than a century. First, because the whitewashed jail accommodated twenty-five paying guests, feeding them (an 1848 poem says) "good pies and oyster soup" in the same rooms with inmates. By the time this facility closed (in the 1950s), the Newfane Inn—which incorporates much of its hilltop structure—was beginning to acquire a reputation for gourmet fare. Economist John Kenneth Galbraith, a summer resident in the area since 1947, helped publicize the charms of both the village and inn—whose one-time chef eventually opened the Four Columns Inn at the rear of the Green.

Newfane has bred as well as fed famous men. In the Windham County Historical Society (open Memorial Day through October, Sundays, holidays 2–5 and for special events), you learn that Eugene Field of nursery rhyme fame (Wynken, Blynken, and Nod, etc.) came from a line of local Fields; a portrait of his father Roswell, who defended Dred Scott in *U.S. v. Scott* hangs in the Courtroom.

Newfane Village is more than just a fine place to dine, sleep, and stroll. It is the site of one of the state's oldest and biggest Sunday flea markets. There are two general stores: one is owned by former flatlanders, specializing in exquisite quilts; the other supplies local needs, and has been run by the same family for decades. Beyond the stores and the remnants of the railway station (which served the narrow-gauge Brattleboro-Londonderry line from 1880 to 1936), there is an unusually fine cemetery in which a local, Sir Isaac Newton (his given name), lies buried beneath a marble obelisk.

Townshend. The next full village center above Newfane is Townshend, a much-photographed community. Its Green is a full two acres bordered on one side by a classic white, 1790 Congregational Church, complete with green blinds, amidst clapboard homes. On the other side of the Green is a columned and towered, stucco town hall and the fine buildings of the new Leland and Gray Union High School (originally founded as a Baptist Seminary in 1834). At the junction of Routes 30 and 35, a short white clapboard block contains an apothecary, a hardware store, and a grocery, even a reasonably priced soda fountain. The big annual event is Hospital Fair Day when the common is filled with booths and games, all to benefit twenty-one-bed Grace Cottage Hospital. The hospital grew, unbelievably, out the backside of a rambling old village home. (Known for the quality of its service, this is Vermont's first hospital to have installed a birthing bed.)

This small town also contains a furniture factory (see *Outlets*), a state forest, public swimming area, Vermont's largest, single-span covered bridge, fifteen cemeteries and, atop one of its wonderfully abrupt hills, a welcoming inn (check Windham Hill under Lodging). An old tannery in West Townshend is now a moderately priced restaurant and tavern.

Westminster. Sited in a mile-wide plain above the Connecticut, this village is one of Vermont's earliest settlements. The unusually wide main street was designed as a militia training ground, and it was here in 1775 that locals barred New York court officials from their courthouse. The uprising, known as the "Westminster Massacre," was quelled and is considered one of the opening shots of the Revolution. Here also at a convention held in 1777, Vermont declared itself a free and independent state. Today, Westminster is a quiet valley town, noted for its farm stands and an outstanding family restaurant (see *Dining*). In the Westminster Historical Society (open Sundays, 2–4), you can see copies of the state's first newspaper (the famous press itself is now in the Vermont Historical Society Museum; see Montpelier).

Marlboro. Turn off busy Route 9 and you enter another, more tranquil world. In summer, flowers brim from window boxes, and the air is filled with the sounds of the Marlboro Music Festival. In other seasons, students purposefully stride from building to building on the small, attractive Marlboro College campus which, incidentally, maintains a fine network of cross-country ski trails. Check under *Shopping* for the three fine crafts studios here and under *Lodging* for details about the delightful Whetstone Inn. The Marlboro Historical Society with its collection of pictures, old farm tools, and antique furniture, is open Saturdays 2–5, July–Labor Day.

Putney. This village's river-side fields have been heavily farmed since the mid-eighteenth century, and its hillsides produce more than one-tenth of all the state's apples. Putney is an unusually fertile place for progressive thinking, too. Back in the 1840s, it spawned a group who practiced "Bible Communism," the sharing of all property, work, and wives. John Humphrey Noyes, the group's leader, was charged with adultery in 1847 and fled with his flock to Oneida, New York, where they founded the famous silverplate company. Today, the town is best known for Putney School, a very unusual co-ed, college preparatory school founded in 1935. It stresses the individual aptitudes of its students and has a regime that entails rising at 6:30 each morning and helping with chores, which include raising animals on the school farm. Landmark College is the country's first college specifically for dyslexic students and occupies the former multi-million dollar Windham College campus designed by Edward Durrell Stone.

The River Valley Playhouse, also on the campus, now stages year-round performances, films, concerts, lectures, and art shows.

Many young people who come to Putney for schooling never move away. The changing population is evidenced by the range of gourmet items available in the Putney Food Coop (one in a lineup of three general stores at the Village center) and in the fact that more than forty established craftsmen now live in town (see *Shopping*). Putney's native sons are no slouches either. They include the late George Aiken, who founded and developed the Putney Nursery and served as governor before going on to Washington as a Senator in 1941, a post he held until retirement in 1975. He was also the author of the classic *Pioneering with Wildflowers*. Frank Wilson, a genuine Yankee trader, who was one of the first merchants to enter Red China, built the first of his six Basketvilles, "The World's Largest Basket Stores," in the Village. We could go on. The Putney Historical Museum, open Wednesdays and Saturdays 2–5, is housed in the town hall. There is a seasonal information booth just off Route 5 at the I-91 access ramp in front of the Putney Inn.

GUIDANCE   Brattleboro Area Chamber of Commerce (254-4565), 180 Main

Street, Brattleboro, 05301. Open year-round, Monday–Friday 8–5. Besides the Main Street office, there are two seasonal information booths, run by knowledgeable senior citizens in warm weather months—on Route 9 in West Brattleboro and on Route 5 at the Common, just north of the junction with Route 30. There is also a seasonal information booth, maintained by Putney merchants, in front of the Putney Inn, just off Route 5.

GETTING THERE   By bus: Greyhound/Vermont Transit offers service from New York and Connecticut. Peter Pan Bus Co. serves Boston via Springfield. The bus stop is on route 5 at the junction with Route 9 West.

By train: see *Amtrak* in *What's Where.*

By plane: Eastern Express (800-451-4221) flies from Boston and New York to Keene, NH

TO SEE AND DO   **Brattleboro Museum and Art Center** (257-0124), Canal and Bridge Streets, Brattleboro. Open April–December 15, Tuesday–Friday, 12–4, also for special events. The town's 1915 rail station makes a handsome home for historical exhibits such as an Estey organ, a photo of Naulahka (the—now private—house in which Rudyard Kipling wrote his *Jungle Books*) and photos of the Brattleboro Kipling knew during his 1892–96 stay. There are also changing exhibits, frequent concerts, and other live presentations.

Brooks Memorial Library, Main Street, Brattleboro. This modern facility includes changing exhibits of art and sculpture, also a permanent collection of works by Larkin G. Mead, the Brattleboro boy who first achieved national fame by sculpting an eight-foot high angel from snow one night and placing it at the junction of Routes 30 and 5. The replica of this snow angel is here.

Santa's Land (387-5550), Route 5, Putney. Open May through December 24th daily; Igloo Pancake House open all year. A Christmas theme park with some unusual animals. Sleigh rides are available January–March by appointment, minimum 10 people.

MG Car Museum (722-3708), Westminster. (See Bellows Falls.)

Molly Stark Trail, Route 9 between Brattleboro and Bennington, is dedicated to the wife of General John Stark, hero of the battle of Bennington. It is a winding, heavily trafficked route, lined for much of the way with tourist-oriented shops and restaurants. We advise avoiding it in foliage season.

Vermont Yankee (257-1416), Vernon. An Energy Information Center at this (Vermont's only) nuclear power plant on Governor Hunt Road is open weekdays, 7:30–4, weekends, 1–5. Phone to check because hours may change. The simulator on Ferry Road, Brattleboro, is also open for tours by appointment.

FARMS TO VISIT   One of the state's concentrations of farms and orchards is here in the lower Connecticut River Valley, some offering "pick-your-own," others welcoming visitors to their farm stands, sugaring houses, or barns.

Harlow's Sugar House (387-5852), Route 5 in Putney, is one of the most visitor-oriented operations, permitting you to pick your own apples, blueberries and strawberries and offering sleigh rides during sugaring season. Syrup prices tend to be high.

Hickins Mountain Mowings (254-2146), Black Road, Dummerston. Located off the high, wooded back route that my children call the "Gnome Road" (between Route 5 in Putney and Route 30 in West Dummerston), this is an outstanding family farm, noted for the quality and variety of its vegetables, flowers, maple syrup, pickles, jams, jellies and fruitcakes. Open year-round until sunset.

Green Mountain Orchards (387-5851), West-Hill Road, Putney. Open daily in season. Pick-your-own apples and blueberries, cider available in season.

Dwight Miller & Son (254-9158), Putney. Open daily year-round, offering pick-your-own apples, strawberries and peaches. Also selling pears, plums, and turnips; follow signs from Route 5 across from KOA campground.

H & M Orchard (254-8100), Dummerston Center. Selling apples and strawberries, offering pick-your-own strawberries. One of the most accessible sugar shacks to observe "boiling" during sugaring season.

Allen Brothers Farms & Orchards (722-3395), Bellows Falls. Open year-round, daily; located on Route 5 two miles south of Bellows Falls, offering pick-your-own apples and potatoes, also selling vegetables, plants, and seeds, honey, syrup, and Vermont gifts.

Dutton Berry Farm and Stand (365-4168), Newfane. You can pick-your-own vegetables and berries at the farm on the Brookline Road or buy from the ample stand on Route 30.

Whetstone Valley Farm (254-9638), Route 9, West Brattleboro, opens its sugar house to visitors and sells syrup year-round.

COVERED BRIDGES   In Brattleboro the reconstructed Creamery Bridge forms the entrance to Living Memorial Park on Route 9. North on Route 30 in West Dummerston a Town Lattice bridge across the West River is the longest still-used covered bridge in the state (for the best view jump into the cool waters on either side; this is a popular swimming hole on a hot summer day). Vermont's longest single span bridge stands by Route 30 in West Townshend just below the Townshend Dam but is closed to traffic. There is also a covered bridge across the Green River in Guilford and another in the delightful backroad town of Williamsville.

PARKS AND FORESTS   **Fort Dummer State Park** (254-2610), R.F.D. #3, Brattleboro 05301. Located two miles south of Brattleboro on South Main Street. There are 61 campsites, including 9 lean-tos, a dump station, playfield, and a hiking trail through hardwoods with views of the river valley.

Dutton Pines State Park (254-2277), Brattleboro. On Route 5, 5 miles north of town this is a picnic area with a shelter. 75¢ per adult, 25¢ per person under 14.

Townshend State Forest (365-7500), Townshend. There are 30 campsites here (camping fees same as Fort Dummer); there is swimming nearby at Townshend Dam and a short (2.7 miles) but very steep climb to the summit of Bald Mountain; trail maps are available at the park office; adults pay 75¢, children 25¢.

Living Memorial Park, just west of Brattleboro on Route 9. This is an unusual facility for any community. It includes a swimming pool (mid-June–Labor Day, 50¢), ice-skating rink (early December to mid-March, $1.75 adults, $1.00 students), tennis courts and playground, camping sites ($4.00 per site per night), lawn games, a 9-hole golf course, and a ski hill serviced by a T-bar.

BICYCLING **Putney Bicycle Club**, the oldest in Vermont, sponsors an extensive program of tours through the nearby backroads. Check the **West Hill Shop** (387-5718), just off Exit 4 of I-91, across from the Putney Inn, good for local information, advice, and rentals, including mountain bikes. **The Country Inn** in Williamsville (348-7148) rents mountain bikes.

CANOEING   The 32 miles from Bellows Falls to the Vernon Dam is slow-moving water, as is the 6 mile stretch from below the dam to the Massachusetts border.

West River Canoe (896-6209), Route 100, Townshend, rents canoes by the hour, day, week, or month in season; sailboats, sailboards, and paddleboats also available.

FISHING   In the **Connecticut River** you can catch bass, trout, pike, pickerel, and yellow perch. There is an access on Old Ferry Road, two miles north of Brattleboro on Route 5, another from River Road on the New Hampshire shore in Westmoreland (Route 9 east then north on Route 63).

In Vernon there is a boat access on **Lily Pond** and in Guilford on **Weatherhead Hollow Pond** (see the *Vermont Atlas and Gazetteer*, DeLorme).

GOLF   **Brattleboro Country Club** (257-7380), Upper Dummerston Road, nine holes.

HIKING   In Brattleboro there are two pleasant walks. One is along the West River, following the abandoned West River Railroad bed. Access is off Route 5 north of town; take the second left turn after crossing the iron bridge; look for the trail by the Maple Farms milk plant. There is also a pleasant path up to the Retreat Tower, a nineteenth-century overlook. The trail begins beside Linden Lodge on Route 30. **Wantastiquet Mountain**, overlooking Brattleboro from across the Connecticut River in New Hampshire, is a good 1½-hour hike from downtown and is great for picnics and views of southeastern Vermont. Also see **Fort Dummer State Park** for a wooded trail south of town, overlooking the Connecticut, and a steep trek up **Bald Mountain**; see **Townshend State Forest**. There is a trail to the top of **Putney Mountain** between Putney and Brookline, off the Putney Mountain Road.

   Charles Marchant (365-7937) Townshend, offers hiking tours of old cemeteries, wilderness, moonlight trips, featuring local history and lore; $20 per person per day, $14 per half day; group rates.

HORSEBACK RIDING   **West River Lodge and Stable** (365-7745), Hill Road, Brookline. The small inn, stable, and riding school were all established in 1930 and have a loyal, year-round following. Guests are encouraged to bring their own mounts, but neophytes are also welcome. Trail rides offered, also sleighing in winter. Just two miles from Newfane, a short ways off Route 30, this is a frequently bypassed place, a real find for anyone who loves horses.

   South Mowing Stables (254-2831), Hinesburg Road. Lucile Bump offers instruction.

   Taffy Morgan (365-4228 or 874-4384) Townshend, offers buggy rides to elegant picnics (see *Dining Out*).

   Robinson Winchester Farm (464-8402 days; 464-2922 evenings), off Higley Hill, Marlboro. One- and two-horse carriage rides and sleigh rides, all in authentic period vehicles.

HORSE RACING   **Hinsdale Racetrack** (336-5382), Route 119, Hinsdale, NH. Pari-Mutuel Betting. Tuesday–Saturday 8:00 PM. Saturday & Sunday Matinee at 1:30. Runs year-round. Greyhounds mid-August to mid-June. Harness Racing mid-June to mid-August. Full dining room. Closed Monday.

SAIL BOARDING   **New England Sailboard Co.** (874-4178), Route 30, Jamaica and **West River Canoe** (896-6209), Route 100 (off Route 30), Townshend, both offer sailboard instruction and rentals.

RIVER TOURS   **Connecticut River Cruises** (254-8080), 91 Chestnut Street, Brattleboro. *Belle of Brattleboro* offers sightseeing, moonlight dinner, foliage, sunset, and Sunday brunch cruises. The 49-passenger riverboat is mahogany trimmed with a canopy roof. Captain Andy Bowen tells stories about the river and points of interest. From $6 adult ($4 per child 12 and under) for the two-hour cruise to $29.95 for Dinner-on-the-River. The *Belle* docks at a site on Route 142 (Vernon Road).

SWIMMING   In Brattleboro there is a pool in **Living Memorial Park** (mid-June to Labor Day, 50¢). The nearest beach for this area is Wares Grove in Chesterfield, NH (9 miles east on Route 9, the next left after the junction with Route 63). This pleasant beach on **Spofford Lake** is good for children; there is a snack bar and makeshift changing facilities. In Guilford there is swimming at **Weatherhead Hollow Pond**. The biggest swimming hole by far is at the **Townshend Dam**, off Route 30, in West Townshend. You drive across the top of this massive structure, completed in 1961 as a major flood prevention measure for the Southern Connecticut River Valley. Swimming is in the reservoir behind the dam, ideal for children. Changing facilities provided, small fee.

CROSS-COUNTRY SKIING   **Brattleboro Outing Club Ski Hut** (254-4081) Upper Dummerston Road. Trails through woods and golf course, 15 km machine tracked, rentals, instruction.

Guided Ski Tours. Charles Marchant (365-7937), Box 132, Townshend 05353, offers guided moonlight and other cross-country tours in the Townshend area.

In **Living Memorial Park**, Brattleboro (354-6700), a 6 km trail through the woods is not only set but lighted for night skiing.

DOWNHILL SKIING   The big ski areas are a short drive west into the Green Mountains, either to Mount Snow (Route 9 from Brattleboro and then up Route 100 to East Dover; see The Mount Snow Area) or up Route 30 to Stratton and beyond to Bromley and Magic Mountains (see Manchester and the Mountains).

Maple Valley (254-6083), West Dummerston, Route 30.

Lifts: 2 double chairlifts, 1 T-bar.

Trails: 13 trails and slopes.

Vertical drop: 1000 feet.

Facilities: cafeteria, ski shop, lounge, rentals, repairs, snowmaking.

Ski School: American technique, PSIA certified.

Open: Tuesday–Sunday, 9–4. Night skiing: Thursday–Saturday, 5–10.

Rates: $19 adult, $16 junior (ages 7–13) on weekends, $14 adult, $12 junior, midweek; 1/2 day available, also night skiing.

In Brattleboro itself a T-bar serves the ski hill in **Living Memorial Park** and there is a ski jump near the Brattleboro Retreat.

SKATING   **Living Memorial Park**, Brattleboro; rink is open daily, evenings until 9. $1.75 adults, $1 students.

Rollerdome. Route 5 north of Brattleboro, roller skating Friday & Saturday, 7:30–10:30; Saturday & Sunday, 2–5.

LODGING   **Whetstone Inn** (254-2500), Marlboro 05344. Open year-round. This 200-year-old tavern stands next to the Congregational Church, the natural gathering place in a classic Vermont village. During the Marlboro Music Festival it is *the* place to stay and week-long stays are frequently booked a year in advance. It is well worth the effort to book ahead. There are ten guest rooms, all bright and comfortable as are the public rooms, well supplied with books and games. Breakfasts are bountiful and dinners include desserts such as brandy Alexander pie and maple mousse. There is a pond and cross-country trails are maintained in winter by Marlboro College. Jean and Harry Boardman are genial hosts. Rates: $45–70 double, $35–60 single. Three efficiency apartments, $60–80 double, plus $15 per extra adult, $3–12 for children. Meals are extra: $5–7 per breakfast, $14–18 per dinner.

Old Newfane Inn (365-4427), Newfane 05345. The long, low-beamed dining room was a part of the original inn built up on Newfane Hill (see Newfane Village), and there is a seemly sense of age to this landmark. The ten guest rooms, nine with baths, furnished with antiques are spotless, as are the public rooms. Formal atmosphere. Closed in November and April. Rates: $70–85 double with bath, $90–95 for a suite (living room, bath and bedroom), $15 for each additional person. Continental breakfast.

Four Columns Inn (365-7713), Newfane 05345. Built in 1830 by General Pardon Kimball to remind his Southern wife of her girlhood home. This is a classic Greek revival mansion, now converted to 16 rooms, each with private bath and brass beds. Sandy and Jacques Allembert have created a genuinely gracious country inn, nicely complemented by the large and highly rated restaurant, housed in the attached barn. In winter there is skating on the trout pond and in summer, swimming in the pool. $65–105 double occupancy, including breakfast.

Windham Hill Inn (874-4080), West Townshend 05359. Poised high above the West River Valley, this 1825 brick farmhouse offers a comfortable retreat. Each of the 15 guest rooms (all with private bath) is carefully furnished with antiques and interesting art. Downstairs rooms are "country elegant," with oriental carpets, wing chairs, silver candelabra on the formal, central dining table. There are also informal spaces for relaxing. Guests congregate for cocktails before dinner—a four-course, candlelit affair. In winter there is a small pond for skating and you can ski on trails right on the property or head for alpine trails at Stratton, less than a half hour drive up Route 30. $85–95 per person MAP single occupancy, $65–75 per person, double; three and five-day packages available.

The Inn at South Newfane (348-7191), South Newfane 05351. This elegant inn is sited just off the beaten track in a picture-perfect village, complete with covered bridge. There are six large guest rooms, all with high ceilings and private bath. The public rooms are nicely appointed and the porch, a great place for evening cocktails, overlooks a sweeping lawn shaded by weeping willows (a hammock is strung between two), with a swimming pond at its center. The innkeepers are Connie and Herb Borst and their daughter, Lisa, a graduate of the Culinary Institute of America, the chef who has put this place on the Vermont dining map. $72.50–$90 per person per day MAP, double occupancy, $15 less B&B.

Hickory Ridge House (387-5709), RFD 3, Box 1410, Putney 05346. This is a find: an 1808 brick mansion, complete with Palladian window, set on 13 acres on a country road near the Connecticut River. There are seven airy guest rooms, painted in soft, authentic colors like lime and peach, decorated with antiques and interesting art, but not enough to clutter. The original Federal-era bedrooms are large, with Rumford fireplaces. Hosts Jacquie Walker and Steve Anderson come to innkeeping from backgrounds that include college teaching, cooking, and chimney-sweeping. Steve can greet you in German, Russian, and French. Breakfast features their own jams and jellies, baked goods, eggs from their chickens, honey from their bees and, with luck, their own maple syrup. In summer a swimming hole lies within walking distance and in winter, there are miles of cross-country touring trails, maintained by the Putney School. Dinner is available by reservation. $40–65 per room, B&B, $12 for an extra person in the room.

West River Lodge (365-7745), RR1, Box 693, Newfane 05345. Since the 1930s this inn has catered to horse lovers, doing so exclusively through the 1970s and up until Gill (pronounced Jill, short for Gillian) and Jack Warner, both former college professors, bought it a few years ago. Riding is still a big draw: English-style riding instruction is offered in the big barn or ring, and there are trail rides. This is also a place you can bring your own horse or carriage. Some of the finest back road bridle paths are right out the door. In winter there are sleigh rides. Non-riders too can enjoy the isolated feel of this white farmhouse, just a mile or two off busy Route 30. Rooms are cheerful, unpretentious, and country comfortable. Meals are what Gill describes as country cooking but with a Welsh accent to match her own. Guests dine around a common table in the low-beamed dining room and also in the friendly, old-style parlor. $55–65 per double room B&B, $85–95 double room MAP; weekly rates also available.

The Country Inn at Williamsville (348-7148), Grimes Hill Road, PO Box 166, Williamsville 05362. Bill and Sandra Cassill spent four years renovating this 1795 farmhouse before inviting guests in. The Federal-style inn offers six guest rooms, all with private bath, one with a hand-painted scene covering its walls. The dining room is large and formal and there is a spacious living room with a grand piano, also a smaller, inviting library with cable TV. Five-course dinners are served Friday, Saturday, and Sunday evenings, prepared by Sandra who has studied cooking in London, Paris, and at the Vermont Culinary Institute in Montpelier. In summer you can swim in the pond or swimming hole on the property, or explore these back roads on mountain bikes (available to guests for $9 per day). In winter there are more than 4 miles of cross-country ski trails on the property and Mount Snow's alpine trails are less than a half-hour's drive away. $65–105 per room B&B, $75–145 MAP, $15 B&B, $30 MAP for extra person in the room.

Longwood Inn (257-1545), Marlboro 05344. Formerly a dairy farm set back above Route 9, this attractive inn has nine nicely furnished guest rooms and there are four efficiency studios (accommodating three to six) in the Carriage House. The more expensive rooms have fireplaces and one has a whirlpool. Two comfortable rooms are reserved for guests to relax downstairs in the inn, and there is a large public dining room with an ambitious menu and strong local following. The fish pond out front is well-stocked. In winter a cross-country trail leads to Hidden Lake. Rates are $85–135 per room B&B, $125–174 MAP, $95–105 B&B, and $135–145 for the apartments.

The Putney Inn (387-5517), Putney 05346. One of the oldest farmhouses in the area, this red clapboard landmark was built by the first settlers. In the early 1960s, when the land was divided for construction of I-91, it was sold to local residents who converted the original building into handsome public rooms, including a large dining room, and added motel units with twin or double beds, phones, and cable TV, some efficiency units. While it has little of the feel of a country inn, this is a pleasant, comfortable place to stay. $48 double, $33 single. Also inquire about the 13 budget-priced rooms (sharing 4 baths), in the "Lodge," geared to groups and large families.

Chamberlain House Inn (365-4210), PO Box 387, Townshend 05353. This mid-nineteenth century village house is a comfortable, reasonably priced alternative to the valley's more elegant inns. Newly converted to a bed and breakfast, it has a large living room with chairs near the woodstove and rooms furnished with antiques and handmade quilts. Continental breakfast is included in $45 per double room.

Mapleton Farm (257-5252), Route 5, East Dummerston 05346. The former Dutton Farm, built in 1803, is set on 25 acres; rates are $45–55 double, including breakfast.

Dalem's Chalet (254-4323), West Brattleboro 05301. Set back from Route 9, this chalet-style motel is a family find, offering tidy rooms with two double beds and TV, indoor and outdoor swimming pools, game room and sauna, a pond with swans, and best of all, a fine little restaurant specializing in Swiss dishes, $36–54 per room.

Massey Farm (365-4716), Grassy Brook Road, Brookline 05345. This eighteenth-century farmhouse is located amidst 122 acres of rolling meadow. Penny and Frank Massey offer a wide range of year-round activities: all-weather tennis court, hiking trails and stocked pond; miles of groomed cross-country trails in winter. There are elegantly cosy rooms (with either shared or private bath), a game room, lounge with VCR, formal dining room and country kitchen eating area. Continental breakfast is served daily from 8:00–10:00. $55.00–75.00 per room.

DINING OUT   **Inn at South Newfane** (348-7191), Dover Road, South Newfane. A nicely decorated dining room in a former mansion (see *Lodging*) is the setting for gourmet meals prepared by Lisa Borst, a graduate of the Culinary Institute of America. The menu is unusually varied. You might begin with char-grilled quail in Yucatan-style marinade or with fresh shucked mussels, sweet sausage and tomato in white wine, followed by boneless breast of duck with a green peppercorn-mustard sauce, milk-fed veal with apple-wine sauce, or a wild game special. Figure $30 per person plus wine. No credit cards.

The Four Columns Inn (365-7713), Newfane. The dining room is housed in a converted barn with a large brick fireplace as its centerpiece. Current owners, Sandra and Jacques Allembert, formerly owned Le Bistro in New York City. The menu is French with emphasis on herbs (homegrown) and locally raised lamb, trout from the adjacent pond. Appetizers might include cold, smoked salmon mousse and smoked trout with chive cream cheese, black bread and horseradish sauce, and the wide choice of entrées might include sauté of lobster and shrimp, assorted vegetables, with green and red pepper corn bread or venison loin with wild rice. Dinner runs $35–40 per person plus wine. Sunday Brunch averages $15.

Longwood Inn (257-1545), Route 9, Marlboro. The attractive dining room in this old inn is well known for the quality of its fare. You might dine on poached salmon in Scotch cream sauce, on roasted Cornish game hen with herbed rice stuffing, or twin lamb chops with Zinfandel sauce, rosemary mustard. Appetizers might include smoked duck sausage or skewered shrimp. Dinner averages $30 per person plus wine; brunch, $12.

Townshend Country Inn (365-4141), Route 30, Townshend. This pleasant country restaurant may just offer the best dining value in southern Vermont. Since acquiring this old house—the oldest part dates back to 1776 and was a summer home for Grandma Moses—a few years ago, Joe Peters (fresh from seven years of managing the Yankee Pedlar in Holyoke, MA) has created a mix of ambiance and quality dining at prices well below the norm. You had better come early for the Sunday Vermont Buffet Brunch ($7.95). The dinner menu features a large seafood selection, including salmon poached in white wine ($9.95) and lobster pie ($14.95). Roast Long Island duck is $11.25 and chicken Kiev (stuffed with sweet butter, garlic, fine herbs, and poulette sauce) is $8.25. January through May there are monthly wine tastings that include a six-course dinner at $25 per person. Lunch prices run $2.50–6.50. Closed Tuesday and Wednesday off-season.

The **Putney Inn** (387-5517), just off I-91, Exit 4 in Putney. An eighteenth-century house is now a popular restaurant, good for "just a plain ole burger" ($3.25) or unlimited salad bar ($4.95) at lunch, or for dependable fare, ranging from baked lasagna ($7.95) to broiled lamb chops ($15.95) for dinner. Try the maple mousse for dessert. All three meals are served.

Old Newfane Inn (365-4427), Route 30, Newfane Village. The low-beamed old dining room is very formal, open for both lunch and dinner. The pricey menu is continental and varied, including unusual soups and memorable desserts. Closed Mondays.

EATING OUT   Taffy Morgan's Elegant Picnics (365-4228 or 874-4384), Townshend. Taffy transports guests in an open buggy or enclosed rockaway to a grassy field or mountain top where she lays out a gourmet picnic lunch, served on linen, with crystal and china. The feast might begin with lobster quiche, include braised Cornish game hens or butterflied leg of lamb.

The Common Ground (257-0855), 25 Elliot Street, Brattleboro. By no means the most elegant or expensive restaurant in town, this is a unique and rewarding place (see chapter introduction). The dining rooms occupy the high-ceilinged second floor of an old industrial building, and there is a pleasant glass-walled solar terrace. At the beginning of each month a leaflet is printed up, showing the specialties available each day; these run the gamut from Russian vegetable pie through lasagna to spanakopita. Other specialties include fresh fish, organic chicken, and sandwiches, depending on the day. Customers help themselves to tea, coffee, and side dishes. Strangers are encouraged to sit down at the same table and talk to each other; there is a rare friendly feel to this place. Beer and wine are available, and there are monthly art shows, occasional lectures and live entertainment. Monday–Friday for three meals except Tuesday nights; Saturdays, 11:30–4 and Sundays for brunch, 10:30–1:30. Dinner from $3.50.

Jade Wah (254-2392), 40 Main Street, Brattleboro. One of the better Chinese restaurants in Vermont, this unpretentious family place offers Szechuan-Mandarin cuisine, some Cantonese dishes, Chinese Hors d'Oeuvres, seafood dishes and some American food. It has a full liquor license. Open Monday–Thursday, 11:30–11:00, Fridays and Saturdays, 11:30–midnight, Sundays, noon–11:00.

Taft's (257-5222), 142 Elliot Street, Brattleboro, serves dinner Monday–Saturday, in a relaxed, contemporary setting, featuring fresh seafood, Cajun dishes, $9.95–14.95, plus lighter fare like crêpes Mont Vert ($7.50).

Westminster Restaurant (722-3541), Route 5, Westminster Village. A true family restaurant, known locally as the best value around. Open daily for breakfast, lunch, and dinner. Chef/owner Ed Cray is a graduate of the Culinary Institute of America and the food reflects it; dinner entrées, however, begin at $6.25. Children's menu and cocktails are both available.

Via Condotti, Ristorante & Pizzaria (257-0094), 69 Elliot Street, Brattleboro. Besides assorted pizza ($5.50 and up) and pastas ($5.50 and up), there are veal, chicken, and seafood dishes ($8 and up). The attached LaGrotta Lounge is fully licensed; house wines are available. Open daily for lunch (11:30–4) featuring burgers, grinders, and salads; dinner until 1:00.

West Townshend Village Cafe (874-4162), Route 30, West Townshend. Hidden down below the road by the West River, this former tannery makes a delightful lunch or dinner stop. There is a children's menu with $1.75 burger and $1.50 hot dog, also a variety of salads and sandwiches served all day, but you can also dine on shrimp parmesan ($12.95), baked stuffed rainbow trout ($11.50), or prime rib au jus ($10.95). In summer there is dining on the deck.

Dalem's Chalet (254-4323), off Route 9, South Street, Brattleboro. Swiss, German, and Austrian specialties, open to the public for dinner only. Reservations requested. Moderately-priced.

Jad's Family Restaurant (257-4559), Canal St., Brattleboro. A good bet for families; homemade soup, diner fare, fried foods, children's menu. $2.75–7.95.

Scottie's Place (365-7684), Harmonyville. Located in the village of Harmonyville, south of Townshend on Route 30. This is a dependable family restaurant open for breakfast and lunch, 7–3. Good for homemade soups, salads, and sandwiches.

Shin La Restaurant (257-5226), 57 Main Street (across from the Latchis Hotel), Brattleboro. Open 11–9, a small, new Korean restaurant specializing in homemade soups, dumplings, and Korean dishes. There are sushi specials on Tuesdays. Entrées average $6.

Walker's Restaurant (254-6046), 132 Main Street, Brattleboro, closed Sundays except during foliage and Christmas. This is a great downtown waystop: spacious dining rooms with bare brick walls, oak tables and bar, soft lighting. For lunch there is a wide choice of burgers, soups, quiche, and sandwiches (note that only fresh potatoes, cut on the premises, are used for french fries). The dinner menu includes steak, seafood, fish and chicken, basics like fried clams and sirloin steak, not-so-basics like mustard-herbed baked chicken. Entrées average $10.

West River Marina (257-7563), Route 5 just north of Brattleboro. Spring through Fall, 11:30–midnight, Sundays, 10–9. Live music, Thursday and Friday. Sandwiches, soups, fresh fish entrées served on a riverside deck. Reasonably priced.

Curtis' Barbeque. On fair summer days follow your nose to the blue school bus parked on Route 5 in Putney, just off I-91 Exit 4. Curtis cooks up pork ribs and chicken, seasoned with his secret barbecue sauce, also foil-wrapped potatoes, grilled corn, and beans flavored with Vermont maple syrup. By far the best barbeque in the Northeast! He's there Thursday–Sunday, 9–9.

ICE CREAM AND SNACKS   Page's Ice Cream, Route 9, West Brattleboro. Outstanding ice cream with frequent special flavors, made on the spot. Good coffee shop, too. Open 7–2, 4–9, closed Tuesdays, also on Wednesdays in Fall and Winter.

The Upper Crust (257-1991), Brooks House Mall, Brattleboro. Located just off the Harmony Parking Lot, this irresistible store is a source of a variety of good breads, cakes, croissants, cookies, linzers, tarts, eclairs, and such. There is a small sit-down area; juices, sodas, coffee, and a variety of teas are served. Monday–Thursday, 7–5:30; Friday, 7–6; Saturday, 7–5. Closed Sundays.

Hamelman's Bakery, Elliot Street, Brattleboro. European pastries, breads, rolls, cakes. Many locals prefer it to the Upper Crust.

MUSIC   Marlboro Music Festival at Persons Auditorium, Marlboro College (254-8163 or 254-2394). Concerts, primarily chamber music, are offered on Fridays, Saturdays, and Sundays, early July through mid-August. Tickets are usually sold out by May, but seats can often be found on the screened-in porch attached to the concert hall. Pablo Casals preceded Rudolf Serkin as artistic director here. Festival members are limited to 70 and their public performances are incidental to their work together. For advance tickets write: Marlboro Music Festival, 135 South 18th Street, Philadelphia, PA 19103 (215-569-4690); after June 6: Marlboro Music Festival, Marlboro 05344.

Yellow Barn Music Festival (387-6637) Putney. Begun in 1969, this is a series of three evening chamber music concerts each week in July and August. Performances are in a 150-seat barn located behind the Public Library in Putney Village. Artists include both well-known professionals and students from leading conservatories.

Brattleboro Music Center (254-5080), 15 Walnut Street, Brattleboro. Housed in a former convent, this burgeoning music school sponsors a wide variety of local music events and festivals, some of them staged at the River Valley Playhouse and Art Center (see below).

PLAYS, CONCERTS, LECTURES   River Valley Playhouse and Art Center (387-4355), on the Landmark College campus, Route 5, Putney. Built as the art center for former Windham College, this facility now serves the community with its 400 and 100-seat theaters.

NIGHT CLUBS   Mole's Eye Cafe (257-0771), Brattleboro. A live music club.

Flat Street (254-8257), Brattleboro. Good for disco and rock music.

River Bend Inn's Echo Room (365-7352), Newfane. Lively band Saturday nights until 1 AM.

FILMS   **Actor's Theater** (257-1129), at the Latchis Hotel Ballroom, 2 Flat Street, Brattleboro. Film classics are often shown here. Call for information on forthcoming programs.

Capra Theater (257-0021), 46 Main Street, Brattleboro. First run films. Two shows nightly.

SELECTIVE SHOPPING   **Vermont Artisan Design** (257-7044), 115 Main Street, Brattleboro. This attractive shop displays the work of more than 80 Vermont craftspeople.

Sam's Army & Navy Dept. Store (254-2933), 74 Main Street, Brattleboro. This family business now fills two floors of two buildings with a full stock of hunting, camping, and sports equipment. Prices are reasonable but people don't shop here for bargains. The big thing is the service, skilled help in selecting the right fishing rod, tennis racket, or gun. There are also name brand sports clothes and standard army & navy gear. Sam's is usually open 8–6, until 9 on Fridays, closed Sundays. On the first day of hunting season (early November) the store opens at dawn and serves a hunter's breakfast (it also sells licenses).

Guilford Cheese Company has been steadily expanding its production of French-style soft cheese over the past few years. Unfortunately the farm in Guilford is not set up for visitors, but the Verde-Mont, Crême Fraiche Camembert, and other cheeses can be found at **Straw and Hay** (257-1277), 71 Main Street, Brattleboro.

Spring Tree Chocolate Factory Outlet, Route 5, Exit 3 (I-91), Putney Road, Brattleboro. Over 150 fine sweets and snacks from bins. Open Monday–Saturday, 10–5:30; noon to 5 Sundays.

The Putney Woodshed and Putney Artisans (387-4481), Route 5, Putney Village, 05346. Open daily 9:30–4:30, Sunday by appointment, closed February. In the barn behind her house Margot Torrey has created a showcase for work by some of the more than 40 craftsmen who live in and around Putney. Woodcuts, cards, things woven, sculpted, forged, and printed are among the unusual wares for sale here. You can also pick up a copy of the Putney Artisans Directory, good for hunting down individual craftsmen. Products range from custom-made, cross-country racing suits through hand-woven clothing to hand-wrought iron and enamel jewelry, not to mention hand-blown glass. All craftsmen are listed with phone numbers. Note that the Putney Artisans stage a festival at the town hall one Saturday in early September.

Carol Brown (387-5875), PO Box C-100, Putney, 05345. This yellow hilltop home contains a treasure trove of imported natural-fiber fabrics: Irish tweeds in richly colored weaves; cottons from

Holland, Switzerland and India; silks from Italy, China, and numerous other spots around the globe. There is also a tantalizing selection of specially made clothes, featuring capes, sweaters, scarves and mittens. "Carefully chosen fabrics from all over the world in pleasant surroundings," is the way Carol Brown, who is now retired at the age of 98, described this unique collection when we first visited her. She explained that it all began with a 1926 bicycle trip through Ireland. Miss Brown returned to Boston and began importing the isle's tweeds, subsequently moving to Putney when her nephew, Lawrie, attended Putney School. Since his aunt's retirement, Lawrie Brown has continued this homey business with a national reputation and following. Open year-round; Monday–Saturday, 9:30–4:30; Sunday by appointment. The way is marked from West Hill Road.

Green Mountain Spinnery (387-4528), Putney, 05346. At the Spinnery you can watch undyed, unbleached wool from local flocks being sorted, scoured, picked, carded, spun, skeined, and labeled. You can also buy the resulting wool in various plys—all in natural colors. Knit-kits and patterns are sold too. Just off I-91 Exit 4. Open Monday–Saturday, 10–5:30.

Basketville (387-5509), Putney Village, 05346. The first of the "world's largest basket stores" now scattered between Venice, Florida and Milo, Maine. Founded by Frank Wilson, an enterprising Yankee Trader in the real sense, this is a family-run business. The vast store features woodenware, wicker furniture (filling the entire upstairs), wooden toys, and exquisite artificial flowers as well as baskets and myriad other things, large and small. Prices are generally 40 percent below retail. Open daily from 8–9 in busy seasons, and 8–5 in slack seasons.

Putney Nursery (387-5577), Route 5, Putney 05346. This roadside nursery, begun and fostered by former Senator George Aiken, offers an unusually wide selection of wildflowers, also ferns, perennials, and herbs. Open Monday–Saturday, 8–5.

Turnpike Road Pottery (245-2168), Marlboro. Open Saturdays 1–4. Malcolm Wright makes wood-fired pottery.

Applewoods (254-2908), Marlboro. Daily 10–6. There are furnishings made from burls and other wood forms.

Newfane Country Store (365-7916). Mary and Peter Loring have filled their store with quilts, herbs, Vermont Cheese and maple syrup plus toys and Christmas ornaments. The quilts and things quilted are truly outstanding.

Carriage House Comforters (348-6633), Williamsville (2 miles west on the Dover Road from Route 30, south of Newfane). Goosedown comforters.

Lawrence's Smoke House (365-7751), Route 30, Newfane 05345.

Corncob smoked hams, bacon, poultry, fish, specialty meats, and cheese are the specialty of the house. Catalog and mail order.

Delectable Mountain (257-4456), 6 Elliot St., Brattleboro. Fine fabrics, Harris tweeds, silks, all natural imported laces, museum quality quilts (owner Jan Norris makes them all).

BOOKSTORES   **The Book Cellar** (254-6026), 120 Main Street, Brattleboro. An outstanding, long-established full service bookstore, particularly strong on Vermont and New England titles.

Green Mountain Bookstore (257-7777), 29 High Street, Brattleboro. Another fine bookstore in which browsing is encouraged, and there are occasional poetry readings and other special events.

Basket's Paperback Exchange (257-4221), 36 Elliot Street, Brattleboro. A great selection of new and used paperbacks.

Everyone's Books (254-8160), 71 Elliot Street, Brattleboro. This is an earnest and interesting alternative bookstore, specializing in women's books, also a great selection of children's titles.

OUTLETS   **The Outlet Center** (254-4594), Canal Street, Brattleboro. Open daily 9–9; Exit 1 off I-91. This former factory building produced handbags up until a few years ago. The Factory Handbag Store still carries the brand which was made here (it's now manufactured in Massachusetts), and a variety of other bags of all sizes. A dozen stores now fill the building; ample parking.

Londontown Factory Outlet Store (257-7056), Fairfield Plaza north of Brattleboro on Route 5. Open Monday–Saturday, 10–6; Friday until 9. A large selection of discounted rainwear, outerwear, jackets, leathers, and slacks for men, women, and children.

Townshend Furniture Company (365-7720), Route 30, Townshend. Attached to the factory itself is a genuine outlet for the colonial-style pine furniture; also the Back Store selling used Townshend furniture and antiques. Open daily, Monday–Friday, 9–5; Saturday and Sunday, 10–5.

Pine Tree Table Store Route 142 in Vernon, next to the Fire Department, open daily. Firsts and seconds of all the pine furniture manufactured in the plant next door.

SPECIAL EVENTS   February: **Brattleboro Winter Carnival**. Many events in Living Memorial Park, a full week of celebrations climaxed with the Washington's Birthday Race.

Late June: **Dummerston Center Annual Strawberry Supper**, Grange Hall, Dummerston.

July and August: **Marlboro Music Festival** in Marlboro, **Yellow Barn Music Festival** in Putney.

July 3: **Annual Banjo Contest** in Newfane.

July 4: A big parade winds through Brattleboro at 10 AM; games, exhibits, refreshments in Living Memorial Park; fireworks at 9PM.

Late July (last Saturday): annual sale and supper sponsored by the Ladies Benevolent Society of Brookline; old-fashioned affairs with quality crafts.

Early August: **Grace Cottage Hospital Fair Day**: exhibits, booths, games, rides on the Green in Townshend.

Early September: **Heritage Festival Benefit** in Newfane, sponsored by Newfane Congregational Church. **Putney Artisans Festival**, Putney Town Hall.

Labor Day Weekend: **Annual two-day music festival** in Guilford's Organ Barn (257-1961). Concerts are free.

October: **Bach Festival**, sponsored by the Brattleboro Music Center.

Early December: **Christmas Bazaar** on the Common, Newfane. Frequent auctions, bazaars, and church suppers are listed with the Chamber of Commerce and in the *Brattleboro Reformer*, the area's daily newspaper. **Farmer's Markets** are held weekly with time and place heavily promoted in the *Brattleboro Reformer*.

MEDICAL EMERGENCY   Brattleboro, Dummerston, Marlboro, Putney (254-2010); Brookline, Newfane, Townshend (365-7676); Westminster (463-4223). **Brattleboro Memorial Hospital** (257-0341), 9 Belmont Avenue, Brattleboro. **Grace Cottage Hospital** (365-7676), Townshend.

Mount Snow/Wilmington Area

Mount Snow made its splashy debut as a ski destination in 1954. Reuben Snow's farm was transformed by ski lifts and trails, lodges, a skating rink, and an immense, floodlit geyser. Ski lodges mushroomed for miles around, varying in style from Tyrolian to fifties futuristic. The impact of all of this hasty development on the small village of West Dover helped to trigger Vermont's environmental protection law, Act 250.

By the early 1970s bust had followed boom, and the ski area was absorbed by one company after another, finally acquired in 1977 by the company now known as S.K.I., owner of Killington (Vermont's largest ski resort by far). Mount Snow is now Vermont's second largest ski resort. Haystack, a few miles down the valley, has also expanded in recent years and draws its own loyal following. A cross-country ski ridge trail connects the two downhill areas. There are also three commercial cross-country ski centers maintaining an extensive system of touring trails.

The town of Dover, which includes Mount Snow, remains Vermont's fastest growing community. But the shape of growth has changed since Act 250. Instead of hundreds of new houses, each on a separate plot, there are now hundreds of new condominium units each year—all neatly clustered behind screens of greenery. While year-round residents still number less than they did in 1810, the annual growth rate is 17 percent. Of the 2,900 parcels of land on the tax boards, 2,200 are owned by nonresidents. And there is still no zoning in town.

The village of Dover is a small knot of white clapboard buildings on the crest of a hill. It isn't even marked from Dover Hill Road. West Dover, down on Route 100, is the actual center of town. It remains picturesque enough, a lineup of church, inn, and town offices. But much of Route 100 between Wilmington and Mount Snow is a visual history of the ups and downs of the ski industry, beginning in the late fifties.

Beyond this narrow, nine-mile long strip of motels and shops, however, mountains rise steeply. On the west, the upper Deerfield Valley is edged with the backbone of the Green Mountains, and on the east, the hills rise tier upon tier. Drive north a mile beyond

Mount Snow and you enter some of the least touristed countryside in Vermont. The same is true a mile south of Wilmington.

Although the surrounding hills were once lumbered extensively, they are now hauntingly empty. At one time, there were more local lumbering villages than there are ski areas today. Many are now ghost towns, two of them—Mountain Mills and Somerset—at the bottom of reservoirs. Wilmington, the village at the junction of Routes 9 and 100, looks much the way it did when sheep were being herded down its streets.

GUIDANCE   **Mount Snow/Haystack Region Chamber of Commerce** (464-8092) P.O. Box 3, Wilmington 05363. Good for inquiries by phone or in writing. A seasonal information booth is maintained at the junction of Route 100 south and Route 9. *Valley News*, the local weekly is good for current events information.

GETTING THERE   By train: see *Amtrak* in *What's Where*.

By air: Eastern Express serves Keene, NH, an hour drive to the east. Albany Airport is served by major carriers. Mount Snow Airport (North Air 464-2196) is open for small planes.

By bus: Greyhound/Vermont Transit to Bennington and Brattleboro, connecting service to Wilmington. The Skier's Express (718-596-4227), runs from New York City regularly during ski season.

Limousine/Taxi Service: New England Shuttle Service (464-8660), meets trains, planes, and buses. Mount Snow Vermont Tours, Inc., also known as Buzzy's Taxi and Shuttle Service, (464-2076) offers charter service to Boston, NYC, Hartford, Albany, and Keene, also meets buses, planes, and trains.

TO SEE AND DO   **Whitingham Village**. Brigham Young, the Mormon prophet who led his people into Utah and is hailed as the founder of Salt Lake City, was born on a hill farm here, the son of a poor basket maker. Two sites in town commemorate Young: one is a monument that sits high on Town Hill (the view is spectacular), near picnic benches, grills, a playground, and parking area. The second is on Stimpson Hill (turn south at Brown's General Store); on the right a few hundred yards up there is a small marker that proclaims this to be the homestead site of "Brigham Young, born on this spot 1801 . . . a man of much courage and superb equipment." Before leaving the village note the "floating island" in the middle of Sadawga Pond. The village was once a busy resort thanks to a mineral spring, and its accessibility via the Hoosuc Tunnel and Wilmington Railroad. It still retains an inn (see *Lodging*) and an auction barn (see *Shopping*).

Green Mt. Flagship Co. (464-2975), Route 9 west from Wilmington. Richard Joyce offers seasonal excursions on Lake Harriman aboard the *M. V. Mt. Mills* and the *M. V. Heather Sue*, twin-stacked pontoon vessels, each accommodating 50 people. Joyce caters to bus groups, but there are usually at least a half dozen seats left over. His narration of the lumbering history of the area is often accompanied by live music.

North River Winery (368-7557), Route 112, 6 miles south of Wilmington. Open May through October, 11–5 and November through April, Friday through Sunday, 11–5. An 1850s farmhouse and barn in this small village contain an interesting, small winery dedicated to producing fruit wines. We can speak for the full-bodied apple blueberry, neither too dry nor too sweet. Green Mountain Apple, Cranberry Apple, and a number of other blends are offered. Free samples come with the tour.

Luman Nelson Wildlife Museum (464-5494), Route 9, across from the Skyline Restaurant, Marlboro, east of Wilmington. Open year-round, 9–5. This is a great little museum, featuring stuffed birds and animals. Nominal admission; gift shop.

STATE PARK   **Molly Stark State Park** (464-5460), Route 9 east of Wilmington Village. This 158-acre preserve offers 34 campsites, including 8 lean-tos. A hiking trail leads through the forest to 2,415-foot Mt. Olga from which there is a panoramic view. See *State Parks* in *What's Where* for fees, reservations, and information.

SCENIC DRIVES   Dover Hill Road, accessible from Route 100 either via Dorr Fitch Road in the village of West Dover or via the East Dover Road farther south (just below Sitzmark). The road climbs steeply up past the tiny village center of Dover. Here you could detour onto gravel-surfaced Cooper Hill Road for a few miles to take in the panoramic view of mountains that spread away to the northwest. On an ordinary day you can pick out Mount Monadnock in New Hampshire beyond Keene. You can either loop back down to Route 100 via Valley View Road or continue down the other side of the hill, through East Dover to the general store, covered bridge and picturesque village center in South Newfane, returning the way you came (if you are out for a *real* ride, follow this road all the way to Route 30, then continue south to Brattleboro and return via Wilmington on Route 9, the Molly Stark Trail).

Handle Road runs south from Mount Snow, paralleling Route 100, turning into Cold Brook Road when it crosses the Wilmington Line. The old farmhouses along this high, wooded road were bought up by city people to form a summer colony in the late 1880s. It's still a beautiful road, retaining some of the old houses and views.

Kelley Stand Road. The 20-mile road west from Wardsboro through the village of Stratton (very different from the ski area by that name on the other side of the mountain), past the Daniel Webster Monument (Webster spoke here to 1,600 people at an 1840 Whig rally), through National Forest all the way to Arlington. The hiking trail into Stratton Pond that begins near the monument is the most heavily hiked section of the Long Trail.

AIR RIDES   **North Air** (464-2196), Mount Snow Airport off Country Club Road, West Dover, offers scenic air rides.

BOATING   Sailboats, canoes, and rowboats can be rented by the hour or day at **Lake Front Restaurant** (464-5838), located west of Wilmington on Route 9, across from Harriman Reservoir.

FISHING   **Harriman Reservoir** is stocked with trout, bass, perch, and salmon; a boat launch is off Fairview Avenue.

Somerset Reservoir, 5 miles west of Wilmington, then 10 miles on the Somerset Road offers bass, trout, and pike. There is a boat launch at the foot of the 9-mile-long lake. Smaller Sadawga Pond in Whitingham and Lake Raponda in Wilmington are also good for bass and trout; there is a boat launch on the former. Fishing licenses are available at Parmelee & Howe and at Coomb's Sugarhouse.

GOLF   **Mt. Snow Country Club** (464-3333). Weekend and five-day midweek Golf School packages are offered June–October, 18-hole Cornish-designed championship golf course also open on daily basis.

Sitzmark Golf Course (464-3384), Wilmington. 18 holes, club and cart rentals.

Haystack (464-8301), Mann Road, off Cold Brook Road, Wilmington; club house, 18 holes.

HIKING   Aside from the trails already mentioned in the two state parks and a short, self-guiding trail atop Mount Snow, there are a number of overgrown roads leading to ghost towns. The Long Trail passes through the former logging town of Glastenbury (261 residents in 1880) and a former, colonial highway within Woodford State Park leads to a burying ground and eighteenth-century homesites. Somerset is another ghost town.

HORSEBACK RIDING   **Flame Stables** (464-8329), Route 100, Wilmington. Western saddle trail rides, half-hour wagon rides.

SWIMMING   There are two beaches on 11-mile long Harriman Reservoir, also known as Whitingham Lake. **Mt. Mills Beach** is 1 mile from Wilmington Village posted from Castle Hill Road. **Ward's Cave Beach** is on Route 100 south from Wilmington, right at Flame Stables and follow signs. (Ask about skinny-dipping at the Ledges.)

Sitzmark Lodge (464-3384), north of Wilmington on Route 100 has a pool which is open to the public free of charge. Snacks and bar available poolside.

TENNIS   The municipal courts at Baker Field in Wilmington are available, also eight courts at Sitzmark (see above), four courts at the Andirons Motel (464-2114), and six at Tara (464-3050), Route 100 in West Dover.

CROSS-COUNTRY SKIING   **Hermitage Ski Touring Center** (464-3511),

Wilmington. Outstanding 35 km machine-tracked network (50 km total) includes a ridgetop trail with superb views, elevations of 1,867 to 3,556 feet. Instruction, rental, repair, telemark, guided tours (also see *Lodging, Restaurants*). Guided tours are offered along the ridge trail connecting Haystack and Mount Snow; inquire at the Hermitage.

Sitzmark Ski Touring & Learning Center (464-8187), Wilmington. Open fields, golf course with orchards and woodlands above, 25 km total tracked. Rentals, instruction, cafe, change rooms, headlamp tours, telemark lessons, guided tours.

The White House Ski Touring Center (464-2136), Wilmington. A total of 22 groomed trails meander through the woods at elevations of 1,573 to 2,036 feet. Instruction, rentals, lodging, ski weeks.

DOWNHILL SKIING   Mount Snow (main number: 464-3333; information and reservations: 464-8502), West Dover 05356. In the decade that S.K.I. has owned Mount Snow, it has boosted snow-making from 7 percent to 80 percent of the trails, which have also multiplied with the absorption of the former Carinthia ski area. Downplaying its old image as a singles' and snowbunnys' haven, it now stresses family and couples packages, has a strong children's program and extensive expert skiing. It is now Vermont's second largest ski area (the largest being Killington, the Sherburne Corporation flagship).

Lifts: 16, including 1 high-speed quad chair, 5 triple chair lifts, 8 double chair lifts, 1 rope tow and 1 T-bar.

Trails: 75 trails—21 "easier," 41 "more difficult," and 13 "most difficult." There are four distinct areas here: the Main Mountain, the expert North Face, the Sunbrook Area, and the Carinthia Slopes.

Vertical drop: 1,700 feet.

Snow-making: 80% of the mountain.

Facilities: Three base lodges and a Vacation Center (ski week registration and Pumpkin Patch Daycare), also the Snow Barn (night club with entertainment, dancing).

Ski School: 85 instructors, ATM method.

For Children: SKIwee for children ages 6–12, Pumpkin Patch for children aged 6 weeks to age 2, Peewee SKIwee for ages 3–5 (a combination of day care and light lessons).

Special programs: Free skiing for children age 12 and under (non-holiday weeks), "Romancing the Snow" couples' ski weeks.

Rates: $32 daily; $54 for 2 days, adult; $29 for two days, age 12 and under.

Haystack (464-5321), Wilmington 05363. Substantially smaller than Mount Snow, this is a family area with its own loyal following.

Lifts: 2 triple, 3 double chair lifts, 1 T-bar.

Trails: 31 trails—8 expert, 10 novice.

Vertical drop: 1,400 feet.

Snow-making: 80%.

Facilities: Unusually attractive base lodge set above the beginner slopes; ski shop, rentals, ski school nursery.

Rates: $25 (age 7 up); 65 and over, free.

OTHER WINTER RECREATION   **Ice fishing** is available on Harriman and Somerset reservoirs. **Sleigh rides** are available at the William Adams Farm (464-3762), at Flame's Stables (464-8329), and at Matterhorn Lodge (464-8011) where dinner is also served. **Snow Shoe** rentals are available at North Branch (464-3319) and at Mount Snow, adjacent to the National Forest. **Snowmobile** rentals are available from Henry Wheeler (464-5225), Route 100, Wilmington.

HEALTH SPA   **Snow Lake Lodge** (464-3333), at Mount Snow opens its well-equipped Fitness Center on a daily, weekly, and three-month subscription basis.

LODGING   There are some 90 lodging facilities in the area, ranging from intimate country inns to impersonal motel-like facilities, designed to accommodate groups. **The Mount Snow Lodging Bureau** (464-8501), operates year-round: November through March, 8–9; otherwise, 8–5. The Mount Snow brochure, available by writing to the Bureau (200 Mountain Road, Mount Snow 05356), includes descriptive listings of 58 inns and lodges, plus chalet and condo rentals.

INNS   **The Inn at Sawmill Farm** (464-8131), West Dover 05356. "When skiing hit the fan, we went elegant" is the way innkeeper Rodney Williams describes how his family coped with the early 1970s slump in the Valley. Williams is an architect, his wife Ione, an interior decorator, and their son Brill, an accomplished chef. Together the team have created one of Vermont's most elegant inns, filled with antiques. In summer, flowers are everywhere, inside and out; there is a swimming pool, tennis and a trout pond. There are 22 beautifully appointed guest rooms, each different, some with working fireplaces; $90–120 per person, MAP.

The Hermitage (464-3511), Wilmington 05363. Set high above its own rolling acres on Cold Brook Road between Mount Snow and Haystack Mountain, this is an inn that prides itself on its food and ambiance. Of the 15 guest rooms, 4 are in the main house, 4 in a converted Carriage House down the hill near the trout pond, and seven in the new Wine House. All rooms have private baths and a number have working fireplaces. In summer, there is tennis, and guests can use the pool at Brookbound, 1 mile down the road. Pheasants, ducks, quail, and geese parade around the grounds. Innkeeper Jim McGovern breeds the birds for their meat (see *Dining Out*), not looks. He also produces maple syrup, jams and jellies, and in winter maintains a first-rate ski touring center. McGovern is a collector of wine (more than 1,500 bottles, priced from $8–

$1,000), game birds, and French artist Michael Delacroix's work, which papers the dining room and is scattered throughout the inn. Rooms vary in quality; we recommend those in the Farmhouse. Prices are $80–90 per person MAP, a five-day ski-week is $340 per person.

The White House of Wilmington (464-2135), Wilmington 05363. Built in 1915 as a summer mansion for Martin Brown, founder of Brown Paper Co. The public rooms are huge, airy, and light but also manage to be warm in winter—with the help of yawning hearths. There are 12 guest rooms, all with private bath, 3 with fireplaces, and 1 suite. Guests gather around the sunken bar. There is tennis and a fine old pool, cross-country trails in winter, also a health spa complete with indoor pool. Rates: $80 per person MAP.

Deerhill Inn (464-3100), PO Box 397, West Dover 05456. A quiet, elegant retreat set on the shoulder of a hill with lovely views. When we stopped by, the accent here had just changed from Danish to English. Jan Ritchie was in the process of adding "a touch of Old England in New England." It all sounded rather grand but hadn't happened yet. There is a pool and tennis court. $130 per person for a two-day weekend, MAP.

Nutmeg Inn (464-3351), Wilmington 05363. A roadside farmhouse on the edge of the village offering nine rooms, each nicely decorated with new wallpaper, quilts, and braided rugs. There is a cozy living room, library, and BYOB bar. In winter, $101 MAP per person per weekend includes a soups-to-nuts dinner and big breakfast.

Trail's End (464-9396), West Dover 05356. So fancifully designed and decorated that a gnome would feel at home. There are 18 rooms, each decorated differently, all with private baths. In summer, the garden is beautiful and there is a pool out back. In winter, there are cross-country ski trails outside the door. $75 per room B&B.

Shield Lodge (464-3984), West Dover 05356. A small, homey inn offering six rooms with private baths and ample meals. There's a comfortable living room with a fireplace. In summer rooms are $25–30 per person B&B, and in winter it's $79–99 per person on weekends including dinner, $139–179 for a ski week. The new innkeepers are John and Marijke Sims.

Doveberry Inn (464-5652), Route 100, Dover 05356. A snug little inn with wood-stove charm; eight rooms with private baths. Home-cooked meals are served in two candle-lit dining rooms. Afternoon tea and a full country breakfast are included in $65–75 for a room (the latter price for a suite with private sun deck).

Misty Mountain Lodge (464-3961), Wilmington 05363. Just 20 people can be accommodated in this informal old farmhouse set high up on a hillside, surrounded by its 150 acres. Rooms are plain but there is an agreeable feel to the inn which features home-cooked meals and singing around the hearth while innkeeper Buzz Cole plays the guitar after dinner; children feel welcome; $40 per person MAP for a two-day winter weekend, $105 per person for a five-day ski week.

Cooper Hill Lodge (348-6333), East Dover 05341. There is an unbeatable view of the surrounding mountains from this rambling, hilltop inn, especially suited to groups and families with children. $40–45 MAP per adult, $15–25 per child.

Waldwinke Inn (464-5281), West Dover 05356. A family-run Alpine style inn geared to winter, families, and groups. $70 per person per winter weekend with continental breakfast; $120 for a five-day ski week.

Sadawga Lake House (368-2435), Whitingham 05361. 9 miles south of Wilmington, this old resort village still has one fine little inn, managed since 1959 by Lillian Jennings. There is no sign outside since more than 80 percent of guests are repeats. There are nine homey guest rooms (sharing two baths) and inviting common rooms (a fireplace in the living room). Rates are $20 per person MAP, $125 per week.

The Red Shutter Inn (464-3768), Wilmington 05363. A gracious village house with eight nicely furnished guest rooms and pleasant public rooms. The dining room, furnished with an assortment of old oak tables, has a good reputation and is open to the public; $65 per room per day, $55 off-season, full breakfast included; pay for four days and get the fifth free.

Snow Den Inn (464-9355), West Dover 05356. A small country inn in the middle of the village, neat and cozy. Five of the eight rooms have fireplaces and TVs, all have private baths. Summer, $65 per room; $100 on weekdays in fall and winter, $220 weekends; $400 ski weeks (five days); all are B&B.

West Dover Inn (464-5207), Route 100, West Dover 05356. Built as the village inn in 1846, there are eight rooms, seven with private baths and color TV. Guests share a living room with a hearth, and a public dining room. $95 per person per winter weekend, MAP, cheaper other seasons.

BED & BREAKFASTS   Slalom Lodge (464-3783), Wilmington 05363 (south of the traffic light). Five rooms (four with shared baths); full breakfast; lounge with Franklin stove and color TV. $55–65 per person; $25 per person with four sharing a room.

Birch Tree Inn (464-7717), Wilmington 05363 (on the northern fringe of the village). A friendly old house with eight guest rooms, all with private bath and plenty of sitting space around the chess set and fireplace in the living room. In summer, rates are $44 per room B&B on weekends; there's a swimming pool out back. In winter it's $50 per room, including a full breakfast.

LODGES These are distinctly different from inns. They are larger, usually with motel-style rooms, and designed with skiers in mind—with such amenities as pools, saunas, game rooms, and lounges.

Snow Lake Lodge at Mount Snow (800-451-4211), 100 Mountain Rd., Mount Snow 05356. Fifties futuristic and fun, this 105-room lodge is known for its indoor hot and cold "leisure pools" surrounded by a bit of tropical jungle. The building also offers an attractive dining room, game room, lounge, complete fitness center, outdoor pool, and tennis. Rates: $59–63 per person MAP, ski season, half that in summer.

North Branch (464-3319), West Dover 05356. Built as a private, club, this is an unusual and thoroughly delightful complex with 2 studios with fireplaces, and 13 one-bed rooms, each with private bath and balcony. There is a reception area, lounge, and dining room, and also a huge lounge area with exercise equipment, the area's largest indoor pool, and a separate game room for kids. A series of art workshops are held here July–October: week-long sessions taught by established artists with rates of $530–590 per week, which includes tuition, lodging, and meals. $78–99 per person in winter MAP, $329–417 per 5-day ski week.

Schroder Haus (464-2783), Higley Hill Road, Wilmington 05363. A classic ski lodge with a barnboard living room and dining room overlooking a mountain stream. Fireplace, sauna, game and TV room; ice-skating pond and cross-country skiing outside the door. There are 14 rooms, $89 per person, per weekend MAP.

Grey Ghost Inn (464-2472), Box 938, West Dover 05356. On Route 100, 27 rooms with bath, lounges, dining areas, game room, sauna, color cable TV, group rates. $40 per person B&B, $120 per five-day ski week.

MOTELS **The Vintage Motel** (464-8824), Wilmington 05363. The Vintage offers 18 pleasant rooms with baths; comfortable common rooms and a pool. The village shops are just down the road. $48 per room with continental breakfast.

CONDOMINIUM UNITS Condominium development has been recent and intense in this area. The Mount Snow brochure describes a half dozen major complexes. Haystack has its own mushrooming units.

Mount Snow Resort Center Condominiums (464-3333; 800-451-4211). There are three distinct condominium developments at the base of Mount Snow—Snow Tree, Snow Mountain Village, and Seasons (trailside), each with its own pool, sauna, whirlpool, and other amenities. There are a total of 276 units at this writing, more than half of them available to rent. $480 is the average rate for a two-day weekend for a unit sleeping four to six people. These are nicely designed; a real bargain in the summer.

Timber Creek Condominiums (464-2323; 800-437-7350), PO Box 560, Mount Snow 05356. This is one of the most attractive of the new developments: 160 units in nicely landscaped grounds; a central Sugar House with pool and hot tubs, racquetball courts and fitness center; also 12 km of cross-country trails and rental equipment. Two-day weekend rates are from $200 for a one-bedroom to $760 for a four-bedroom; seven nights for a one-bedroom are $760; $1,440 for a four-bedroom; much cheaper in summer.

Crafts Inn (464-2344), West Main Street, Wilmington 05363. The old hotel in the middle of the village (designed by Stanford White in 1896) has been renovated as a time-share resort. The 29 rental units each have a bedroom, sleep sofa in the living room, and kitchen. There is an indoor heated pool, four hot tubs, two saunas, a racquetball court, and a weight room. Summer rates: $100–140, weekdays, $120–160 weekends.

Haystack Mountain Real Estate (464-5321/7458). Two and three-bedroom condo townhouses are spread out along the Golf Club fairways and slope-side at Haystack Mountain Ski Area.

DINING OUT   **Sawmill Farm & Restaurant** (464-8131), West Dover. Dinner only, 6–9. The main dining room is fabricated from the innards of an old barn but hung with fine old portraits, the linen-covered tables set with sterling and garnished with fresh flowers; there is also a smaller, sun and plant-filled dining room. Eighteen main dishes are offered regularly; specialties include roast duck in green peppercorn sauce, rack of lamb, and soft shell crab. Entrées are $15–22; generally there is also a choice of 16 appetizers and irresistible desserts. One of the best in the state.

The Hermitage (464-3759), Wilmington. Lunch and dinner daily; dinner from noon until 11 on Sunday. A widely acclaimed restaurant that has recently been expanded: French doors, fine art on the walls, long tablecloths and a mixture of arm and wing chairs all make for the elegance due the dishes. (Though, truth be told, the large dining room can be noisy, and the service sometimes slow.) You might begin dinner with Norwegian smoked salmon ($7.50), proceed to chicken amandine ($13) or frogs legs Provençal ($16), with a wine chosen from a very wide selection, $8–$1000.

The Carriage Stop Restaurant (368-2882), Route 112, Jacksonville. Closed Mondays. Open for lunch and dinner. This small, out-of-the-way village (actually it's right on a shortcut to Mount Snow if you are coming up from Route 2 in Massachusetts) has a hot new gourmet restaurant tucked away in a house. The decor is a zany mix of milk cans, old postcards, and painted tree branches

Marvelous views surround golfers at the Mt. Snow Country Club

hung with Christmas lights. The menu goes from $9.95 for Stan's Country Cajun to $19.95 for rack of lamb; specialties include Creole dishes, veal and roast duck. Desserts are freshly baked. Crêpes are a luncheon specialty ($4.95).

Le Petit Chef (464-8437), Wilmington, Route 100 north. Open daily except Tuesdays, 6–9. Elegant French dining in an old road-side house; dinners, $11–$18.25.

Deerhill Inn (464-9382), West Dover. Applauded as one of the best places to dine in the valley. There are two dining rooms in this hillside inn, one with a cozy fireplace and a larger room with windows and French doors overlooking Mount Snow. Tables are elegantly set with candles, linen, and crystal. The menu may begin with escargot in puff pastry ($5.50), include oven-poached shrimp and scallops ($16), or roast duck with lingonberry sauce ($15); all desserts are made on the premises: fresh fruit tarts, truffle cake, "sin pie," homemade ice cream.

The White House of Wilmington (464-2135). The wood paneled dining room is warmed by a glowing hearth. The menu is ambitious, including Wiener Schnitzel, Coquilles St. Jacques, boneless duck stuffed with apple, grape, and walnut stuffing, and Veal Marsala plus 13 other entrées, $12.50–17.95.

The Old Barn Inn (896-6100), Route 100, West Wardsboro. Open for dinner, May–October, 6–10 PM. Closed Wednesday. A pleasant country inn atmosphere. Dinners from $14.95.

EATING OUT   **Poncho's Wreck** (464-9321), Wilmington. Newly rebuilt, open daily for dinner; lunch Friday–Sunday. A delightful, casual atmosphere; specialties are Mexican dishes, fish, and smoked meats. Located in the village, moderately priced, tends to fill up so it's advisable to come very early or late.

Elsa's Epicurean Deli and Cafe (464-8425), Route 100, Wilmington. Popular for lunch, gourmet shop and take-out.

Mainstreet's (464-3183), West Main Street, Wilmington. Open for lunch, dinner; good soups and lighter fare.

Costello's (464-2812), Route 9 west, Wilmington. Northern Italian food. Full dinner menu and separate pizza and sub sandwiches for kids; good for families.

Dot's Restaurant (464-7284), Wilmington, is open from 5:30 AM until 3 PM. This is a cheerful, pine-sided place in the middle of the village. There's a long formica counter as well as tables, fireplace in back, and wine by the glass. Stop by for a bowl of the hottest chili in New England ($1.95 a bowl). The soup and muffins are homemade and the Reubens are first-rate.

Cup'N'Saucer (464-5813), Wilmington. Open 6–6, a small, reasonably priced place on Route 100 north; pies a specialty.

Skyline Restaurant (464-5535) Route 9, Hogback Mountain, Marlboro. For more than 40 years, Joyce and Dick Hamilton have operated this restaurant with "the 100-mile view." The knotty pine dining room has worn shiny tables, fresh flowers, and a traditional New England menu. In winter there's a fire. Specialties include homemade soups, homebaked brownies, pies and turnovers, and a Vermonter Sandwich. Moderately priced.

APRÈS SKI   During ski season the following establishments feature live entertainment or DJs on most nights. In summer, they come to life on weekends. On Route 100, between Wilmington and Mount Snow, look for **The North Country Fair** (464-5697), **Sitzmark Lodge** (464-3384), **Andirons** (464-2114), **Deacon's Den** (464-9361), **Silo Saloon** (464-5820), and **Snow Barn Entertainment Center** (the old Rubin's Barn at Mount Snow). In town, check out **Poncho's Wreck** (464-9320). **Michael's** (Route 100) features musical reviews in summer.

SELECTIVE SHOPPING   **Quaigh Design Centre** (464-2780), Main Street, Wilmington. This is a long established showcase for top Vermont crafts, imported Scottish woolens are also a specialty.

John McLeod, Ltd. (464-8175), Route 9, Wilmington. Unusual wooden shapes to decorate your homes (clocks, mirrors, cuttingboards, etc.) are sold in the showroom of this woodworking shop on the western verge of the village; open daily.

Coomb's Sugarhouse, Wilmington. Located at the junction of Routes 9 and 100 south, this is one of the region's biggest maple

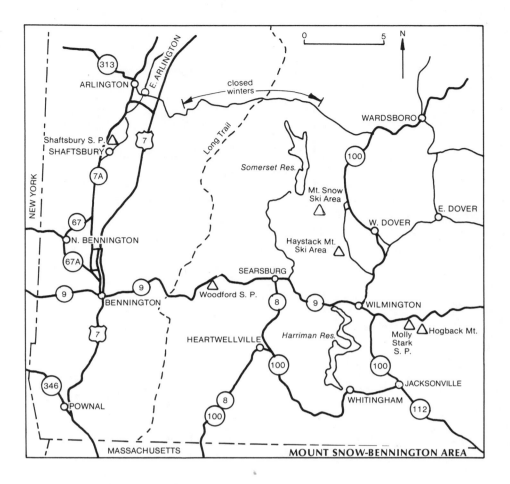

producers and vendors, selling syrup, cheese, honey, jams and Vermont souvenirs.

Parmelee & Howe (464-5435), Wilmington. Under the same ownership for the past four generations, this is a serious pharmacy, a first-rate hardware store, and a good bet for most summer vacation needs, from toys to fishing licenses.

Craft-haus (464-2164), Wilmington. Set high on a hillside, this is a gallery in Ursula and Ed Tancrel's home. The big attractions are Ursula's cloisonne and enamel-plated jewelry that sells for far higher prices in urban stores. Open weekends 10–5 and at other times by appointment.

Swe Den Nor Ltd. (464-2788), Route 100, West Dover. A long-established (recently moved) store with a wide selection of Scandinavian, contemporary, and country furniture; also lamps, paintings, and gifts.

Klara Simpla (464-5257), Wilmington. A "Holistic Country Store" with a following stretching the length of Route 9: vitamins, homeopathic remedies, natural foods, a wide selection of books and, of course, Birkenstock sandals. Upstairs are weekly sessions in massage therapy, Yoga, chiropractics, acupuncture, also special workshops in nutrition, dowsing, etc.

Stone Soldier Pottery (368-7077), Route 100 south, Jacksonville. A nice selection of Vermont-made crafts in wood and ceramics, including Robert Burnell's work, made on the premises.

Country Store Village, Wilmington. The Norton House is a 1770s centerpiece for a collection of gift shops selling hand-crafted jewelry, candles, calicos, quilting supplies, and more.

SPECIAL EVENTS   March (St. Patrick's Day weekend): valley-wide snow sculpture contest, torchlight ski parade.

April (Easter weekend): nondenominational sunrise service on Mount Snow summit, eggs hidden all over mountain, good for prizes, season's pass.

Late May–early October: Mount Snow Golf School.

July–early October: **The Pepsi Mount Snow Concert Series**. Friday and Saturday concerts by big name performers in Memorial Hall, Wilmington.

July to mid-August: **Marlboro Music Festival**.

Early August: **Art on the Mountain, Haystack**: a nine-day exhibit, one of the largest and best gatherings of craftspeople and their wares, displayed in Haystack's unusual glass and wood baselodge, daily 10–5.

Late August (last August weekend): **Deerfield Valley Farmers Day**. Old fashioned agricultural fair with midway, livestock exhibits, Wilmington.

October (Columbus Day Weekend): **Mount Snow Craft Fair**.

MEDICAL EMERGENCY   Whitingham (368-2323); East Dover (365-7676). **Deerfield Valley Health Center** (464-5311) Wilmington. Staffed by four doctors, four nurses, lab technician.

Deerfield Valley Rescue Squad (464-5335), Wilmington.

Bennington/Arlington Area

Vermont's southwest corner is dominated by Bennington, the state's third largest city (15,815), which is undergoing something of an industrial renaissance, while retaining its historic luster. This has, in turn, spawned several new places to stay and eat. The first town settled west of the Connecticut River in the New Hampshire Grants, in 1749, and named for the avaricious Governor Benning Wentworth, Bennington became a hotbed of sedition when the "Bennington Mob," or Green Mountain Boys, formed in 1770 at Fay's Catamount Tavern under the leadership of Seth Warner and Ethan Allen to expel both the 'Yorkers (who claimed the territory) and later the British.

The Battle of Bennington (more precisely the Battle *for* Bennington) on August 16, 1777, deflected General Burgoyne's occupation of the Colonies when New Hampshire General John Stark's hastily mobilized militiamen beat the tar out of Colonel Baum's overdressed Hessians on high ground near the Wallomsac River, across the New York border.

Today, Bennington is nationally known as the home of distinguished Bennington College, established in the early 1930s (now the most expensive private college in the country) and remembered by collectors of Bennington pottery.

Although never formally the capital of Vermont, Arlington, on Route 7A, was the *de facto* seat of government during most of the Revolutionary period. Fearing British attacks in the north, Vermont's first governor, Thomas Chittenden, moved south from Williston, liberated a Tory property in Arlington (the area known as "Tory Hollow") and conducted affairs of state from there.

Many older visitors to Arlington fondly remember Dorothy Canfield Fisher, the author of fifty immensely popular, warm-hearted novels, and a judge of the Book-of-the-Month Club for twenty-five years. Five years before her death in 1958, Mrs. Fisher published *Vermont Tradition, The Biography of an Outlook on Life,* in which she captured the essence of the state's character: ". . . Travel through Vermont—north, south, east, west, from Pownal to Canaan, Guilford to Highgate—nowhere will you find a township where overwhelming majority opinion does not support this unwritten law:

that, except where the safety of others is in danger, everyone must be allowed to do, think, believe whatever seems best to him; that equality before the law is only the first step. Equality must extend to the protection of everybody's personal dignity, within the community; for the backroad farmer and his wife bringing butter and eggs to the kitchen door, no less and no more for the owner of the plywood factory."

Another famous resident was illustrator Norman Rockwell, who lived in West Arlington from 1939 to 1953. Many of his illustrations of small-town Americans were done in and around Arlington.

GUIDANCE   A good visitor's guide to Bennington County is provided by the **Greater Bennington Area Chamber of Commerce** (447-3311), Veterans Memorial Drive, 05201, which also has a well-supplied information center.

GETTING THERE   By car: Bennington lies at the convergence of Routes 7, 7A, 9, 67, and 67A. Going north can be confusing; watch the signs carefully to choose between the limited-access Route 7 to Manchester, or the more interesting but slower Historic Route 7A, to Shrewsbury and Arlington.

By bus: Vermont Transit from Albany or hubs in Connecticut and Massachusetts.

TO SEE AND DO   **Historic Bennington Walking Tours**, self-guided with a keyed map-brochure from the Chamber of Commerce which describes Old Bennington, including the 306-foot, blue limestone shaft of the Bennington Battle Monument, dedicated in 1891; all the fine early houses along Monument Avenue; the Old Academy; Old First Church; the Burying Ground, where five Vermont Governors and Robert Frost repose; and the venerable Walloomsac Inn, which has been in continuous operation since 1766.

A second walking tour of the downtown area includes the 1898 railroad depot (now a restaurant), constructed of blue marble cut to resemble granite, old mills, and Victorian homes.

Bennington Museum (447-1571), West Main Street, Route 9, Bennington. Features memorabilia from the Battle of Bennington, especially the oldest American Revolutionary flag in existence, early American glass, furniture, dolls and toys, plus historic Bennington pottery, notably an extraordinary ten-foot ceramic piece created for the 1853 Crystal Palace Exhibition. Particularly popular is a gallery of paintings by "Grandma Moses" (Anna Mary Robertson, 1860–1961), who lived in the vicinity. Open daily 9–5 except for the months of December, January and February. Admission: adults $4; seniors and college students $3; aged 12–17, $2.50; under 12, free.

The Park-McCullough House (442-5441), Route 67A in North Bennington. A splendid 35-room Victorian mansion built in 1865 by Trenor W. Park, a Forty-Niner who struck it rich as a lawyer in

Robert Frost reposes beside First Church, Old Bennington

California and later as a railroader. He built the house on part of the farm owned by his father-in-law, Hiland Hall, a representative to congress and governor of Vermont. Park's son-in-law, John G. McCullough, became governor of Vermont in 1902 and raised his family in this capacious house. It has been open to the public since 1965 and is on the National Register of Historic Sites, functioning as a community arts center. There's an appealing children's play-house replica of the mansion and a stable full of carriages; gift shop; lunch counter; afternoon tea on the verandah. Open for tours late May through October, Monday–Friday 10–4, Saturday 10–2; admission.

The Shaftsbury Historical Society, Route 7A, is gradually developing a cluster of five historic buildings, including two schools. Open summer weekends 2–4 and serendipitously when the curator happens to be handy.

Norman Rockwell Exhibition (375-6423), Route 7A, Arlington. Housed in a "Hudson River Gothic" church are some 500 of the artist's *Saturday Evening Post* cover illustrations and prints, plus a 20-minute film showing and a gift shop. Open daily, 9–7, admission.

The Dr. George A. Russell Collection of Vermontiana, believed to be the third largest such collection, is housed in quarters behind the Martha Canfield Public Library, Arlington. Dr. Russell, the country doctor immortalized in the Rockwell print that hangs in thousands of doctors' offices, collected Vermontiana for most of his long life and left his collection to the town. The collection includes a fine collection of Dorothy Canfield Fisher materials, a large selection of Norman Rockwell's work, many photographs from the period 1860–1890, an extensive selection of town and country histories for Vermont and neighboring states, and a wealth of genealogical materials (deeds, letters, wills, account books, diaries, etc.) for the Arlington area and the state as a whole. Although not a museum (there are no displays), the collection is open to the public on Tuesdays or by appointment with the curators, David and Mary Lou Thomas (375-6307).

The Martha Canfield Library, Arlington (named for Dorothy Canfield Fisher's grandmother), holds a book sale under a tent on its lawn 10–5 on Fridays and Saturdays and 1–5 on Sundays from June 15 through foliage season. Books are sold at prices ranging from 15¢ to 50¢ per copy, and records and jig-saw puzzles are also available at moderate prices. During peak holiday seasons, the sale is sometimes held on weekdays as well.

Oldcastle Theatre Company (447-0564), Bennington. Based at Southern Vermont College (lodged in the Norman-style Everett mansion on the slopes of Mount Anthony), the Company offers a full summer season of plays, sometimes performing also at Bennington College.

Sage City Symphony. For information about performances, call Bennington College (442-5401 or 442-5441).

COVERED BRIDGES   Three just off Route 67A in North Bennington: Silk Road, Paper Mill Village, and the Burt Henry.

STATE PARKS   Shaftsbury State Park (375-9979), 10½ miles north on Route 7A, has facilities for swimming, picnicking, boating, nature trail, on 26-acre Lake Shaftsbury.

Woodford State Park (447-4169), Route 9 east of Bennington. This 400-acre area includes 104 camping sites, 16 of them with lean-tos, swimming in Adams reservoir, a children's playground, picnic spots, canoe and rowboat rentals.

CANOEING   Battenkill Canoe Ltd. (375-9559), River Road, off 7A, Arlington, is the center for day trips—with van service—canoe camping, instruction, rentals, and equipment. Customized inn-to-inn tours arranged.

SKIING   Prospect Mountain (442-2575/442-5283), Route 9 east of Bennington. An intimate, friendly family ski area, with cross-country (25 km), downhill and telemark facilities, ski school, rentals and repairs, learn-to-ski packages, group rates, cafeteria and bar. Moderate prices for all.

OTHER RECREATION   Mt. Anthony Club (442-2617), Bank Street (just below the Battle Monument): 18-hole golf course, tennis and paddle courts, pool, lunch, and dinner.

Green Mountain Racetrack (823-7311), Route 7 south in Pownal, just this side of the Massachusetts border, was built for horse racing, but now has a parimutuel season of Greyhound races from the end of February to early October, Wednesday–Saturday, 7:45 PM; Sundays, holidays, 1:30 PM doubleheaders. Admission $1.00.

**LODGING   *Bennington.*   All places listed below are in the 05201 zip code unless otherwise noted.

Greenwood Lodge (summer 442-2547; winter 914-472-2575), 8 miles east of Bennington on Route 9. Open July through Labor Day, this rustic lodge/hostel and its tent sites occupy 120 acres in Woodford, adjacent to the Prospect Mountain ski area. There are $10 a night dorms for American Youth Hostel members, and $25 private family rooms; bring your own linen or sleeping bags. Three small ponds for swimming and fishing. Inquire about winter rates and exclusive group use.

BED & BREAKFASTS   South Shire Inn (447-3839), 124 Elm Street. Mark and Suzanne Gashi have transformed this turn-of-the-century Victorian mansion into a most attractive guest house, featuring ten-foot ceilings with plaster moldings, a library with a massive mahogany fireplace, an Italianate formal dining room, and comfortable bedrooms furnished with antiques. The five guest rooms have private baths, some with fireplaces; two can be joined as a suite. $55–95 with breakfast; limited smoking; older children preferred.

Safford Manor (442-5934), 722 Main Street, Route 9 east, has six rooms in a 1774 house that displays some fine examples of colonial workmanship, plus a Victorian main parlor and library, $48–75.

Molly Stark Inn (442-9631), 1067 East Main Street. Five rooms, one with private bath, $57–65.

The Colonial Guest House (442-2263), Route 7A north, is a pleasant, five-bedroom place, $20–25 per room.

The Four Chimneys Inn (447-3500), 21 West Road, Route 9, Old Bennington. This stately home offers three redecorated, luxurious rooms ($100–125) as adjuncts to Alex Koks' latest upscale restaurant (see below).

The Walloomsac Inn (442-4865), Monument Avenue, Old Bennington, could advertise itself (as one posh Berkshire resort once did) as "two centuries behind the times," for it has changed little since its birth as a tavern around 1766. A magnet for curiosity-seekers, it is calmly carried on by the Berry family, and *may* (one can never be certain ahead of time) provide clean and simple rooms with baths for about $25 from Memorial Day to November 1. No meals.

Country Cousin (375-6985), Old Depot Road, off Route 7A, Shaftsbury, 05262. This 1824 Greek Revival house has three bedrooms and baths, plus living and dining area, library and music room. $31 single, $46 double including macrobiotic or continental breakfast.

MOTELS Among them, **Harwood Hill** (442-6278), Route 7A north, has economy and deluxe units, $36–44; **Ramada Inn** (442-8145), intersection of Routes 7 and 7A, Kocher Drive, $74.

Arlington   All places listed below are in the 05250 zip code unless otherwise noted.

The Arlington Inn (375-6532), on Route 7A in the center of Arlington, occupies the 1848 Greek Revival mansion built by Martin Chester Deming, a Vermont railroad magnate, and has been used as an inn off and on since 1889. Attractively restored rooms are spacious and furnished with Victorian antiques. The inn serves excellent French-Italian-American dinners. Room rates range from $50 double occupancy, to $125, including continental breakfast. Open all year.

Sycamore Inn (362-2284), Route 7A, Arlington. An old roadside home with 11 guest rooms, some set up for families. Innkeepers Tom and April Erwinski have children of their own and the large living room is well-stocked with games. Full breakfasts are served year-round, even brought to your room if you wish. Dinners featuring homemade soups and desserts are available in ski season and by reservation other times. The inn's property across Route 7 fronts on the Batten Kill, good for trout fishing and, for the warm blooded, a dip in a 10-foot deep swimming hole. Three rooms with private bath, seven shared: $20–23.50 per person, B&B.

West Mountain Inn (375-6516), on Route 313 west of Arlington. A former summer home with splendid views of the mountains and valley converted and expanded into an inn. The attractive rooms are named after famous people associated with Arlington, and a copy of Dorothy Canfield Fisher's *Vermont Tradition* is in every room. Breakfast, dinner and Sunday brunch served (no dinner on Sunday). The Inn's property includes over 5 miles of walking and cross-country skiing trails. A number of special events are featured, such as a fly-tying weekend two weeks before trout season and a wild leek and fiddlehead fern weekend later in the spring. Innkeepers Mary Ann and Wes Carlson give complimentary African Violet plants to guests who promise to take care of them. Rates $120–140 MAP. A two-bedroom housekeeping apartment is available on short-term or seasonal lease. Open all year.

Hill Farm Inn (375-2269), RR 2, Box 2015, Arlington. Located off Route 7A north of the village, this historic farmstead, now owned by the Hardy family, is set on 50 acres of land bordering the Batten Kill. There are 6 bedrooms on the second floor of the main building and 5 in the adjacent 1790 guest house; 5 of the 11 rooms have private baths. Several cabins are available in the summer and fall, and a two-room housekeeping apartment is available for weekly or seasonal rental. Guests can have a four-course dinner at 6:30 and full country breakfast. Licensed for beer and wine; smoking only in the common rooms. Double room rates range from $76 (hall bath or cabin) to $84 (private bath), MAP; $52–60 B&B.

BED & BREAKFASTS **The Inn on Covered Bridge Green** (375-9489), off Route 313, West Arlington. Fans of Norman Rockwell can now actually stay in his former home, a pretty white colonial next to a red covered bridge on the village green where Ethan Allen mustered his Green Mountain Boys. Ron and Anne Weber opened the place in 1987, and offer five bedrooms (semi-private baths), furnished with antiques. There's a tennis court, and full country breakfasts are events, served on bone china, with Waterford glass and silver. Rates range from $45 single to $125 for a family room for four. No smoking.

Shenandoah Farm (375-6372), 5 miles west of Arlington on Route 313, has three rooms with private baths and two shared in an 1820 colonial house. $25–30 per person with full breakfast.

DINING OUT **The Four Chimneys Inn** (447-3500), 21 West Road, Route 9, Old Bennington. Alex Koks, one of Vermont's preeminent chefs, has transferred his talents from the Village Auberge in Dorset to this recently redecorated stately home. The elegantly sophisticated setting—three dining areas with pale rose walls and table linens, and a screened porch with red and white striped canvas ceiling—reflects the equally superior cuisine. For lunch, one might savor a salad of grilled duck with spiced pecans ($7.25), home-cured Gravad Lox with sourdough toast and lemon-lime mustard ($6.50), or sautéed shrimp with garlic pasta and chive butter ($9.25). At dinner, appetizers range from $4.75 to $8.50 for a galantine of goose liver mousse, and entrées from $12.50 for roast chicken, $17.50 for steak, $21.50 for rack of lamb, to $16.50 per person for a ribeye steak flambéed with cognac and green peppercorns. Open daily, but check ahead, especially in late fall or early spring.

Bennington Station (447-1080), Depot Street, Bennington. Train buffs love this place, a splendidly converted romanesque railroad station built in 1897 of rough-hewn blue marble for the Bennington & Rutland Railroad. The exceptionally attractive restaurant features a collection of historic photos and is open for lunch and dinner daily. For lunch, one could have Iron Horse Chili ($3.95) to start; Railroad Spikes (marinated and grilled beef strips, $4.95), or a variety of salads and sandwiches. The dinner menu includes grilled duck salad ($6.95), prime rib ($13.95), New England chicken pot pie ($9.50), fish, and various teriyakis and BBQ ribs.

The Publyck House (442-9861), Route 7A north, Bennington, is a remodeled barn with an indoor greenhouse and a fine view of Mt. Anthony. Open for dinner daily; moderate prices.

The Arlington Inn (375-6532), Arlington, serves moderately priced, imaginative dinners nightly that might include scallion pasta with oysters poached in Riesling, Maine crab cakes, scallops *capicola* served on red-pepper pasta. Sunday brunch, luncheons on Friday and Saturday.

West Mountain Inn (375-6516), Arlington, offers a six-course dinner (beef, pork tenderloin, duck or fish) at $18.50.

EATING OUT **The Brasserie** (447-7922), 324 County Street, Bennington (in Pottery Yard), is open daily except Tuesday, 11:30–8, serving inexpensive, exceptional, lighter fare—imaginative combinations of hearty soups (black-eyed pea with ham hocks and vegetables), quiche, pâté, salads, and such specialties as Mozzarella Loaf (cheese baked through a small loaf of French bread with anchovy-herb butter, $3.95), or Rotelle with spinach, onions and prosciutto in cream with parmesan ($8.95).

Blue Benn Diner (442-8977), Route 7, near Deer Park, Bennington, open from 5:00: breakfast all day, or lunch, which combines "road fare" with more esoteric items like eggs benedict, tabouli, felafel, and herb teas.

Mother Hubbard's Cookies and Ice Cream, 431 Main Street, Bennington.

Mainly Yoghurt Natural Food Restaurant, 452 Main Street, Bennington.

Phyllis' Food and Et Cetera, East Arlington, open May through October, combines a profusion of collectibles with church-supper goodies: chicken and biscuits, French silk pie, cheddar and ham sandwiches.

The Pepper Mill (375-9910), Route 7A, Arlington, open daily 6–9; very affordable fare.

The Riverbank Restaurant, Route 7A north, Arlington; good for families or for take-out box lunches; eight different pastas served nightly.

SELECTIVE SHOPPING   **Hawkins House** (447-0488), 262 North Street, Route 7, Bennington, is a crafts market complex for the work of some 250 artisans in silver and gold, unusual textiles, handblown glass, pottery, quilts, cards, books, music, prints and woodcuts, stained glass, candles, and more. Open daily except for Christmas and New Year's.

The Antique Center of Old Bennington & The Camelot Gift Gallery, Route 9 west, Bennington, which has several high-quality shops under one roof.

Bennington Potters Yard, downtown on County Street, Bennington, is the hi-tech place to get contemporary Bennington Pottery, Catamount Glass, well-designed ovenproof cookware manufactured in North Bennington, and to eat at the Brasserie.

Jonathan Logan Outlet, West Main Street, Bennington, at the Paradise Motel, has name-brand ladies apparel at discount.

CB Sports Outlet (447-0482), 190 North Street, Route 7 north, Bennington. Offers seconds, samples, and discontinued items from their popular sportswear line.

Fairdale Farms (442-6391), Route 9 west, Old Bennington. Gift shop, antiques, homemade ice cream, and snacks; small animal barn; outside view of dairy processing.

The Nut Factory, 520 Main Street, Bennington, turns out ribbon candy and canes, plus more sophisticated chocolates.

Williams Smoke House Country Store, Route 9 east, Bennington, offers a free pound of bacon with its bone-in-hams; gift packs.

Hale Company Factory Outlet, East Arlington. Hardrock maple and red oak chairs and tables available in seconds and discontinued designs.

The Chocolate Barn, Route 7A north of Shaftsbury, is an unusual combination: two floors of antiques, 56 varieties of hand-dipped chocolates, fudge, and special orders from antique candy molds. (There's another store at Routes 30 and 100 in Jamaica.)

Candle Mill Village in East Arlington is a charming hamlet of specialty shops next to two waterfalls. It is located in the Candle Mill, operated locally, stocking 50,000 candles from all over the world, including one that weighs 248 pounds. There's also The Happy Cook, The Music Box Shop, (and in the "Little Red Building" complex) Where Did You Get That Hat?; the Rosebud Toy Company; Aunt Dudy's; and the Bearatorium. One of the ubiquitous Green Mountain Boys, Remember Baker, the builder and first owner of the mill, is remembered by a monument.

The Beside Myself Gallery, Lathrop Lane, 4 miles north of Arlington off Route 7A. Open May 15–October 15, this gallery displays the work of contemporary regional artists: paintings, handmade paper, sculpture and collages. Open 2–5 daily or by appointment.

SPECIAL EVENTS   Late May: **Bennington Mayfest**: street festival, crafts, entertainment.

July: **Annual Bennington Museum Antique Show**.

August 16–18: **Bennington Battle Day Weekend**.

Mid-September: **Antique and Classic Car Show**.

October 3–5: **Annual Antique Show**.

January 29: **Bennington Winter Carnival**.

MEDICAL EMERGENCY   Bennington (442-5464); Arlington (375-6313). **Southwestern Vermont Medical Center** (442-6361), Bennington.

Manchester and the Mountains

Manchester is an up-and-down town consisting of several villages that seem to vary in status with their altitude. The highest, Manchester Village, is an elegant gathering of mansions, spread along marble sidewalks, around the venerable Equinox Hotel, the gold-domed county courthouse, and historic Hildene, a lavish summer retreat built by Robert Todd Lincoln, son of the president. Fine summer homes are sequestered away from view on River Road and up country lanes that radiate from Manchester Center and Manchester Depot. With art, music, nearby summer theater, and three golf clubs (only one of which is open to the public), Manchester remains a top summer address.

Manchester's old Dowager Queen Mary atmosphere has been replaced by a Princess Di quality, as moneyed young professionals flock to the snowy slopes of Bromley and Stratton, setting a faster pace than their leisured patrician predecessors. But beneath the town's bustling resort glamour lies—as reliable as Harris tweed—the fabric of a thriving small town, woven by farmers, merchants, lawyers, carpenters, teachers, clergymen, doctors, housewives, and innkeepers.

It was the sharp contrast between old money and local poverty that prompted Manchester's Socialist poet Sarah Cleghorn to write her famous quatrain:

The golf links lie so near the mill
That almost every day
The laboring children can look out
And see the men at play.

The stark contrast between the nineteenth-century resort village and mill town have disappeared with the mills, and the lines between the Center and Depot have been blurred by the lineup of dozens of factory direct stores, augmented by new boutiques and restaurants.

Manchester's "Mountains" are Mt. Equinox, a stray member of the Taconic Range, looming grandly above Manchester Village on the west, and the march of Green Mountains on the east. You can drive and hike up Mt. Equinox, but in winter the action shifts to skiing at Bromley. So, Manchester has distinct summer and winter

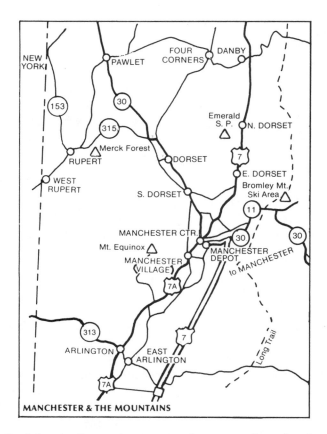

MANCHESTER & THE MOUNTAINS

faces. Lodging in the eastern parts of town tends to be cheaper in summer, while motels and inns on the western side are cheaper in winter.

In addition to Manchester, there are three other unusually picturesque resort villages: **Dorset**, 7 miles north of Manchester at the narrow head of the valley; **Pawlet**, another 7 miles north on Route 30; and **Danby**, 13 miles north on Route 7. (Dorset and Pawlet are also served by the Manchester Chamber of Commerce.)

GUIDANCE   **Manchester and the Mountains** (362-2100), at Manchester Center, this clapboard Chamber of Commerce information booth is walled with pamphlets, good for general walk-in information. The Chamber does not make reservations, but does keep a running tally on space in member lodging places, short-term condo and cottage rentals.

For year-round help with local lodging, phone the **Area Lodging Service**: 824-6915.

Vermont News Guide, Box 1265, Manchester Center. Based in an old storefront across from the Chamber of Commerce, this publication is a weekly compendium of news and advertising, helpful guides to local events, shopping, and dining. It also publishes semi-annual guidebooks of the same.

GETTING THERE   From Bennington north, Route 7 to Manchester is a limited-access highway that's speedy but dull, except for viewing Mt. Equinox. One gets a more interesting taste of the area, especially around Arlington, by clinging to Historic Route 7A.

By bus: Vermont Transit offers good service from New York and Montreal; connections with Boston are via Williamstown, MA or Rutland.

By air: Eastern Express (800-451-4221) serves Rutland and a wider choice of regularly scheduled airlines serve Albany, 70 miles distant.

GETTING AROUND   **Equinox Limousine** (362-2365) provides luxury sedans and stretch limousines to and from airports and other points.

Taxis: **Andrews** (362-2626), **Linihan's** (362-3765).

TO SEE AND DO   **Historic Hildene** (362-1788), Manchester. Late May–late October, 10–4; $5.00 per adult, $1 for children under 15, free under 6. A house among historic houses, this 24-room Georgian Revival manor is set on 412 acres, including formal gardens and paths that lead down into the Batten Kill Valley. Bring a picnic lunch and plan to stay half the day. The tour begins with a wagon ride to the Carriage Barn, now a sophisticated Visitors Center with a slide show about Robert Todd Lincoln. You learn that he first came to the village as a boy with his mother for a stay at the Equinox House; his father was assassinated before the family could return, as they had intended, the following summer. It was Todd's law partner who later persuaded him to build this summer home adjacent to his own mansion. Todd died here in 1926 and members of the family lived here until 1975. Guides are familiar with at least one Lincoln and with the true character of the authentically furnished house. Tours include the restored formal gardens (the peony collection alone is worth the $5 gate), a brief demonstration of the 1,000-pipe organ, which can be played both manually and with one of 240 player rolls on hand. Formal concerts are given Sunday evenings. Picnic tables outside command a view of the valley below and there are numerous trails to stroll or—in winter when the Carriage Barn becomes a warming hut—to explore on skis (see *Cross-Country Skiing*). In the summer, Sunday afternoon polo matches are a popular spectator sport.

Southern Vermont Art Center (362-1405), West Road, Manchester Center. June to mid-October, daily except Monday, 10–5; Sunday, noon–5; admission, but free for children under 13 and on Tuesdays. This gracious old mansion, set on 375 acres of grounds, offers changing exhibits: paintings, sculpture, prints and photography, also a summer-long session of classes in various art forms for both adults and children and a series of both concerts (held in the adjacent, 430-seat Pavilion hall) and films. Light lunches are also served in the Garden Cafe, and there are extensive trails through the woods, among them a botany trail featuring rock formations, 67 varieties of wildflowers and birches.

The American Museum of Fly Fishing, Seminary Avenue and Route 7A, Manchester. Open 10–4 daily, the museum displays more than a thousand rods and reels made by famous rodbuilders and owned by such luminaries as Daniel Webster, Bing Crosby, Ernest Hemingway, and Presidents Hoover and Eisenhower. Don't miss it.

MOUNTAIN TOPS   Mount Equinox (362-1113). The 3,825-foot high summit of Mount Equinox, most of the mountain in fact, is owned by the Carthusian monks who occupy the Monastery, which can be seen from the top. A toll road (open May through October, 8–10; $4.50 per car) climbs more than 5 miles from Route 7 to the **Sky Line Inn** on top. The Inn (362-1113), is open from mid-May to mid-October for lodging, lunch, and dinner.

Bromley Mountain. This 3,284-foot high mountain offers excellent views of Stratton and Equinox mountains. It is traversed by the Long Trail (see *Hiking*) and is also accessible by hiking up the ski trails from the midpoint get-off on the chairlift. This lift serves the **Alpine Slide**, 9:30–6 (just until 5 in October), $3.75 adults, $3 junior, $15 for all day midweek. The Alpine Slide is the first in this country. Lunch, snacks and drinks are available at the base lodge, 8 miles east of Manchester on Route 11 in Peru (824-5522).

PARKS, FORESTS, AND A DAM   Green Mountain National Forest (362-2307), District Ranger Office. A public information office serving the southern third of the 275,000-acre Green Mountain National Forest is located on Routes 30 and 11 east of Manchester, open Monday–Friday, 8–4:30. Maps and details are available about where to fish, hike, cross-country ski, and camp. All National Forest campsites are available on a first-come, first-serve basis.

Emerald State Park (362-1655), North Dorset. On Route 7 this area offers 105 campsites, including 36 lean-tos, also hiking and nature trails, among them a 3.4 mile round-trip trek to a natural bridge.

Merck Forest and Farmland Center (394-7836), Route 315, Rupert 05768. Some 2,500 acres of near wilderness, including Mt. Antone, were set aside in the 1950s as a foundation by George Merck of the Merck Drug Company. The forest area offers year-round facilities: foot and horse trails, picnic areas, a swimming pond, 12 shelters, a farm museum, and a sugar house that produces 400 gallons of syrup. The Merck Forest Summer Camp has six one-week sessions for children. Reservations are required for overnight use of the shelters. An extensive network of trails is marked for cross-country skiing.

BICYCLING   Bike rentals and touring information are available from **Vermont Pedal Pushers and Battenkill Sports**, both in Manchester Center.

CANOEING   The **Batten Kill** makes for satisfying canoeing in the spring; the Manchester to Arlington section is relatively flat water but gets difficult a mile above Arlington. (See Arlington for rentals from **Battenkill Canoe**.

FISHING   Fly fishing has been serious business in the **Batten Kill** since the mid-nineteenth century. Orvis Company began manufacturing bamboo rods in Manchester Village near the spot where they are still produced.

The **Batten Kill** is generally recognized as Vermont's best wild trout stream; access is available at a number of places off Route 8. Brown trout can also be found in **Gale Meadows Pond**, accessible via gravel road from Route 30 at Bondville. **Emerald Lake** in North Dorset is stocked with pike, bass, and perch; rental boats available at the State Park facility.

The **Orvis Fly Fishing School** (362-3900), Manchester, offers basic instruction in the art and skill of fly casting in a three-day, hands-on course with experts, weekly from April to October. Weekday sessions cost $415 including room and board ($430 over weekends).

Gloria Jordan Productions (362-1721), Route 7 north, Manchester, is run by a woman who grew up catching brook trout in the area and learned her craft as a rod maker at Orvis. Jordan makes and sells rods, ties, flies, and conducts a fly fishing school in cooperation with the Dorset Inn and the Red Sled Motel. She can also be hired as a guide to the best spots on the Batten Kill and Mettawee River for $100 for two people.

GOLF   There is an 18-hole golf course at the **Equinox Country Club** (362-3223), which was established in the 1920s for guests of the Equinox House; the club also offers pleasant noontime dining.

HIKING AND CAMPING   **Green Mountain National Forest** (362-2307), District Ranger Office, Manchester. Request maps to two hiking trails: the 2⅓-mile trail to the Lye Brook Waterfalls in the 14,600-acre Lye Brook Wilderness south of Manchester and the easy trails around Grout Pond, west of the town of Stratton.

Mount Equinox. Details about the rewarding, 6-mile Burr and Burton Trail from Manchester Village to the summit are available in *Day Hiker's Guide to Vermont* (Green Mountain Club) and *Fifty Hikes in Vermont* (Backcountry Publications). At 3,825 feet, this is the highest mountain in the state that is not traversed by the Long Trail.

The Long Trail. This Massachusetts to Quebec path doubles as the Appalachian Trail throughout this area; portions of the Trail make good day hikes, either north over Bromley Mountain or south over Spruce Peak from Routes 11 and 30. The most heavily hiked stretch of the entire trail is the relatively level trek in from the Kelley Stand Road to Stratton Pond; there are three shelters in the immediate area and swimming is permitted. Griffith Lake, accessible from Peru and Danby, is a less crowded swimming and camping site on the Trail. For details consult the *Green Mountain Club Guide Book of the Long Trail*. In **Emerald Lake State Park** there are extensive hiking and nature trails. Inquire at the Green Mountain National Forest District Office in Manchester (362-2307) for details about hiking in the Lye Brook Wilderness.

HORSEBACK RIDING   **Windhill Farm Stable** (362-2604), Manchester, North Road. Trail rides and lessons offered, open daily in riding season. Sleigh rides.

Village Carriage Company (447-1769), based at The Equinox, offers carriage rides around Manchester Village, 10¢ a minute.

SWIMMING   **Dana L. Thompson Recreation Area** (362-1439), Route 30 north, Manchester, is open daily in summer but hours for general swimming are limited; nominal fee.

Dorset Quarry, off Route 30 on Kelly Stand Road between Manchester and Dorset, is a deep, satisfying pool but not recommended for children. The upper quarry is the local skinny-dipping spot.

TENNIS   **Dana L. Thompson Recreation Area**, Manchester. Public courts are available with weekly memberships or on a per hour basis.

CROSS-COUNTRY SKIING   **Hildene Ski Touring Center** (362-1788), Manchester. The Lincoln Carriage Barn serves as a warming hut for this system of 21 kilometers of groomed and mapped trails on the estate built by Robert Todd Lincoln. Trails meander through woods and fields on a promontory overlooking the Batten Kill Valley between Mount Equinox and Lye Brook Wilderness. Lessons and equipment are available. Trail fees.

DOWNHILL SKIING   **Bromley** (824-5522). Located on Route 11 in Peru, 8 miles east of Manchester. Founded in 1937 by the late Fred Pabst of the Milwaukee brewing family, this is among the oldest ski areas in the country. It was also one of the first to have snowmaking, snow farming, a slopeside nursery, and condominiums. It retains its own following of those who like its friendly atmosphere and sunny trails. (Now under the same ownership as Magic Mountain; lift tickets for both are interchangeable.)

Lifts: 6 double chairlifts and 1 T-bar.

Trails: 35 trails—50% intermediate, 25% beginner, 25% expert.

Vertical drop: 1,334 feet.

Snowmaking: 83% of terrain from base to summit.

Facilities: The base lodge offers two cafeterias, two more formal areas. Skiers unloaded right at the base lodge; the driver then parks in an area across Route 11 and rides back on a shuttle bus.

Ski School: GLM/ATM combined method.

For Children: Nursery for ages one month to 6 years. Ski and Play House for ages 3 to 5, Snoopy Ski School for 6 to 14 year olds.

Special program: Telemark Skiing, combining Alpine with cross-country, is taught.

Rates: $29 per adult, $19 per junior weekends; $15 adult, $10 junior weekdays; also half-day and five-day rates; free under age 6.

SLEIGH RIDES   Inquire at **Windhill Farm Stable** (362-2604), North Road in Manchester, at the **Village Carriage Co.** (447-1769).

SNOWMOBILING   A "Winter Recreation Map," available free from the Green Mountain National Forest District Ranger Office, Manchester (362-2307) shows trails presently maintained in this area by the Vermont Association of Snow Travelers.

HOT TUBS   The **Calidarium** at Bromley View Inn (297-1459) is open daily 2–10.

RESORT INNS   **The Equinox** (362-4700; 362-4747), Manchester Village 05254. More like sleeping beauty than Rip Van Winkle, The Equinox House has emerged from an 11-year snooze. The white columned inn, made up of 17 distinct parts, has been painstakingly restored from its underpinnings to the turnings on its stair rails. The resulting resort is as posh as ever. Public rooms are plushly decorated in high Victorian style and the oval dining room, facing Mt. Equinox, is light and airy, under a sky-blue, vaulted ceiling. There are 154 rooms and suites and a ten-unit, three-bedroom condo lodge. (The place is so vast that guests quickly become acquainted in the halls, helping each other find the way in and out.) Amenities include clay tennis courts, outdoor and indoor swimming pools, an 18-hole golf course, a fitness center and spa program.

Staying in this grande dame of Vermont resort hotels evokes the sense of gratitude that music lovers feel about the newly renovated Carnegie Hall. Requisite modernization (sprinklers, smoke alarms, air conditioning, color TV) accompanies the exquisitely detailed restoration. The spacious, color-coordinated bedrooms are furnished with antiques and pine reproductions, including armoires and big, firm beds. Service is friendly and impeccable. Meals are memorable (see *Dining Out*). Our one criticism is the hotel's policy of mixing groups with individual guests who, inevitably, are the losers.

Harking back to Manchester's nineteenth-century heyday as a mineral spa, the Equinox offers an Evolution Spa Optimum Health, Fitness & Beauty Program, designed and supervised by an Albany-based doctor. Individually tailored three or seven-night plans include a medical analysis, cardiopulmonary assessment and nutritional profile, followed by exercise, whirlpool, sauna, steamroom, massage, loofah, cosmetology treatments, and a calorie-controlled diet. Use of the Spa facilities and services are also available to guests on an à la carte basis ($10 per aerobic class, $5 per Nautilus use, $30 per herbal wrap).

Summer rates begin at $65 per person weekdays in a standard room and go to $190 per person in a cupola suite (add $38 per person for MAP), slightly less in winter. A seven-night spa package is $1,550 per person, double occupancy, $728 for three nights. Golf, ski, and fly-fishing packages are available.

The Inn at Willow Pond (362-4733; 800-533-3533, outside of Vermont), Box 1429, Manchester Center 05255, five minutes north on Route 7, is southern Vermont's newest year-round mini-resort (opened in the spring of 1987). An outstanding addition to the state's hospitality scene, its 40 spacious guest rooms and suites occupy 3 separate contemporary colonial-style buildings on a hillside overlooking the Manchester Country Club's golf course. The Meeting House reception building contains the lofty main lounge, conference facilities for up to 200, fitness equipment—including an outdoor lap pool—and the Williamsburg-like restaurant in a renovated 1780 house makes the fifth unit of this campus. Tennis courts are to be added.

The sleek main lobby's furnishings do double duty: most of the sofas, tables, and chairs are for sale. The larger guest rooms with fireplaces and sitting areas are perhaps the most attractive and luxuriously comfortable of any of the state's larger inns and hotels. Winter and spring rates are $75 per room, double occupancy; $130 with fireplace or a two-room with parlor; $195 for a three-room, two-bath, parlor suite for four people. In summer, foliage, and holidays these rates rise, respectively, to $95, $165, and $250; $250–700 for a five-night ski week. Meals are not included, but modestly priced breakfasts are served in the restaurant (see *Dining Out*).

1811 House (362-1811), Manchester 05254. "A place to feel pampered" is the way the owners of this magnificent building describe what they offer. Parts of this mansion date back to the 1770s. It has been an inn since 1811, except for the few years during which it was owned by President Lincoln's granddaughter, Mary Lincoln Isham. Public rooms are as elegant as any to be found in New England and the 13 guest rooms are in keeping, each with private bath, many with hearths; TV and phones are available on request. Innkeepers Mary and Jack Hirst dispel any stuffiness in this rarified world. Guests are invited to kick off their shoes, wander into the kitchen and make a cup of tea. There is a game room downstairs, an authentic-looking pub room with exposed rafters, and an expansive lawn overlooking the Equinox Golf Course. There are also English-style flower gardens. A full English breakfast is included in the room rate, from $80 for a cozy double to $120 for the Jeremiah French Suite (queen four-poster canopy bed, fireplace and sitting room).

Birch Hill Inn (362-2761), West Road, PO Box 346, Manchester 05254. A gracious, bright, and airy old home set away by itself up on West Road, amid lovely mountain scenery. Innkeepers Pat and Jim Lee welcome guests as they would into their own home, presiding over the dinner table, which seats 14. There are just five guest rooms plus a summer cottage. The house has been in Pat's family since 1917, which may be the reason the rooms look so homey and right. There is an endless jigsaw puzzle and supply of games in the living room (children over 6 are welcome), a kidney-shaped pool and trout pond for warm weather use and miles of touring trails for the winter. Hors d'oeuvres and set-ups are provided at the cocktail hour. $46 per person MAP, $48 in the cottage; $92–114 per room B&B. Closed April and November. No dinner served Wednesdays.

Reluctant Panther Inn (362-2568), Box 678, Manchester 05254. Renowned for its gourmet fare (see *Restaurants*) this purple-painted village home also has seven guest rooms, each flamboyantly decorated with bright wallpapers and antiques. Four rooms have fireplaces. All have private baths, room phones, and cable TV. Breakfast is served to guests only; and with the exception of dining hours, the living room and unique pubs make a peaceful and pleasant retreat. Innkeepers are Ed and Loretta Friihauf. Closed after foliage until early December, again in Mud Season. $79–160 per room, B&B; less in winter. No children or pets.

Wilburton Inn (362-2500), River Road, Manchester 05254. A turn-of-the-century mansion that has served as a summer retreat for ladies and gentlemen since the 1940s. The new proprietors have sought to retain the Wilburton's air of gentility while livening things up just a tad, as, for example, with the new main floor art gallery. There are a total of 35 rooms: 14 in the manor house, the remainder in cottages scattered over the property, which also includes a pool and tennis courts. Open late May until mid-October. $80–110 per room, B&B. (Dining room open to the public, except Tuesdays.)

The Wiley Inn (824-6600), Route 11, Peru 05152. This homey old inn is just 1 mile from Bromley. Its core is an 1835 house containing a delightful living room, library, and dining room and a 1940s motel-style wing, obviously tacked on to serve early skiers. There are 13 units, two of them two-bedroom suites, and the remaining 11 are double rooms—all have private bath. Request a room in the old inn; these are just a few dollars more and much nicer than those in the new wing. Summer facilities include a backyard pool and play area. Children are welcome. $30 per person B&B, $60 per person MAP, $200 MAP for a two-bedroom suite sleeping four (MAP rates only in winter).

The Inn at Manchester (362-1793), Box 452, Manchester 05254. A gracious old Main Street home with an expansive porch, big windows, gables and a carriage house in back. There are 22 rooms, named for flowers and herbs, all but five with private bath. There are several two-bedroom suites with connecting bath. The dining room and parlors are imaginatively and comfortably furnished and there is a game room, warmed by an antique woodstove. In summer there is a pool in back. Breakfast and—on holidays and winter weekends—dinner is prepared with flare and care by innkeepers Harriet and Stan Rosenberg. $55–125 per room B&B. Dinner by advance reservation is $15.

The Village Country Inn (362-1782), Manchester Village 05254. This century-old inn (formerly The Worthy Inn) has been resurrected in lace and roses. There are 30 rooms and suites, all with private bath. The rooms are small but fun, furnished in antiques, dressed in lace curtains. Downstairs there are roses on the curtains and couches and the predominant color is rose. There is an attractive dining room, an inviting pub and a pool out back. $115–200 double (the high end is for a suite with sitting room and TV).

Manchester Highlands Inn (362-4565) PO Box 1754, Highland Ave., Manchester Center 05255. A spacious Victorian home on a quiet side street with an expansive view of Mt. Equinox from the rockers on its porch. There are 13 guest rooms, decorated with family antiques and personal touches. Innkeepers Harry and Donna Williams and Marge Bellestri take their cooking seriously. Breakfast and dinner (also wine and cocktails) are served. $66–96 per room, B&B.

SKI LODGES   at Bromley, **Johnny Seesaw's** (824-5533), Peru 05152. Built as a dance hall in 1926 and converted into one of Vermont's first ski lodges in the 1930s, this is a wonderfully weathered, comfortable place. Within walking distance of the slopes in winter, it offers tennis and a pool in summer. There are two dozen rooms, ranging from dorms to doubles and master bedrooms with fireplaces in the main house, also four cottages with fireplaces, good for large families and small groups. The living room boasts Vermont's first circular fireplace, a long row of upholstered pads known as the "seducerie" and red leather chairs from the 1936 Republican Committee Headquarters in New York City. $45–65 per person MAP in winter, less in summer.

Bromley Sun Lodge (824-6941 or 6400), Peru 05152. A five-story chalet-roofed lodge with an Alpine feel. Just down Route 11 from Bromley base lodge, it offers 51 rooms, each with 2 double beds, cable color TVs, phones, and private baths. The lounges and restaurant reflect the tastes of Austrian owners Erwin and Cheri Dostal. There are game rooms and an indoor pool, $62 per person, MAP on winter weekends.

Bromley View Inn (297-1459), Route 30, Box 161, Bondville 05340. 3 miles from Bromley, 5 from Stratton, this comfortable lodge overlooks a deep, wooded valley with Bromley on the far side. Amy and Bick Atherton pride themselves on the breakfasts served up with this view; public rooms offer a variety of games, a licensed bar, and TV. The 12 rooms all have private baths. The "calidarium" (hot tub and spa rooms) downstairs is open to the public. Bick prides himself on offering the largest selection of beers and ales in Vermont. Rates: $39–52 per person MAP, $25–28 per person, B&B.

Bromley Village (824-5522), PO Box 1130, Manchester Center 05255, is a complex of attractive one and two bedroom units adjacent to the ski area. Summer facilities include a pool and tennis courts. In winter you can walk to the lifts; there is also a shuttle bus. From $28 per person midweek in winter.

BED & BREAKFASTS   Brook-n-Hearth (362-3604), Box 508, Manchester 05255. A gracious home, built in the 1940s to accommodate guests in four nicely furnished second-floor rooms sharing a bath with shower. Guests have full use of the living room with its inviting hearthside sofas, games, books and TV; also the pool table in the basement. The house sits high on the crest of Routes 11 & 30 overlooking the town and there are trails running back to the brook, from which to enjoy the view. Hosts Larry and Terry Greene are unusually knowledgeable about the area and eager to help you enjoy it. $42–46 per room, B&B.

River Meadow Farm (362-1602/3700), Sugarhouse Lane, PO Box 822, Manchester 05255. Off by itself down near the Batten Kill south of Manchester, this is a beautiful old farm, built early in the nineteenth century to house the town's paupers. There are five bedrooms sharing two baths; guests have the run of the downstairs with its welcoming kitchen, pleasant living room and dining room. Outside there is ample space to hike and ski cross-country with a splendid view of Mount Equinox. Rates are $18 per person, full breakfast included.

The Inn at Sunderland (362-4213), Route 7A, Manchester 05254, at the foot of the Equinox Skyline Drive, is an 1840 Victorian farmhouse with fine woodwork. Tom and Peggy Wall make this small B&B hospitable, with complimentary canapes at the bar. There are ten rooms, eight with private bath, four with fireplaces. $75–95 per couple.

MOTELS   The Barnstead Motel (362-1619), Box 88, Manchester 05255. Just up Bonnet Street, 2 blocks from the amenities of the Center, this is a genuine former hay barn, converted by owners Virginia and

Gordon Barnes into motel units. It's all been done with consummate grace and charm, many small touches like braided rugs and exposed old beams. There is also a "gathering room" and outdoor pool. Rooms: $51–69.

The Weathervane (362-2444), Route 7, Manchester 05254. Set back from the road with two picture windows in each of its 20 large units, each room has TV, free coffee, and hot chocolate. There is also a "courtesy room" with books, games, and magazines and a pool. $15–34 per person.

Best Western Palmer House (362-3600), Manchester 05255. A luxury motel with 31 rooms with color TV, free coffee. There are also meeting rooms, a pool, whirlpool and sauna. $26–30 per person.

Four Winds (362-1105), Box 1234, Manchester Center 05255, 2 miles north on Route 7, combines an 1854 house with pleasant motel units. A full-service breakfast is served in the inn; golf, tennis and luncheon privileges at the Manchester Country Club. Double occupancy rates $58–76.

DINING OUT   There are so many places to eat in these hills and dells that we don't have room to mention them all. What follows is a sampler, ones which are, for one reason or another, unusual.

Chantecleer (362-1616), East Dorset, 5:30–9:30, closed Tuesdays. Long respected as one of Vermont's outstanding restaurants, this chef-owned restaurant prepares such specialties as veal sweetbreads and shrimp basilik, braised rabbit maison, cajun-style seafood and pheasant à Laile. Leave room for profiterole maison or coup Matterhorn. The setting is an elegantly remodeled old dairy barn. Entrees run $12.50–$20 and there is an extensive wine list.

Reluctant Panther Inn (362-2568), Manchester Village. Dinner only, closed Wednesdays; $17–22 for five-course dinners. In imaginatively decorated rooms, 60 lucky people a night sit down to feasts that begin with such hors d'oeuvres as peach sparkle and salmon mousse, followed by a choice of hot and cold soups, salad, a choice of brace of quail, steak, duckling, lamb, pork, trout, or chicken. Since you have already paid for it, you will probably also be able to digest a selection from the delectable dessert tray. Innkeeper Loretta Friihauf is the chef.

Toll Gate Lodge (362-1779), off Route 11/30 east of Manchester. 5:30–10 daily, 4–9 on Sundays. From $11. A very continental restaurant in the old toll house once serving the Boston to Saratoga road. During warm weather months there is the sound of the brook, rushing by just under the windows. Specialties such as imported Dover sole and rack of lamb are accompanied by a very long wine list.

The Equinox (362-4700), Manchester Village. Dinner here in the big vaulted blue and yellow dining room (or perhaps the buffet in the more intimate Marsh Tavern) can be eminently satisfying. Appetizers include a terrine of scallops, lobster, and vegetables with chilled saffron and tomato coulis ($5.75); for entrées, sautéed veal sweetbreads with maple and Madeira glaze ($16.75), roast lamb ($18), or the evening's seafood or poultry specials.

The Black Swan (362-3807), Manchester Village (next to the Jelly Mill). Open for lunch and dinner daily except Wednesday, the food in this crisply decorated and managed old brick Colonial house is a treat for the senses. A representative dinner might begin with chilled strawberry soup ($3.75) or escargots en Bouchée ($5.75) and proceed to Filet of Beef Nancy ($17) or scallops Navarin ($15.75). A satisfying summer lunch featured curried chicken salad ($6.50).

Harvest Inn (362-2125), Route 7A, Manchester Village. Open May through October and mid-December through mid-March from 5:00 and Sunday from 1:00. Closed Mondays. Still under the same management that opened it in 1947, this fine dining landmark has a menu that has changed with the years from hearty American to something lighter and more imaginative. We counted 16 different fish dishes and seafood tempters like shrimp and crawfish etouffeé ($12.95); veal scallopini sauté with wild mushrooms costs the same. The menu also includes Cajun spice blackened boneless loin of lamb with wild rice. Entrées run $9.75–18.

Greenbaum & Gilhooley's (362-4837), Route 11/30, 2.5 miles east of Manchester Village. One of the area's newer and livelier restaurants, this steak and seafood house has earned kudos. Entrées include grilled swordfish ($12.95), lobster tails ($17.95), and prime rib of beef ($14.95 for an extra thick cut); there are daily blackboard specials, also a reasonably priced children's menu. Open daily except Christmas.

The Inn at Willow Pond (362-4733), Route 7 north of Manchester Center. This meticulously renovated 1780 farmhouse, with exposed beams, traditional three-sided fireplaces and raised colonial paneling, resembles a Williamsburg tavern. Open for dinner daily, the restaurant offers a seductive (and expensive) menu: for starters, salad of grilled duck, spiced pecans and cranberries ($5.25) or ragoût of rabbit ($4.95); entrées include rack of lamb ($18.50), Black Angus sirloin ($19.50), and grilled fresh quail ($18.50). A six-course tasting menu can be yours for $32.50: soup, chèvre and pear salad, lemon fettucine with smoked salmon and caviar, sorbet, rack of lamb or grilled fresh tuna, dessert, and coffee. (See also Dorset.)

EATING OUT   Garden Cafe at the Southern Vermont Arts Center (262-1405), West Road, Manchester Center, open for lunch, June through mid-October, Tuesday–Saturday 11:30–2:30, brunch on Sunday at the same time. The food is fine and the setting is superb: a pleasant indoor room with views over the sculpture garden and the terrace outside; reasonably priced.

Golden Royal Dragon (362-4569/4560), Route 11/30, Manchester Center, open daily for lunch and dinner. This is a relatively small, attractive Chinese restaurant with a standard selection, also some really spicy Szechuan dishes, and reasonable prices: Moo Shu Beef for $7.25, sweet and sour pork for $5.95. Luncheon specials begin at $3.75.

Quality Restaurant (362-9839), Main Street, Manchester Center. This used to be the local little place you stopped by for breakfast, lunch, and dinner, but with the gentrification of Manchester, the atmosphere and prices have risen. It's still a good bet for lunch and dinner. Seafood fettucini is now $13.50, broiled, herbed lamb chops, $14.95.

Garlic John's (362-9843), Route 11/30, Manchester. Open daily from 5:00. Newly renovated with a more upscale atmosphere and prices than of yore, but still not a bad bet for pasta with garlic and oil (add anchovy if you dare) or a dozen other pasta dishes, not to mention eggplant parmigiana (an old family recipe), veal Marsala or shrimp parmigiana.

Grabber's (362-3394), Manchester. Lunch and dinner. Dinner $7.50–$13.75. Formerly the "Palace," this high Victorian brick building makes a colorful dining space; you can choose to dine in the pub, library, parlor, or garden room; specialties are barbecued spare ribs, prime ribs, and seafood, or you can dine from the salad bar.

Gurry's (362-9878), Route 11/30, east of Manchester Depot. Open daily, 5–12. This is a locally favored, rather dark but friendly place for pizza, burgers, fried seafood, and such.

Sirloin Saloon (362-2600), Route 11/30, Manchester Center. This is a large, many-cornered, Tiffany lamp-lit, polished brass place that's always packed; entrées run $6.95–14.95 and there's a children's menu.

The Gourmet Cafe (362-1254), Factory Point Square, Manchester Center. Lunch year-round, daily, extended hours in summer. Tucked away in a corner of one of many shopping clusters, this attractive small dining room has deli food, an outdoor cafe weather permitting. Soups, salads, sandwiches, beers, and wine spritzers. Picnics-to-go.

Park Bench Cafe (362-2557), open from 5 PM daily, the town's singles' bar, featuring munchies like fried zucchini, veggies, and nachos, deli sandwiches and more substantial New York sirloin, ribs.

Double Hex (362-1270), Route 11/30, Manchester. Daily except Wednesday, 11–9. From $1.25. The feel is friendly inside this six-sided building where customers line up to place their orders for every conceivable variety of hamburger, hot dogs, fried chicken, and the like; all good, available with plenty of greens and shakes, coffee, beer, or wine. If every town had a place like this, McDonald's would be out of business.

Marbleledge Lodge (362-1518), 5 miles north of Manchester Center on Route 7. A great find for reasonably priced home cooking; German specialties.

Manchester Pancake House (362-3496), Route 7A, Manchester Center. This small brown house has no connection with the Pancake House chain; it's a family find for breakfast and lunch.

ICE CREAM AND FUDGE   **Wilcox Brothers Dairy** (362-1223), Route 7A south, Manchester. Some of the creamiest, most delectable flavors in Vermont are made in this family-owned and run dairy, available at the farm and a variety of local restaurants.

Mother Myrick's Ice Cream Parlor & Fudge Factory (362-1223), Route 7A, Manchester Center. Open daily at 11, until midnight in summer; fountain treats, cappuccino, baked goods, handmade chocolates, and fudge concocted daily.

SELECTIVE SHOPPING   **Orvis Retail Store**, Manchester Center. Supplying the needs of fishermen and Manchester's other visiting sportsmen since 1856. Known widely for its mail-order catalog, the second oldest in the country, Orvis specializes in the fishing rods made in the factory out back, also other fishing tackle and gear, country clothes and other small luxury items—from silk underwear to welcome mats—which make the difference in country, or would-be country, living. Don't miss the "bargain-basement."

The Jelly Mill, Route 7A, Manchester Center. Daily 10–6. A three-story barn filled with folk art, crystal, cards, crafts, and other assorted gifts. You can watch the resident woodcarver and silversmith. Snacks and light meals available in the Buttery Restaurant on the second floor.

Equinox Village Shops, in the restored buildings across the green from The Equinox, include the **Irish House** for classic and contemporary crafts; the **Village Store**, for Vermont products; **Equinox Antiques**, and **Pat Estey Stencils**.

Equinox Valley Nursery, Route 7A south, Manchester. An outstanding farmstand and spread managed by three generations of a family, good for picking vegetables, berries in season; especially famous in the fall for 100,000 pounds of pumpkins it produces, also for its display of scarecrows and pumpkin faces; sells pumpkin bread, pie, ice cream and marmalade along with other farmstand staples; during January and February the family usually makes 1,000 jars of jams and jellies.

Herdsmen Leather, Manchester Center. Open daily, year-round, billing itself as "New England's finest leathershop," coats, boots, shoes, and accessories; watch for sales.

Landau, Factory Point Square and Route 7A, across from Jelly Mill, Manchester Center. Billing itself as "the world's largest collection of Icelandic woolens," an unusual choice of Icelandic jackets, blankets, sweaters, coats, and accessories.

The Enchanted Doll House, Route 7, north of Manchester Center. Daily 9–5, Sundays 10–5. Twelve rooms full of dolls, doll houses, toys, miniatures, games, and books. For children as well as collectors.

BOOK STORES   **Johnny Appleseed**, Manchester. A bookstore for book lovers, in the square brick building built to house the Battenkill Bank in the early nineteenth century. In 1930 Ruth Hard opened the bookstore, relinquishing it in 1935 to her famous parents—newspaper columnist, state legislator, and poet Walter Hard and novelist and general Vermont raconteur Margaret Hard—who acquired a following of other famous writers as well as the celebrities staying at the neighboring Equinox House. Since 1965 the store has been owned by Fred Taylor, who likes to talk books—both old and new. There is an extensive stock of used books upstairs, while downstairs there are cards along with Vermont lore, humor, fishing, hunting, and general titles.

The Northshire Bookstore, Main Street, Manchester Center, is highly regarded as one of the most complete in New England. The Morrows have moved the shop into the venerable Colburn House diagonally across the street from the store's former location. Children's books are featured, along with an extraordinarily comprehensive stock of current and classic paperbacks.

FACTORY DIRECT SHOPS   Manchester merchants refuse to call these stores "outlets." Prices are slightly higher than factory stores, lower than retail. The list is lengthening quickly. At present it includes Polo/Ralph Lauren, Anne Klein, CB Sports, Van Heusen, Timberland, Hathaway, Kidsport USA, and John Roberts. Shops that carry a number of brands include: **Manchester Commons, Campus Factory Outlet,** and **Battenkill Place**.

ANTIQUE SHOPS   Two dozen dealers and shops are listed in a folder-guide to local antique shops, available from the **Manchester and the Mountains Chamber of Commerce**.

Antiques Centers (more than one dealer) include: **Center Hill,** Manchester Center; the **1812 House**, Route 7 north, Manchester Center; and the **Carriage Trade**, Route 7 north, Manchester Center.

ENTERTAINMENT   **Dorset Playhouse** (867-5777). The Dorset Players, a community theatre group formed in 1927, actually owns the beautiful playhouse in Dorset. Winter performances by the Dorset Players. Mid-June to October, 8:30 nightly, 5 PM and 9 PM Saturday.

In summer the "Dorset Theatre Festival": new plays as well as classics by a resident professional group.

Manchester Cinema (362-1229), Manchester Center.

Equinox Twin Cinema (262-2633), Manchester Center.

Bromley Summer Music Series (824-5222), at the Outdoor Deck Cafe, Bromley.

Manchester Music Festival (362-1956), summer, at the Southern Vermont Arts Center.

SPECIAL EVENTS   March: Spring skiing, sugaring.

April: Trout season opens, Easter parades and egg hunts at ski areas.

May: **Vermont Symphony Orchestra** performs, Hildene opens.

June: **Strawberry festivals** in Dorset, the annual vintage car climb to Equinox Summit, Southern Vermont Art series opens.

July: Fireworks and old-fashioned Fourth celebrations; Dorset Theater and Weston Playhouse open; a major antiques show held at Hildene in even years, at Dorset in odd ones.

August (first weekend): **Southern Vermont Crafts Fair** juried exhibitors, entertainment, food, and music.

September: **Annual Maple Leaf Half-Marathon, Stratton Wurstfest** on Labor Day Weekend; **Stratton Arts Festival** (beginning second weekend, running through mid-October), a major display of Vermont crafts and art, and a performing arts series in the base lodge at Stratton Mountain. The **Manchester Autumnfest** is a concurrent presentation of dance, theater, and music.

October: **Peru Fair** (crafts, exhibits, food, entertainment).

December: **Candlelight Tours of Hildene**, including sleigh rides, refreshments in the barn, music on the organ.

MEDICAL EMERGENCY   Manchester/Dorset Rescue Squad (362-2121).

Northshire Medical Associates (362-4440) Manchester Center.

Manchester Medical Center (362-1263).

Dorset

Eight miles northwest of Manchester on Route 30, the pristine village of Dorset is visible evidence that it takes money to "prevent the future." A fashionable summer refuge for years, few signs of commerce mar its state of carefully manicured nature. Today's tranquility, making it a haven for artists and writers as well as for the affluent, contrasts sharply with its hotheaded youth. In 1776, the Green Mountain Boys gathered in Cephas Kent's Tavern and issued their first declaration of independence from the New Hampshire Grants, signed by Thomas Chittenden, Ira Allen, Matthew Lyon, Seth Warner, and other Founding Fathers of Vermont.

Today the venerable **Dorset Inn** is the village focal point, along with the **Playhouse** (see *Entertainment*, above) at the far end of the green. The theater has been in continuous operation since it was a stage for a resident professional summer group and for the Dorset Players (876-5777), a community group, in winter. The first marble to be quarried in North America came from Dorset and a local quarry is one of the most popular swimming holes for miles around. There is also an 18-hole golf course and a choice of places to stay.

All places listed below are in Dorset (05251) unless otherwise noted. Just the name of the place, Dorset, Vermont 05251 is sufficient address.

LODGING   The **Barrows House** (867-4455). This exceptional mini-resort features attractive, flexibly-arranged accommodations in the main house and seven adjacent cottages. Guests have the use of a swimming pool and tennis court in the summer, plus bike rentals, and access to the nearby Dorset Golf Club (also used for cross-country skiing). There are comfortable sitting rooms in the main house and the larger cottages, where large families or several friendly couples can be lodged. A convivial bar and game room is wallpapered to resemble a private library. Room rates range upward from $75 single and $145 double, MAP, to $180 for one of the suites. The dining room is outstanding (see below).

The Dorset Inn (867-5500), Dorset Village, a National Historic Site and the state's most venerable hostelry, has been stylishly renovated by its relatively new owners, Sissy Hicks, former chef at the Barrows House, and Henneke Koks (also proprietor of the nearby Village Auberge). Known for its excellent cuisine and relaxing atmosphere, the Inn has 29 guest rooms at $120 double, MAP.

The Village Auberge (867-5715), Dorset Village, is a small, well-groomed lodge with an appealing personality, known especially for its exceptional French and continental cuisine. There are six rooms, from $65 double to $85 for a small suite.

Cornucopia of Dorset (867-5751). This newly renovated nineteenth-century Colonial home run by Bill and Linda Ley has four bedrooms, each with canopy or four-poster bed and private bath, plus a separate cottage suite with a loft bedroom, living room with fireplace, kitchen and sun deck. Guests can relax in the study, living and sun rooms, or on a patio and porch. Rates are $65–115 single, $85–135 double including continental breakfast.

The Little Lodge at Dorset (867-4040). Allen and Nancy Norris have opened their attractive home to guests. Handy to the Playhouse and shops in the village, there are five guest rooms big enough to squeeze in an extra child or two. In winter there is cross-country skiing, skating on the Norris's own small pond, and Bromley is just 20 minutes away. Guests are invited to store picnic fixings in the icebox, share the cocktail hour (set-ups and cheese provided) and socialize by the hearth. Rates: $33–38 per person B&B.

Dovetail Inn (867-5747), PO Box 976. Federal-style inn on the Dorset Green with 11 bedrooms (all with private bath). Breakfast served in rooms or in the dining room; wine and beer served in the "keeping room"; outdoor pool. Rates: $47–65 per day double, breakfast included.

Country Lane Motor Lodge (362-1208), RD 1, Box 501, Route 7, East Dorset 05253. Seven miles north of Manchester Center, this exceptional motel sits on a well-landscaped hillside up and off Route 7 traffic. There's a swimming pool for guests as well as croquet, badminton, and volleyball. Rates range from $47 double to $60 (in foliage season).

Emerald Lake Motel & Chalets (362-1636), Route 7, 8 miles north of Manchester, North Dorset 05253 (next to Emerald Lake State Park). Motel units are available from $32 daily, $175 weekly. Its chalets accommodate from 2 to 12 people, with living rooms and color TV, and fully equipped kitchens, with linens, dishes, and cookware (but no maid service). Upwards of $20 per person with a $60 minimum in the smaller units, $80 in the larger or $425 weekly.

DINING OUT   The Barrows House (876-4455). Dorset Village. In a spacious, rather formal country dining room and its attached conservatory, both conscientiously appointed, diners can select à la carte or the $20.95 prix fixe menu. Appetizers include grilled quail, a hearty leek and rice soup, and among the entrées could be sautéed scallops with fresh dill and gin, roast loin of pork with pear and walnut sauce, sautéed breast of duck with raspberry vinegar, and medallions of lamb with thyme sauce. Vegetables are treated imaginatively—carrots in Dijon maple sauce, for instance. Desserts are sinfully tempting. This is one of the better restaurants in the state.

Dorset Inn (867-5500). Chef Sissy Hicks can be relied on for outstanding New England fare, seven days a week. Begin dinner with French fried mushrooms ($2.50) or New England Cheese Chowder ($2.50), graduate to pork tenderloin with apple butter in puff pastry ($13.50), veal medallions with lime ginger sauce ($14.50) or rack of lamb ($17.50), and end with chocolate mousse cake or pumpkin pecan pie.

The Village Auberge (867-5715). French and continental cuisine in an elegantly intimate setting: after smoked salmon, mussel soup or escargots, entrées ($12–20) might be stuffed breast of pheasant with wild mushrooms, medallions of veal with Calvados cream sauce, or poached salmon with cream of chives. Closed Mondays and best to check ahead for winter day closings.

SELECTIVE SHOPPING   Peltier's General Merchandise (867-4400). A village landmark since 1816: staples and then some, including almost any kind of fish on request, baking to order, Vermont products, wines and gourmet items like hearts of palm and Tiptree jams. Since there are no lunch or snack shops in Dorset this also serves the purpose; good for picnic fare.

Patchcraft. Joan Stewart creates fabric hangings, quilts, pillows, and quilted portraits or paintings of an individual's home or business.

J. K. Adams Co., Factory and Factory Store, Route 30, has a complete line of its fine wood products: sugar maple butcher blocks, knife racks, spice racks, cheese and carving boards, with complementary accessories. Discounted "seconds" on the second floor.

The Wood Duck Carving Studio (362-2413) stocks hand-carved and painted decorated and working decoys of Marilyn Morrissey.

Pawlet

Not far north of Dorset, this hamlet on Route 30 is an unexpected delight, with an intriguing mix of architectural styles in the buildings that cling to the rather steep slopes leading up from Flower Brook, over which **Johnny Mach's General Store** extends. Mach rebuilt the millpond and a waterwheel to generate electricity. A glassed hole in the store's floor provides an unusual overview.

The Old Station Restaurant and Ice Cream Parlor is where the town's business is conducted mornings over coffee from cups bearing the sippers' names. It's a popular stop for bike tours in the summer. In winter it's open from 6:00 AM to 3:00 PM.

The Pawlet Potter (325-3100). Marion Waldo McChesney works in her studio in the basement of her restored brick landmark house, where customers can watch her turn out spongeware, an old method of glazing that resembles the early Bennington pottery. Her work is in the American Folk Art Museum.

East-West Antiques (325-3466), Route 30, offers antiques and artifacts from Indonesia and Ireland.

Authentic Designs (394-7713), The Mill Road, Route 315, West Rupert 05776, creates fine reproduction colonial and early American lighting fixtures, electrified or left unwired for candles, made of brass or maple. Open Monday–Friday, 9–4, or by appointment on weekends.

Danby

A by-passed hamlet on Route 7 north of Manchester and south of Wallingford, Danby is being re-born—again. In this vintage village known for its fine marble quarries, home base for Silas Griffith, who made himself Vermont's first millionaire in the 1850s with his lumber empire, seven buildings owned by the late Pearl Buck, who started renovations before her death in 1969, are being restored by a new group of private investor/benefactors, creating an attraction for travelers interested in antiquities.

LODGING   **Silas Griffith Inn** (293-5567), Danby (05739), is the renovated, 33-room establishment that once housed Danby's timber baron. Lois and Paul Dansereau, the new owners of the Victorian mansion, have restored the hardwood floors, carved birdseye, curly maple and cherry woodwork, and provide 18 guest rooms, many with private bath, divided among the main house, converted carriage house, and annex. There are three spacious common rooms, furnished with Victorian antiques or reproductions. Weekend rates are $75 for a room with private bath, $65 shared, including full breakfast, discounts for weekdays or for a stay of several days. The dining room recently opened to the public with an eclectic dinner menu, including some ethnic specialties, with entrées in the $10–15 class.

   The Quail's Nest (293-5099), Box 21, Main Street, Danby 05739, is a simple, pleasant B&B in an 1835 house. Each of its five guest rooms is furnished with antiques and handmade country quilts ($35 single, $45 double). The Edsons serve a tempting full breakfast.

EATING OUT   **White Dog Tavern** (293-5477), Route 7, Danby, a nicely renovated 1812 farmhouse with a central chimney and four fireplaces, serves light lunches Wednesday through Sunday; dinner Tuesday through Sunday. There's a cheery bar, and an outdoor deck in summer. The blackboard menu includes clams, shrimp, sandwiches, and the house special, chicken breasts à la Tom, served up with herbs, garlic, and melted cheese over spaghetti.

SELECTIVE SHOPPING   **The Gallery of Danby Green** (293-5550), Main Street, occupies the restored Greek revival Hawden House. From parlor to kitchen, dining room to nursery, each room is appropriately decorated and stocked with upscale gifts and gadgets, mostly from Vermont, including wood and marble carvings.

The Danby Antiques Center (293-5484), Main Street, displays American country and formal furniture and accessories from 24 dealers in 11 rooms and the barn. Open 10–5, daily April–December; Thursday–Monday, January–March.

Main Street Antiques Center (293-9919), two doors away, has antiques and collectibles from several dealers.

Danby Marble Company & Yankee Vineyard (293-5425), on Route 7, are open daily from May 1 to October 30 and from November 20 to December 30. The first is a factory store stocking a dazzling array of marble bookends, lamps, chessboards, candle holders, trivets, vases, custom-cut "English Pub" tables and other marble counter tops. The Vineyard barn holds about a half acre of baskets, oak kegs, sheepskin/deerskin gloves, syrup, cheese, and preserves.

The Peel Gallery (293-5230), Route 7, 2 miles north of Danby, represents 50 American artists whose works are dramatically displayed in a remodeled barn. Margaret and Harris Peel launched this showcase 12 years ago and schedule shows between May 23 and October 10. Among the Vermont artists represented are Janet McKenzie, Richard Clark, and Patrick Farrow, whose sinuous steel figures are outstanding. The gallery is closed Tuesdays except July and August, but otherwise open year-round 10–5.

Mountain Villages

The spine of the Green Mountains is traced on the map by one road, Route 100. The road hugs the base, rather than ridge of the mountains, and twists with the rivers which, in some places, have carved valleys just wide enough to hold small villages.

Nowhere in Vermont is this sense of high mountains, deep valleys, and small villages more pronounced than along the 30 miles of Route 100 that follow the West River, up from Jamaica through Rawsonville, the Londonderries, and Weston. Three ski areas—posh and prosperous Stratton, and the recently expanded Magic Mountain—are all just off this road (as is Bromley which we have described in the"Manchester and the Mountains" section), and there is excellent cross-country skiing, available well into the spring after snow has faded from the lower, broader valleys farther north.

The most famous village here is Weston, at the north end of the West River Valley. The oval common is shaded with majestic maples. A band plays in the bandstand and theatricals are performed in the Weston Playhouse, one of the oldest summer theaters in the country. Down the street stands The Vermont Country Store, New England's number one nostalgia outlet. A number of small inns, restaurants, and shops round out the scene.

The West River actually rises in Londonderry, an old mill village that has turned its surviving mill—and several other old buildings—into restaurants. Routes 11 and 100 cross here, and there are an amazing number of amenities (including the area movie house and lodging service) for one tiny village.

Rawsonville is simply the name for the junction of Routes 100 and 30, in the way Bondville designates the huddle of houses two miles west. But the resort community here is hidden four miles up the Stratton Mountain access road, and it is unexpectedly suburban-looking with high-rise condominiums gathered around a monumental parking garage and the Mountain Market place.

Jamaica, the southernmost community in this region, was once the terminus of a railroad that ran up the West River Valley from Brattleboro. The former rail yards are now the core of Jamaica State Park, a great camping spot with a swimming hole. There are two general stores, Munroe's, which has been in the same family since

1852 (it stocks Woolrich shirts for stray tourists), and the Jamaica General Store, with a stash of reasonably priced nonessentials upstairs. The inn at the core of the village is steadily expanding, absorbing surrounding houses, and eliminating front porch washlines.

On the northwestern fringe of this area is the small, picturesque village of Peru and, on a delightful gravel road halfway between Peru and Weston, the hamlet of Landgrove, a beautiful by-way with an inn.

GUIDANCE   Londonderry Area Chamber of Commerce (824-8178), PO Box 58, Londonderry 05148, is a source of information for this entire region. Look for the information booth in the Londonderry Shopping Center, staffed 11–4 weekdays, 10–5 weekends in summer and fall; there's an information board here year-round and brochures are available in the office directly across the way.

Area Lodging Service (824-6915), PO Box 519, Londonderry 05148, is a reservation service for a region which also includes the area covered in "Manchester and the Mountains." Manchester and the

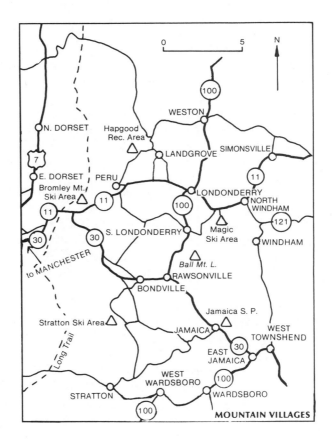

MOUNTAIN VILLAGES

Mountains Chamber of Commerce (362-2100), Manchester Center 05255 also covers this area.

GETTING THERE   From the Boston area the access is via Route 30, and from New York it is up Route 11 from Manchester.

TO SEE AND DO   The Museum of Vermont Guild of Old-Time Crafts & Industries, Weston, open in summer months 9–5, closed Tuesdays. This is a working restoration of a vintage 1900 mill with resident craftspeople—a woodworker, a basket maker, spinner, and weaver, all plying their trades.

Farrar Mansur House (824-5894), Weston. Built in 1797 as a tavern and inn, this is a rewarding museum of local history. Open weekends in late May, June, and Labor Day to Columbus Day; in July and August, Wednesday–Saturday, 1–5, Sundays, 2–5, $1 (free under 10).

Weston Priory (824-5409) north of Weston on Route 155. A small community of Benedictine monks welcome guests who come to share their regimen. There are no formal retreats, but groups and individuals can be accommodated in the guest house. Visitors are also welcome at daily and Sunday liturgies. Times vary from season to season. A small gift store sells, among other things, records of the warm-hearted music for which the Priory is famed.

A PARK, A FOREST, AND A DAM   Jamaica State Park (874-4600), Jamaica 05343. This 758-acre wooded area offers riverside camping, swimming in a great swimming hole, a picnic area, and an organized program of guided hikes. An old railroad bed along the river serves as a trail to the Ball Mountain Dam. One weekend in spring and fall is set aside for white water canoe races. There are 40 tent sites, including 15 lean-tos.

Hapgood Pond Recreation Area, Peru. (Contact the local Green Mountain National Forest office on Route 11 between Manchester and Peru: 362-2307). Acquired in 1931, this was the beginning of the Green Mountain National Forest. There is swimming, fishing, and limited boating on the 7-acre pond. Removed from the picnic ground and beach, there are 28 campsites (first come, first serve basis). A pleasant, .8 mile forest trail threads the woods.

Ball Mountain Lake (886-8111), Jamaica 05343. This 85-acre lake, a dramatic sight among the wooded, steep mountains, can be viewed from the access road off Route 30. 107 campsites are available on Winhall Brook at the other end of the reservoir, open mid-May to mid-September; accessible off Route 100 in South Londonderry, free. It is controlled release from this flood dam that provides the outstanding canoeing available on the West River below Jamaica each spring. This area is maintained by the U.S. Army Corp of Engineers.

Greendale Campground, 2 miles north of Weston on Route 100.

There are 14 sites, $5 per day; contact the Green Mountain National Forest (362-2307), District Ranger Office, Manchester.

BICYCLING   Mountain bikes are available from **Stratton Sports Center** (297-2525) at Stratton Mountain. (See also Manchester.)

CANOEING   The West River between Ball Mountain and Townshend dams is one of the major centers for white water canoeing and kayaking in the East. The annual West River Slalom Races in April draw thousands to the bank of the river. Rentals are available from **West River Canoe** (896-6209), Route 100 just south of East Jamaica.

CAMPING, HIKING, AND SWIMMING   See Jamaica State Park and Hapgood Pond. The Long Trail also passes through this region.

GOLF   **Tater Hill** (875-2517), Windham. A 9-hole course, pro shop, carts, dressing rooms, and showers. (*Note*: there is also a swimming pool for nongolfing members of the family).

HORSEBACK RIDING   **Woodwind Stables** (297-1687), Kendall Farm Road, Bondville. Trail rides.

TENNIS   **Stratton Mountain** (297-2200), home of the prestigious Volvo International Tennis Tournament in early August, offers weekend and five-day instructional programs. There are 15 outdoor and 4 indoor courts. (*Note*: these facilities are not available on a drop-in basis.)

Tater Hill (875-2517). Red clay and all-weather surface courts, available on an hourly basis.

CROSS-COUNTRY SKIING   **Viking Ski Touring Centre** (824-3933), Little Pond Road, Londonderry. Brothers Lee and Stanton Allaban began renting out cross-country equipment and teaching folks how to use it back in 1970. They were among the first commercial "centres" in the state and both brothers continue to pioneer the paying possibilities of the sport. The Viking Trail system now includes 40 km of groomed trails, 2 km lighted on Friday and Saturday evenings. There is a rental and retail shop and a cafe serving drinks, light breakfasts, and lunches. There are lessons, lunch tours to Weston, bed and breakfast, and Inn-to-Inn tours using a total of four local hostelries.

Wild Wings Ski Touring Center (824-6793), Peru. Tracy and Chuck Black run a family-oriented touring center located within the boundaries of the Green Mountain National Forest, 2½ miles north of Peru. Trails are narrow, geared to the intermediate skier, and adjoin an extensive public system which connects the center with Landgrove. This area tends to get a heavier snowfall than other local touring centers; the 20 km of trail are at elevations of between 1,650 and 2,040 feet. Instruction, rentals, and free hot bouillon are found in the warming hut.

Stratton Ski Touring Center (297-1880), Stratton Mountain. The touring network here has atrophied in recent years as condominiums have appeared in the middle of old trails. There are now just 10 km of set trails, mostly on the golf course, some limited wooded stretches. Veteran touring leader Charles Marchant offers Wednesday moonlight tours, other daytime tours in the local area.

Nordic Inn Ski Touring Center (824-6444), Route 11, Londonderry. The center has 20 km of trails through neighboring woods. Lunch and dinner are served.

Magic Mountains (824-5566), Timberside, Route 121, just off Route 11, Windham. There are 34 km of trails and a touring center at the recently re-opened Timberside Ski Area (formerly Timber Ridge), now part of Magic. This is a long-established network, formerly known as Globe Mountain Farm.

Tater Hill (875-2517), 4 miles east of Londonderry, 1 mile off Routes 11 and 121 in Windham. Rentals and a 20 km trail network.

DOWNHILL SKIING   **Stratton** (297-2200). Located atop a 5-mile access road from Route 30 in Bondville. Snow Phone: 297-2211. Stratton is an unusually well groomed mountain: this goes for its trails, its facilities, lodges, and clientele. It ranks highly among Vermont's major ski resorts, a big mountain with two separate areas: the original North Face and the distinctly sunnier Sun Bowl. Thanks to the quantity of lifts, skiers are generally dispersed over the trail network. Stratton Village, a complex that includes 30 shops, 3 restaurants, a 91-room condo-hotel, a conference center, a 750-car garage, and 170 condominiums, dwarfs the base facility. A sports center includes a 25-yard long pool, whirlpool, indoor tennis courts, and racquetball courts, exercise equipment, and a lounge. (Also see *Lodging*.)

Lifts: 6 double chairlifts, 1 triple, 3 quads.

Trails and Slopes: 86

Vertical drop: 2,003 feet

Snowmaking: 240 acres.

Facilities: A restaurant and cafeteria in the base lodge, also cafeterias mid-mountain and in the Sun Bowl lodges. Chapel of the Snows at the parking lot, a little Bavarian-style church, has frequent nondenominational and Roman Catholic services. A shuttle bus brings skiers from inns on the mountain to the base lodge, with service to Bromley. The First Run Ski Shop offers rentals and repairs.

Ski School: ATM and GLM methods.

For Children: Day Care for six month to three years old. A separate base lodge for "Cubs"; combined ski and play programs are offered. Little Cubs (aged 3–6) and Big Cubs (aged 6–12).

Special Program: Stratton Mountain School, a coed prep school for Alpine and cross-country racers, academic year and summer programs.

Rates: $34 per day adult, $19 junior, free under 6, special packages.

Magic Mountains (824-5566), Londonderry. Magic Mountain has magically turned its 22 trails into 72 by annexing the former Timber Ridge ski area in Windham. The two trail systems (now interlinked as Magicside and Timberside) have been carved on opposite sides of Glebe Mountain, which the area's first settlers farmed, the same Glebe Mountain now hanging in major museums, captured in a number of paintings by Aldro Hibbard. Ordov Ski Area Development Corporation, a major investor in the Magics, is now also joint-owner of Bromley, 9 miles away (see "Manchester and the Mountains"); lift tickets are interchangeable.

Lifts: 3 triple chairs, 1 double Magicside; 1 double and a T-bar, Timberside.

Trails: 72 (24 are on Timberside)

Vertical drop: 1,700 feet

Snowmaking: 80% of Magicside; not much on Timberside

Facilities: 2 base lodges, 2 rental shops

Rates: $30 adult, $20 junior, $15 midweek.

SLEIGH RIDES   Check with the **Stratton Touring Center** (297-1880), the **Inn at Bear Creek** (297-1700), the **Village Inn at Landgrove** (824-6673). **Pfisters** (824-6320) also offers hay rides.

LODGING   See **Guidance** for details about the local reservations service and chamber of commerce.

COUNTRY INNS   The Village Inn (824-6673), R.D. Box 215, Landgrove 05148. This red brick building rambles back and around, beginning with the 1820 house, ending an acre or two away with a 1976 addition housing a whirlpool. The "Vermont continuous architecture" draws guests from a handsome lobby, past 20 crisp, bright rooms that meander off in all directions, through the inviting Rafter Room Lounge (huge, filled with games and books) to the attractive dining room in the original house. During warm weather there is a heated pool, tennis, 3-hole pitch'n'put, and lawn games. In winter you step out onto the 15-mile cross-country trail system which leads through the picturesque village of Landgrove (just a church, former school, and salting of homes, cupped in a hollow), on into surrounding National Forest. Six miles from the Magics on one hand and from Bromley on the other, this is also a good base for downhill skiers. There are also sleigh rides. Dining is by candlelight and the menu is imaginative. The Snyder family has been running this very special place for many years; the Snyders currently at the helm are Else and Ron. $35–65 per person MAP in fall and winter ($20–30 per child in the same room); $40–63 per room, B&B in summer; dinner is still served in summer except Wednesdays.

Three Mountain Inn (874-4140), Route 30/100, Jamaica 05343. A 1780s house in the village of Jamaica forms the core of a delightful inn offering 14 guest rooms. Charles and Elaine Murray have constantly upgraded the inn, subtly expanded during the past decade. The rooms—whether in the old house, above the former stables or in the cottage across the street—are all beautifully decorated. The public rooms include a cozy pub and living room with wide-planked floors and a friendly hearth. (For details about the two dining rooms see *Dining Out*.) In summer there is a lovely garden pool, and you can stroll to the walking trails in Jamaica State Park. In winter Stratton Ski Resort is just down the road, or you can ski the old railroad bed along the West River. There are also meeting facilities and the cottage across the road can be rented as one unit. $50–75 per person MAP.

The Londonderry Inn (824-5226), PO Box 301, South Londonderry 05155. A large, handsome old summer inn that went year-round when it found itself handy to Stratton as well as Magic and Bromley. There are 25 guest rooms, 20 with baths. Public rooms are large, bright, and warm. Jim and Jean Cavanagh delight in helping plan guests' daily itineraries. Children are welcome. Rooms come big and small, and all are cheerful. There is a big dining room, a tavern, a game room with table tennis, and a swimming pool. Rates are $53–65 per couple including breakfast; $14–17 extra per person in a family room.

The Highland House (824-3019). Route 100, Londonderry 05148 (but fairly close to Weston). An especially handsome establishment with nine rooms (two with shared baths), plus four doubles, and four suites in the renovated carriage house; sitting and dining room. Singles $40–60, doubles $50–70, including full breakfast. Dinner entrées range from $9.75 for the "Chef's Drunken Chicken" to $14.75 for steak au Poivre.

Colonial House Inn & Motel (824-6286), Box 138, Weston 05161. A rare and delightful combination of nine motel units and six traditional inn rooms, connected by a very pleasant dining room, a comfortable lounge with fireplace, and game room. Innkeepers John and Betty Nunnikhoven make guests of all ages feel very welcome. Rates include memorable breakfasts; dinners are served family style. BYOB. In winter this is one of the stops on local cross-country inn-to-inn tours. Rates are $22–40 per person, B&B, $8 per child 4–12 (free for infants), less 15 percent for five days midweek; dinners are $8–15.

The Darling Family Inn (824-3223), Route 100, Weston 05161. An 1830s house, exquisitely furnished with family antiques by Joan and Chapin Darling. The five guest rooms have canopied beds, fine quilts and artistic touches. Two rooms have private baths, the others share two. There are wide-planked floors throughout, and Joan has expertly stenciled the walls. Full country breakfasts are included in the rates, lunches and candlelit dinners can be reserved. In summer the pool adds a nice touch. $55–70 per room B&B, $58 per couple in one of the two attractive cottages out back (breakfast not included).

The Inn at Weston (824-5804), Box 56, Weston 05161. This clapboard inn at the edge of the picturesque village has earned rave reviews for food as well as atmosphere. The 14 guest rooms, most with private bath, are small but nicely furnished, and the dining room is walled in barnboard. There are separate children's and adult game rooms, and hot drinks and pastries are served at 4 PM in the winter. Jeanne and Bob Wilder are the new owners. Rates: $44–70 per person, MAP.

The Three Clock Inn (824-6327), Londonderry 05148. This is a little gem, tucked up on a hilly village back street. Better known as a restaurant (see *Dining Out*), there are four lovely upstairs rooms, one with a canopy bed and fireplace, also an upstairs sitting room to provide complete privacy from the dining crowd. In summer the garden is a profusion of flowers and in winter the Magics are just a few minutes' drive, as are the cross-country trails at Viking. $55 per room or $55 per person MAP.

SKI LODGES   *Stratton Mountain 05155*   Most of these facilities are open year-round but are designed for skiers.

Stratton Mountain Resort Lodging (800-843-6867), open 24 hours daily, is—if you can get through—a reservation service for rooms at the Stratton Mountain Inn, Stratton Village Lodge, and Stratton Mountain Villas. The 125-room inn is the largest lodging facility on the mountain. Recently refurbished, it offers private baths, phones, TVs, a large dining room, saunas, and whirlpools on the premises. The 91-room Lodge, opened in 1985, adjacent to the Stratton base lodge, features studio-style units with kitchenettes. The villas are condominium units in a range of sizes and shapes; roughly 100 are in the rental pool at any given time. Room rates run $135–200 without meals but usually less when combined with golf, tennis, or ski packages; condo units run $175 per night for a one-bedroom to $350 for a four-bedroom unit. All resort guests have access to the sports center with its indoor pool, exercise machines, racquetball, and tennis courts.

Birkenhaus Village (297-2000). A modern but intimate lodge owned by Emo Henrich, founder of Stratton's ski school. There are 18 rooms plus 3 efficiency apartments and a bunkroom; the decor and dining is Austrian. There is a bier stube, a beauty shop, and afternoon tea. $75 per person, MAP.

Liftline Lodge (297-2600). This Austrian-style hostelry is the smallest and coziest at Stratton. Rooms have two double beds and color TV, but are definitely one-up from motel rooms, and the public rooms are delightful; there are exercise machines and a tennis court along with the Sports Center across the way. Pleasant dining in Victoria's Konditorei. $44 per person MAP. (For details on The New Life Spa housed here, see *Health Spa*.)

Bear Creek (297-1700), is a sport hotel and condominium resort located near the bottom of the Stratton Access Road on Route 30. In winter it offers free shuttle service to the lifts. Amenities include a Jacuzzi, sauna, two pools, tennis courts, dining in Feather's Saloon and Restaurant, and sleigh rides. From $45 per person.

Alpenrose Inn (297-2750), Winhall Hollow Road, Bondville 05340. Ski lodge-style rooms and a pleasant lounge with a huge stone fireplace, a dining room with hand hewn beams and cathedral ceilings; $58 per person B&B.

At Magic Mountains, Londonderry, Landgrove 05148   **Blue Gentian Lodge** (824-5908), Swiss-style lodge; 14 rooms with private baths. There is an attractive lounge, game room, and dining room with meals featuring homemade bread and pastries. $28 per person EP.

The Country Hare (824-3131), is a chalet-style hostelry on Route 11, at the bottom of the access road to the ski area. Formerly The Post-Horn, it offers 15 rooms with private baths, color TVs, a bar, restaurant, and game room. $32.50 per person B&B.

Dostal's (824-6700). Very Austrian and very clean with 50 rooms. Public rooms fulfill expectations of what a ski lodge should be: hearths, comfortable lounges, a cozy bar, an indoor pool, and whirlpool. In summer there is tennis, an outdoor pool, lawn games. $34.50 per person EP.

(See also **Bromley Sun Lodge, Johnny Seesaw's,** and **The Wiley Inn** under Manchester and the Mountains.)

Nordic Inn (824-6444), Route 11, Landgrove 05148. Although technically in Landgrove, this pleasant lodging place is right down the main drag from Bromley. There are just five guest rooms, the largest of which has a private bath and woodburning fireplace. The dining room is the famous thing here (see *Dining Out*), and there is a large, friendly pub, plus 20 km of cross-country trails open to the public.

Swiss Inn (824-3442), Route 11, Londonderry 05148. From the exterior, this looks like a standard motel, but once inside, you are somewhere special. Hans and Lisa Gegenschatz have created a true Swiss lodge atmosphere, crisp and cozy. The 19 rooms all have private baths, and public space is inviting and comfortable. There is a game room, lounge, and dining room—where the specialties are continental as well as Swiss (see *Restaurants*). In winter, it's handy to both Bromley and Magic and in summer, there's a pool and tennis court. Rates: $27 per person B&B.

SPA PROGRAM   New Life Spa (297-2600), Liftline Lodge, Stratton 05155.

This is the oldest spa program in Vermont, and director Jimmy LeSage has honed it into a combination of exercise, diet, and lectures that work well. The six-night programs are offered year-round. Guests weigh in at check-in (Sunday at 3:30) and usually weigh out the following Saturday pounds lighter. But the focus here isn't just on losing weight; it's on understanding how to eat and exercise to keep your body humming healthily. Guests have access to Stratton's sports center, and to cross-country and alpine slopes in season. Rates average $895 for six nights, seven days.

DINING OUT **Three Clock Inn** (824-6327), South Londonderry. Closed Mondays. Chef Heinrich Tschernitz has a well-earned reputation for the quality of a varied menu that includes escargots maison and unusual veal dishes. You might begin with scampi maison ($6.75), proceed to cutlet of veal zingara ($15.50), and finish with chocolate mousse ($2.50). Dining rooms are small and simple. In summer, request the porch.

Three Mountain Inn (874-4140), Route 30/100 in the village of Jamaica. Reservations please. Closed to the public Wednesday. The two front rooms of this eighteenth-century house are a fine setting for candlelit dinners. The menu changes every day, and there is a fair choice. You might begin with smoked trout or fresh-made soup, proceed to chicken paprika or veal Swiss, finish with Jamaican ice cream or strawberry cheese cake. Entrées range $9.50–14.50.

Nordic Inn (824-6444), Londonderry. Lunch 12–3, Dinner 6–10. Sunday Brunch 11–3. Entrées $10.50–16.00. The glass-sided, greens-filled dining rooms at the rear of this inn welcome cross-country skiers for lunch, but at dinner this is a serious dining place.

Restaurant Hasenpfeffer and Victoria's Terrace Cafe at Liftline Lodge (297-2600), Stratton Mountain. Open for breakfast, lunch, and dinner. The dining rooms at Liftline are unexpectedly attractive, bright and Tyrolian with alpine specialties like *Viennese Schlemmer Suppe* and *Kassler Rippchen mit Sauerkraut* and, of course, *apfelstrudel mit schlag*. The Sunday buffet is served 12:30–3.

Birkenhaus (297-2000), Stratton Mountain. This small, modern-style lodge has a fine reputation for dining. The five-course, daily changing menu includes French and Austrian specialties. It's priced at $29. Dinner might begin with smoked goose breasts in lingonberry sauce, followed by gingered pear bisque, then endive and watercress salad, then maybe noisettes of pork, *poive verte creme* or quenelles of salmon, saffron beurre, topped off with dark and white chocolate mousse or *Schwarzwalder Kirch Torte*. Reservations are a must.

The Weston Playhouse Dinner Theater Cabaret (824-5288), Thursday through Monday from 6 PM, July–September. You might dine on lobster pie ($13.95) or chicken "Evita" (same price) while watching the cabaret; there are also matinee lunches on Saturdays, from 11:30.

Swiss Inn (824-3442), Londonderry. Open for dinner to the public with a strong local following. Specialties include Geschnetzeltes (veal à la Swiss), beef fondue and chicken "Lugano" (chicken breast dipped in Gruyere cheese batter), also continental dishes like Shrimp à la Marseille and veal tarragon, all prepared by chef-owner Hans Gegenschatz. Entrées range from $9.50–13.50.

The Mill Tavern Restaurant (824-3247), Londonderry. Open for dinner only, 5–9:30 nightly. A genuine old mill building, its interior festooned with 10,000 handmade tools dating from the early 1700s through the late nineteenth century. In winter there is a blazing hearth and après-ski atmosphere. $8.95–14.

The Londonderry Inn (824-5226), Route 100, South Londonderry. Closed Tuesdays. The large, attractive dining room is a pleasant place to dine on baked brie followed by duckling soup, then maybe bouillabaisse or veal marsala topped off by chocolate walnut pie. There is a broad choice. Entrées are priced from $8.95–15. The huge tavern hearth is also a nice place to linger.

The Highland House (824-3019), Route 100, Londonderry. There are just six tables in the dining room of this old inn. Specialties include drunken chicken, also roast New England duckling ($12), and baked shrimp with crabmeat ($13.95).

The Inn at Weston (824-5804), Weston Village. The dining rooms are fairly large and the inn has a tradition of fine dining. Under its present ownership, specialties include blackened salmon ($15.95) and steak *au poivre* ($17.95).

EATING OUT   **Stoddards** (824-3505), Londonderry, Route 11, attached to Stoddard's Market. This is a real breakfast and lunch find, open 5 AM–3 PM. The walls are decorated with customers' hats and the atmosphere is spic'n'span homey. There is a counter and a half dozen tables. One egg and home fries costs $1.65 and most sandwiches are under $2. There are salads, and the soups are homemade. And when was the last time you had tapioca pudding for dessert? Actually we preferred the strawberry rhubarb cobbler. Linda and Terry Stoddard sell fishing and hunting licenses next door. In summer, there's a dairy bar and deck, open until 8:30.

Hearthstone Country Grill (824-5060), Route 100 between Londonderry and South Londonderry. Open Wednesday–Sunday from 5 PM. Casual country dining in a former horse barn. The dining menu includes some Cajun-style entrées, $6.95–14.95; half portions at half price are also available.

The Bryant House (824-6287), Weston. Owned by the neighboring Vermont Country Store, this fine old house has belonged to one family—the Bryants—from the time it was built in 1827 until the family line petered out. Upstairs a special room is set aside to look as it did in the 1890s. The $1.95 on the "Bill of Fare" is for a "Bowl of cold milk, a hunk of Vermont Cheddar and Common Crackers." There are also plenty of salads, sandwiches and Vermont-style chicken pie. Lunch and afternoon tea served 11:30–2:30.

ENTERTAINMENT   Weston Playhouse (824-5288). This popular summer theater on the Common has been active for over 50 years and gives nightly performances from mid-July through September. The cabaret downstairs is open after performances.

Kinhaven Music School (824-9592), Lawrence Hill Road, Weston, presents free concerts Fridays at 4:30, Saturdays at 2:30, July to mid-August; inquire about details.

Haig's in Bondville is the place for live music and dancing in the winter.

Derry Twin Cinema (824-2221), Routes 11 and 100, Londonderry Shopping Center, includes a bar, tables in rear rows, and shows two first-run movies nightly.

GENERAL STORES   The Vermont Country Store, Weston, year-round, Monday through Saturday, 9–5. Back in 1944 the late Vrest Orton revived the business established by his grandfather and father in northern Vermont before the turn of the century. Gradually that business—selling sensible clothing, gadgets, old-fashioned yard goods, and kitchen utensils—has expanded into a national tourist attraction, complete with a hefty mail-order catalog. Orton prided himself on reviving, among other things, the Vermont Common Cracker, first made in 1820, now produced in his Rockingham store. Son, Lyman, is now in charge.

J. J. Hapgood Store, Peru. Daily, 8:30–6. A genuine general store with a pot belly stove, old-fashioned counters filled with food, and some clothing staples; geared to locals rather than tourists.

The Weston Village Store, Weston. Open daily. A standard country emporium catering to visitors; stocking gifts, clothing, fishing gear, food, and books. If you can't find anything just ask Bob Ballard, the friendly proprietor. There is also a pleasant sandwich and coffee shop on the side, and a porch with extra benches for writing postcards.

SELECTIVE SHOPPING   The Village Square at Stratton Mountain is a Tyroleanesque showcase for some of Vermont's poshest shops and industries. **Bogner** and **CB**, both ski ware manufacturers, have stores here as does **Overland Outfitters**. There is also an art gallery, bookstore, and a cafe.

Mountain Stitchery (824-6431), Weston Village (next to Weston Village Store). Best supply of needle work materials for miles around! Yarns, calico materials, stenciling, quilting, embroidery thread, needlepoint—both supplies and kits.

Challenging white water on the West River

The Barn (clothing) and **Shoe Barn**, Londonderry, corner of Routes 100 and 11. Open daily, year-round, 10–5:30. Casual clothing, sweaters, brand names, shoes and boots for children.

OUTLETS **Weston Bowl Mill**, Weston. Open year-round, 8–6 in summer, 9–5 in winter; 10–5 on Sundays. This classic old wood mill has long produced quality wooden ware, available throughout the state and here at factory prices.

SPECIAL EVENTS

January–March: skiing

April: Whitewater canoeing on the West River.

July–Labor Day: **Weston Playhouse** season.

July–mid-August: **Kinhaven Music School** concerts.

August (first week): **Volvo International Tennis Tournament** (297-2945), Stratton Mountain, matches between the world's top players, usually a sellout.

September: **Stratton Wurstfest** on Labor Day Weekend; **Stratton Arts Festival** (beginning second weekend, running through mid-October), a major display of Vermont crafts and art, and a performing arts series in the base lodge at Stratton Mountain.

October: **Peru Fair**: crafts, exhibits, food, entertainment; Stratton Arts Festival continues.

MEDICAL EMERGENCY **Mountain Valley Health Center** (824-6901), Route 11, opposite the Flood Brook School, 2 miles west of Londonderry, 3 miles east of Peru.

Rescue Squad: 824-3166.

Grafton, Chester, and Bellows Falls

These three, strikingly different towns form a collage of Vermont's past, present, even future—from the once-thriving industrial center of Bellows Falls to the oases for travelers in the villages of Grafton and Chester.

Grafton is Vermont's Cinderella. Unquestionably queenly today, it was—and not too long ago—a forgotten, decaying village.

Prior to the Civil War, Grafton boasted more than 1,480 souls and 10,000 sheep. Wool was turned to 75,000 yards of Grafton cloth annually, soapstone from thirteen local quarries left town in the shape of sinks, stoves, ink wells, and footwarmers.

But then one in three of Grafton's men marched off to the Civil War and few returned. An 1869 flood destroyed the town's six dams and its road. The new highway bypassed Grafton. The town's Tavern, however, built in 1801, entered a golden era. Innkeeper Marlan Phelps invested his entire California Gold Rush fortune in adding a third floor and double porches and his brother Francis organized a still extant coronet band. Guests included Emerson, Thoreau, and Kipling; later both Woodrow Wilson and Teddy Roosevelt visited.

But by 1940 the Tavern was sagging and nearly all the eighty-some houses were selling—with plenty of acreage—for $3000–$5000.

Enter Matthew Hall, a New York financier and descendant of the town's first pastor, who had been summering here since 1936. Hall's "Aunt Pauline" Fiske, who often joined him, financed restoration of some fine three-dimensional murals in the Congregational Church. On her death Miss Fiske left a fortune in trust to her two nephews, Hall and Dean Mathey of Princeton, New Jersey. A note requested its use be for an unusual worthy cause, something she would have liked. For five years the men couldn't hit on a suitable scheme. Then one Vermont morning Mathey woke Hall with the news that he had "found the answer to Aunt Pauline's money . . . Grafton."

Incorporated in 1963 under the name "Windham," the Foundation immediately focused on the town's rotting core. A restored version of the last store was opened, complete with lunch counter.

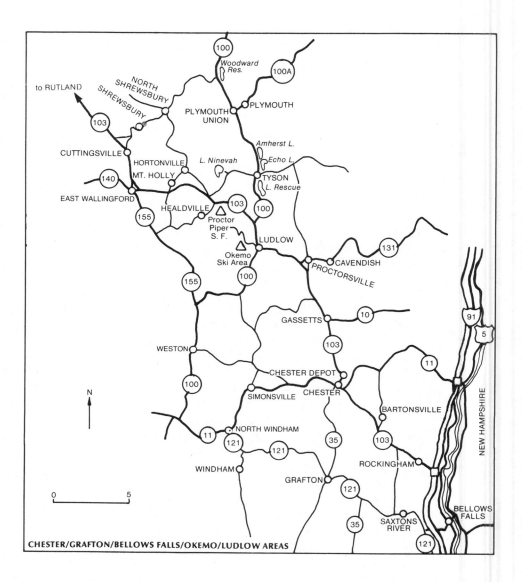

100

Woodward
Res.

100A

to RUTLAND

NORTH
SHREWSBURY
SHREWSBURY

PLYMOUTH

PLYMOUTH
UNION

103

Amherst L.

CUTTINGSVILLE

HORTONVILLE

L. Ninevah

Echo L.

140

MT. HOLLY

TYSON

L. Rescue

EAST WALLINGFORD

HEALDVILLE

103

155

Proctor
Piper
S. F.

100

LUDLOW

131

Okemo
Ski Area

CAVENDISH

PROCTORSVILLE

155

100

GASSETTS

10

91

5

103

N

WESTON

11

100

CHESTER DEPOT

SIMONSVILLE

CHESTER

BARTONSVILLE

NEW HAMPSHIRE

11

NORTH WINDHAM

121

121

35

103

WINDHAM

ROCKINGHAM

0   5

GRAFTON

121

BELLOWS
FALLS

35

SAXTONS
RIVER

121

CHESTER/GRAFTON/BELLOWS FALLS/OKEMO/LUDLOW AREAS

After roofing a blacksmith shop, the Foundation went on to tackle the unwinterized Tavern. The architects of Old Deerfield left the rocking chairs on the Tavern's front porch and its handsome face unchanged. New heating, wiring, an elevator, twenty guest rooms, and fourteen private baths were added.

The Windham Foundation has expanded the inn by adding sixteen double rooms in restored homes across the way, also four complete houses and a luxurious stable for guests who want to bring a horse. It owns twenty-one buildings in town, and among other things, has built a cheese factory, opened a nursery and gift shop, and buried the Village's electric, phone, and cable TV wires. There is a museum with old vehicles, tools, and the innards of an old time country store, also displays on the wildlife management of its 1,300 acres. The Windham Foundation maintains a demonstration flock of twenty sheep and marked footpaths on which visitors can wander down past the sheep and pond, into the woods and home again.

Over the past few years some fine guesthouses have opened around town—along with art galleries and assorted shops. It all adds up to the biggest tourist destination within a radius of ten miles—a sweep that happens to include the fine old Rockingham Meeting House and the Vermont Country Store in the village of Rockingham, the delightfully unrestored village of Windham, the village of Saxtons River (known for its own picturesque inn) and the town of Chester with its fine Historical Society and Art Guild, its outstanding shops and inns. The roads connecting these places are particularly scenic.

GUIDANCE   The **Bellows Falls Chamber of Commerce** (463-4280), Box 554, 55 Village Square, Bellows Falls, 05101, maintains a downtown office generally open year-round; offers information about the town of Rockingham—which includes Bellows Falls, Rockingham Village, and Saxtons River.

The Chamber has a most informative "Guided Walking Tour" brochure for the town's historic district, where adaptive preservation is under way.

The **Chester Chamber of Commerce** (875-3827), Chester 05143, maintains a booth in the center of town.

GETTING THERE   By bus: Vermont Transit from points in Connecticut and Massachusetts stops at Bellows Falls (at Fletcher's drugstore in the Square) and in Chester (at the Rexall next to the Chester Inn).

By train: see *Amtrak*.

By air: Eastern Express serves Keene, N.H.

Taxi service for Bellows Falls: **Rick's Taxi Service** (463-9414).

TO SEE AND DO   **Green Mountain Flyer** (463-3069), PO Box 498, Bellows Falls 05101. Created in 1984 to fill the void left by Steamtown USA, this fledgling railroad operates May–October between the stations in Chester Depot and in Bellows Falls. Passengers can board and detrain at either end of the line. Rolling stock includes some turn-of-the-century cars and the 13-mile (one-way) route is along the Connecticut River, past covered bridges, small villages and farms, through wooded rock cuts, which include the spectacular Brockway Mills gorge.

MG Car Museum (722-3708), Route 5, Westminster, between Bellows Falls and Brattleboro. Assembled by Gerard Goguen, a former trumpet player with the Boston Symphony and sports car race driver, the museum is "the world's largest private exhibit of a single marque." Twenty-seven of the sleek models are on display, with 10 more being restored. There's a 1927 14/28 Tourer Flatnose, the oldest MG in the United States, and one of six known to exist; the J-4 which nearly took Goguen's head off at Watkins Glen; the 1955 EX-182 race car and the prototype of the MGA. The most elegant is a 1932 custom convertible created for Bernice Marshall of Montreal, Canada. Open daily except Monday 10-5, July and August; weekends June, September and up to Columbus Day.

Chester encompasses three distinct villages within a few miles, each of them worth noting. There is the old core with the double-porched Chester Inn at its center, flanked by an attractive lineup of shops and restaurants, set back from the old highway (Route 11) by a stringbean green. Across the road stands a fine old brick schoolhouse, now the **Historical Society and Art Guild** (open June to October, daily except Mondays, 2–5) in which you can see changing art exhibits and learn about the town's colorful history, including the story of Clarence Adams, one of Chester's most prominent citizens who broke into more than 50 businesses and homes between 1886 and 1902 when he was finally apprehended.

Don't miss Chester's **Stone Village** up on North Street (Route 103); a double line of 30 buildings faced in "gneiss," a rough-hewn, gleaming mica schist quarried from nearby Flamstead Mountain. Cool in summer, warm in winter, stone house are a rarity in New England. All of these are said to have been built by two brothers in the pre-Civil War decade, with hiding spaces enough to make them a significant stop on the Underground Railroad.

Midway between Main and North Streets is **Chester Depot,** a pleasant old traffic center which resembles neither of these places. The well-kept Victorian depot serves as northern terminus for the Green Mountain Flyer (see above), spilling more than a hundred passengers at a time into the village center to browse in Cummings Hardware and Jameson's Food Market and stroll by the steepled town hall. It's an appropriate terminus for a country railroad.

The peaceful village of **Rockingham** just off Route 103 between Chester and Bellows Falls is well worth a stop to visit the **Old Rockingham Meeting House,** Vermont's oldest unchanged public building. Built in 1787, this Federal-style structure contains "pig-pen" style pews, each accommodating 10 to 15 people, some with their backs to the minister. The old burying ground is filled with thin old markers bearing readable epitaphs.

Sited by one of the biggest natural falls in the entire course of the Connecticut River, **Bellows Falls** itself cascades down a hill so steep that a stairway connects the commercial Westminster Street with the residential neighborhood above. Old paper mills and railroad-era buildings are crowded on yet another level down by the river—where you can still see carvings made centuries ago by members of the Pennacook Tribe who gathered by the falls to fish. You can also see the remains of one of America's first canals, built in 1802 to ease river traffic around the great falls.

Fish Ladder and Visitors Center (463-3226), New England Power Company, Bridge Street. One of a series of ladders constructed on the Connecticut River to return Atlantic salmon and American shad to their native spawning grounds.

Here, too, is the **Adams Old Stone Gristmill Museum.** The mill ground grain from 1831 until 1961; the old machinery is all in place and the adjacent museum exhibits relics of the town's long and varied industrial history (open usually Saturday and Sunday 2–4 and by appointment: 463-4280). There are more relics of local history to be found in the **Rockingham Free Library and Museum** (65 Westminster Street; open year-round, Monday–Friday 2–4.).

Most shops and businesses are contained in nineteenth-century brick buildings lining the widened stretch of Westminster Street (Route 5) known as "The Village Square." There is a Florentine tower atop the town hall (which includes the Falls Cinema and Fletchers Drug). The bus stops here.

Bellows Falls was the home of Hetty Green (1835-1916), who parlayed a substantial inheritance into a $100 million fortune; she was called the "witch of Wall Street," to which she traveled by day coach, looking like a bag-lady in threadbare bombazine.

Even if you do not stay in **Grafton,** you must come to see this restored village center, to visit the village shops, walk the well-marked paths through the woods and fields and look into the **Grafton Historical Society Museum** (open Memorial Day–Columbus Day, 2:30–4:40 on Saturdays; also on Sundays in July and August plus holiday weekends and holiday Mondays: 843-2388). There are also wildlife exhibits, a replica of a country store, horse-drawn vehicles and before and after pictures of the town—all housed next to the Windham Foundation on Townshend Road (open June–November, daily: 8:30–5).

The unusually-shaped inn (see *Lodging)* and Vermont Academy (now a private, coed prep school) are the two most striking buildings in **Saxtons River.** The **Historical Museum,** housing a nineteenth-century parlor and kitchen as well as other local memorabilia, is open Saturday and Sunday, 2:30–5 in summer.

FARMS TO VISIT   **Saxtons River Orchards.** (869-2443) Pick your own apples during September and October and enjoy the foliage from these hilltop orchards; choice of McIntosh, Cortland, Delicious, and Spys. Off Route 121 west of the village.

COVERED BRIDGES   There are five covered bridges in the area: two in Bartonsville (one and a half miles north of Route 103, the other east off Route 103), two in Grafton and one in Saxtons River off

Route 121, noteworthy for its "flying buttresses" (replaced in 1982).
SUGAR HOUSES   Butternut Acres (843-2429), Route 121, Grafton; **Valley Brook Farm** (843-2452), 3 miles south of Grafton on the Townshend Road; **Grouse Hill Farm,** Grafton, 1 mile north on Middletown Road; **Grafton Village Apple Company** (843-2406), Route 121, Grafton.

RECREATION   Tavern Recreation Service (843-2231), Grafton, arranges for bicycle rentals and tours, cross-country skiing, fishing and canoeing.

GOLF   **Tater Hill Club** (875-2517), Popple Dungeon Road, Windham (off Route 11, 2 miles south from junction of Windham Road and Route 121), Offers 18 holes, a pro shop, instruction, and a restaurant.

The Bellows Falls Country Club (463-9809), Rockingham. Scenic 9-hole course, club house with bar and lunch room.

HORSEBACK RIDING   Tater Hill Club (875-2517), Windham. Popple Dungeon Road off Route 11 near North Windham. Hourly trail rides, 10–4. Also picnic, evening and hay rides.

CROSS-COUNTRY SKIING   Tater Hill Cross-Country Ski Center (875-2517), Popple Dungeon Road, Windham. A total of 40 km of trails, 20 tracked: a mix of meadows and forests at elevations of 1,786-2,000 feet. Instruction, rentals, showers, change rooms and restaurant, guided and headlamp tours.

**LODGING   *Grafton*   All places listed below are in the 05146 zip code area unless otherwise noted.

The Old Tavern (843-2231). The brick core of this splendid building dates back to 1788, but the double-porched facade is mid-nineteenth-century. The stylish interior (vintage 1965) tastefully recreates a formal early-American setting worthy of Williamsburg or Old Deerfield. The 20 beautifully decorated bedrooms in the main building are supplemented by 16 more in a less formal wing and four rental houses, accommodating 100 guests in all, far fewer than want to come here during the summer and in foliage season. It's open year-round; in the summer there are tennis courts and a sand-bottomed swimming pond; in winter, cross-country skiing arranged by the recreation director. Doubles cost $50–105 per night; meals are extra. There's a 20 percent discount for midweek stays of two or more nights in the winter. (Contrary to what we implied in the last edition of this book, youngsters are welcome—in the annex.)

Gabriel's Woodchuck Hill Farm (843-2398; winter 869-2309). Open May 1–November 1, this 1780s farmhouse located 2 miles from the village is an elegant, antique-furnished place to stay, accommodating 20 guests. Rooms with private bath are $80, a studio apartment $85, and a barn apartment $100 per couple, or $150 for four.

Afternoon tea is served, and a five-course gourmet dinner is available by arrangement. Country antiques, stoneware jugs, and other old kitchenware are sold in the barn.

Eaglebrook of Grafton (843-2564), a stately home diagonally across from the Tavern, has opened three guest rooms in addition to its gift and textile shop; $60 or $65 (private bath).

The Wayfarer at Grafton (843-2332) has spool beds and country antiques. This 1834 brick house is up-street from the Tavern and has four guest rooms, two with private bath, two shared, each with fireplace. $65–80 including continental breakfast. This, too, has a barn full of antiques. Open year-round, except during the Parks' vacations.

Stronghold Inn (843-2203), Route 121 east, is an 1820s roadside house on the edge of the village that offers four nicely furnished guest rooms, three with private bath. Rates ($45-65) include a full breakfast; children are welcome.

Hayes Guest House (843-2461), Water Street, is located on a pleasant back street by a covered bridge. This is a comfortable old house with four guest rooms, the gem being on the first floor with a private bath, fireplace, and four-poster so high you need a stool to climb aboard. Reasonable rates ($25–50) include continental breakfast. Children and (a rarity) dogs are welcome.

Other Bed and Breakfasts: Round the Bend (843-2515/2385), Old Farmhouse Road; **Stiles Brook** (843-2582), 4 miles south of the village on Townshend Road.

Chester   All places listed below are in the 05142 zip code unless otherwise noted.

The Inn at Long Last (875-2444) (formerly the Chester Inn) is the revitalized centerpiece of this lively village, recently purchased by Jack Coleman and his family. Coleman, the former president of Haverford College, received a lot of national publicity when he worked incognito as a garbage man in Maryland and a ditch-digger (while returning to chair meetings of the Federal Reserve Bank of Philadelphia). He recorded these sabbaticals in a book, *Blue Collar Journal*, and then headed the Clark Foundation in New York, again impersonating a homeless vagabond and prison inmate. The 32 individualized guest rooms in the renovated inn have been named for people he admires, Currier & Ives, Frederick Law Olmstead, George Orwell, and Lord Peter Wimsey. And it has the only private dining/meeting room in New England dedicated to the memory of Ichabod Onion (whose identity will be revealed to visitors). The inn boasts a swimming pool, tennis courts, and a fishing stream. Rates are $75-95 per person, with dinner and breakfast. Holiday rates are somewhat higher because "we try to make each of them more special."

Hugging Bear Inn & Shoppe (875-2412), Main Street, Chester, is a handsome Victorian home in the middle of an unusually handsome Vermont town, with a giant teddy bear sitting on its front porch. Inside there are teddy bears on the beds of six spacious guest rooms (each with private bath), and in the "Shoppe" out back are more than 500 stuffed bears. Innkeepers Georgette and Paul Thomas (he is a former attorney and she is a personal counselor) believe that people don't hug enough, period. Everyone is invited to hug any bear in the house and the atmosphere here is contagiously friendly. Rates are $65 per couple, and $50 single (plus $5 during foliage season), $10 for children under age 14, breakfast included.

The Chester House (875-2205), on the green across from the Inn at Long Last, was opened in 1987 by Irene and Norm Wright. A distinctive 1790s house on the National Register of Historic Places, the inn has a downstairs parlor, Keeping Room, and dining room decorated in early-American style, and the bedrooms are quite luxurious. Of the two large front rooms with queen-size beds, one has a whirlpool in its bathroom. The third guest room has twin beds and an adjacent bath. $35–65 B&B, less for four nights or more.

The Stone Hearth Inn (875-2525), is an 1810 farmhouse. Its many additions (formerly the Cranberry Inn) ramble along behind a stockade-like row of fir trees that shield it from Route 11. The 10 guest rooms are nicely decorated with the same quality antiques that you see in the living room—which has a fieldstone fireplace. The dining room serves breakfast, lunch (Tuesday–Saturday), and dinner (Wednesday–Saturday). There is also an inviting Pub Room with a full liquor license and player piano. A large game room has ping pong, pool tables, and exercise equipment. $35–45 per person including breakfast. Open year-round.

Old Town Farm Inn (875-2346), Route 10, Gassetts. Ruth and Dick Lewis are the latest owners of this large 1860s farmhouse (once the town poor farm) with a graceful semi-circular staircase, and they have been joined by a son who is a trained chef. There are nine guest rooms, two with private bath. The place needed the anticipated refurbishing when we visited in the fall of 1987. Rates: $50 per person, private bath, MAP; $45 shared bath; less for B&B.

Rowell's Inn (875-3658), Route 11, Simonsville 05143. Truly exceptional, this place was obviously built as a brick, double-porched stage stop in 1820 by Major Edward Simons. It has been serving the public off and on since then. After decades of neglect it was meticulously restored in 1985 by Lee and Beth Davis. Inside are Victorian touches like tin ceilings and some stained glass; tavern, parlor, dining room and five comfortable guest rooms with private baths, one with a working fireplace. Midweek room rates (Sunday through Thursday) are $65–75 B&B or $100–120 with five-course dinner as well as breakfast; on Fridays, Saturdays, and holiday weekends, MAP only, $120–140, which includes afternoon tea as well. Now licensed for beer and wine. **The Carriage Shed Antiques Shop** is in the attached barn. Located midway between Londonderry, Weston, and Chester, it's off by itself with some fine walks and cross-country skiing out the back door.

Other Bed & Breakfasts: Stone Village (875-3914), Route 103, Chester; **Quail Hollow** (875-3401), Route 11, Chester; **Greenleaf Inn** (875-3171), Chester; **The Henry Farm** (875-2674), off Route 11, Chester; **Glen Finert Farm** (875-2160).

Bellows Falls   All places listed below are in the 05101 zip code area unless otherwise noted.

Rockingham Motor Inn (463-4536, 800-255-4756 outside Vermont), Route 5, north of town. Richard Ticino and his family, who took over the place in 1987, are making this a popular spot for family gatherings and community benefits. Its friendly atmosphere outweighs its rather utilitarian appearance. Rick has upgraded its telephone service to accommodate business travelers' computers. Doubles are $45 (foliage season surcharge); a two-day, midweek ski package including lift tickets at Magic Mountain, breakfasts and dinner is available for $110 per person.

The Highlands Lodge (463-9840), strategically located off Exit 6, 1–91, and the junction of Routes 5 and 103, is a 24-unit motel, under new management (David Savoy). Rates range from $38 to $46 for a room with two double beds, including continental breakfast (commercial and truckers, $26 per person).

Saxtons River Inn (869-2110), Saxtons River 05154. Each of the 16 rooms (7 with private baths) has its own name and decor. All feature splashy wallpapers and colors coordinated to the turn-of-the-century look of the inn inside and out. Across the street in the Colvin House there are five more rooms all with private baths and a gift shop open weekends. The sunny breakfast room with its picture window overlooking Main Street is a place where guests tend to linger. The dining room is open to the public and there is a zany pub room with a copper bar; there is also a TV, a game room, and reading room for guests. Doubles cost $40–65, continental breakfast included.

DINING OUT   The Old Tavern (843-2231), Grafton, serves lunch, dinner, and Sunday brunch in the formal dining rooms or in the more casual sun room. The new chef's menu includes a baked cheddar turnover as an appetizer ($4.75), and such entrées as chicken breast stuffed with pecans and Vermont goat cheese ($13.85), grilled quail with currant BBQ sauce ($18.75), venison stew ($16.95), and buffalo rib eye steak ($21). Lunches are under $10, and there's a winter series of Renaissance Sunday Brunches featuring recitals.

The Inn at Long Last (875-2444), Chester, is open to the public for dinner Tuesday–Saturday and for Sunday brunch. The imaginative menu might include seafarer's fishpot soup with tomato, saffron, and fennel seed ($3.25); a summer dinner salad special composed of warm sweetbreads with local greens and vegetables served with raspberry vinegar ($9.50); grilled veal chop with sun-dried tomato-orange salsa ($17.25).

Leslie's (463-4929) Rockingham. Conveniently placed a short distance off the Interstate, this one-time tavern with seven fireplaces and a Dutch oven serves lunch and dinner daily. There's a selection of beef entrées, including Leslie's Combo (sautéed shrimp and a 7-ounce sirloin) at $13.75, plus seafood (Cajun seafood stuffed shrimp, $12.95), and such specialties as Veal Zurichoise ($9.95) and Leslie's Alfredo (strips of chicken breast sautéed with garlic, tomatoes, mushroooms, parmesan, and cream served over fettuccini) at $9.95.

Joy Wah (463-9761), Rockingham Road (Route 5), Bellows Falls. Full-service Chinese fare in a Victorian farmhouse perched on a knoll overlooking the Connecticut River includes all the familiar dishes on its lengthy menu, plus a selection of special family dinners at $10 per person. The Szechuan group ranges from $7.85-10.25. Open daily for lunch and dinner.

Rockingham Motor Inn (463-4536), Route 5, Bellows Falls. Open for lunch and dinner, with moderate prices. Friday and Saturday specials include prime rib at $9.95, clams $10.95, shrimp scampi $12.95, roast turkey $8.95, all served to the accompaniment of live music for dancing.

Saxtons River Inn (869-2110), Saxtons River. Dinner à la carte, with several veal specialties ($11–16) among the 14 entrées. (You might even be there when venison chops are in season.)

EATING OUT   **The Village Green Deli** (875-3898), on the green, Chester. Outstanding soups, salads, sandwiches in a Victorian setting.

Beverly Restaurant & White Parrot Lounge (875-2400), on the green, Chester. An unusual, offbeat sort of place; moderate prices, presumably open every day till 10, but better check because we've twice found it closed.

Miss Bellows Falls Diner, downtown Bellows Falls, is one of the few remaining Worcester Lunch Cars, and as such is on the National Register of Historic Places. Open daily till 8, it serves customary roadside fare and a few specials, like American Chop Suey at $3.95.

SELECTIVE SHOPPING   **Grafton Village Cheese Co.** (843-2221), Grafton Village. You cannot tour this exceedingly tidy operation but you can look through the large viewing window and watch the cheese being made. The shop, open Monday–Friday: 9–4, and Saturdays June 1–October 21, sells its Covered Bridge Cheddar (the covered bridge has been positioned out back). It is milder than Cabot or Crowley cheese and comes both plain and sage: $4.15 per pound for the plain.

Bonnie's Bundles (875-2114), Stone Village, Route 103, Chester; and Townshend Road, Grafton. A doll-lover's find. More than 100 original handcrafted stuffed dolls. Open daily February–December: 9–5; Sundays: 1–5.

Grafton Village Store (843-2348), Grafton, combines staples and convenience with Vermont crafts, syrup, cheese, and an upscale room full of "Goodjam" products—vinegars, herbs, old and new kitchenware.

Tickle Your Fancy Gifts (843-2384), Main Street, Grafton. Unusual cards, among other things.

Pickle Street Antiques (843-2203), Route 121 east, Grafton, stocks country furniture, folk art, tinware, quilts, and collectibles.

Wildacre Enterprises (843-2324), Grafton, offers custom cabinetry with one-of-a-kind and limited production furniture, including rosewood, black walnut, ebony, and bubinga.

Flamstead of Vermont (875-3267), Chester. Flamstead is one name under which Chester was originally chartered and it still represents the town throughout the world—on the labels of silk-screen garnished clothing. A long-established business, Flamstead has been owned since 1975 by Tory and Tom Spater and employs some 25 people in the cutting and screening rooms upstairs over the store in the middle of Chester. Some 30,000–40,000 skirts alone are shipped annually to far-flung stores. There are also jumpers, dresses, shirts, evening wear, and accessories, all stamped with designs of local mushrooms, weeds, and flowers. In addition to the clothing the shop carries a full stock of toys, gifts, books and craft items. Open Monday–Saturday: 9–5.

The National Survey (875-2121), Chester. Founded in 1912 by two sons of Chester's Baptist minister, the National Survey publishes maps for many states, foreign governments, industries, and groups throughout the world. In their Charthouse store—which occupies the ground floor of a lacy Victorian house on Main Street—you can find maps, books about Vermont, also arts and crafts supplies. Open Monday–Friday: 9–5, Saturday: 10–4.

Brick Cottage Collectibles (875-3431), Route 11 east, Chester, stocks antiques and used books.

Misty Valley Books (875-3400), on the Green, Chester, has an exceptionally well-tailored stock of new books.

Weird Wood (875-3535), Route 11, Chester, connected to the Green Mountain Log Homes center, has racks of cherry, butternut,

The Old Tavern in Grafton

pine, maple, walnut, redwood, teak, rosewood, and even cherry burls for wood carvers and do-it-yourself projects.

Chester Marble Mart (875-4099), Route 11, Chester. Open daily late May through October, this store sells marble lamp bases, book ends, and many other objects (including some translucent bowls made in Pakistan!).

Forlie-Ballou (875-2090), Chester. Upscale women's clothes, accessories, and gifts.

Oak Unlimited, Route 103, Chester, offers furniture and marvelous handcarved animals.

Vermont Country Store, Rockingham Village. An offshoot of the famous Vermont Country Store in Weston, this is also owned by Lyman Orton and actually houses his common cracker machine, which visitors can watch stamping out the hard round biscuits. The store also sells whole-grain breads and cookies baked here, along with a line of calico material, soapstone griddles, woodenware gadgets, natural-fiber clothing, and much more; there is an upstairs bargain room.

Allen Brothers Farm Market, Bellows Falls. Located 2 miles south of Bellows Falls on Route 5, this major farmstand offers pick-your-own apples, strawberries and flowers depending on the season, also sells Vermont products such as cheese and syrup. Open daily, year-round.

Big Red Barn, Route 5, south of Bellows Falls. Four floors of a 150-year-old barn are filled with baskets, candles, Vermont products, souvenirs, antiques. Open year-round.

Jelly Bean Tree (869-2326), Saxtons River. A craft cooperative run by several local artisans and carrying the work of many more on consignment: pottery, macrame, leather, weaving, batik, hand sewn, knit, and crocheted items. Open daily 12–5.

ART GALLERIES   **Gallery North Star** (843-2465), Grafton. There are six rooms in this Grafton Village house, all hung with landscapes and graphic prints of birds, horses and other animals, most of them by Mel Hunter whose "atelier" in the back is also open to visitors. Hunter specializes in minutely detailed graphic prints. Hunter's signed, limited graphics, which he prints on the premises, are priced from $125 up.

Thistledown Gallery (843-2340), Grafton (next to the Old Tavern). Open Memorial Day through October for New England crafts and fine art.

Crow Hill Gallery (875-3763), Flamstead Road, Chester, shows the work of Jeanne Carbonetti and other local artists.

MORE ANTIQUES   Antique stores are particularly thick in this area. In Grafton they include **Gabriel's Barn Antiques** at Woodchuck Hill Farm (843-2398), **Woodshed Antiques** (843-2365), **Frank E. Jones** (843-2424). In Saxtons River: **Studio Antiques** (869-2326), **Agape Antiques** (869-2273), **Sign of the Raven** (869-2500), and **Schoolhouse Antiques** (869-2332). In Chester: **Chester House Antiques** (875-2871), **Bill Lindsey** (875-2671), and **Lamplighter Antiques** (875-2612).

SPECIAL EVENTS   February: **Chester Winter Carnival.**

July: In Chester: **St. Josephs Carnival, Horse Show and Community Picnic, Congregational Country Fair.** In Bellows Falls: **The Vermont State Certified Championship Old Time Fiddlers Contest.**

August: In Chester: **Outdoor Art Show.** In Rockingham (first weekend in August): **Old Rockingham Days,** a full weekend of events: dancing, live entertainment, sidewalk dining, contests, fireworks.

MEDICAL EMERGENCY   Chester (875-2233); Bellows Falls, Grafton, Rockingham (463-4223); Gassetts (365-7676).

Rockingham Memorial Hospital (463-3903), Bellows Falls.

Okemo Mountain/Ludlow Area

In contrast to all other Vermont ski towns, Ludlow is neither a tiny picturesque village, nor a long-established resort. It boomed with the production of "shoddy" (fabric made from reworked wool) after the Civil War, a period frozen in the red brick of its commercial block, Victorian mansions, magnificent library, and academy (now the Black River Museum). In the wake of the wool, the General Electric Company moved into the steepled mill at the heart of town and kept people employed making small aircraft engine parts until 1977. Cashmere is still produced in the town's old Jewel Brook Mill, and an assortment of small industries have opened in the new Dean Brown Industrial Park. Ludlow is, furthermore, a crossroads market town with stores supplying most of the needs for the small surrounding towns.

Ludlow also has 3,343 foot high Okemo mountain rising right from its heart. The ski area here dates from 1956, but until recently, it was a sleeper—a big mountain with antiquated lifts on the edge of a former mill town. Ski clubs nested in the Victorian homes, and a few inns catered to serious skiers.

Since 1982, however, when Tim and Diane Mueller bought Okemo, the old T-bars and Poma lifts have all been replaced with fast-moving, high-capacity chair lifts. Snowmaking equipment and more than two dozen trails have been added, along with more than 300 new condominiums. A total of 2,400 people can presently bed down on the mountain—which has doubled its number of patrons in as many years.

The effect on Ludlow has been dramatic. The old General Electric plant has been condoed, inns have multiplied, and the fire chief has tacked a tidy motel on the back of his house. Local dining options now include a choice of six-course gourmet meals as well as well-sauced dishes and stained-glass atmosphere at Nikki's and pasta at Valentes (where Mama pinches a child's cheek and tells him to "eata the meatballs").

Summer visitors tend to own or rent a cottage on Lake Pauline, Reservoir Pond, or Lake Rescue. Lake Ninevah, Echo and Amherst Lakes are just north of the town line. There are also those who come for programs at Fletcher Farm Crafts School or simply because

Ludlow's location makes an ideal base from which to explore much of Southern and Central Vermont.

"The resort business is the number-one employer now" observes Bob Gilmore, owner of Nikki's. "But this is still a real town."

West from Ludlow, Route 103 climbs steeply in beautiful hill country, through Cuttingsville and Shrewsbury to Rutland. At Healdville you turn off to see the state's oldest and most colorful cheese factory, and a turn off through Mount Holly and Hortonville will be rewarded with spectacular views of the surrounding hills.

North from Ludlow, Route 100 links together the chain of lakes. South from town, it climbs Terrible Mountain for nine full miles before its descent into Weston. To the east Route 131 follows the Black River through the picturesque mill villages of Proctorsville and Cavendish. Route 103 follows the Williams River to Chester. Handy to Weston, Grafton, Killington, and numerous activities, Ludlow is just far enough from everywhere to retain its own unmistakable identity.

GUIDANCE   Ludlow Area Chamber of Commerce (228-5318/7936), Ludlow 05149. A walk-in information office in the Jewell Brook Plaza, Route 100/103 in the middle of the village, is filled with menus, events listings, and lodging brochures, staffed daily in summer, also on weekends in winter—when the job of lodging visitors shifts to the **Okemo Area Lodging Service** (228-5571) at Okemo Mountain.

GETTING THERE   By bus: Direct service from Boston, via Bellows Falls for New York and Connecticut, from Rutland for points north and west; Vermont Transit.

By train: Those determined to come by train from Manhattan are advised to take it to Springfield, Massachusetts, where an easy connection can be made to Vermont Transit. See *Amtrak*.

By air: Eastern Express serves Springfield, 14 miles in one direction, and Rutland, 21 miles in the other. Refer to Rutland listings for information on ground transfers.

TO SEE AND DO   Black River Academy Historical Museum (228-5050), Ludlow. Open May–Labor Day, Wednesday–Sunday: 12–4. A steepled, brick school building, built in 1889. The Academy's reputation drew students from throughout New England. One large room is dedicated to President Calvin Coolidge, class of 1890. Other rooms in the four-floor building are filled with exhibits about mining, lumbering, railroading, farming, and other segments in the history of the Black River Valley. Children and donations are welcome.

Crowley Cheese Factory (259-2340), Healdville. Open year-round, Monday–Saturday: 8–4, Sunday 11–5. Five miles west of Ludlow on Route 103 look for the Crowley Cheese store and ask directions there for the factory, a picturesque three-story wooden building, essentially unchanged since 1882. Here cheese is still "cut" and "raked" by hand, pressed in old crank presses, aged without additives or preservatives. When the Crowleys died out in 1967 the business was assumed by a neighbor, retired New York City educator Randolf Smith and his son Peter. Now four employees produce between 500 and 800 pounds of cheese a day, beginning at 7AM when fresh milk is poured into the vats. It's best to come between 11–1 to see the raking and kneading. The cheese is smoother, moister than cheddar. It is sold in varying degrees of sharpness and is available by mail order. Don't fail to stop by the retail store (open 10–5 except Sundays, 11–5; 259-2210), where Mrs. Smith (a former NYU professor) sells cookies, pottery, syrup, and woodenware as well as cheese.

Joseph Cerniglia Winery, Inc. (226-7575; 800-654-6382), #1 Box 119A, Proctorsville 05153. We found both the winery and the wine disappointing. The winery is a large brick building, open daily, 10–5 year-round. Geared to bus groups, it can be crowded. There are tours every 15 minutes and wine tastings constantly. The wines are apple blends, ranging from hard cider ($5.99 for a 1.5 liter bottle) to a half dozen varieties of apple wines.

Fletcher Library, Ludlow. (Monday–Friday, 10–5:30: Saturday 10–1, 6:30–8:30). One of Vermont's most beautiful town libraries: reading rooms contain marble inlays, fireplaces, old-style green-shaded lights, and century-old paintings of local landscapes.

Cavendish Historical Society Museum, Cavendish. Open June to October, Sunday 2–5, housed in the former Baptist Church; this is a collection of weaving implements, old photographs, farm tools, articles used or made in Cavendish, changing exhibits and a lecture program.

SUGAR HOUSE **Green Mountain Sugar House** (228-7151), Route 100, 4 miles north of Ludlow. You can watch syrup being produced at this roadside sugar house in March and April; maple candy is made throughout the year on a weekly basis. Gift and produce shop open 9–6 "most of the time."

FISHING   Public access has been provided to Lake Rescue, Echo Lake, Lake Ninevah, Woodward Reservoir, and Amherst Lake. Fishing licenses are required (even for canoeing on these lakes), and this is strictly enforced. The catch includes rainbow trout, bass, pickerel. There is also fly fishing in the Black River.

BACK ROAD TOURS   **Vermont Backroad Tours** (266-7910), Box 64, Carlton Road, Cavendish. The Phillips family offer tours, June through mid-October, 9–4, Monday, Tuesday, Saturday, and Sunday. Tours frequently include the Crown Point Military Road, Cavendish Gorge, visits to local craftspeople, and a soapstone factory. $35 per person per day.

BICYCLING AND WALKING   Cycle Inn Vermont (228-8799), Box 243, Ludlow 05149-0243. Five inns in and around Ludlow combine to offer a flexible service for bikers. It includes route planning, luggage transport from inn to inn, bike rentals and emergency assistance. You can tour for two days or two weeks, cycle or walk a few or 50 miles. The local inns involved are The Okemo Inn and Combes Family Inn.

BOATING   Echo Lake Inn (228-8602) rents canoes and other boats. Rentals are also available at Camp Plymouth State Park (see *Swimming)* and at Hawk at Salt Ash (see Killington).

HORSEBACK RIDING   Holly Hills Trails (259-2650), Mount Holly. The same trails are used for riding and cross-country skiing.

Trail rides are also offered at **Salt Ash Stables** (see Killington.)

RAILROAD EXCURSION   The Green Mountain Flyer (463-3069), based in Bellows Falls, makes daily summer and foliage season excursions to Ludlow (the vintage 1849 depot has been restored in its honor), also weekends in early September and late October. $16 round trip.

GOLF   Fox Run Resort (228-8871), Ludlow. A 9-hole course with a restaurant, lounge.

SWIMMING   The Town Recreation Area on West Hill includes a man-made beach (with lifeguard) on a small, spring-fed reservoir, also a snack bar and playground/picnic area.

Buttermilk Falls, near the junction of Routes 100 and 103. There is a swimming hole off Route 103. Turn at the VFW post just west of the intersection.

Camp Plymouth State Park, off Route 100 at Tyson. Beach on Echo Lake, picnic area, food concession.

TENNIS   Town Recreation Park on West Hill (end of Pond Street). Two courts available to the public.

CROSS-COUNTRY SKIING   Fox Run Ski Touring Center (228-8871), junction Routes 100 and 103, Ludlow. A cafe and rental shop are surrounded by the open roll of the golf course; there are also wooded and mountain trails adding up to 20 kms, most of it tracked; guided tours.

Holly Hill Trails (259-2650), Mount Holly.

DOWNHILL SKIING   Okemo (228-4041/snow reports 228-5222), Ludlow. "Rip Van Mountain" is the image Okemo is presently projecting: a BIG mountain (boasting Vermont's fourth highest vertical drop) that's been sleeping since the fifties but is making up for lost time. Okemo is now a big destination mountain with a small resort feel. The trails are easily accessible. Just beyond the middle of town you turn up a short access road to a relatively small parking lot. You walk through a hotel complex, find the smallish base lodge and are off on a fast-moving chair lift (no wait). Surprises begin at the top of these lifts—where you meet a wall of three-story condominiums, find your way down to the spacious Sugar House base lodge from which the true size of the mountain becomes apparent. This is a mountain of many parts. Beginners and lower intermediate skiers can enjoy not only the lower southwest but also the upper northeast sides of the mountain—entirely different places in view and feel. From the summit beginners can actually run a full 4½ miles to the base. Expert skiers, on the other hand, have the entire northwestern face of the mountain, served by its own chair. There are also a number of wide, central fall line runs down the face of Okemo. Basically, however, this is upper intermediate heaven—with literally dozens of trails with varying terrain. We became addicted to Upper and Lower World Cup, a long and steep but forgiving run with sweeping views off across the Black River Valley to the Connecticut River.

Lifts: 9; 2 quad chairs, 3 triple chairs, 3 double chairs, and 1 Poma lift.

Trails and Slopes: 68: 30% novice, 50% intermediate, 20% expert.

Vertical drop: 2,150 feet.

Snowmaking: covers 80% of trails, some with top to bottom snow.

Facilities: Base lodge with cafeteria; mid-mountain Sugar House base lodge with cafeteria; Beach House snack bar just below summit; two restaurants, hotel, rental shops, nursery, condo lodging.

Ski School: 75 instructors, ATM (American Teaching Method), Nastar races.

Rates: $56 for two days adults, $30 weekdays.

LODGING   Okemo Area Lodging Service (228-5571) refers less than half its inquiries to slope-side condominiums. A wide variety of inns can be found within a 10-mile radius.

COUNTRY INNS   Castle Inn (226-7222) Box 157, Proctorsville 05153. Open except for November and Mud Season. Built in 1904 by Allen Fletcher, another Vermont governor, this is a truly palatial stone mansion with an abundance of mahogany and oak paneling, ten hearths, elaborately carved ceilings and mantels. An inn since 1964, offering ten guest rooms, eight with private baths. It need refurbishing. Breakfast is served to guests, dinner is open to the public (see *Dining*); $70–90 per person MAP in winter, less in summer. The hot tub, sauna, and winterized tennis courts are under separate ownership.

Okemo Lantern Lodge (226-7770), Box 247, Proctorsville 05153. A former mill owner's mansion, rich in ornately carved butternut and stained glass. There are seven guest rooms, including a two-room suite with bath. $65 per person MAP.

The Golden Stage Inn (226-7744), PO Box 218, Proctorsville 05153.

Under new owners—Kristen Murphy and Marcel Perret—this inn is still a find, offering exceptional food and elegantly comfortable rooms at the right price. Built as a stage stop in 1796, this spacious white clapboard house also served as a stop on the underground railroad and as home for actress and writer Cornelia Otis Skinner. There are six guest rooms with private baths, four that share two baths. There are antique quilts on the beds, rockers where you want them. The large, plant-filled living room is lined with books round a cheery fireplace. For summer there is an outdoor pool set in four acres of rolling lawns; note the large herb garden from which Marcel culls seasonings. Both are former professionals in the food business. Dinner is a five-course gourmet event, included along with evening hors d'oeuvres and a full breakfast in the $150 per couple room rate.

The Okemo Inn (228-8700), Ludlow 05149. Ron Parry has been here longer than any other local innkeeper and this 1810 home is well-kept, effortlessly welcoming. There are 12 nicely furnished guest rooms, most with two double beds and private bath. There is a living room with a table made from old bellows in front of the hearth and a dining room with low, notched beams, also a TV room with color cable. In winter it's $57–67 per person MAP; in summer $33 per person B&B.

Echo Lake Inn (228-8602), Tyson 05149. One of the few survivors of the many Victorian-style summer hotels (although parts of the building are older) which once graced Vermont lakes, the inn is four stories tall with a long, white porch, lined in summer with red rockers. Now winterized, it offers 27 rooms, 12 with bath. The rooms under the eaves have recently been turned into suites, some of the nicest rooms in the house; there are six condo units in the adjacent Victorian Carriage House. Common rooms are homey, informal as is the pink dining room and the Stoned Tavern, both open to the public. Summer facilities include tennis, swimming in the pool or at the private beach on Echo Lake across the road, where rental boats are available. No smoking in guest rooms. $45–78 per person MAP.

The Governor's Inn (228-8830), 86 Main Street, Ludlow 05149. William Wallace Stickney, governor of Vermont from 1900–1902, built this fine Victorian house with its ornate slate, hand-painted fireplace. The eight guest rooms, all with private baths, are smallish but antique-filled, coated with flowery paper, windows fitted with country curtains; guests find cordials and other nice touches next to their quilt-covered beds. There is a small pub and game room as well as the elegant living room and dining room, open to the public, featuring a table d'hote menu of five courses (see *Dining*);

three-course breakfasts are served in a cheery back room, warmed by the sun and a woodstove. $75 per person double occupancy. MAP.

Black River Inn (228-5585), 100 Main Street, Ludlow 05149. A fine, 1835 Federal-style home with hand-carved oak staircases and marble fireplaces is now a very gracious inn. Boasting Ludlow's first indoor tub and a carved bed in which Lincoln slept, it offers eight antique-furnished guest chambers, four with private bath (there are antique bath fixtures and new Vermont marble showers). Guests have a choice of breakfast in bed, in the dining room or— in summer—on a porch overlooking the Black River. Rates are $44.50 (B&B); $62.50 (MAP) per person. Weekend packages are also available.

Combes Family Inn (228-8799), RFD 1, Ludlow 05149. On a lake road, this inn stands on a high knoll surrounded by 50 acres. The farmhouse has seven guest rooms, four with shared bath; and five more units in the attached motel, each with double beds. $98 per couple MAP.

The Inn at Weathersfield (263-9217). Outstanding and not that far, listed under the Upper Connecticut Valley.

BED & BREAKFASTS **The Buckmaster Inn** (492-3485), Lincoln Hill Road, Shrewsbury Center 05738, was built as the Buckmaster Tavern in 1801. Now owned by Sam and Grace Husselman, it accommodates six guests ($30 for a room with a shared bath, $50 for the room with private bath); breakfast specialties include Grace's cranberry or banana bread.

Maple Crest Farm (492-3367), Cuttingsville 05738. Set high on a ridge across from the old hilltop center of Shrewsbury (closest to the 1986-87 "Jessica and the Moose" phenomenon), the handsome brick farmhouse was built in 1869 as Gleason's Tavern. Still in the same family, it offers bed & breakfast in four antique-filled rooms at $40 per couple, and in two charming apartments ($50), which can accommodate small families. The Smiths are noted for the quality of their maple syrup, produced in the sugar house at the peak of the hill; the same sweeping view can be enjoyed in winter on cross-country skis.

Austria Haus (259-2441), Box 2, Mount Holly 05758 (off Route 103). A century-old farmhouse surrounded by 100 acres, it offers four guest rooms, two with private bath, grand views and cross-country skiing outside the door. $20 single, $40 double with full breakfast.

Hortonville Inn (259-2587), off Route 103 in Hortonville, RFD #1, Mount Holly 05758. This large white house sits high on a hill and, along with the classic church across the road, forms the center (in fact, about all there is) of Hortonville. One room has a private

Calvin Coolidge studied at Ludlow's Black River Academy

bath, the other four share another. Each room has a VCR; 250 tapes on hand. There's a swimming pool, and you can rent a horse or bikes. The views are magnificent and there are 13 acres out back with trails cut for hiking and cross-country skiing. The $49 per couple rates include a continental breakfast with homemade pastries.

MOTEL   **Ludlow Colonial Motel** (228-8188), 93 Main Street, Ludlow 05149. A few years ago, Fire Chief Rick Harrison built a 14-unit motel unit onto the back of his 1825 home, and he built it well. His wife Betty Ann tastefully decorated the standard rooms (two double beds, TV, phone) and family suites. They added a two-bedroom unit with a full bath and living room in their home, then built another building full of condominiums next door and rehabbed an old house at the other end of the village (near the Okemo access road) into more condominiums with a laundromat downstairs. Everything is nicely done and reasonably priced. Foliage prices are $39 per standard room, $43–46 per family unit, $52–65 for an apartment; on winter weekends a standard room goes for $65.

CONDOMINIUMS   **Okemo Mountain Lodge** (228-5571), RFD #1, Ludlow 05149. This three-story condo hotel fans out around the base area; each unit has one bedroom and a sleeping couch in the living room. There's a compact kitchen with eating counter and a fireplace, enough space for a couple and two children. Winter rates are $160 per day on weekends for two adults (children under 12 are free); cheaper off-season.

Kettle Brook Condominiums at Okemo, same phone and address as the Lodge. Salted along trails, units range from efficiencies to three-bedrooom units, nicely built. $135-320 per unit on winter weekends. Cheaper midweek and off-season.

Winterplace, same phone and address as the Lodge. These are Okemo's luxury condominiums, set high on a mountain shelf with access to an indoor pool and, in summer, tennis courts. Winter weekend rates run $240 for two bedrooms to $325 for three bedrooms with loft, sleeping eight. Cheaper midweek and off-season.

Okemo Trailside Condominiums (228-8255), PO Box 165, Ludlow 05149. Scattered along the Lower Sachem trail, many of these condos date back more than 15 years; the 100-acre development is under different management from Okemo Mountain. There are some 200 one-to-four-bedroom units, half of them in the rental pool; priced $150-250 per night.

The Mill Motel (228-5566), 145 Main St., Ludlow 05149. The town's beautiful centerpiece has been converted into one-to-three-room condo units from $75-149. These are attractive but rather dark rooms with back balconies overlooking the Black River. Offers the advantage of being able to walk to all amenities in town.

Tiki & Associates (228-3500), Ludlow, manages rental properties ranging from condos to farmhouses, good for all seasons.

SELF-IMPROVING VACATIONS **Fletcher Farm** (228-8770), Ludlow 05149. Operated since 1948 by the Society of Vermont Craftsmen, this old farm on the eastern edge of town offers dorm-style lodging, pleasant studio and relaxing space, and June–October programs (basically two-week sessions) in weaving, spinning, potting, other crafts, art and folk dancing. Meals are family-style. The store sells handcrafted items, art and craft supplies.

Green Mountain at Fox Run (228-8885), Box 164, Ludlow 05149. A former resort, now "an educational community for weight and health management," directed by Thelma Wayler. Rates on request.

DINING OUT **Nikki's** (228-7797), Sunshine Market Place, Ludlow. Positioned at the foot of Okemo's access road, this is one of Vermont's pleasantest restaurants. Bob Gilmore has been in business a dozen years now and his chef, Robert McIntyre, has won in all categories at the "Taste of Vermont" contest. The dining rooms are up-and-down spaces with plenty of stained and beveled glass, exposed wood and brick, booths, with-it prints and naperies. You might start with stuffed mushroom caps or smoked provolone with fresh fruit. The large selection of entrees includes a mixed grill, broiled New England scallops, grilled Black Angus sirloin, and veal sautéed with wine and mushrooms. Prices begin at $7.25 for chef's salad and hover in the $12–14 range. There is a wine bar and large wine selection. Children's menu available.

Clock Works (228-2800) at Okemo Mountain, Ludlow. Named for the new clock tower at Okemo's entrance, this is a full-service restaurant with wood and brass decor, and a flexible approach to satisfying dining. Breakfast begins at 7 AM and can be either buffet or special-order style (waffles are the specialty). Lunch may be soup and salad, a burger, or seafood on a croissant. Dinner is fairly elegant: coquille Saint-Jacques au cidre ($12.95) or filet mignon with a wine sauce ($14.50). There's a Sunday buffet and a children's menu.

Golden Stage Inn (226-7744), Proctorsville (between Route 103 and 131). The dining rooms are attractive and the food is receiving rave reviews. Innkeepers Marcel Perret and Kristen Murphy were both formerly "flavor experts" employed by a national company. They grow most of their vegetables, fruit, berries, and herbs. Marcel is the entrée chef and Kristen supervises the baking and desserts. Meals are $22 prix fixe. A much abridged sample menu features potato chervil soup with Pernod to begin, and includes salmon steaks with chive sauce, tortellini with pesto, lime sorbet with gin, chicken proscuitto in cream sauce with fresh sage, and a walnut tart.

The Governor's Inn (228-8830), 86 Main Street, Ludlow. Owned by Chef Deedy Marble and her husband Charlie, this is Ludlow's most famous restaurant. Dining begins at 6 PM with hot hors d'oevres and cocktails served in the parlor. Dinner is promptly at 7:00, a single seating in the Victorian dining rooms served by waitresses in period dress. Each evening's six-course, $35 menu is fixed and might include sherried apricot soup, Lobster coquille in brandy cream sauce or the Governor's Braised Quail.

Echo Lake Inn (228-8602), Route 100 north in Tyson. Open to the public for breakfast, lunch, and dinner, it presents a dinner menu with such specialties as chilled Vermont apple soup, roast pheasant with hazelnut sauce, and rabbit terrine. Roast duckling with blueberry sauce is another chef's favorite. Entrées are $10-15. Friday night buffet.

Castle Inn (226-7222), Ludlow. The interior of this stone mansion is a rich blend of American oak, Mexican Mahogany, and French marble. Before dinner guests are invited to meet in the library for cocktails, then move to the paneled dining room for a five-course meal that can commence with pâté or escargots and include roast duckling ($16.95) or veal scallopini ($17.95).

Chuckles (228-5530), Ludlow. Route 103 north near Okemo. An 1890s barn with live entertainment and a satisfying menu: scampi, veal cordon bleu, Geshnetzletes (medaillions of veal in white cream sauce), and crab legs. There are also specials—like pasta (from $3.95) on Thursdays and lobster ($10.95) on Fridays.

Black River Inn (228-5585), 100 Main Street, Ludlow. Next door to the Governor's Inn, another elegant dining room offers another, rather expensive elegant meal with one 7 PM seating and a five-course menu-du-jour. This one might begin with salmon mousse and include beef roulades in a rich Burgundy sauce. Prix fixe: $20.00 per person; reservations must be made by 3:00 for the day you dine.

Michael's Seafood and Steak House (228-5622), Main Street, Ludlow. A large old dining landmark with a large upscale pub. Open for dinner nightly with mid-week specials, a Sunday buffet lunch and entrées geared to six guests: coq au vin for six is $29.75, vegetable lasagna $27.75, while seafood newburg is $48.95. The regular menu is large with chicken teriyaki at $9.95 and seafood kabob, $12.75.

EATING OUT   Pot Belly (228-8989), 130 Main Street, Ludlow. First opened in a store front in 1974, this zany place is good for live entertainment and victuals ranging from popcorn shrimp through pot belly chicken or ribs ($6.50) to chocolate peanut butter pie.

Valente's Italian Restaurant (228-2671), Main Street, Ludlow. Open Monday, Thursday, Friday, Saturday, 9–5, Sundays 5–8. An old-fashioned downtown restaurant, this is locally respected Italian food the way mama makes it.

The Hatchery (228-8654), Main Street at the stoplight, Ludlow. Open 5 AM–2. A storefront coffee shop with a cafe atmosphere, great for breakfast omelets or pancakes, for luncheon quiche or soups.

D.J.'s Restaurant (228-5374), Main Street, Ludlow. Open weekdays 11–9, Sundays 12–9. The best kind of downtown restaurant. A shiny formica counter accommodates single patrons and there are deep booths as well. A big, big hamburger goes for $1.95 but the place is best known for its broiled scallops and shrimp, fried platters of fish and "Roman fingers" (fried, boneless chicken); there are also children's plates, all reasonably priced.

Pace's Family Restaurant (228-8495). Owned by Frank Pace (also proprietor of The Hatchery), this is the place where locals eat. Good coffee shop food with a few booths and a lot of counter.

SNACKS   **Sweet Surrender,** Sunshine Marketplace, Ludlow. Open 5 AM when Kate Welch arrives to begin making fresh doughnuts and breads; there are a few tables; coffee, cream soda, and papers are also sold.

Baba-à Louis Bakery (226-7178), corner of Depot Street and Route 131 in Proctorsville (across from the Post Office). Open 7–6, Tuesday–Saturday, it developed a wide following in Chester before moving to this location in 1984. Everything is made on the spot from fresh ingredients. The breads are outstanding, so are the croissants, the cheese twists, and a wide assortment of munchies.

APRÈS SKI   **Dadd's** (228-9820), just down the road from Okemo's base lodge, is where the ski patrol hangs out after work. Known for its sandwiches, Mexican nights; also a limited dinner menu, electronic games.

Chuckles (228-5530) is on Route 103 north, in Ludlow (see *Eating Out*). Features live, late entertainment on weekends.

Herchel's (228-7447) specializes in music from the fifties, sixties, and seventies; music for dancing and listening Wednesday–Sunday.

Pot Belly (228-8989) jumps with dance music—swing and blues bands, jug band music, rock 'n' roll.

SELECTIVE SHOPPING   In **Sunshine Marketplace** at the Okemo access road check out **Pottery Works** featuring owner Susan Wishnatizki's work, also **Mountain High,** an artist's workshop selling handmade jewelry.

Quarry Road Studios (226-7331), off Route 131 between Proctorsville and Cavendish. Open by appointment, year-round. Alan and Wendy Regier have created an unusual exhibit space for their pottery and weavings. Alan works with white stoneware clay that he digs and prepares himself; Wendy weaves rugs from hand-dyed cotton yarns and calico fabric.

Green Mountain Sugar House (228-7151), Route 100, 4 miles north of Ludlow. You can watch syrup being produced in March and April; maple candy is made throughout the year on a weekly basis. This is also a place to pick strawberries in June and July, to find freshly pressed cider in September; the gift and produce shop is open daily 9–6 "most of the time."

The Haunted Mansion Bookshop (492-3462), Cuttingsville. This is a classic Victorian-style haunted house, set across from an unusual cemetery—with a chilling tale to link the two. Late in the nineteenth-century, tannery owner John Bowman built the extraordinary mausoleum by the road (into which you can peek); a life-sized Mr. Bowman stands beside it, hat in hand, mourning for his wife and two daughters, all of whom had died of various diseases. After completing this memorial to them, Bowman built the mansion across the road and then died. The mansion is now owned by Clint and Lucille Fiske who have filled it with antiquarian books. Open daily, spring–late fall, 9–5.

Castle Hill Stained Glass Studio (492-3525/259-2333), Cuttingsville. The interior of a former general store is filled with stained-glass creations. Master craftsmen William O'Connor and Jim Osborne affably interrupt their work to explain the different kinds of glass and how it is shaped.

The Etc. Shop, Route 103 east of Cuttingsville. This small store by the road and river, under the RR trestle, is operated by a painter and an artist in stained glass; they also carry a number of pieces by other local craftsmen.

Vermont Industries (800-826-4766, 492-3451), Route 103, Box 301, Cuttingsville, occupies a big barn full of hand-forged wrought iron products—free-standing sundials, sconces, candle holders, corn driers, hanging planters, chandeliers, and a wide range of fireplace accessories.

W. E. Pierce General Store, North Shrewsbury. Closed Sundays, otherwise open 7:30–6. Located at a four corners at which signs point variously to Rutland 10, Cuttingsville 4, Shrewsbury Center 2, Bridgewater 9, Plymouth 9. Two brothers carry on the business that their father began in 1918. It remains one of the most genuine, old fashioned, and beloved general stores in all Vermont. Pot belly stove and all!

Meadowsweet Herb Farm (492-3566), North Shrewsbury. The Herbshed attached to Polly Hayne's handsome old farmhouse on a backroad (follow the signs), is a studio and retail shop in which herb wreaths, potpourri and culinary blends are made from more than 175 herbs and scented geraniums. A number of perennial herbs and geraniums are grown year-round in the solar greenhouse and sold as seedlings and seeds. The farm and Renaissance Gardens are open daily, May–October, Monday–Saturday during November and December.

SPECIAL EVENTS   July 4–Labor Day: Band concerts on the Green. January: **Okemo Winter Carnival** is celebrated for nine days, including two weekends in the middle of the month: tug-of-war, tobogganing, snow sculpture contest, fireworks, ski races, torch light parade, etc.

MEDICAL EMERGENCY   Ludlow (228-4411); Cavendish (226-7283); Mount Holly (775-3133).

Black River Medical Group (226-7262), Cavendish.

Upper Connecticut Valley

Introduction

Occupying a broad oval on both sides of the Connecticut River from Bellows Falls north to St. Johnsbury, the "Upper Valley" region is one of the most rapidly developing areas of New England. On the Vermont side, Windsor County is, in many respects, New England in miniature: The roots and limbs of the state's independence and its constitution, the technological innovations that stimulated America's industrial revolution, carefully preserved architectural landmarks, centers for the study and advancement of law and medicine, and tangible evidence of environmental conservation can be found here. Windsor County bred an unusual number of foresighted legislators and governors, inventors and industrialists. So much American history in microcosm is reflected in Windsor County that it has been suggested as a candidate for National Park status along the lines of a British "preserve"—like the Lake District.

Within its boundaries are the machine tool centers of Springfield and Windsor; White River Junction, once an important railroad intersection; Woodstock, the County seat and a century-old resort; and the distinctive riverbank towns from Norwich north to Bradford. Because of their proximity and historic associations, we are including excursions into Cornish, Hanover, Lyme, and Orford, New Hampshire.

GETTING THERE By car: Interstates 91 and 89 converge in the White River Junction/Lebanon, New Hampshire sector, where they also meet Route 5, north and south, and Route 4, the main east-west highway through central Vermont.

By bus: Greyhound/Vermont Transit to White River Junction.

By air: Flights to and from the Lebanon Regional Airport on Eastern Express (800-451-4221).

GUIDANCE Area chambers of commerce are identified below. For a useful well-edited and printed booklet, pick up a copy of the *Upper Valley Guide,* published quarterly by Teago Publishing Company, South Pomfret, Vermont 05067; single copies are $1, but mostly they are free in participating establishments. Look, too, for complimentary copies of the seasonal *Dining Guide for the Upper Connecticut River Valley,* published by Mammoth Enterprises, Box 61, Thetford, Vermont 05074, which contains sample menus from some of the area's restaurants. See also the glossy *Upper Valley* magazine.

GETTING AROUND   Taxis: **Willette** (295-2440); **Ed's** (448-5407); **Airport** (298-9951); **LaBombard** (448-2340).

Stretch-limousine Service: **Doyle & Son** (298-8989); **Hallmark** (295-LIMO); **Bentley's** (457-3232; 603-643-4075); **Montgomery & Morgan** (457-4848).

Springfield

Springfield (10,063), on the cascades of the Black River, has been the capital of Vermont's machine tool industry, famous for the past hundred years, thanks to the inventiveness of the men who built up the Jones & Lamson Machine Company, Fellows Gear Shaper, and Bryant Chucking Grinder. These are now mostly owned by out-of-state conglomerates, and operating at far less than their capacity.

One of the notable shapers of Springfield's industrial fame was James Hartness, astronomer and aviation pioneer who patented 120 different machines, president of Jones & Lamson, and governor of Vermont in 1921–23. He entertained Charles Lindbergh when he landed at Vermont's first airport after his trans-Atlantic flight in 1927. Hartness's son-in-law, Ralph Flanders, was one of the few United States Senators with the courage to challenge Senator Joseph McCarthy's reprehensible witch-hunting and red-baiting in 1953.

GUIDANCE   The **Springfield Chamber of Commerce** (885-2779), 55 Clinton Street (Route 11), Springfield 05156.

GETTING THERE   By car: Exit 7, I-91, west on Route 11; which leads to Route 106 from the north, and Route 10 from the west.

By bus: Vermont Transit.

By air: Eastern Express (800-451-4221); **Hartness State Airport** (886-2231), North Springfield.

TO SEE AND DO   **Art & Historical Society** (885-2415), 9 Elm Street. Lodged in a Victorian mansion with collections of pewter, Bennington pottery, toys and dolls, primitive paintings, costumes, and periodic shows by area artists. Open daily, noon–4:30, May–December. Donations welcome.

Eureka Schoolhouse, Route 11 near I–91. The oldest (1790) schoolhouse left in the state. Open 9–5 daily, June to mid-October; free. Nearby is a century-old covered bridge.

Weathersfield Historical Society, 6 miles north of Springfield in Weathersfield Center, south of Route 131. The graciously restored Reverend Dan Foster House is open June through October, Wednesday–Sunday, and features a working blacksmith shop. This nearly secret hamlet is a gem, with its beautiful 1821 Meeting House,

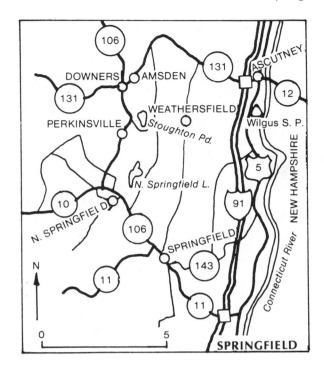

and Civil War memorial, a particularly sobering reminder of how many young Vermonters from tiny towns served, and died, in that war.

   Weathersfield Bow, off Route 5, is where 350 of the original Merino sheep arrived in 1810, imported from Spain by William Jarvis, the American Minister to Madrid, who had a farm here. He managed to spirit 4,000 of these splendid woolies into the United States; by 1840 there were 2 million of them in Vermont and New Hampshire.

GREEN SPACE   Wilgus State Park (674-5422/773-2657), 1½ miles south of Exit 8, I–91, off Route 5. This small, quiet campground on the Connecticut River is ideal for canoeists since many lean-tos and tentsites are on the river bank; car shuttle service available.

   Springweather Nature Trail, (where Weathersfield and Springfield meet). Fifty-five acres of fields and woods on the border of Springfield and Weathersfield have been developed by the Ascutney Mountain Audubon Society, as an environmental area.

GOLF   Crown Point Country Club (885-2703), Weathersfield Station Road, Springfield. 18 holes, rolling terrain.

SWIMMING   Stoughton Pond between Downers and Amsden south off Route 131 or north from Route 106, near Springfield Dam Lake. **North Springfield Lake** offers picnicking and swimming.

HEALTH SPA   Springfield Racquet Club and Fitness Center (885-5580), 333 River Street. Includes whirlpool, sauna, snack and juice bar, as well as the elementals.

LODGING   Hartness House (885-2115), Orchard Street (off Route 143), Springfield 05156. Governor Hartness built the house in 1903 in the "Newport cottage" style on the bluff where the lathe-makers lived. He installed his own Turret Equatorial Telescope at the end of a 240-foot underground corridor connected to the mansion, which has served as the town's principal hostelry since 1954. It has spacious sitting and dining rooms and 42 guest rooms in the main house and attached wings, each with private bath, telephone, color TV. Rates for two people range from $54–59 in the main house to $59–75 for the guest house and suites, EP; and from $49 to $53 per person, MAP. Five-day and weekend package rates available. There's a heated swimming pool, lighted clay tennis court, 33 acres for cross-country skiing, and golf privileges. The dining room serves good, moderately priced lunches and dinners.

    The Inn at Weathersfield (263-9217), Route 106 (near Perkinsville), Weathersfield 05151. If you're yearning for the New England edition of a cozy English county inn or a French provincial *auberge,* here it is. This charming, porticoed eighteenth-century homestead and farm has been through several incarnations: as a stage-coach stop between Rutland and Nashua, New Hampshire; as a station on the Underground Railroad; and reconversion to an inn in 1961. There are 10 antique-furnished guest rooms and 2 two-room suites, all with private bath and several with working fireplaces. Five public rooms offer relaxation and browsing among the 4,000 books in the hosts' library. For working off the calories, an exercise room and sauna beckon; a pond and grass tennis court are being restored. For equestrians, the inn has box stalls, a paddock, and can offer information about inn-to-inn carriage tours. Single occupancy is $88; double, $65 per person, including full breakfast, high tea, and a superior dinner (see *Dining Out*). To insure tranquility, hosts Mary Louise and Ron Thorburn won't accept reservations for children under 8; older ones are welcome only if their behavior "will permit other guests to enjoy the quiet atmosphere of our dining and guest rooms."

MOTELS   The Abbey Lyn Motel (886-2223/2224), Routes 106 and 10, North Springfield, has a swimming pool and miniature golf; **Howard Johnson's** near the I–91 interchange (885-4516), $49–63 weekdays; $70 weekends.

DINING OUT   The Inn at Weathersfield (263-9217), Route 106 (near Perkinsville), Weathersfield. A six-course prix fixe dinner at $21.95 is served every night except Wednesday, with reservations recommended. The menu changes daily, but one might choose the following: Vermont cheddar and pepper soup, lemon sole mousse with dill and carrot, a Romaine salad, raspberry sorbet, quail with shitake mushrooms in cream over Bordelaise, dessert and coffee. Another entrée might be stuffed loin of pork with apricot sauce, white wine and shallots.

See also **Hartness House**

EATING OUT   Penelope's/McKinley's (885-9186), on the square, Springfield, is full of polished woods, stained glass and greenery; homemade bread, soups and desserts accompany beef, lamb, fish, and vegetarian dishes at very reasonable prices. Mexican food Wednesdays. Entertainment most weekends. Dinners range from $7.25–16.95.

The Paddock (885-2720), Paddock Road, Springfield, ¼ mile west of Route 5 and I-91. Continental and substantial American fare in a handsomely converted barn. Complete dinners range from $8.95 to 17.95; children's plates. Dinners 5–9 except Monday; Sunday, noon–3, 5–8.

SELECTIVE SHOPPING   Vermont Soapstone Company north of Perkinsville off Route 106 (look for sign). Soapstone griddles won't stick, and they retain heat amazingly. Soapstone is used for woodstoves and even kitchen sinks. Gift shop outlet open daily 9–5 except Sunday, May–December. Regular mill hours 9–4:30 weekdays, January through April.

Pastimes (885-5819), 218 River Street, junction of Routes 11 and 106, features all sorts of copper utensils, pressed glass, tin sconces, and more.

SPECIAL EVENTS Columbus Day weekend: **Annual Vermont Apple Festival** (885-2779), includes craft show.

MEDICAL EMERGENCY   Springfield Hospital (885-2151), 25 Ridgewood Road, Springfield. **Mount Ascutney Hospital** (674-6711), County Road, Windsor.

Windsor

Windsor is called "the birthplace of Vermont" because on July 2, 1777, delegates from what was then the New Hampshire Grants assembled at Elijah West's tavern and adopted the constitution of Vermont as an independent republic. One of the document's chief drafters was Dr. Thomas Young, generally credited with having coined the name "Vermont" (from the strangled Latin, "Verd Mont") instead of "New Connecticut." Vermont's constitution was modeled on Pennsylvania's except that it was the first to abolish slavery and institute universal (but male) suffrage, regardless of property ownership.

After 1800, the town burgeoned as a manufacturing center for the products of local inventors, starting with Asahel Hubbard's hydraulic pump; Nicanor Kendall's repeating rifle; the long-range Sharps rifle; and B. Taylor Henry's Winchester—all of which made Windsor the cradle of the American firearms industry, prospering from the Mexican, Crimean, and Civil Wars. Windsor also spawned an early sewing machine, was an influential publishing hub, and was once the home of the second press brought to North America. This early affluence explains the handsome residences that line North Main Street. The Vermont State Prison and House of Correction stood in the heart of the town from 1807 until its closing in 1979 and was subsequently converted to low-cost housing units.

Windsor was the summer home for the famous nineteenth-century constitutional lawyer, William Maxwell Evarts, who, as acting Attorney General, successfully defended President Andrew Johnson from impeachment by the Senate. He also served as Secretary of State in the Hayes administration, when his house on Main Street (still occupied by the family) was known as "the little White House." (In an ironic footnote to history, Evarts' great-grandson, Archibald Cox, was fired as special Watergate prosecutor by President Nixon prior to his impeachment proceedings.)

GUIDANCE   **Windsor Area Chamber of Commerce,** Box 5, Windsor 05089 (674-6711).

TO SEE AND DO   **The American Precision Museum** (674-5781), South Main Street. An important, expanding collection of hand and machine

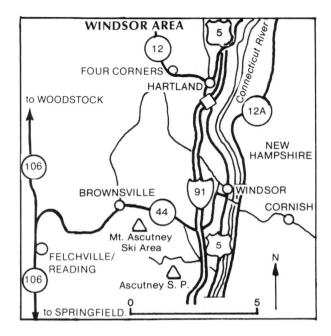

tools, assembled in the 1846 Robbins, Kendall & Lawrence Armory, itself a National Historic Landmark. The firm became world-famous in 1851 because of its displays of "the American system" of manufacturing interchangeable parts especially for what became the renowned Enfield rifle. Open May 30–November 1, 9–5 weekdays, 10–4 weekends and holidays. Small admission fee.

Old Constitution House, North Main Street. This is West's tavern moved from its original location, where delegates gathered around a table to adopt Vermont's constitution. It now holds an intriguing collection of antiques, prints, documents, tools and cooking utensils, table ware, toys, and early fabrics. Open daily from late May to mid-October. A small admission fee is charged.

Vermont State Craft Center (674-6729), Main Street. An attractive retail showcase-gallery for Vermont craftspeople: glass, ceramics, furniture, jewelry, prints, toys, fabrics, plus a series of instructional programs. It is located in historic Windsor House, once an inn, known in 1840 as the best public house between Boston and Montreal, and saved from the wreckers by a band of determined local preservationists, who organized Historic Windsor, Inc., in the early 1970s. Open year-round Monday through Saturday, 9–5.

Baked Bean Suppers. The ladies of Brownsville (West Windsor) have been serving up their famous baked bean and salad suppers since 1935, first for the benefit of the Methodist Church, lately for the Grange and the Historical Society. They start Saturdays in late June and run through the summer. People start lining up at 4:00 PM for the first seating at 5:00.

WALKS AND DRIVES   On your stroll around town, note the **Old South Congregational Church,** designed by the famed Asher Benjamin and built in 1798; it was renovated in 1844, 1879, and again in 1922 but fortunately retains its classic beauty.

St. Francis of Assisi Roman Catholic Church. The most significant example of contemporary religious art since the Rothko chapel in Houston may be seen here in the series of the "Seven Sacraments" panels contributed to the newly-built church by George Tooker, the noted American painter who lives in nearby Hartland.

St. Paul's Episcopal Church, on the common, built in 1832, is the oldest Episcopal church in Vermont still in regular use.

The Townsend Cottage, across the square, dating from 1847, is a striking example of "Hudson River Bracketed" or "Carpenter Gothic" style.

The Saint-Gaudens National Historic Site (603-675-2175), Cornish, New Hampshire. Includes the sculptor's summer home, barn/studio, sculpture court, and formal gardens, which he developed and occupied between 1885 and his death in 1907. The property was accepted by the National Park Service in 1964. Augustus Saint-Gaudens loved the Ravine Trail, a quarter-mile cart path to Blow-Me-Up Brook, now marked for visitors, and other walks laid out through the woodlands and wetlands of the Blow-Me-Down Natural Area. Saint-Gaudens was one of several artists who formed a summer colony in Cornish, a group that included poets Percy MacKaye, Witter Bynner, and William Vaughan Moody; Winston Churchill, the American novelist whose summer estate was used as the vacation White House by President Woodrow Wilson in 1914 and 1915; Ethel Barrymore, Charles Dana Gibson, Finley Peter Dunne, and Maxfield Parrish. Summer visitors can enjoy examples of the artist's work, and bring a picnic lunch for Sunday outdoor concerts. Open daily late May through October.

GREENSPACE   **Ascutney State Park** (674-2060): picnicking, trails, tent and trailer sites, lean-tos; paved road to summit. Granite was quarried here as early as 1808, and there was a popular summit house.

GOLF   **Windsor Country Club** (674-6491), 1 mile north of Windsor on Route 5; 9 holes, hilly terrain, across the road from a farm once owned by Marie Dressler, the movie star of "Tugboat Annie" fame.

CANOEING   **North Star Canoes** (603-542-5802), Cornish, New Hampshire, just across the river from Windsor. John and Linda Hammond offer "Highway for Adventure" half-day, all-day, and overnight canoe trips on the Connecticut River.

SKIING   **Ascutney Mountain Resort** (484-7711 for information; 800-243-0011

The Windsor-Cornish covered bridge

for reservations), Box 129, Route 44, Brownsville 05037. Six miles west of I–91, the full-service, family-oriented Ascutney Alpine and Nordic ski area continues to grow and improve, but remains relatively small and uncrowded in comparison to others in the state. The Ascutney Ski Village now includes the attractive Ascutney Mountain Resort Hotel, base lodge, 2 restaurants, an indoor-outdoor Sports & Fitness Center, a shopping arcade, convention facilities, and is planning a new 18-hole Robert Trent Jones golf course scheduled to open in 1990.

Lifts: 3 triple, 1 double chair lift.

Trails and slopes: 31

Vertical drop: 1,530 feet.

Snowmaking: 70%

Ski School: PSIA member

For children: SKIWee program for 6–12; certified nursery for 1–6; infant care available by prior reservation.

Rates: Adult, $21 midweek, $27 weekends and holidays; junior (12 and under), $14-16; children under 6 free; seniors, $14–18. (See *Lodging* for packages.)

Nordic Center: 20 km groomed cross-country trails

Ski rentals: Carrol Reed, on the premises; Sitzmark, Route 44

Special programs: NASTAR races Thursdays, Saturdays, Sundays; clinics Saturday and Sunday mornings.

LODGING   Ascutney Resort Hotel (484-7711 for information, 800-243-0011 for reservations), Box 129, Brownsville 05037. This gray-clapboard, "neo-colonial" complex is designed for flexible accommodations: from comfortably furnished hotel rooms to one, two, and three-bedroom suites with kitchen, fireplace, and outdoor deck, all readily accessible to the ski area by a lift just outside the door. Adjacent to the hotel is an indoor-outdoor Sports & Fitness Center, which includes tennis courts, swimming pools, raquetball courts, weight and aerobic rooms. There's formal dining in the Ascutney Harvest Inn, lighter fare in nearby Cheddar's, and a roomy, convivial bar. Rates vary according to the season and particular package: for example, slopeside lodging in a suite is $45 per person midweek, $65 weekends and holidays (add $25.50 per person, MAP); a Weekender (2 nights lodging and 2½ days skiing is $130 per person). Lower rates in summer.

Juniper Hill Inn (674-5273), RR 1, Box 79, Windsor 05069, off Route 5 on Juniper Hill Road. With a view of Mt. Ascutney and the Connecticut River Valley, this impressive mansion, built by Maxwell Evarts in 1901, combines Edwardian grandeur with the informal hospitality of its current proprietors, Jim and Krisha Pennino. Adult guests (and children over 12) can relax in the huge main hall, parlors, and cozy library. There are 14 spacious bedrooms ($50 with shared bath; $55 with semi-private; $58–75 with private bath); MAP and five-day midweek plans available. Inn guests dine on single-entrée, four-course dinners ($13.50–$15.50), featuring, for example, roast loin of pork with mustard and brandy sauce. The dining room is open to the public Friday and Saturday nights. Closed November to mid-December and Mud Season.

Wolpert's Mountain Inn Motel (674-5565), on a knoll off Route 5, 1.5 miles north of Windsor 05089. $35 to $45 B&B.

Yankee Village Motel (674-6010), Exit 8, I–91, Route 5, Ascutney 05030. 16 rooms, coffee shop.

BED & BREAKFAST   Ascutney House (674- 2664), junction of Routes 5 and 131, Ascutney 05030. This gracious brick Federal house, circa 1800, has three rooms with private baths for $50 including full breakfast.

The Mill Brook (484-7283), Box 410, Route 44, Brownsville 05037. This 1890s farmhouse near the Ascutney Resort features antiques, art and crafts, and food. Three sitting rooms and game area. Children and some pets welcome; limited smoking. Eight rooms with shared baths/showers, $26–55.

DINING OUT   Ascutney Harvest Inn (484-7711), Brownsville. This spacious dining room has a few old-fashioned summer hotel touches and an elaborate, ambitious (though barely legible) menu that can be studied at tables set far enough apart to prevent competing conversations. Appetizers include oysters on the half shell stuffed with spinach, smoked ham, mushrooms, and served hot with Hollandaise sauce ($3.95), smoked duck ($4.95), pheasant pâté ($6.95); lobster chowder ($3); salads; and entrées from chicken breasts Dijonnaise ($11.95), through duck, tuna steak, red snapper, coquille Pare (sea scallops sautéed in a basil cream sauce over spinach fettuccini) at $15.95, to veal Wellington ($18.95), plus daily specials. Delectable desserts cost $3. (On weekends, old-favorite piano music is played by Tom McDermott, who once played with the Glenn Miller band.

Ascutney House (674-2664), junction of Routes 5 and 131, Ascutney. The owners of this splendid early 1800s brick house serve dinner daily in three soothingly decorated dining rooms. Appetizers include a hearty Russian cabbage soup ($2.25), fettuccini Alfredo ($4.50), or baked brie for two ($6.50). Entrées range in price from Cornish game hen ($10.95) to shrimp scampi ($14.95), plus veal, duck, steak, scallops and sole, prepared and presented competently.

Windsor Station Restaurant (674-2052), Depot Avenue, Windsor. This *was* the mainline station, now natural wood plus velvet and brass, serving reasonably priced dinners with entrées from chicken Kiev or Almondine at $8.50, veal Madeira at $10.50, to the "Station Master" filet mignon topped with shrimp, asparagus, and Hollandaise for $14.25. A children's menu is available.

Skunk Hollow Tavern (436-2139), Hartland Four Corners, off Route 12 north of I–91, Exit 9. People gather downstairs in the closest approximation of a true English pub in Vermont to play darts and backgammon and munch on fish-and-chips, mussels, or pizza ($4.90–$7.95); generally excellent, more formal dining upstairs in the inn's original parlor ($12–16). Open Wednesday through Sunday.

EATING OUT   Green Mountain Land & Cattle Company (674-2032), Route 5, south of Windsor. Open for lunch and dinner Monday through Saturday and for Sunday dinner from noon till 9:00. Pork ribs a specialty; children's menu. Entrées range from $5.95–12.95.

Alice's Restaurant (674-2137), Route 131, Ascutney (off Exit 8, I–91), where "you can get almost anything you want, excepting Alice"; open Monday–Friday 5:30–9, Saturday–Sunday, 6:30–9.

SELECTIVE SHOPPING   Cider Hill Farm (674-5293), Hunt Road, 2½ miles west of State Street, Windsor. Growers of herbs, perennials, creators of herb wreaths, dry flower arrangements, herbal blends, wild apple cider.

The **Windsor Antiques Market** (674-9336), 53 Main Street, Windsor. This Gothic Revival church houses 30 dealers in antiquities whose wares are particularly strong in period pieces (eighteenth and nineteenth centuries), American painting, folk art and artifacts. Open 7 days May–October, 9:30–5:30; November–April, 10–5, closed Tuesday and Wednesday.

Antiques Center at Hartland (436-2441), Route 5, Hartland 05048, 5 miles north of Windsor. Barbara Mills has assembled the stock of some 45 dealers in this exceptional, three-building complex. It's worth the trip just to see her own four-square Federal brick house, where early American, "high country," and formal antiques look very much at home.

Presents, in the Bennington Building at the Ascutney Resort in Brownsville, is a snazzy, upscale gift shop with a variety of arts, crafts, quilts, and other items, imported and Vermont-made.

SPECIAL EVENTS   October: **Festival Windsor:** A celebration of Autumn in Windsor, Vermont.

MEDICAL EMERGENCY   Windsor (674-2112); Ascutney (542-2244); **Mount Ascutney Hospital** (674-6711), County Road, Windsor. **Springfield Hospital, Inc.** (885-2151), 25 Ridgewood Road, Springfield.

Woodstock Area

WOODSTOCK

A moated village cradled in hills around the Ottauquechee River fourteen miles west of White River Junction on Route 4, Woodstock is one of the most cosmopolitan towns in the state and, justifiably, considered one of the half dozen prettiest towns in America. It has been a popular year-round resort for a century: in the 1890s, summer folk settled into the old Woodstock Inn for the season, or returned for lively winter sports parties; and in the mid-1930s, it was mecca for Eastern skiers because of its rope tow—the first in America (1934).

As the Shire Town of Windsor County since the 1790s, Woodstock attracted an influential and prosperous group of professionals, who, with the local merchants and bankers, built the unusual concentration of distinguished Federal houses that surround the elliptical green, forming a long-admired architectural showcase that has been meticulously preserved.

Woodstock produced more than its share of nineteenth-century celebrities, including Hiram Powers, the sculptor whose nude Greek Slave scandalized the nation in 1847; and Senator Jacob Collamer (1791–1865), President Lincoln's confidante, who declared, "The good people of Woodstock have less incentive than others to yearn for heaven." George Perkins Marsh (1801–1882), helped found the Smithsonian when he was serving in Congress, was U.S. Minister to Turkey and Italy, and wrote the pioneering work on environmental conservation, *Man and Nature* (1864), which has long been regarded as the ecologists' bible. John Cotton Dana was an eminent early twentieth-century librarian and museum director, whose innovations made books and art more accessible to the public. The town still feels the influence of Frederick Billings (1823–1890), who became a famous San Francisco lawyer in the Gold Rush years, and later was responsible for the completion of the Northern Pacific Railroad (Billings, Montana, was named for him in 1882). The Billings Mansion, a Historic Landmark and the boyhood home of George Perkins Marsh, and the prize Jersey dairy are now owned by Billings' granddaughter and her husband, Laurence S. Rockefeller. The Rockefellers are responsible for much of Woodstock's

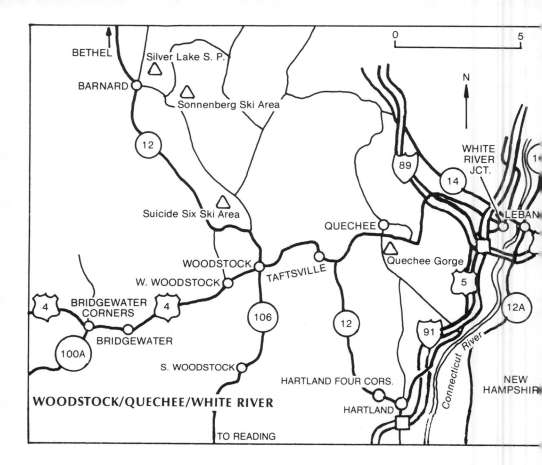

BETHEL
Silver Lake S. P.
BARNARD
Sonnenberg Ski Area
12
Suicide Six Ski Area
WOODSTOCK
W. WOODSTOCK
TAFTSVILLE
QUECHEE
Quechee Gorge
WHITE RIVER JCT.
89
14
LEBAN
5
12A
BRIDGEWATER CORNERS
4
4
106
12
91
NEW HAMPSHIR
100A
BRIDGEWATER
S. WOODSTOCK
HARTLAND FOUR CORS.
Connecticut River
WOODSTOCK/QUECHEE/WHITE RIVER
HARTLAND
TO READING
N
0   5

preservation, outlying green space, and recreational assets. Most of the village itself, and the hamlet of South Woodstock, are on the National Register of Historic Places.

GUIDANCE   The Woodstock Area Chamber of Commerce (457-3555), 4 Central Street, Woodstock 05901, keeps an information booth open on the Green from June through October (457-9823), which does its best to find beds in private homes for fall foliage leaf-peekers stranded without reservations, and from which daily walking tours are conducted in season. The Chamber annually publishes two useful free brochures, *Window on Woodstock* and *Where to Stay and Eat.*

Woodstock Common magazine is published quarterly and is available locally without charge or from the Prosper Publishing Company, Box 206, Barnard 05031.

A detailed schedule of local events is posted daily on the blackboard at the corner of Elm and Central Streets by the indefatigable "town crier," Frank Teagle.

TO SEE AND DO   The Billings Farm & Museum (457-2355), Route 12 north of River Road, holds a beautifully mounted series of exhibits demonstrating farm life in the 1890s: plowing, seeding, cultivating, harvesting and storing crops; making cheese and butter; wood-cutting and sugaring. Visitors can also observe what happens on a modern dairy farm. The tour is preceded by an imaginative audio-visual presentation. Open late May through October; limited capacity; admission charge.

The Dana House (The Woodstock Historical Society, 457-1822) on Elm Street, completed in 1807 and occupied for the next 140 years by the notable Dana family, has an admirable collection of antiques, locally wrought coin silver, portraits, porcelains, fabrics, costumes, toys, and a barn full of early tools, stoves, skis, sleds, and a splendid go-to-meeting sleigh owned by the Billings family. In its Canaday Gallery, given by the maker of the World War II prototype Jeep, is a permanent collection of more than 70 etchings by John Taylor Arms, who had a studio in Pomfret. Open 10–5, June 1–October 15. Admission charge.

The D.A.R. House and Museum, 22 The Green, has an interesting collection of early furniture and memorabilia, especially of the Woodstock Railroad (1875–1933), including a most unusual eight-foot long 1820 primitive painting of the influential Hutchinson family including cross-eyed young Alexander. The house itself was built in 1805 and first served as a boarding house for legislators who met in various towns around the state until Montpelier was chosen as the capital. Open Monday–Saturday, 2–4, June–October. Admission $1.

The Norman Williams Public Library, on The Green, a Romanesque gem, donated and endowed in 1883 by Dr. Edward H. Williams, general manager of the Pennsylvania Railroad and later head of Baldwin Locomotives. It offers children's story hours, poetry readings, brown-bag summer concerts on the lawn. Open daily except Sundays and holidays.

The Green Mountain Perkins Academy and Institute (457-3974), Route 106 in South Woodstock, has exhibits related to its tenure as a famous school between 1848 and 1890. Open Saturdays 2–4:30 in July and August and by appointment.

The Vermont Institute of Natural Science (457-2779), 1.5 miles southeast of the village on Church Hill Road, has a rare herbarium collection, other exhibits of flora and fauna, a library, nature trails, bird-banding station, a Raptor center, and offers lectures, bird-fern-and-wildflower walks. Open year-round, Monday–Friday 9–4.

COVERED BRIDGES   There are three in the town of Woodstock—the Lincoln Bridge (1865), Vermont's only Pratt-type truss, Route 4, West Woodstock; the Middle Bridge, in the center of the village, built in 1969 by Milton Graton, "last of the covered bridge builders," in the Town Lattice style (partially destroyed by vandalism and rebuilt); and the notable red Taftsville Bridge (1836) utilizing multiple king and queenposts and an unusual mongrel truss, Route 4 east. The Taftsville bridge overlooks a hydro dam, still in use, and magnetizes photographers.

BICYCLING   Bike Vermont (457-3553), Box 207, Pleasant Street, Woodstock. Weekend and five-day midweek inn-to-inn tours are arranged through central Vermont, including Grafton and Chester, Middletown Springs, Lake St. Catherine, Manchester, and the Connecticut River Valley. Twleve-speed Univegas are available for rent at $25 for weekends and $70 for midweek tours. Costs in 1987 ranged from $170—190 per person double occupancy for weekends; $455–495 for several midweek days, depending on the season, which begins the second weekend in May and lasts to near the end of October.

The Cyclery (457-3377), Route 4 in West Woodstock, has rentals; a marked bike path leads east from the village along River Road to Taftsville and its covered bridge.

BALLOONING   Green Mountain High Balloon Expedition (Fred Bartrum 457-1991). Rates based on length of flight and number in party.

GOLF AND TENNIS   The 18-hole **Woodstock Country Club** (457-2112) designed by Robert Trent Jones is part of the Woodstock Inn & Resort. Crossing and recrossing the trout-filled Kedron Brook has caused more than one player to remark that this was the first club where he needed a fishing license. Lower greens fees after 4:00 PM on weekdays. Ten tennis and two paddle courts are available.

The Quechee Club (295-9760), off Route 4 east, opens the lower Lakeland 18 holes to the public.

Vail Field. Two public tennis courts and children's playground.

HORSEBACK RIDING   Woodstock has been an equestrian center for generations, especially for the hardy Morgans, which are making a local comeback in South Woodstock.

The Green Mountain Horse Association (457-1509), Route 106, South Woodstock. Sponsor of the original 100-mile ride, an annual event around Labor Day that draws entrants from all over; shows, trials, and other popular events.

Kedron Valley Inn Stables (457-1480), Route 106, South Woodstock. Boarding, rentals, lessons; indoor arena. Inn-to-inn rides by invitation in June.

SWIMMING   Silver Lake State Park (234-9451/773-2657), 10 miles north on Route 12 in Barnard has a nice beach, and there's another smaller one right next to the general store.

The Woodstock Recreation Center has two public pools, mostly for youngsters.

WALKING AND HIKING   Faulkner Park, laid out by its donor, Mrs. Edward Faulkner, one of Woodstock's most thoughtful philanthropists, was modeled on Baden-Baden's "cardiac" walks; marked trails lead upward around Mt. Tom.

CROSS-COUNTRY SKIING   The Ski Touring Center (457-2114) at the **Woodstock Country Club,** Route 106 south of the village, part of the Rockresort properties, has mapped, marked, and groomed 47 miles of varied trails, from gentle terrain to forest and uplands, including Mt. Tom and the Skyline Trail in Pomfret. Group and individual lessons; guided four-hour picnic tours; rentals; sales room; lockers, bar restaurant (and dog-sled carts when the snow fails!).

Wilderness Trails (295-7620), Clubhouse Road at the Quechee Inn, has 8 miles of track-set trails. Most of the trails are good for "entry-level" skiers, and travel through the woods and meadows around Quechee Gorge, offering views of its waterfalls. Complete rentals lessons, available.

DOWNHILL SKIING   Suicide Six (457-1666), 2 miles north of the village on the Pomfret Road, now 50 years old, is the heir—on the other side of the slope—to the first ski tow in the United States, which was cranked up in 1934. The Face of Suicide Six, 655 feet vertical (operated for many years by Ski Hall of Famer, the late Bunny Bertram), is now part of the Woodstock Inn & Resort complex, and has a roomy new base lodge finished with native woodwork. Its beginner's area has a complimentary J-bar; 2 double chair lifts reach 18 trails ranging from easy to "The Show Off" and "Pomfret Plunge." Lift ticket prices start at $9 for youngsters and seniors on weekdays and climb to $22 for adults on weekends and holidays. Lessons; rentals; restaurant.

Sonnenberg Ski Area (234-9874), 12 miles north of Woodstock in Barnard. A small, family area good for beginners and intermediate. It has two Poma lifts and seven trails. Rentals, restaurant and a warming hut. Open only weekends and holiday weeks. The daily lift ticket price of $45 makes it the most expensive in Vermont, but the price includes rentals, lessons, lunch, ice skating, and cross-country trails.

ICE SKATING   Silver Lake, by the general store in Barnard.

Vail Field, Woodstock, maintained by local hockey and skating committee. Free, light for night skating.

Skate rental. **Woodstock Sports** (457-1568), 30 Central Street, Woodstock. $3 per day, $20 deposit. Sharpening ($1.50). Ski rentals also.

HEALTH SPA   The Sports Center (457-1160), part of the Woodstock Inn & Resort, Route 106, has indoor tennis and raquetball, lap pool, whirlpool, aerobic and state-of-the-art fitness equipment, plus restaurant and bar.

LODGING   The Woodstock Inn & Resort (457-1100; 800-223-7637; in New York State 800-442-8198; in New York City 212-586-4459), on The Green, is the lineal descendant of the eighteenth-century Eagle Tavern, and of the famous "old" Woodstock Inn that flourished between 1893 and 1969 and put the town on the year-round resort map. Today's 120-room, air-conditioned, colonial-style edition, owned by Laurence S. Rockefeller, is one of the pearls of the Rock-resort group, and reflects the owner's meticulous standards. The comfortably furnished main lobby is dominated by a huge stone fireplace where five-foot birch logs blaze in the winter. There's a spiffy main dining room, cozy bar, coffee shop, gift shop, conference facilities for up to 300, patio lunching in the summer, putting green and swimming pool, overlooked by a terrace with old-fashioned rocking chairs. Guests have access to the scenic 18-hole Woodstock Country Club for golf and tennis (it's a fine cross-country ski center in the winter) and to a splendid new indoor Sports Center plus downhill skiing at the historic Suicide Six area, wagon and sleigh rides. Current rates range from $92–156 single, $94–158 double, to $300 for a one-bedroom suite. Children under 14 free when staying in the same room with an adult; $10 for a third person; MAP available at an additional $34 per person.

Check out their special packages: Summer Sports, Celebration ($611 per couple, MAP, for three nights and four days, including two days of complimentary sports in season); Serenity Season; Sport Escape, others.

The Kedron Valley Inn (457-1473), Route 106, South Woodstock 05071. Max and Merrily Comins, recently transplanted Gothamites, have gingered up the decor, appointments, and cuisine of this venerable mini-resort without depleting its nineteenth-century charm. The mellow brick main house and historic tavern, plus Vermont log motel unit, are supplemented by an acre-plus swimming pond with sandy beach, adjacent to the Kedron Valley Stables—boarding, lessons, trail rides, indoor arena, surrey and sleigh rides in season. The freshly decorated 30 guest rooms, all with private bath, feature canopy and antique oak beds, some with fireplaces or Franklin stoves. There are so many examples of the Comins' collection of antique quilts on display that the dining room might have been named "The Quilted Pony," reflecting both the superior quality of the food (see *Dining Out*) and the inn's popularity with the horse people who are drawn to South Woodstock as an equestrian center. Room rates range from $55 to $90 per person double occupancy, including dinner and hearty country breakfast. Discounts available for midweek stays during nonholiday periods.

The Village Inn of Woodstock (457-1255), 41 Pleasant Street, is an informal, Victorian manse with fireplaces, oak wainscotting, pressed tin ceilings and all, plus bar and dining room. There are eight comfortable rooms, six with bath, $50–90 including continental breakfast.

The Lincoln Covered Bridge Inn (457-3312), Route 4 west, Woodstock, recently changed hands; Marilyn Dolan is now the innkeeper and is making some changes to this homey lodge on the river, with six bedrooms, sitting room, enclosed porch, lounge and dining room. Continental breakfast is included in the rates: kingsize bedroom, $85–100 ($135 MAP); queen or twin, $75–85 ($125 MAP); single occupancy $60 ($90), third person $15 ($35). All have private baths. Children under 8 and pets are not accommodated, and payment by cash or check is preferred.

The October Country Inn (672-3412), Bridgewater Corners 05035, is 8 miles west of Woodstock on Route 4. Ten rooms, eight with private baths, in a relaxed, casual, farmhouse setting: $49–65 per person, MAP. No pets.

BED & BREAKFASTS   **Three Church Street** (457-1925), Woodstock. In one of the grander Federal houses near The Green, Eleanor Paine holds hospitable court, serving bountiful breakfasts and dinner by arrangement. There are spacious sitting rooms and 11 guest rooms, with private and shared baths ($52–68), plus swimming pool and tennis court. Pets welcome.

The Charleston House (457-3843), 21 Pleasant Street, Woodstock, retains its Carolinian appeal under new ownership. Bill and Barbara Hough make this Federal brick townhouse appealing, with period furniture in seven bedrooms, all with private bath. $75–90, including full breakfast in the dining room, or continental breakfast bedside.

The Jackson House (457-2065), Route 4, West Woodstock 05091. Hosts Jack Foster and Bruce McIllveen have further expanded this spacious 1890 farmhouse with the addition of a pond for swimming and trout fishing. Each of the ten guest rooms is furnished in a different style and named accordingly, such as "Miss Gloria Swanson," in honor of the actress who hid out here in 1948 with her Rolls-Royce while her secretary stayed at the Woodstock Inn. Jackson House has a no-smoking policy "because of the irreplaceable nature of our furnishings and numerous requests from our guests." $90–100 double with big breakfast.

Clay Gates Farm (672-5294), Bridgewater 05034. Beautifully situated on a ridge 1 mile north of Route 4, this handsome Morgan Horse farm residence belonging to Charles and Betsy Clagett offers four attractive guest quarters: the Woodbury and Bulrush Rooms, with queen beds, shower and fireplace, at $85 each; the Sherman Room, with king bed, shower, fireplace and porch at $95; and the

Justin Morgan Suite, which includes a private sitting room with two fireplaces, bath and shower, at $110, all including breakfast. The hosts issue an unusual request: "We ask that all persons please bring slippers. Finished floors are slippery in socks, and street shoes do great damage. Your consideration will be greatly appreciated." [Reeboks, anyone?]

Carrousel Farm (484-9119), RR 1 Box 100, Reading 05062. 13 miles south of Woodstock on Route 106, this B&B has stables and so attracts horseback riders, children and pets. Six rooms with private baths at $60 including full breakfast.

Greystone Bed & Breakfast (484-7200), Box 85, Reading 05062, 11 miles south of Woodstock on Route 106. This restored 1830 stone colonial has three rooms, $50–60 including continental breakfast, but no pets.

The Peeping Cow (484-5036), Box 47, Reading 05062, 13 miles south of Woodstock on Route 106. This 1830 farmhouse is antique-furnished, and is near a swimming hole. No TV, no pets, non-smokers preferred, but French spoken. $45 double.

Beaver Pond Farm (436-2443), RR 1 Box 796, Woodstock. Up Hartland Hill Road 4.5 miles east of Woodstock, Bill and Beverly Garnett offer "lodging for horse and rider" in a Georgian colonial plus dressage ring and barn stalls, swimming and canoeing in the six-acre pond, and riding trails linked to the Green Mountain Horse Association. No children under 10; three large rooms with fireplace and bath in each, $50–75 with country continental breakfast.

Other B&Bs   1826 House (457-1335), 47 River Street ($30–35); **Riverside Guest House** (457-3896), 61 River Street ($45–85); **The Carriage House** (457-4322), Route 4, West Woodstock ($60 plus); **The Winslow House** (457-1820), Route 4, West Woodstock.

GUEST HOUSE   Abbott House (457-3077), 43 Pleasant Street, Woodstock, is the enlarged and renamed Cambria Guest House. The new owners have added two baths, so that two of the five double guest rooms, have private baths, with three sharing two baths. Rates are $40–50, double occupancy; no breakfast.

MOTELS   Braeside (457-1366), Route 4 east; 12 deluxe units, small heated pool ($38–72). **Shire Motel,** 46 Pleasant Street, 18 units ($40–70). **Woodstock Motel** (457-2500), Route 4 east, 15 units ($38 and up). **Pond Ridge** (457-1667), Route 4, West Woodstock, 12 units plus apartments ($39 and up). **Ottauquechee Motel** (672-3404), Route 4, West Woodstock, capacity 38 ($38). **The Valley View** (457-2123), 5 miles north of Woodstock on Route 12, 20 rooms ($48 and up).

DINING OUT   The Prince and the Pauper (457-1818), 24 Elm Street, Woodstock. Provides nouvelle and continental cuisine in a candlelit, elegantly rustic setting. Owner/chef Chris Balcer has, over the years, created and upheld consistently superior standards, now with daily

The Woodstock Country Club doubles as a cross-country ski center

menu changes. Our most recent sampling of the $23 prix fixe dinner included, for starters, smoked marlin, garnished with Raifort sauce and capers, fettuccini Primavera; Escalope de Veau Forestière (veal sautéed with oyster mushrooms, Madeira and creme fraîche), and Paillard of Blackened Tuna seared with Cajun spices. A boneless rack of lamb in puff pastry carried a $2 supplement. Subtle desserts are $2.50–3.95. Patrons tend to linger in the premium winebar, where one can also dine solo. Open daily except for late fall and early spring vacations. One of the state's best; "worth every calorie and dollar," we said in the first edition of this book, and have no reason to change our minds.

The Barnard Inn (234-9961), Barnard, 10 miles north of Woodstock on Route 12 in an impressive 1796 brick house, serves dinner in three beautifully appointed formal rooms. Owner/chef Sepp Schenker is renowned for his classic cuisine, stressing Swiss specialties and seasonal local produce (fiddleheads, morels, wild grapes, wild raspberries). Particularly recommended is the duckling, with various sauces ($20.50). Appetizers $4.75–6.50, entrées $17.50–25. This is one of Vermont's finest. Reservations essential. Closed Mondays, and it's wise to call ahead since hours vary in the off season.

The Woodstock Inn & Resort (457-1100). The cheerfully contemporary main dining room here offers several options. Extravagant buffets are served on Saturday nights ($20) and for Sunday brunch ($12.50). On other nights, an upper-bracket dinner might start with deepfried Camembert with tomato coulis ($5) or sautéed chicken and scallops in puff pastry ($5), followed by broiled medallions of venison with Port sauce ($19) or broiled tenderloin of veal with honey-mustard tomato glace and thyme sauce ($21). Pastries, subtle or lavish, are especially toothsome.

Lighter fare is served at lunch and dinner in the coffee shop, and the main dining room features a tasty soup-salad-coldcuts-dessert buffet for $7 at midday.

The Kedron Valley Inn (457-1473), Route 106, 5 miles south of Woodstock, serves stylish "Nouvelle Vermont" dinners at moderate prices. A small crock of luscious mushroom mousse and crackers accompanies cocktails. Appetizers include soups, pasta with basil pesto ($3.25), oysters, escargots in puff pastry with fennel butter ($5.25). Entrées range from chicken breast with honey, peaches, white wine, and scallions at $10.25 to the delectable house special, filet of Norwegian salmon stuffed with an herb seafood mousse, wrapped in puff pastry at $16.75. Fresh vegetables are especially well-prepared and subtly seasoned.

The Lincoln Covered Bridge Inn (457-3312), West Woodstock. The new menu here offers such appetizers as stuffed mushrooms with melted Provolone ($3.95), shrimp Amaretto ($5.50), and Harvest Chowder ($3.50), pastas at $8.95. Entrées range from $13.50 for chicken Mornay through veal En Croute ($16.95) and Norwegian salmon ($17.98) to grilled filet of lamb with Bordelaise ($18.95).

The Village Inn of Woodstock (457-1255), 41 Pleasant Street, Woodstock. This Victorian guest house serves dinner nightly, featuring roast Vermont turkey at $10.95, roast duck at $14.25, prime rib at $16.25, or rack of lamb at $18.95.

EATING OUT   **Spooner's** (457-4022), Route 4 east (in the Sunset Farm Barn), is a nifty, informal, relatively inexpensive restaurant open for dinner daily and for Sunday brunch (seasonal), featuring beef, fresh seafood, salad bar, and children's menu. Prime rib comes at $12.95 or $14.95, shrimp scampi and sirloin at $11.95, plus nightly specials and mesquite-broiled fish, chicken, and steak in various combinations. Steak kabob on the children's dinner is only $4.95.

Rumbleseat Rathskeller (457-3609), Woodstock East (located in the basement of the 1834 Stone House), is a popular local hangout with a pleasant awninged patio in the summer. Inexpensive soups, salads, burgers, sandwiches at lunch; special entrées at dinner in the $9-16 class.

Bentley's Restaurant (457-3232), Elm Street, Woodstock. This popular spot serves lunch, dinner, and brunch in an eclectic hanging-plant, bentwood-chair setting. Its lighter menu includes Torta Rustica ($6.95), deepfried mushrooms ($3.75), hefty burgers at $4.25, croissants with various fillings ($6.95) served with lots of fresh fruit. Dinner entrées include a vegetarian stir-fry ($12.95), Jamaican Pecan Chicken ($13.95), Jack Daniels Steak ($17.50), plus various Cajun and Creole specials. Live entertainment weekends.

The Corners Inn (672-9968), Routes 4 and 100A, Bridgewater Corners. Charlie Robbins, the chef, a graduate of the Culinary Institute of America, is responsible for the new and broader menu (dinner Wednesday–Sunday), which includes seasonal specialties like fiddlehead soup, soft shell crabs with basil, tomatoes, and aioli sauce, angel hair pasta with three seafoods in a light shallot cream sauce, salmon grilled with buerre blanc sauce, as well as the more traditional duckling and strip steak. For dessert, Robbins whips up raspberry and strawberry mousse and strawberry butter cream torte. Entrées $6.95–14.95.

Enes' Table (457-2512), at the Valley View Motel, 5 miles north of Woodstock on Route 12, serves zesty Italian fare. The daily specials are especially recommended. Various pasta selections at $8.50; variations on veal or chicken ($10–11), or shrimp sautéed in white wine and garlic ($11.75).

SNACKS PLUS   The Deli in Woodstock (457-1062), Gallery Place, Route 4 east, Woodstock, is *the* place for light lunches, on the premises or to take out, open Monday–Saturday 7:30–7. This is the town's very own Dean & DeLucca, with gourmet cheeses, meats, pâtés, wines and sweets, as well as a superior catering service.

Downtown Deli (457-3286), located in the former firehouse over the Kedron Brook, this branch of the above serves breakfast, luncheon sandwiches, quiches, soups, salads. Open daily 7–5, Sunday 7:30–5.

Woodstock Country Club (457-2112). Light lunch and excellent Sunday brunch buffet.

Mountain Creamery (457-1715), Central Street, serves breakfast daily 7–11:30, plus sandwiches and luncheon specials, and homemade ice cream.

The Village Butcher (457-2756), 18 Elm Street, provides tasty deli specials to go, along with its top-flight meats, wines and baked goods.

The Wasp Diner, Pleasant Street, is unsigned, but if you can find it, join Woodstock's hard-working fraternity for breakfast or lunch at the counter.

Cole Farm Restaurant (672-3419), 4 miles west of Woodstock on Route 4, serves good, inexpensive roadside food.

White Cottage Snack Bar, West Woodstock, open late spring to mid-October, snacks and ice-cream drive-in.

SELECTIVE SHOPPING   Woodstock is full of antique and gift shops, boutiques, and specialty stores for toys, candy, linen, sports and children's clothes, silver, leather, wool and needlework. Among the established or unusual:

F.H. Gillingham & Sons (457-2100) Elm Street, owned and run by the same family since 1886, is something of an institution, retaining a lot of its old-fashioned general store flavor in which plain and fancy groceries, wine, housewares and hardware for home, garden, and farm can be found. Mail-order catalog.

Gallery 2 (457-1171), in two locations (on Elm Street and around the corner on Central Street), has won special awards for its consistent promotion of the work of Vermont painters, sculptors, and glass blowers. Folk art and prints round out its distinctive examples of contemporary art.

The Lamp Shop (457-2280), 49 Central Street, offers antiques, lighting fixtures, custom-made lamp shades.

The Looking Glass (457-1301), Central Street, stocks upscale children's clothing, featuring its locally-made Elizabeth Anne collection.

Unicorn (457-2480), 15 Central Street, is a veritable treasure trove of unusual gifts, cards, games, toys, and unclassifiable finds.

Woodstock Potters (457-1298), Mechanic Street (off Central), is a studio workshop where Kathy Myers and Robin Scully make stoneware pottery and hand-painted porcelains.

The Yankee Bookshop (457-2411), Central Street, carries a large stock of hardbound and paperback books for adults and children, plus cards; features the work of local authors and publishers.

Who is Sylvia? (457-1110), 26 Central Street, features vintage clothing and accessories.

The Vermont Workshop (457-1400), 73 Central Street (formerly run by the late Nancy Wickham, the well-known potter) features a wide selection of gifts and crafts.

Log Cabin Quilts (457-2725), 9 Central Street. Calicos, stencils, and supplies; imaginative works by Vermont artisans.

James S. Keefer Birdcarver (457-3977), Route 12 north. Duck, swan, goose, and snipe decoys.

Woodstock Gallery & Design Center (457-1900), Gallery Place,

Route 4 east, shows and sells paintings, photographs and prints; custom framing.

HSI (457-3804), Routes 12 and 4, Taftsville. Factory outlet store for the designers and manufacturers of contemporary oak furniture.

The Market Place at Bridgewater Mill (672-3332), Route 4, Bridgewater. When an 1825 woolen mill on the Ottauquechee finally gave up the ghost in the early 1970s, a local bootstrap effort was mounted to convert it to an indoor shopping center. After several precarious years, the Market Place has come into its own, housing over 50 shops on 3 floors, and sponsoring periodic crafts fairs and other events. Among the individual specialty shops of interest are the **Sun of the Heart Bookstore, Deertan Leather, Fabrics and Findings,** and **Vermont Clock Craft.** There's a food court for grazers, and factory outlets for Manhattan, Prestige Fragrances & Cosmetics, Van Heusen, Dunham, Kids Port, Outdoorsmen, the Weston Bowl Mill, Townshend Furniture, Vermont Shaker, and more.

Sugarbush Farm (457-1757), Pomfret. Route 4 to Taftsville, cross covered bridge, go up the hill and turn left on Hillside Road, then follow signs. Sample seven Vermont cheeses packaged there and watch maple sugaring.

Country Stores: for maple syrup, honey, cheese, jams and jellies, and other Vermont products—**The Taftsville Country Store** and **The Red Cupboard,** West Woodstock.

ANTIQUES **Wigren & Barlow** (457-2453), 29 Pleasant Street, is closed in the winter; **Church Street Antiques** (457-2628), west of The Green, is open daily; **Sheila Barton** (457-1320), 53 Central Street, may be closed in the winter; **M.V.Coker** (457-4312), Route 4, 3 miles west of Woodstock (June–November or by appointment); **Frasers'** (457-3437), Taftsville.

SPECIAL EVENTS February (Washington's Birthday) A week of **Winter Carnival** events sponsored by the Woodstock Recreation Center (457-1502); concerts, Fisk Trophy Race, sleigh rides, square dance, "casino" night, Torchlight ski parade.

April: **Annual Ottauquechee Raft Race** sponsored by Woodstock Recreational Center (457-1502) draws a large number of unusual and amusing entries.

July (Fourth) **Crafts Fair;** fireworks display in the evening at the High School. **AKC Dog Show,** Woodstock Union High School. Woodstock Road Race, 7.4 miles (457-1502).

Mid-August: Sidewalk sale

Mid-October: **Apple & Crafts Fair**

Thanksgiving Weekend: **Christmas Crafts Bazaar**

Early December: **Christmas Wassail Weekend.**
MEDICAL EMERGENCY   Woodstock (457-2323), Barnard (728-9600). **Ot-tauquechee Health Center** (457-3030), 32 Pleasant Street, Woodstock.

QUECHEE

Quechee, on Route 4, four miles east of Woodstock, once a thriving woolen milltown, has been almost completely swallowed in the past fifteen years by the 6000-acre Quechee Lakes Corporation, probably the largest second-home and condominium development in the state. As such enterprises go, this one has been well-planned, allowing for a maximum of greenspace, but hilltops crowned by townhouses can't help but make rural preservationists wince. Still, it's an attractive colony of suburbanites. In the wake of this leviathan, village resources have been preserved and expanded, including a replicated covered bridge across the river near what was Downer's Mill.

GUIDANCE   The Quechee Chamber of Commerce (295-7900).
TO SEE AND DO   **Quechee Gorge,** Route 4, is one of Vermont's natural wonders, its 165-foot chasm bridged by a span that used to carry Woodstock Railroad trains. The nearby **Quechee Gorge Recreation Area** (295-2990/773-2657) has picnic grounds, tent and trailer sites, and trails leading down into the gorge, which should be approached carefully; at the north end of the gorge, under a spillway, is a fine rockbound swimming hole, accessible by easy stages through the pine woods at the west end of the bridge.

Quechee Polo Club. Matches most Saturdays in July and August on field near the center of the village.

Quechee Hot Air Balloon Festival (295-7900), late June. Ascensions, flights, races, craft show, entertainment.

Timber Rail Village (295-1550), the latest attraction at Quechee Gorge, Route 4, combines a huge country store, a 225-dealer antique mall, Bunk-House Restaurant, and a miniature train ride for kiddies.

Four Seasons Sports (295-7620), Clubhouse Road at the Quechee Inn. Complete equipment rental for the whole family: daily bike trips; canoeing and fishing on Dewey's lake.

LODGING   All places listed below are in Quechee (zip code 05059) unless otherwise noted.

Quechee Lakes Corp. (295-7527, rentals 295-7525) Box 85, Quechee. House and rental condo properties include cable TV, fireplace or stove, fully-equipped kitchens; some accommodations have Jacuzzi and sauna; rental fee includes linens, firewood, utilities. Sam-

The annual Balloon Festival draws crowds to Quechee

ple rates: for three nights, $350 for a cozy one-bedroom to $790 for a deluxe three-bedroom, three-bath, plus loft, Jacuzzi/sauna; or $1,400–3,150 for a seven-day stay, respectively.

The Quechee Inn at Marshland Farm (295-3133), Clubhouse Road, Quechee, is an extremely attractive restored and enlarged eighteenth-century farmhouse once the home of Vermont's first lieutenant-governor. It's near the Ottauchequee River just above the dramatic gorge. The sitting and 24 guest rooms have a romantic aura, and the dining room is above average. Guests have access to the nearby Quechee Club for golf, downhill skiing, and swimming pool. The inn maintains its own 18 km of groomed cross-country ski trails. Rates range from $128 double MAP, lower midweek from November to May.

The Parker House (295-6077), Main Street, Quechee, a handsome Victorian mansion has four spacious guest rooms at $75–95 with full breakfast, served in your room if you prefer. Formal dining, too (see *Dining Out*). Closed Wednesday.

Quechee Bed & Breakfast (295-1776), Route 4. Six comfortable guest rooms with private baths, $85 with full breakfast.

Carefree Quechee (295-9500) provides weekend and seasonal rentals of homes and townhouses.

Quechee Gorge Friendship Inn (295-7600), Route 4. This motel has 75 rooms with rates from $36–63, suites $62–73, plus efficiencies.

DINING OUT   **The Parker House** (295-6077), Main Street, Quechee, is the latest contender for culinary honors in the Upper Valley. In its three attractive dining rooms or on the back porch in clement weather, you can dine exceedingly well on a $25 prix fixe menu, or on soup, entrée, and salad for $18. For openers, try veal and chicken pâté with pink peppercorns, or puff pastry-wrapped seafood. Among the main dishes are duck with homemade chutney, sweetbreads sautéed with wild mushrooms, *poisson du jour*, or (our current favorite) tender New Zealand venison medallions with peppercorn sauce. Rich desserts tempt, and the carefully selected wine list has some reasonably priced vintages. The Parker House is now owned by Roger Nicolas, the accomplished owner-chef of Home Hill, Plainfield, New Hampshire.

Quechee Inn at Marshland Farm (295-3133), Clubhouse Road, Quechee. Open seven evenings a week, this romantically rustic dining room features, for example, avocado with Boursin, or escargot as appetizers, and entrees in the $14–20 class, which might include duckling with raspberry sauce, pork with peaches, or New Zealand rack of lamb. Their French Silk Pie is not to be missed.

Simon Pearce Restaurant (295-1470), The Mill, Quechee, is a cheerful, upbeat contemporary place for lunch and dinner, served with its own pottery and glass, overlooking the waterfall. The patio is open in the summer, and its Irish soda bread and Ballymaloe brown bread alone is worth a visit. Lunch entrées ($5.25–9) could be spinach and cheddar cheese in puff pastry or beef and Guiness stew; at dinner ($10.50–18.50), duck with mango chutney sauce, veal with two-mustard sauce, or beef tenderloin pressed in cracked pepper and sautéed with brandy and mustard. Open daily during the summer and fall, but check ahead for dinner in the winter.

EATING OUT   **Rosalita's** (295-1600), Waterman Place, Route 4, is the area's Tex-Mex hangout, with adobe walls and Mexican tiles, where you can quaff Dos Equis beer and cheese soup served in a deepfried tortilla bowl ($2.50), munch hamburgers or Nachos Fajita ($5.95) anytime, or add Louisiana Blackened sole ($11.95) for a dinner entrée.

Sevi's House of Seafood (295-9351), Route 4. In pleasant nautical surroundings, Mike and Sevi Guryel offer hearty, consistently well-prepared dinners daily, featuring lobster, broiled scrod ($8.95), baked stuffed shrimp ($12.95), a broiled shore dinner ($12.95), steak or tender prime ribs ($10.95–14.95), all accompanied by Greek salad. Their homemade New England clam chowder is rich, and daily specials are good values. From 4:00 to midnight, it's pizza time, in the lounge or take-out.

Red Pines Restaurant (295-7600), Route 4, Quechee (near the Gorge). An above-average road-food place, often crowded with bus tours during the summer and early fall. Folks who yearn for good brown gravy (and rarely find it in these *nouvelle* days) can comfort themselves with its meat loaf ($6.25) or roast turkey dinner ($6.95). Most other entrées are moderately priced, too: London broil at $9.95, baked stuffed shrimp at $11.75.

SELECTIVE SHOPPING   **Simon Pearce Glass** (295-2711), The Mill, Main Street, Quechee. Pearce, who operated his own glassworks in Ireland for a decade, moved here in 1981, acquired the venerable Downer's Mill and is now harnessing the dam's hydro power for the glass furnace. Visitors can watch glass being blown and shop for individual pieces from the retail shop, where seconds with imperceptible flaws are also stocked, along with rugged wool clothing and distinctive pottery. The shop is open from 10:00 to 5:00 daily; glass blowing can be viewed during those hours on weekdays and on summer weekends.

Waterman Place, Route 4. Once past the outlandish, salmon-colored "neo-Etruscan" facade of this indoor shopping center, you can pause for ice cream at the **Atrium Cafe** next to Rosalita's, browse through six gift shops on three floors, buy books, cards, records, tapes and toys at **Waterman Exchange,** indulge your sweet teeth in **Truffles** (at $1.40 *per truffle*), or stock up at the **Quechee Wine and Cheese Shop.**

Laro's Farmstand, Route 4 between Taftsville and Quechee, open in summer and early fall, is a superior produce market that also sells well-selected wooden ware, woven place mats, syrup, honey, preserves, Ben & Jerry's ice cream, an unlimited variety of baskets, and a barn full of old things. Fresh corn on the cob roasted while you wait.

Scotland by the Yard (295-5351), Route 4, 3 miles east of Woodstock, imports tartans and tweeds, kilts, capes, coats, sweaters, skirts, canes, books, records, oatcakes, and shortbreads.

Talbot's Herb & Perennial Farm (436-2085), Harland-Quechee Road, 3 miles south of the blinker off Route 4. Field-grown herbs, dried flowers and wreaths, greenhouse. Open daily 9–5, from early April through October.

Henderson's Ski Systems (295-1973), Route 4, Quechee. Full-line ski shop, with adult and junior rental or lease plans for downhill and cross-country equipment.

Sugar Pine Farm (295-1266), Route 4, Quechee. Old and contemporary folk art and other gifts, in a 1740s replica house. Closed Wednesdays, usually open other days from 10:30.

Yankee Musket Shop (295-2284), in Quechee village, is a mini-museum of antique and modern firearms; archery equipment, too.

WHITE RIVER JUNCTION

Located at the confluence of the Connecticut and White Rivers and the intersection of Interstates 91 and 89 and once a bustling, often raucous railroad hub, White River Junction is expanding its peripheral reach to accommodate the concentration of brand-name motels, a new post office, professional offices, and fast-food stops. The downtown seems to resist renewal, except for the venerable Hotel Coolidge, and you can almost feel the aura of steam and cinders that cling to the locomotive and railroad cars parked across from the hotel. (And how many residents or visitors know that Horace Wells of White River Junction was the first person to use laughing gas as an anesthetic for pulling teeth in 1844?)

GUIDANCE   **White River Junction Chamber of Commerce** (295-6200), Box 697, White River Junction 05001.

GETTING THERE   **Vermont Transit** (295-3011) Interchange Plaza. This is the hub of the area's bus transportation; also noteworthy in that it is one of the New England's few pleasant bus stations with clean, friendly dining and snack rooms.

TO SEE AND DO   **Summer Theater** (295-6228), **Green Mountain Guild.** Musical comedies and reviews and special shows for children at the Junction Playhouse, White River Junction, and at the Killington Playhouse, Snowshed Baselodge.

The Catamount Brewery (296-2248), 28 South Main Street, White River Junction. Grateful quaffers applauded the recent introduction of this zesty English-type ale; tours and tastings by appointment.

LODGING   **The Hotel Coolidge** (295-3118; 800-622-1124) deserves attention as one of the last of the old railroad hotels. Recently renovated, it has inexpensive accommodations and an above-average dining room—in short, a "find" for the economy-minded traveler. $31 single to $45 double.

OTHER LODGING   Since several kinds of transportation converge on White River Junction, it has a clutch of the major motor inns: **Holiday Inn** (295-7537); **Howard Johnson's Motor Lodge and Restaurant** (295-3015); The **Susse Chalet Motor Lodge** (295-3051); and, across the river in Lebanon, NH, the **Sheraton North Country Inn** (603-298-5906).

RESTAURANTS   **Than Wheeler's Restaurant** (295-9717), Main Street. Offers good food at very reasonable prices. Open from 11:30 AM until around midnight, closed Sunday. Weekend entertainment.

The Hotel Coolidge (see *Loding*).

SELECTIVE SHOPPING   **Vermont Salvage Exchange** (295-7616), Railroad Row, White River Junction, for doors, chandeliers, moldings, mantels, old bricks and other architectural relics.

Norwich, Hanover, and the Upper River Towns

Norwich, on Route 5 and reachable from Exit 13, I–91, is one of the prettiest towns in Vermont, settled in 1761 by a group from Marshfield, Connecticut. It has always had close ties to its neighbor in New Hampshire, Hanover, with which it shares the Dresden School District, one of the few such bi-state jurisdictions. Lots of Dartmouth College faculty members live in Norwich, which once was the home for the American Literary, Scientific and Military Academy, founded in 1819 and named Norwich University in 1834; it was moved to Northfield after the Civil War. Like Woodstock, Norwich is an architectural showcase for fine brick and frame Federal homes. One particularly unusual example is known as The Seven Nations House, across from the Norwich Inn, built as a commercial "tenement" in 1832 and now occupied by professional offices.

The impressive campus of Dartmouth College dominates the town of **Hanover;** parts of the white brick Old Dartmouth Row on the east side of the central quadrangle date from 1784. The college itself was founded by Eleazer Wheelock in 1769 and is now even more famous for its medical school than for its Winter Carnival.

North of Hanover on Route 10, which follows the Connecticut River, lie **Lyme** and **Orford,** two lovely villages. Orford is known for its "Bulfinch Row" tier of seven elegant houses built between 1773 and 1839 by merchants and professional men. The Bulfinch-style house (1814–1816) of John B. Wheeler at the southernmost end of the ridge was probably designed by Asher Benjamin of Boston, an associate of Bulfinch.

A bridge from Orford to Thetford brings one back to Route 5 in Vermont. **Thetford** has an unusual distinction in that the six different post offices established in the township are still functioning. Thetford Hill, site of Thetford Academy, is one of the most perfect hamlets left in the state. The stretch of the Connecticut River north from Wilder Dam to its Ox Bow at Newbury is especially beautiful. Route 5 follows and sometimes overlooks the river's graceful curves,

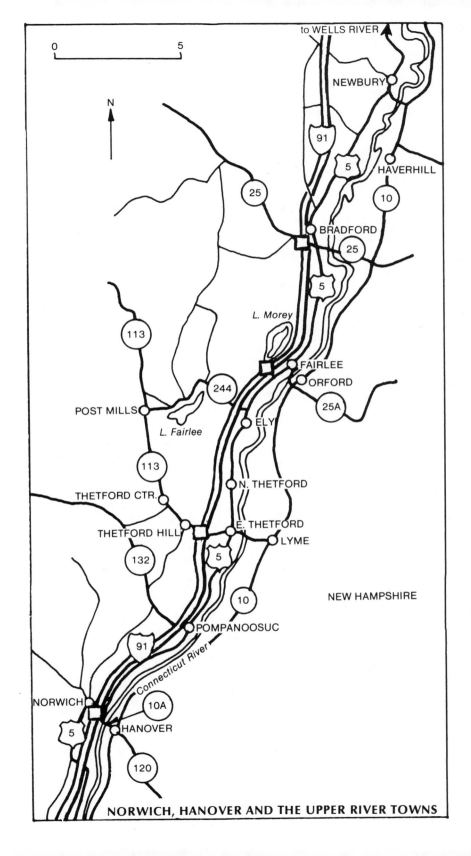

NORWICH, HANOVER AND THE UPPER RIVER TOWNS

accenting the vista of the Presidential Range on the New Hampshire side. This waterway is ideal for canoeing (see *Canoeing*). Between East Thetford and Bradford are Ely and Fairlee, where two lakes, Fairlee and Morey, offer resort facilities.

Samuel Morey, a resident of Orford and a lumberman in Fairlee, was the inventor of the first steamboat: in 1793, fourteen years before Fulton launched his *Clermont,* Morey was puffing up and down the river in a primitive craft barely big enough to hold him and his firewood; the remains of this little steamer are believed to lie at the bottom of Lake Morey, scuttled by its builder when the $100,000 in stock offered him by Robert Fulton turned out to be worthless. Morey also patented an internal combustion engine in 1825.

Bradford, where the Waits River flows into the Connecticut, is unique in Vermont because it is the only town to have been settled, in the late 1760s, without any deed, grant, or charter, thus setting an early example of contrariness for which Vermont is famous. Bradford was home to James Wilson, an ingenious farmer who made America's first geographical globes in the early 1800s, and the birthplace of Captain Charles Clark, who commanded the battleship *Oregon* on its strategic 15,000-mile dash around Cape Horn from the Pacific to help defeat the Spanish fleet at Santiago Bay in 1898. His exploit, on the heels of Commodore George Dewey's victory in Manila, and Vermont Senator Redfield Proctor's jingoistic call for the liberation of Cuba, prompted the *Rutland Herald* to call this conflict "the Vermont-Spanish War."

TO SEE AND DO   Dartmouth College. Guide-service tours in the summer from the information booth at the east side of the green. The Baker Memorial Library has a set of murals by the famous Mexican painter, Jose Orozco, which some alumni once demanded be removed or covered because of the artist's left-wing reputation.

Hopkins Center for the Arts (603-646-2422) has two theaters, a recital hall, art galleries for permanent and seasonal exhibits, a cafeteria, studios, and a year-round program of plays, concerts, film society showings. It serves as home base for the accomplished Dartmouth Symphony Orchestra, which includes both amateurs and professionals.

The Hood Museum of Art (603-646-2808), Hanover, is attached to Dartmouth's Hopkins Center. The museum frequently holds outstanding special exhibits alongside its distinguished small permanent collection of paintings, silver, and folk art.

Montshire Museum of Science (603-643-5672), 45 Lyme Road, Hanover. This increasingly popular and expanding natural science center offers permanent and changing exhibits, lectures, films, field trips, many of which are geared for families and young children.

Open 10–5, Tuesday–Saturday; 2–5 Sunday. Contributions welcome.

East Thetford Commission Livestock Auctions (785-2161), Route 5. Attending these Monday evening auctions of cattle, sheep, pigs, goats, rabbits, and poultry is the best show around. (We were once highly amused by watching a goat nonchalantly chewing the wool off a complacent old ewe, in the holding pen.)

Annual Wild Game Supper. Bradford nearly doubles its population of 1,700 on the Saturday before Thanksgiving when hungry visitors pour into the Congregational Church for this feast, now in its 27th year. Some 2,800 pounds of buffalo, venison, moose, pheasant, coon, rabbit, wild boar, and bear, cooked up by parishioners as roasts, steaks, hamburger, stews, and sausage, are devoured along with salad, vegetables, and gingerbread with whipped cream. Tickets ($15 for adults, $7 for children) are limited to 1,000, doors open at 3:00 PM.

Reservations are accepted only on or after the "middle Monday of October," postmarked or in person. Contact Mrs. Eris Eastman, Box 182, Bradford 05033. For information call Mrs. Raymond Green (222-4670), Box 356, Bradford.

SUMMER THEATER   **The Parish Players** (785-4344), based in the Eclipse Grange Hall on Thetford Hill, is a vigorous young company with a growing reputation.

CANOEING   Since this 55-mile section of the Connecticut River is so seductive to paddlers, three country inns collaborate in a leisurely two-day trip from the end of June through August, beginning at the **Haverill Inn,** Haverill, New Hampshire, with the second night at the **Stone House Inn,** and ending at the **Moose Mountain Lodge** in Hanover. The tab is $225 per person, double occupancy, for everything except canoe rentals, which can be arranged by the Stone House Inn for $45. For reservations: write the **Stone House Inn,** Box 47, North Thetford 05054.

The Ledyard Canoe Club of Dartmouth (603-646-2753) sponsors a variety of canoe and kayak events during the summer, including safaris to Maine and Connecticut, kayak and windsurfer clinics. Memberships are extended to Dartmouth students, faculty, employees, alumni and to the public.

GOLF   **Hanover Country Club** (603-646-2000), Rope Ferry Road, off Route 10, Hanover, New Hampshire. A classy 18-hole course with pro shop and lounge, open May through October.

Lake Morey Country Club (333-4311), Fairlee, Exit 15 off I-91. Relatively flat 18-hole course, home of the Vermont State Open for many years. Tennis and racquetball courts are also available to the public.

Bradford Country Club (222-5207). 9 holes.

OTHER RECREATION   Swimming: **Union Village Dam Recreation Area,** west on Route 132 from Pompanoosuc, offers swimming, picnicking, and fishing. Soaring: **Post Mills Airport** (333-9254), Post Mills 05058. Airplane and sailplane rides, rentals and instruction.

LODGING   **The Inn at Norwich** (649-1143), 225 Main Street, Norwich 05055. Originally built as a stage stop in 1797, the Inn has 25 individualized guest rooms with private baths in the main building and a motel unit. Some feature four-poster or brass beds. The sitting and dining rooms are semi-formal, and the informal Jasper Murdock tavern serves a light menu from 11:30 AM to closing. Peak-season room rates (September–October) are $60–85 single, $70–95 double, with suites at $95–115.

  Lake House (333-4025), Route 244, Post Mills 05058. Built as an inn in 1870, this comfortable big house, a hundred yards from the shore of Lake Fairlee, has two rooms with private bath, ten shared. Rates for bed and full breakfast $22.50–29.50 per person. Open all year.

  The Stone House Inn (333-9124), North Thetford 05054, is the old farmhouse centerpiece of canoeing inn-to-inn (see *Canoeing*), but you don't need to canoe to get there, because it's right on Route 5. It has six rooms (shared baths) at $21 per person, including continental breakfast. Rooms are available all year.

  Silver Maple Lodge & Cottages (333-4326), RR 1, Box 8, Fairlee 05045. Situated just south of the village on Route 5, Silver Maples was built as a farmhouse in 1855 and has been welcoming travelers for nearly 60 years. Now run by Scott and Sharon Wright, it has nine modestly priced, nicely appointed guest rooms in the lodge and five separate pine-paneled, shaded hideaway cabins. The farmhouse has cheerful sitting rooms, screened porch, and a dining/breakfast room where fresh breads appear with other continental breakfast goodies. Play horseshoes, croquet, badminton or shuffleboard on the lawn, or borrow a bike. Open year-round, rooms in the lodge with shared bath range from $24 single to $34 double; in the cottages with private bath, $34 to $36 single, $36 to $38 double, all including breakfast.

CLASSIC LAKE RESORTS   **The Lake Morey Inn Resort,** Fairlee 05045 (800-423-1211, outside Vermont, otherwise 333-4311), keeps pace with the times, constantly upgrading its attractive guest and conference facilities. Perched on the shore of the sparkling 600-acre Lake Morey, and incorporating an 18-hole golf course where the Vermont Open has been played for 33 years, the traditionally homey inn boasts an indoor pool and fitness facilities as well as outdoor pool and tennis courts.

  Per person, double-occupancy rates (including breakfast and dinner) range from $60 in the Lakeside Cottages to $100 in the Waterlot

Wing and $130 in the newest Terrace Wing. Unlimited golf and tennis packages are available from $79 to $129, MAP. The resort is open all year; convention, winter and spring rates are somewhat lower; "Winter in Vermont" packages cover New Year's Eve, a January Snowmobile Ride-in weekend, a pre-Valentine getaway weekend special, plus specials for Washington's Birthday and St. Patrick's Day. The latter, for example, costs $110 per person for two nights lodging, two dinners, two breakfasts and Sunday brunch.

Rutledge Inn & Cottages (333-9722), Fairlee 05045. Another Lake Morey family resort, with lots of activities. American Plan rates $42–58 per person, double occupancy; European Plan May 31 to June 22, $30 single, $54 double, includes use of boats, canoes, etc.

Eagle's Nest Resort (333-4302/4303), East Lakeshore Road, Fairlee 05045. This modernized-rustic, all-season family lodge on Lake Morey (formerly Bonnie Oaks) offers a wide range of accommo-dations and activities plus conference facilities. There are spacious new rooms overlooking the lake, waterfront cottages with fire-places, two-story townhouses with kitchenettes, secluded cottages by the tennis club, beachside apartments and two-bedroom suites. The lodge itself has a glass-walled dining room, library, and card room. Swimming, boating, canoeing, sailing, ice skating, and fish-ing are all right there, and golf is handy. Rates range generally from $50–95 per person MAP for adults, less for children; write for brochure listing all the variations.

BED & BREAKFASTS **The Village Inn of Bradford** (222-9303), Main Street, Route 5, Bradford 05033. Five rooms in a fine old Federal house, two with private bath $20–30 per person, including continental breakfast.

A Century Past (866-3358), Route 5, Newbury 05051. Four homey rooms with shared baths in a 1790s house; $35 per person with continental breakfast.

The Welches (866-5969), Route 5, Newbury, open their farm house to visitors: 3 bedrooms with 2 shared baths, with the patch-work common room: $28 per couple, continental breakfast; $3 ad-ditional for a big country breakfast.

DINING OUT **D'Artagnan** (603-795-2137) in the Ambrose Publick House, 7 miles north of Hanover on Route 10, Lyme, New Hampshire, is probably the best (and most expensive) restaurant in this stretch of the Upper Valley. Decidedly French in atmosphere, it's open for dinner Wednesday through Sunday and for lunch on Sunday. A typical prix fixe dinner might include a light soup of oysters with curry or halibut quenelles to start, salmon with asparagus or duck breast, house salad and dessert for $25. Reservations essential.

The Norwich Inn (649-1143). Lunch and dinner in the dining or sun room tasty and locally popular. Begin dinner with baked chevre in grape leaves ($5.95), proceed to veal piccatta ($13.50), frog legs provençale ($14.95), mushroom and broccoli Stroganoff ($11.75), or bouillabaisse ($33 for two).

Carpenter Street Restaurant (649-2922), in the historic 1820 House, Main Street, Norwich. Open for dinner Monday through Saturday, this attractive, often crowded restaurant, offers, for example, clams casino ($4.95), Chicken Dijon ($13.95), Veal Allemand ($13.95), or broiled salmon with dill sauce ($15.50).

Italian Gardens Restaurant (649-8824), Main Street, Norwich. The landmark Emerson House contains this "Italian restaurant with the French connection," serving lunch Monday–Friday, dinner daily except Monday. Antipasto ($6.95 for two) could be followed by Chicken Tetrazini with angel hair spaghetti ($10.75), Saltimbocca ($12.50) or Scampi ($13.95).

EATING OUT   The Third Rail (333-9797), Route 5, Fairlee, is a low-key, congenial, and casual place for dinner in one of three different rooms, specializing in fish and Italian dishes at reasonable prices.

Melissa's (333-9735), Route 5, Fairlee (formerly the Kettledrum) is open daily from 11:00 AM, specializing in American cookery, with lunch prices from $3.50 for a BLT to $5.95 for chicken teriyaki. Dinner entrées are from $6–11.95 and include New England pot roast. Open daily May–November, Wednesday–Sunday December–April; closed in March.

Colatina Exit (222-9008), Main Street, Bradford. Dinner daily. A justifiably popular place for its Italian specialties: pizza to veal scallopini ($9.95) and a Sicilian mushroom and clam soup.

The Fairlee Diner, Route 5, Fairlee. Afficionados of road food love this place, a real diner that serves up such tasty daily specials as a cup of vegetable soup, creamed chipped beef on toast, peas, and onions, rich homemade rolls and apple crisp for $4.75.

Happy Hours Restaurant (757-3466), Wells River. This solid, pine-paneled family restaurant in the middle of town is good for breakfast, lunch, and dinner at moderate prices. Fully licensed.

P&H Truck Stop (429-2144), Wells River. Just off I-91, a genuine truckers' haven, complete with showers and hearty grub.

SELECTIVE SHOPPING   Dan & Whit's (649-1602), in the center of Norwich, is a sprawling country store and community nerve and message center that has practically everything on its shelves.

R. Voake, Toymaker (785-2837), route 133, Thetford Center, four miles from Exit 14, I-91. Hardwood toys in traditional and original designs made in the workshop where visitors can watch. Open 10–5 all year, but call ahead.

Pompanoosuc Mills (785-4851), Route 5, East Thetford 05043 is a small but growing outfit that specializes in contemporary hardwood furniture. The white pine, sugar maple, yellow birch, and red oak comes from the surrounding area, black cherry and walnut, from away. Factory outlet prices here on desks, tables, chests, beds, and bunks.

South Road at the Mill and **The Country Duckling** (222-9222) are both in the newly-restored Grist Mill on Main Street in Bradford, the former selling distinctive work by Vermont and New Hampshire craftspeople, the latter antiques and gifts.

Lilac Hedge Bookshop (649-2921), Main Street, Norwich. Pleasant browsing for antiquarians, students, and "Dear Readers" of all kinds; large stock of not-so-new fiction, art, history, and regional titles, well-arranged.

Stave Puzzles (649-1450), Main Street, Norwich. The handcrafted wooden jigsaw puzzles made here are the Rolls-Royces of this pastime, some being cut and put together in multiple-choice fashion. Their prices are impressive, too: a 275-piece, 16-inch Snowflake costs $550. The 900-piece, 18" x 25" Bruegel wedding dance scene can be yours for $1,425. Stave also has some Petite Puzzles of famous paintings in the $140–215 class.

Bush Galleries (649-1075), Main Street, Norwich, is most unusual in that it displays and sells original art work for children's books by some of America's best illustrators. Open daily 12–6.

MEDICAL EMERGENCY Norwich (643-3610); Hanover (603-643-2222); Thetford/Fairlee/Bradford (353-4347). **Dartmouth-Hitchcock Medical Center** (603-646-5000), Hanover.

Central Vermont

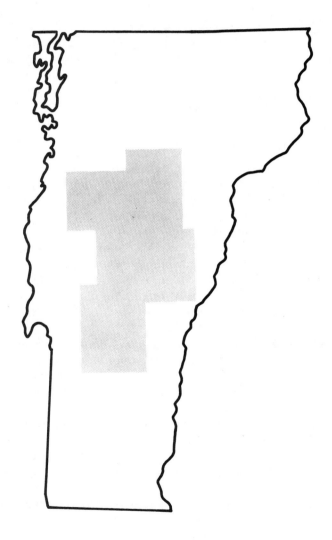

The White River Valley

The White River rises high in the Green Mountains—near Bread Loaf Mountain—to be precise—and rushes down through the villages of Granville, Hancock, and Rochester, keeping company with Route 100 until Stockbridge, where its course dictates a dog leg in the highway. It then turns sharply northeast, carving a narrow valley for Route 107. This section is an especially challenging one for kayakers during spring freshets. Flowing through the village of Gaysville, devastated by the great Flood of 1927, the White River reaches Bethel, where it begins to parallel Route 14 and I–89. Vestiges of an old railroad connecting Rochester to Bethel can occasionally be seen from Routes 100 and 107. As the river continues through the Royaltons and Sharon on its way to the Connecticut River, the input of its three northern branches swells its waters, making it particular rich in swimming and fishing holes. A federal salmon hatchery in Bethel promises to make the White River even more attractive to fishermen in years to come. In the winter, the route from White River Junction to the upper reaches in Granville is heavily trafficked by skiers bound for the Mad River Valley.

GETTING THERE By train: see *Amtrak* in *What's Where.*

By bus: Daily service from Boston, connecting in White River Junction with Connecticut, NYC service; stops in Sharon, South Royalton, Bethel.

TO SEE AND DO **South Royalton Village** 05068. Cupped between a bend in the river and the straight line of Route 14, this is a small but unusually attractive village gathered around an outsized green with an elevated bandstand in the middle. A granite arch at one end of the park recalls the 1780 raid on nearby Royalton by more than 300 Indians commanded by an English lieutenant. Stagecoach inn at one end of the green and a train depot on another recall later eras in village history. Many of the clapboard buildings within eyeshot, including the old inn, have received a new coat of paint and lease on life as part of Vermont's first and only law school, headquartered in a tower-topped old school building. Founded in 1972, accredited in 1975, Vermont Law School now has a full-time faculty of 20 and a student body of 340 men and women from around the country.

Memorabilia from the town's colorful past can be seen in the Royalton Historical Society Museum (763-8830) in the 1840 Town House in Royalton, open by appointment.

Rochester, tucked into a narrow valley between the Green Mountains and the Braintree Range, is almost equidistant between—and just far enough from—Waitsfield to the north and Killington to the south, thereby escaping some of the ravages of resort development. It's still a quiet, unhurried sort of place, with a picturesque village green and reclusive summer population. A drive through the Hollows, situated above the village on the flanks of the Braintree Range, provides superb views and a delightful alternation of field and forest. The largely uninhabited western portion of the town lies within the Green Mountain National Forest and is used by sportsmen, picnickers, and hikers. The Bingo area, in particular, offers swimming holes, abandoned town roads, cellar holes, and Civil War-era cemeteries to poke around in.

Joseph Smith Memorial and Birthplace, Sharon. One mile south of South Royalton, a marker on Route 14 points you up a steep two-mile hill to a complex maintained by the Mormon Church. Open year-round, daylight hours, is a museum devoted to the telling of the life of the founder of the Chruch of Jesus Christ of Latter Day Saints. A 38½-foot high obelisk, cut from Barre granite in 1908, marks the site of the farm in which Joseph Smith was born in 1805 and lived until he was ten. Each foot on the shaft marks a year in the life of the prophet, who was murdered by a mob in Carthage, Illinois, in 1844. There are a total of 360 beautifully maintained acres here, including picnic tables and camp sites.

Bethel National Fish Hatchery, Gaysville (Bethel). Established in 1977 to raise imprint salmon for the Connecticut River restoration program, the hatchery produces 1 million salmon smolts per year.

GREEN MOUNTAIN NATIONAL FOREST   Among the highlights in the Rochester district of the GMNF are the **Long Trail** and the **Texas Falls Recreation Area** (off Route 125), offering 17 picnic sites and an interesting series of cascades hollowed through bedrock. **Chittenden Brook** (off Route 73) is the developed campground near Rochester. A good short hike is from Brandon Gap north six-tenths of a mile to the cliffs of Mount Horrid, where there are views to the east. Because of the abundance of other things to do in this area, be sure to drop in to the district ranger's office on Main Street in Rochester (767-4777 or Box 108, 05767), and ask about their Recreation Opportunity Guides.

BOATING   While most of the White River is navigable in high water, the 20-mile stretch from Rochester to Bethel is especially popular with canoeists, tubers, and kayakers. A good place to put in is at the cement bridge just south of Rochester. Camping available at Rud Memorial Park, 7 miles from Bethel. The river has white water in spring and some steep grades.

FISHING   Trout abound at the junction of Tweed & White Rivers, downstream to Bethel, above Randolph and below Royalton. Fly-fishing enthusiasts find the Bethel area good for large rainbows and brown trout, while below Royalton there are bass, spring walleye, and trout. **Bud's Bait and Tackle Shop,** on Route 14 between Sharon and South Royalton, is a source of fishing tackle and supplies.

HIKING   There are two short nature trails near Granville Gulf. At Moss Glen Falls, the ½-mile loop on the west side of the road is more rugged than the 1-mile loop on the east side.

CROSS-COUNTRY SKIING   **Trail Head Ski Touring Center** (746-8038), Stockbridge. A total of 45 km of trails, 20 km set on flat, easy meadows and surrounding woodlands. Food, rentals, and instruction are available, along with guided tours, mountaineering, inn-to-inn tours.

   Nordic Adventures (767-3996) Box 155, Rochester 05767. Cross-country ski tours are tailored to your needs in the neighboring National Forest and adjacent areas. Day trips, inn-to-inn tours, instruction, and rentals.

LODGING   **Tupper Farm Lodge** (767-4243), Box 43F, Rochester 05767. An 1820s farmhouse on Route 100, known for its friendly atmosphere and good cooking. Roger and Anne Verme can accommodate 18 guests in 10 rooms with 6 baths. They cater to skiers and bicyclists with bountiful breakfasts and candlelit dinners. The swimming hole is across the road in the White River. $38–48 per person MAP double occupancy.

   Harvey's Mountain View Inn (767-4273), Rochester 05767. Situated in the North Hollow area, this spot offers spectacular views of the Green Mountains and the Braintree Range. Don and Maggie Harvey have been specializing in farm-style family vacations for years, and have developed a strong following so book well in advance. Heated pool in summer. Open year-round. $38–42 per person MAP, $26 for children 3–12.

   Liberty Hill Farm (767-3926), Rochester 05767. This is a working, 100-head dairy farm set in a broad meadow off Route 100—a great place for families. Bob and Beth Kennett have two boys (aged 10 and 8 at this writing) and there are plenty of toys, three horses, some chicks and kittens. There are five guest rooms; families can spread into two rooms sharing a sitting room and bath. Meals are served family-style and Beth makes everything from scratch. In summer you can hear the gurgle of the White River (good for trout fishing, and there's a swimming hole) from the porch, and in winter you can ski off into the village across the meadows. $30 per adult,

$20 per child aged 2–12, $10 under that, including a full breakfast and dinner.

Huntington House (767-3926), Rochester 05767. An 1806 house on the Green with four double guest rooms. There is no common room for guests downstairs; instead there is a fully licensed bar and a dining room that's open to the public for dinner. $38–60 per couple B&B.

The Kincroft Inn (767-3734), PO Box 96, Hancock 05734. This is a handsome old home with six guest rooms upstairs, nothing fancy, but cozy spaces to spend the night. Downstairs there is a comfortable living room with an organ and a pleasant dining room; dinner is available by reservation and breakfast is included in $20 per person; the MAP rate is $28. Innkeeper Ken Neitzel makes the furniture and Irene, the knitted goods, quilts, and other handcrafted items on sale in their craft shop.

Hawk North (746-8911), PO Box 529, Route 100, Pittsfield 05762. Hawk homes are nicely designed vacation homes, each hidden away in the woods on sites scattered between Hancock, Rochester, and Pittsfield. There is a health center in the Barn with squash courts and assorted swim ponds. Rates vary wildly with the season. As of this writing the rates are $190 (for a two-bedroom house) to $280 (for a four-bedroom house) per night. Inquire about special packages.

Fox Stand Inn (763-8437), Royalton 05063. An 1818 stage stop on Route 14, established as a restaurant, Jean and Gary Curley now also offer six guest rooms (share two baths) with their own large, comfortable common room. $20–25 per person MAP.

Greenhurst Inn (234-9474), Bethel 05032. A Victorian mansion, it stands alone on the western fringe of Bethel, across Route 107 from the river. There are ten guest rooms, six with private baths; amenities include a tennis court, eight fireplaces, and a library of 4,000 books; $20–40 per person with breakfast.

Poplar Manor (234-9265), Bethel 05032. 2 miles west of Bethel on Route 107, this gracious Federal-era home offers a family suite with two double beds, two rooms with antique double beds and two rooms with twin beds; $20 single, $32 double B&B.

The New Homestead (767-4751), Rochester 05767. This handsome old house on the fringe of town has one room with private bath, four which share three baths. $16–20 per person includes a sumptuous breakfast of homegrown ingredients; not for children.

Loalke Lodge (234-9205), Gaysville 05746. Olive Pratt serves family-style meals in her rustic log cabin that accommodates 20 (shared baths). $28 per person MAP, $15 EP.

The Columns Motor Lodge (763-7040), Sharon 05065. A small, neat motel attached to an old house. Located in Sharon village, just off I–89 and within walking distance of both the general store and Brooksies Family Restaurant, a good waystop. $24–28 double, $3 per extra person, $4 per cot.

Cobble House Inn (234-5458), off Route 107, Gaysville 05746. Set high on a hillside overlooking the White River, the capacious house built by Dr. Sparhawk in 1864 has been transformed into a distinctive, welcoming inn by the Bensons. There are two parlors, framed in natural woods, a dining room, and six period bedrooms with private baths, which go for $70 including full breakfast. Dinner is served ($15.50–20) by reservation only, cooked by Beau Anne Benson, a graduate of the Academie de Cuisine of Bethesda, Maryland.

The Silver Lake House (234-9957), North Road, Barnard 05031. An 1810 gingerbread-trimmed house with three rooms, shared baths, $45–48 including continental breakfast. Open June–November.

Eastwood House (234-9686), Route 107, Bethel. Six rooms, two baths, stenciled walls, handmade quilts, Children welcome but not pets. $30–50 with full breakfast.

CONDOMINIUMS   See Killington/Pico area for **Hawk Mountain Condominiums** in Pittsfield, Stockbridge, and Rochester.

HOSTEL   Schoolhouse Youth Hostel (767-9384), Main Street, Rochester 05767. This 150-year-old former church has long been a favorite of ski and bike groups, but drop-ins, including motorists, are also welcome. Open May 15–October 15; November 15–April 15.

DINING OUT   **Annabelle's** (746-8552), Stockbridge. Located near the junction of Routes 100 and 107, this restaurant offers a memorable dining experience, in part because of its glass-walled light and plant-filled decor but primarily because the entrées are imaginative and well-prepared. Entrées range from $12.75–17.50.

Huntington House (767-3511), On the Park, Rochester. The dining rooms are small and elegant. The hand-written menu offers an interesting choice, ranging from a burrito filled with a spicy mixture of red kidney beans, carrots, peppers, and onions ($7.95) to tenderloin of beef grilled and served with sautéed onions, red and green peppers, and fresh thyme ($13.50). Desserts include rum-cognac caramel custard.

Cobble House Inn (234-5458), Gaysville. The dinner menu changes weekly but includes hot rolls, salad, a pasta or pâté appetizer, and main entrée, which could be veal marsala, veal "Thief Style" (with sage, mushrooms, shallots, roasted pine nuts and wine), each $18.50; chicken stuffed with brie, proscuitto ham with shallots and wine ($16.50) or chicken Normandy, stuffed with apples, maple, spices, cream, and brandy ($15.50).

EATING OUT   Fox Stand (763-8437), Route 14, Royalton. Homegrown beef and farm produce served in a landmark 1818 stagecoach inn. Lunch and dinner, Tuesday–Saturday; Sunday noon buffet.

Brooksies Family Restaurant (763-8407), Sharon. A genuine family restaurant with counter service on one side and a slightly classier addition on the other. The diner opens early for breakfast and has a full lunch and dinner menu. Dinners on the restaurant side can begin with baked stuffed mushroom caps ($2.25) and include roast duckling flambé ($8.95), filet mignon ($9.95), or spaghetti with meatballs ($5.95). Just off I–89, this is a traditional stop for many ski-bound families.

Vermont Sugar House, Inc. Located at the junction of Routes 14 and 107 in Royalton, a restaurant featuring pancakes and local syrup, also Vermont cheese and other products are sold.

Wilson's Diner. Junction of Routes 12 and 107; dependable for breakfast, lunch, supper, homemade bread.

SELECTIVE SHOPPING   **Tontine Press** (763-7092) RFD 2, (East Barnard) South Royalton 05068. Sabra Field's woodcuts of Vermont landscapes and people are among the most popular works of art presently produced in the state. The artist welcomes visitors (call before) in the studio attached to her home in the village of East Barnard— 5 miles up Broad Brook Road from the river road (cross the iron bridge at Tracy's Garage, on Route 14, just west of the general store in Sharon). The bright, distinctive prints are exhibited in the gallery at Tontine where they are available as postcards or full-sized prints either mounted or framed ($30–500).

The Silk Purse and the Sow's Ear (234-5368), Bethel. Located at the junction of Routes 12 and 107, open Monday–Saturday, 9–5. A fine selection of Vermont and New England crafts, including weavings, pottery, kaleidoscopes, and other items; also custom furniture made and repaired.

Creek House Country Gifts, Cook's Cure (234-5609), Routes 107 and 12, Bethel 05032. All sorts of gifts, kitchen gadgets, gourmet seasonings, and a Christmas shop, brightly displayed in a thoughtfully renovated 1836 stage shop (with ballroom).

The Featherstitch Quilter (234-5010), Bethel. Open by appointment only: quilts, soft sculpture, wall hangings.

Emerson Farm Pottery (767-3942), 3 miles south of Rochester on Route 100. In addition to stoneware, porcelain and tiles, and herb wreaths, this working sheep farm also sells raw wool for handspinning and yarn from Vermont sheep.

Frecks, in South Royalton. Open weekdays 9–5, Saturdays 9–12, an old-fashioned family store selling clothes, stationery, toys, and an incredible variety of basics.

Just Vermont Shop, junction of Routes 100 and 125, in the old

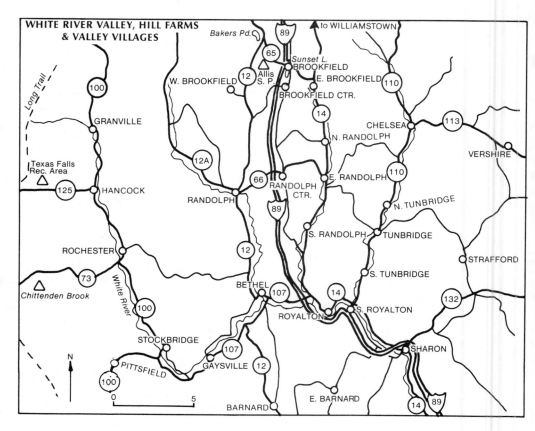

WHITE RIVER VALLEY, HILL FARMS & VALLEY VILLAGES

Hancock Hotel building. Books, cards, preserves, T-shirts, Christmas decorations.

Je-Mel Wood Products, on Route 100 in Granville, manufactures native wood products, and its retail store features its own finished and unfinished woodenware, including "seconds," and other gifts. Open daily; year-round.

Vermont Only Village Store (767-4711), Route 100, Granville. Central Vermont's largest selection of Vermont-made products are housed in an old farmhouse, good for woodenware, toys, crafts, cards, books, clothing, baskets, smoked meats, cheeses, maple products, specialty foods, antiques.

Vermont Wood Specialties, also on Route 100 in Granville, is the state's largest maker of wooden lazy susans, ice buckets, and other items, available at retail and wholesale, including "seconds." Shop open daily; factory on weekends.

MEDICAL EMERGENCY   Bethel, Stockbridge (728-9600); Rochester (767-4211).

Hill Farms and Valley Villages

From Montpelier and Barre four streams and parallel roads thread their way south through four valleys—separated by some of the most remote woodland and uncommercial farm country in all Vermont. Route 110 follows the First Branch of the White River through the classic farming towns of Chelsea and Tunbridge, flanked by high, open country, webbed with back roads on which the sky seems very near. To the east, roads slope gently off this high plateau through the academic communities of Vershire and Strafford. To the west Route 14 and Route 12 both traverse lonely valleys that steepen in spots into gulfs, and are linked by a particularly rewarding road through the photogenic village of Brookfield. Further to the west Route 12A follows the Third Branch of the White River along the base of the majestic Roxbury and Randolph ranges. Three streams and their three accompanying roads (Route 12A, 12, and 14) meet like threads in a string purse in the town of Randolph—itself a combination of hill farms, a gracious old village in Randolph Center, and Randolph itself, the area's commercial center.

GUIDANCE   **Chamber of Commerce** (728-9027), Box 9, Randolph 05060. Phone answered year-round, information center maintained at State Plaza, just off I-89 Exit 4 (next to the Mobil Station). Good for info on the Randolph area. For leads on cottage rentals and details about special events in other communities, check with their respective **Town Clerks**: Brookfield (276-3352), Chelsea (685-4460), Tunbridge (889-5521), Strafford (765-4411). *The White River Valley Herald*, (728-3232), Box 309, Randolph, carries local news and events for all of Orange County.

GETTING THERE   Vermont Transit buses stop just off I-89 in Randolph; otherwise see Montpelier/Barre.

VILLAGES   **Randolph**   Randolph Center is clearly the oldest of the five Randolphs, a lineup of brick and clapboard Federal-era mansions along a main street that was cut unusually wide with the idea that this might be the state capital. Instead it is now a soul-satisfying village in which life centers around Floyds General Store and the nearby complex of Vermont Technical College, grown from the grammar school built here in 1806. A historical marker informs us

Summer days in Rochester bring out the tubers

that musician and school master Justin Morgan of Randolph Center brought a young stallion from Massachusetts to his home here in 1795 (Justin Morgan the man lies buried in the nearby cemetery; the grave of Justin Morgan the horse is marked by a simple stone off Route 110 in Chelsea). Randolph remains an unusually horsey community (see *Horseback Riding*). But with the arrival of the railroad in the mid-nineteenth century population shifted from the Center to the valley three miles west where a red brick Main Street now serves as a shopping, dining, and entertainment center for surrounding villages. Vermont Castings, housed in a nineteenth-century foundry hidden away down under the railroad bridge, claims to manufacture the world's best-selling cast iron woodstoves; its steady stream of customers sustain limited local lodging.

Brookfield   Easily one of the most picturesque four corners in all New England, this sleepy community belies its vivid past. Among its boasts are the state's oldest, continuously operating library (established 1791) and a house in which the Prince of Wales, father of Queen Victoria, not only slept, but received a kick in the pants. The sole survivor of the thirteen mills that once lined Brookfield's Pond is a former pitchfork factory, now the Fork Shop Restaurant. Its view is the sheet of water known variously as Sunset Lake, Clinton and Mirror Pond, traversed by a floating bridge, buoyed by 380 barrels (the lake is too deep to support a pillared span). During the summer much of its traffic stops midway to fish and on the last Saturday in January it is a much-coveted viewing point for one of New England's last ice harvest festivals. A few of the village buildings now form Green Trails, an inn catering to bikers in summer, cross-country skiers in winter. Unfortunately the sound of traffic on I-89 less than a mile from the village breaks the otherwise perfect sense of remoteness. Allis State Park a few miles west offers camping, picnicking, and a sweeping view.

Chelsea   Chelsea has been hailed as one of the few remaining bastions of "Vermont character." It is a town with an unusual survival rate of dairy farms and maple producers. It has a classic, steepled church and courthouse, a brick library and its own bank (since 1822), an abundance of Federal-era homes and not one but two handsome commons. An amazing number of services—post office, restaurant, barber, food stores, sewing shop, and fish and game office—are compressed in a small space. The commercial heart of town revolves around two twin 1818 brick buildings, one housing a general store, the second a pharmacy better known as "Fred's Ice Cream." Fred has been here since 1944 and small cones of his homemade ice cream were selling for 30¢ in 1985; his building itself still bears the inscription "The Old Hood Store." The Hood brothers loom large in town history, one brother having invented a lucrative sarsaparilla promising "instant relief from all ailments of mankind" and another, the Boston-based Hood Milk company. The Orange County Hotel, a substantial hostelry built in 1857, burned in 1917; its site is now occupied by a combination gas station and harness shop. The early nineteenth-century grist mill still stands but a giant wind harp, set high on a Chelsea hill in 1970, tumbled down in 1973, to residents' relief.

Tunbridge   Some 20,000 people jam into this village of 400 souls for four days each September. They come for the World's Fair, said to originate in 1761 when the town received its charter from George III to hold two fairs each year. In fact it dates back to 1867 when it was first sponsored by the Union Agricultural Society. Sited in a grassy, natural bowl by a bend in the river it still has everything an agricultural fair should have: a midway, livestock displays and contests, a Floral Hall, collection of old time relics, dancing, sulky racing, a fiddlers' contest, horse pulls, a grandstand and more. Known as the "Drunkards Reunion" during a prolonged era when it was claimed that anyone found sober after 3 PM was expelled as a nuisance, it is now billed as a family event; drinking is confined to the parking lot and beer hall. The other 361 days of the year Tunbridge dozes, devoid of tourist attractions unless you count its five covered bridges, the fishing hole by the Strafford River, or the photogenic brick Methodist Church in South Tunbridge.

Strafford   East from Tunbridge the road climbs steeply through woods and fields, finally cresting and beginning its downhill run through a new kind of landscape: beautifully restored farms with ponds out back (pools would be too garish), stables and other signs of wealth not evident back on the other side of the mountain. You are in Strafford, a physically beautiful community that has grown greatly in recent decades because it is within an easy commute of Dartmouth College and the Vermont Law School, also within the outstanding bi-state Dresden School District. Aristocratic homes—which include the Gothic Revival mansion built by U.S. Senator Justin Morrill in 1848—are clustered along and below a sloping green above which rises the exquisite white clapboard Town House, built in 1799. South Strafford is a crossroads community with an unusually pleasant general store at its center.

SIGHTS TO SEE   **Justin Morrill Homestead** (828-3226), Strafford. A striking, 17-room Gothic Revival mansion built by Justin Morrill who served as a congressman and senator in Washington from 1855 until 1898 and is best remembered for the Land Grant Colleges Act. Morrill built this as his retirement home but never managed to spend much time here because he kept getting reelected. It is a fascinating Victorian house, well maintained by the Vermont Division for Historic Preservation, free. Open mid-March to mid-October, Wednesday–Sunday, 9:30–5:30.

Floating Bridge at Sunset Lake, Brookfield. First built in 1820 and replaced six times since, this is the only heavily used bridge of its kind in the country and very picturesque.

Marvin Newton House, Ridge Road, Brookfield Center. An eight-room house built in 1835, this displays historical exhibits for the area and serves as the site for weekly lecture programs in summer; open Sundays in July and August, 2–5.

Chandler Music Hall (728-5884), Main Street, Randolph. A fine, acoustically outstanding music hall built in 1907, recently restored to mint condition, open March–December for a concert series, also for weekend appearances by top performers. The Chandler Players, a local amateur group, perform a Broadway show, usually with rave reviews, beginning the July 4 weekend.

Chandler Art Gallery (728-5884), Main Street, Randolph. Part of the Chandler complex, open April–December for changing exhibits; Friday 3–8, Saturday 10–4, Sunday 11–1, and after events in the music hall.

Randolph Historical Society Museum, Randolph. Located upstairs in the Town Hall, this is a fine collection of local memorabilia, with emphasis on railroading; three rooms are furnished in circa 1900 style. Open July 4–October; Sunday 2–4; adults 50¢, children, free.

FARMS TO VISIT   **Vermont Technical College** maintains a demonstration farm in Randolph Center (728-3395). Visitors can tour the sugar house, apple orchard, and dairy barn.

The Reynolds Farm (728-5295), East Randolph, and the **Circle Saw Farm** (728-9082), Randolph, also welcome visitors to tour their dairy operations.

COVERED BRIDGES   There are five covered bridges in the town of Tunbridge: the Mill and Cilley bridges, both south of the junction of Route 110 with the Strafford Road, both built in 1883; the Howe Bridge (1879), east off Route 110 in South Tunbridge; and in North Tunbridge the 1845 Flint Bridge and 1902 Larkin Bridge, both east of Route 110.

In Randolph two Multiple Kingpost bridges, both built in 1904, are just off Route 14 between East Randolph and South Randolph.

In Chelsea there is the Moxley or Guy Bridge, an 1886 Queenpost, east off Route 110.

SUGAR HOUSES   These maple producers all sell syrup from their homes year-round and welcome visitors into their sugar shacks during March production periods.

In Chelsea: **David Gilman** (685-4402), Route 110 north of the village, has a wood-fired evaporator, fed by buckets and pipeline.

In Brookfield: **Robert Churchill** (276-3300), West Street, permits up to six at a time in his sugarhouse.

In Tunbridge: **Roger Ingoldsby** (889-3349), Heffalump Hill, off Spring Road, can accommodate 15–20 visitors at a time.

In Randolph: **Paul Silloway** and **Laurence Boudro** (728-5253), Randolph Center, welcome up to 20 visitors in their sugarhouse, also at other times to view dairy operations.

Armstrong's Cider Mill and Sugarhouse (728-9763), Randolph Center, can fit up to 75 into its operation, which boils off the yield of 4,000 taps.

Maple Valley Sugarbush in Randolph produces syrup from 1,800 taps and the **Howard Wight Family** on Gifford Hill Road, Randolph Center, makes candy as well as syrup.

STATE PARK   **Allis State Park** (276-3175), Brookfield. Open May 30–September 15, a camping area with 22 sites, 4 with lean-tos, no hook-ups, each on a wooded loop road, separate from the picnic area in which you can choose from tables on a windy hilltop or under a pavilion. A hiking trail (see *Hiking*) commands a fine view of the valley northward.

BICYCLING   This is some of the most rewarding biking country in Vermont. **The Brick Store** on the Green, Strafford (765-6941) offers repairs and touring advice but no rentals. Organized bicycle tours frequent Green Trails in Brookfield. Given the scenic North/South roads and choice of East/West links, also the abundance of back roads not shown on the State Highway Map, the potential for do-it-yourself tours is immense.

FISHING   **Baker's Pond** on Route 12 in Brookfield has a parking area and boat launch, for trout; there is a boat access on Road Pond in Williamstown and a canoe access on Sunset Lake in Brookfield, also stocked with trout; the floating bridge is a popular fishing spot.

GOLF   **Montague Course** (728-9172), 9 holes, Randolph.

HIKING   In **Allis State Park**, Brookfield (off Route 12) a 2½ mile trail circles down through meadows, back up through woods. Access is from the fire tower beyond the picnic area; views are exceptional.

HORSEBACK RIDING   **Royalton Stable** at Green Mountain Stock Farm (728-3009), Randolph, off Route 66; trail rides and lessons, Morgan horses.

Room for One More Farm, Thelma and Cliff Murray (728-9426), Randolph. Trail rides.

Foggy Bottom Farm, Braintree (Randolph). Sara Fields boards horses and gives lessons.

PICNICKING   See Allis State Park. Also Brookfield Gulf, Route 12 west of Brookfield: picnic facility, nature trail.

Unique floating bridge on Sunset Lake in Brookfield

SWIMMING   Ask locally about various swimming holes in the first, second and third branches of the White River. In Randolph Center there is a man-made beach, bath house and picnic area. At **Lake Champagne**, there is swimming at a private campground that charges admission.

TENNIS   **Green Mountain Tennis Center**, Green Mountain Stock Farm (729-9122), Randolph.

CROSS-COUNTRY SKIING   **Green Trails Ski Touring Center** (276-3412), Brookfield. 40 km of trails meander around frozen ponds, through woods and over meadows at elevations of 1,132 to 1,572 feet. A ski shop offering rentals and instruction is open weekends, holidays; inn-to-inn tours may also be arranged. Much, but far from all, of this trail system is within earshot of the highway. Fee.

    Green Mountain Sports Center (728-9122), Randolph. More than 20 miles of groomed and tracked trails through woods and meadows; instruction and rentals available from the shop at Three Stallion Inn, marked from Route 66.

OTHER WINTER RECREATION   See Northfield, under Barre/Montpelier for downhill skiing. Sleigh Rides: **Morris Lasell** (433-6290), in Williamstown.

LODGING   **Green Trails Inn** (276-3412), Brookfield 05036. The unusual shape of this inn is explained by its history. It began as a scattering of rooms owned by friends and relatives of Jessie Fiske, a Brookfield native who became one of the first women professors at Rutgers University in New Jersey. The rooms were rented out to her students and associates who spent summers horseback riding and "botanizing" with Miss Fiske. The present inn consists of 15 rooms, some in a 1790s house called "The Lodge." More in "The Inn" and an efficiency unit. $21–31 per person (for a room with private bath) breakfast included; group rates available.

    Three Stallion Inn (728-5575), Randolph 05060. A nineteenth-century farmhouse, part of the 1,300-acre Green Mountain Stock Farm, a former estate which is presently being developed. The inn can accommodate 40 guests in 8 rooms. The property offers tennis, horseback riding, and cross-country skiing; golf is down the road and swimming in a pool or in the White River. Room rates $55 single, $75 double, with private bath; $45–55 shared. Breakfast, lunch and dinner served.

    The Shire Inn (685-3031), Chelsea 05038. An exceptional 1832 Federal-era brick mansion furnished with fine antiques, offering six rooms, four with working fireplaces, all with private bath ($65 to $75 per couple). Rates include breakfast, and dinner can be reserved a day in advance. The new owners, De and Ingeborg Davis, have modernized the kitchen and take pride in what they serve.

Watercourse Way (765-4314), Route 132, South Strafford 05070. Lincoln Alden offers three rooms in his 1850 farmhouse (wide pine floors, a flagstone fireplace). The property backs on the Ompomponoosuc River and there is summer fishing, winter ski touring. $40 per couple including a breakfast of fresh baked muffins and fruit. A cut-your-own Christmas tree farm is an added attraction.

Randolph Motor Inn. This 60-unit motel, at Exit 4 I-89 with conference center, spa, and restaurant, is scheduled to open in the fall of 1988. Room rates are expected to be $45–50.

DINING OUT   **Shire Inn** (685-3031), Chelsea, serves a six-course $25 prix-fixe dinner, by advance reservation and mostly family style, at 7. Marylee Papa, the chef, features regional and other specialties like pumpkin soup, filet mignon with cranberry brandy, and especially rich desserts.

Stone Soup Restaurant (765-4301), Strafford. Open Wednesday–Sunday, 6–11, dinner served until 9:15. Reservations suggested. This elegant little restaurant has acquired a strong following over the past decade. There are daily blackboard specials like maple country spare ribs and roasted Cornish game hen; all entrées are under $10. Owner George Tidman also operates the adjacent ice-cream parlor (open Friday, Saturday, and Sunday) and the art gallery.

August Lion (728-5043), Randolph. Located on Main Street across from Chandler Music Hall in a nineteenth-century house with high tin ceilings, plants, and stained glass. At lunch the menu features soups, salads, and sandwiches, at dinner the specialty is Maine seafood, also veal; most entrées are priced under $15. Closed Tuesdays.

SELECTIVE SHOPPING   **Vermont Castings** (728-0560), Prince Street, Randolph. Even if you are not interested in buying a wood or coal-burning stove, the showrooms are worth a stop. Since its founding in the mid-1970s, the company has established a reputation for cast-iron stoves that keep a fire overnight, ornament the house, and do not take up much space. Their first model was the Defiant, followed by the smaller Vigilant, and even smaller Resolute. At present the plant produces 90 stoves an hour, recycling old engine blocks in the process. Open weekdays 8–5, Saturday 8–4.

Farrow Farm Forge (728-3310), Randolph Center. Fireplace tools, kitchen utensils, a variety of wrought iron pieces forged on the spot by John Farrow.

The Bittersweet (685-4508), Chelsea. Marcia Hammond exhibits and sells the exquisite woven clothing sold in top urban stores.

Fred's Ice Cream, Chelsea. Fred Dickinson presides over his unique pharmacy that stocks an eclectic mix of pharmaceutical items, fishing gear and penny candy. His ice cream is justly famous, made on the spot in a variety of delectable flavors that can be consumed at old-style ice-cream parlor tables. Homey touches include a TV and plants a'plenty.

SPECIAL EVENTS   January (last Saturday): Brookfield—**Ice Harvest Festival**

February: **Strafford Winter Carnival**

March: Sugaring in an exceptional number of open sugarhouses.

May: **Chelsea Arts Day**—flea market covers both greens, music, crafts.

July: July 4 parade in Strafford, a bigger one in Randolph. Randolph Players performance at Chandler Music Hall, Randolph.

July, August: Summer music school, workshops at the Mountain School, Vershire.

Early August: **Huntington Farm Show**, Strafford.

Mid-August: **Stove Owners Outing** at Vermont Castings, Randolph—some 8,000 customers gather from far and near for games, food, and live entertainment; everyone welcome.

September: **World's Fair**, Tunbridge.

October (Columbus Day Weekend):—**Lord's Acre Supper**, sale and auction, Barrett Hall, Strafford.

November: **Annual Hunters' Supper**, Barrett Hall, Strafford.

MEDICAL EMERGENCY   Randolph (728-9600); Chelsea, Tunbridge (685-3610).

Chelsea Health Center (685-4400), Chelsea. **Gifford Memorial Hospital** (728-3366), 44 South Main Street, Randolph.

Killington/Pico Area

Killington is the largest ski resort in the East. It boasts six mountains, the longest ski run and season in the Northeast, the longest gondola line in the country, and the most extensive snowmaking in the world. Just down the road is Pico, "the friendly mountain": older, smaller, family-run and geared. It's said that some 11,000 visitors can bed down within twenty miles of these two ski destinations.

The rugged lay of this land, however, precludes any chance of a real resort village. Killington is the second highest peak in the state: it is flanked by other mountains and faces another majestic range across Sherburne Pass. Although the road through this upland village has been heavily traveled since the settling of Rutland (eleven miles to the west) and Woodstock (fourteen miles to the east) there was never much of anything here. In 1924 an elaborate rustic-style inn was built at the junction of the road (Route 4), the Appalachian Trail and the newly established Long Trail. A winter annex across the road was added in 1938 when Pico installed one of the country's first T-bars. But the lumbering village of Sherburne Center was practically a ghost town in 1957 when Killington began.

Lodging is strung along the four-mile length of Killington's access road and on Route 4 as it slopes ever-downward toward Rutland. The hill village of Chittenden, sequestered six miles up a back road from Route 4, is blessed with a large reservoir and a few inns. Ski lodges are also salted along Route 100 north to the pleasant old town of Pittsfield. Killington's Northeast Passage chairlift from Route 100 also puts the inns of both Woodstock and Ludlow within fourteen miles.

In summer this is exceptional hiking country. The view from the summit of Killington is also accessible via gondola and chairlift. Other things to do include visiting the restored village of Plymouth, birthplace of Calvin Coolidge, and the Alpine Slide at Pico. Killington offers its own tennis and golf packages and a few inns have full resort facilities, a number have tennis courts and swimming pools. There is also summer theater, a series of musical, horsey, and other events, and—because this is still primarily a winter resort area—substantial savings on summer lodging prices.

GUIDANCE   See Lodging for winter reservations services. In summer:
    Killington-Pico Area Association (775-7070), Box 14, Killington, is the source of an excellent guide to lodging. The Association maintains an information booth next to the Lothlorien in the small shopping complex, junction Routes 100 north and 4, open June through Foliage, daily: 10–6. (See also *Lodging*.)

GETTING THERE   By bus: Vermont Transit stops en route from Rutland to White River Junction at Killington Depot, Route 4 near the access road. Most inns will pick up guests.
    By plane: Eastern Express connects both Boston and New York to the Rutland Airport, 21 miles from Killington, where car rentals are available.

GETTING AROUND   **Green Mountain Limousine Service** (773-1313), **Mike's Cab** (773-2328), **Scottie's Taxi** (773-9317). For other limousine services, see Rutland.

TO SEE AND DO   **Plymouth Notch Historic District**, (672-3650), Route 100A, is dedicated to Calvin Coolidge. This tiny white clapboard hamlet is where the thirtieth President of the United States was born in 1872, worked on his father's farm, was awakened 52 years later at 2 AM one August morning to take the oath of office as successor to President Warren G. Harding, and where he is buried. A modest photo-history in the granite Visitors Center summarizes Coolidge's life. The old vehicles in the Wilder Barn, the plainly furnished homestead, the recreated general store which was run by the President's father are all tangible reminders of the simplicity and frugality of the Coolidge aura.
    The Plymouth Cheese Company, founded by the elder Coolidge in 1890 and revived in 1960 by his grandson, John Coolidge (who summers in the village) welcomes visitors year-round (closed Sundays in winter). Cheese is made weekdays and sold on the premises along with Common Crackers. **The Wilder House**, an old village home, serves soups and sandwiches in its pretty dining room and has counter service. Picnic tables available.
    Killington Peak. At 4,241 feet, this is the second highest in the state, said to be the spot where a Reverend Samuel Peters in 1763 may have called the state "Verd monts." The summit restaurant serves also as terminal for the **Killington Gondola** (422-3333), which operates practically nonstop in the ski season, on weekends August through Labor Day and mid-September to Columbus Day (spectacular in foliage); $11 per adult, $7 per child 12 and under. The shorter ride to the summit on the **Chairlifts** runs daily, mid-July to Labor Day and mid-September to Columbus Day, $7 per adult, $5 per child 12 and under.
    Pico Alpine Slide (775-4345), Route 4, Sherburne. Late June–Labor Day, 10–6, 10–5 in slower periods. $3.75 per adult, $2.75

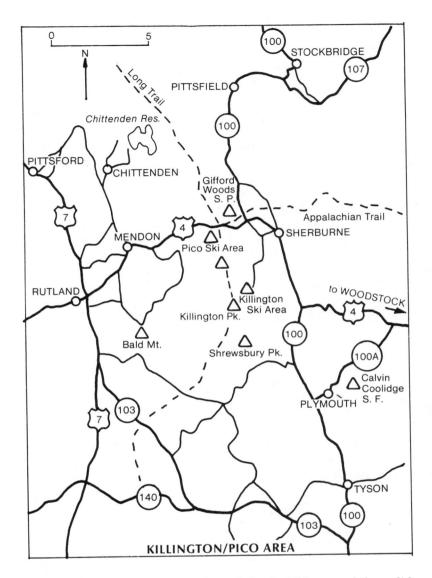

KILLINGTON/PICO AREA

per child, age 6–12. Patrons ride a triple chairlift up and then slide down a total of 3,410 feet; the slide begins near the summit with a sweeping view of the valley to the west. Lunch and snacks are served in the base lodge at the bottom.

Pittsfield National Fish Hatchery (483-6618), Furnace Road. Open 8–4 daily. The Fish and Wildlife Service raises landlocked salmon and lake trout here.

PARKS AND FORESTS   **Calvin Coolidge State Forest** (672-3612), Plymouth 05056. A 16,165-acre preserve that offers 60 campsites including 35 lean-tos, a dump station, picnic area and shelter, hiking, and snow-mobile trails. Killington Peak is actually within this area. Primitive camping is permitted in specified parts of the forest. Facilities are handy to the Calvin Coolidge Birthplace and to the Shrewsbury Peak Trail. $5.50 for a tentsite, $7.50 for a lean-to; 75¢ day use fee for adults, 25¢ for children 3–14.

Gifford Woods State Park (775-5354), Sherburne 05751. 114 acres located ½ mile north of Route 4 on Route 100: 47 campsites including 21 lean-tos, a dump station, picnic area, fishing access to Kent Pond, hiking on the Appalachian Trail, also near Deer Leap; fees same as above.

Camp Plymouth State Park, off Route 100 at Tyson. Beach on Echo Lake picnic area, food concession.

BICYCLING   Vermont Mountain Bike Tours (746-8943), Pittsfield. Tom Yennerell, owner of the Pittsfield Inn, offers tours that range from four hours to five days. Tours are limited to ten riders and are geared to novices as well as experienced bikers. Participants tour dirt roads, abandoned farm lanes, and logging trails. Two-day tours are $159, lodging and meals included.

CANOEING   The Mustard Seed (483-6081), Dam Road, Chittenden, rents and transports canoes to the nearby reservoir.

FISHING   Licenses are available from the Sherburne Town Clerk, River Road, and also from sporting goods stores, and State Park rangers.

Landlocked salmon and trout can be had in Chittenden Reservoir; trout are the catch in Mendon Brook. There also is fishing in Kent Pond, Colton Pond, White River, Tweed River, Ottauquechee River.

GOLF   Killington Resort (422-3333), has its own 18-hole golf course. Weekend clinics and golf packages.

HIKING   Deer Leap Trail off Route 4 behind The Inn at Long Trail is the most popular short hike: a two-hour round-trip trek up a winding, steep path that yields a panoramic view from the top of a 2,490 foot cliff. See *Fifty Hikes in Vermont* (Backcountry Publications, Woodstock 05091).

For details about hiking the Appalachian/Long Trails south from Sherburne Pass (Route 4) and the Long Trail north consult *Guide Book to the Long Trail* published by the Green Mountain Club.

Shrewsbury Peak. A rewarding, five hour round-trip hike begins in the abandoned Northam Picnic Area on the steep, wooded North Shrewsbury Road off Route 100 south of West Bridgewater (See *Fifty Hikes in Vermont* and *Day Hiker's Guide to Vermont*).

Bald Mountain. This 3-mile, 3-hour round-trip hike is in Aiken State Forest, off Stratton Road from Route 4 in Mendon. The blue-blazed circle trail begins opposite the entrance to Tamarack Notch Camp.

Two local inns, **Mountain Meadows Lodge** and **Tulip Tree Inn**, cater to hikers on the "Hike . . . inn to inn" program; for details write: Churchill House Inn, R.D. 3, Brandon, VT 05733. **The Inn at Long Trail** also offers hikers a special rate (see *Lodging*).

HORSEBACK RIDING   Mountain Top Equestrian (483-2311), Chittenden: pony and trail rides.

Hawk Center (672-3811), at Salt Ash, Route 100, in Plymouth offers lessons, trail and hay rides.

TENNIS   Killington School for Tennis (422-3613), Killington. Weekend and five-day, midweek packages are available: Memorial Day to early September, using nine outdoor courts and the Village at Killington.

Cortina Inn (773-3331), Route 4, Killington. A resort with eight outdoor courts, also available to the public.

Summit Lodge (422-3535), Killington Road. Six outdoor courts available to guests, also to the public.

Public Courts are also maintained by the towns of Chittenden and Sherburne.

YEAR-ROUND   Cortina Health Club (773-3331), Cortina Inn, Route 4, Killington. Heated indoor pool, whirlpool, exercise room, saunas, massage, facials, exercise classes. Open daily 6 AM–10 PM. Special short-term memberships.

Summit Lodge Racquet Club (422-3535), Killington Road. Racquetball courts, instruction, racquet rental, volleyball, whirlpool, saunas, massage, ice skating and skate rentals.

Killington Health Club (422-9370), Killington Road just below Snowshed base lodge. Located in the Mountain Green complex, a club with a 54-foot indoor lap pool, Jacuzzi, cardiovascular conditioning room, aerobics classes, steam rooms, sauna, tanning bed, racquetball court, massage, and juice bar. Open 6 AM–11 PM weekdays, 'till 3 AM Friday and Saturday, 7–11 Sundays. Monthly memberships.

CROSS-COUNTRY SKIING   Mountain Meadows Ski Touring Center (775-7077), Killington. One of Vermont's oldest and most serious touring centers set high (1,500-1,800 feet) on the rolling acreage of the Mountain Inn; 40 km total, 25 km set, 2 km lit; instruction, rentals, headlamp and inn-to-inn tours all offered. Free.

Mountain Top Ski Touring Center (483-6089), Chittenden. A total of 91 km of trails (50 km set) begin at Mountain Top Inn, an ideal location at 1,495–2,165 feet with sweeping views of Chittenden Mountain and Reservoir; rentals and lessons plus guided tours, limited snowmaking and a log cabin warming hut in the woods at the intersection of trails; $6 trail use fee.

Trail Head Ski Touring Center (see White River Valley).

Woodstock Ski Touring Center (see Woodstock).

Nordic Adventures (see White River Valley).

DOWNHILL SKIING   Killington Ski Area (422-3333), Killington. Among its boasts, Killington claims twice the uphill capacity of any other ski resort in the East. With six parking lots, six base lodges, six interconnected mountains, an entirely separate novice area, Killington is unquestionably big. Thanks to its three entry points and far-flung network of lifts and trails, the crowds are neatly dispersed throughout the area.

Lifts: 6 double chairs, 4 triple chairs, 5 quads, one 3½-mile gondola.
Trails and slopes: 107.
Vertical drop: 3,060 feet.
Snowmaking: services all 18 lifts from the 6 summits and connecting trails, meaning nearly 7 months of skiing.
Facilities: five cafeterias, five ski rental shops, one mountaintop restaurant, four lounges.
Ski School: Accelerated Ski Method (a refined version of GLM that was developed here); two- and five-day programs available for all levels; novices have their own Snowshed Area; "terrain gardens" have been constructed as learning areas for various abilities.
For Children: Children from 6 months are accepted in the nursery; the combination nursery and ski school program for ages 2 to 12 is available on a drop-in to seven-day basis.
Special Programs: a two-hour Meet the Mountain Tour, geared to varied ability levels, introduces patrons to the full extent of terrain within their ability levels. Offered several times daily, December to mid-April, free with lift ticket.
Rates: $55 adult, $29 child for two days; $60 and $15 during holidays; a wide variety of packages.

Pico (775-4345), Sherburne Pass, Rutland 05701. Dating back to 1937, this is a low-key, friendly, expanding area, which offers plenty of first rate skiing on four mountains.

Lifts: 4 double chairs, 2 triple chairs, 1 T-bar, 1 Poma Lift, 1 Quad.
Vertical drop: 1,967 feet vertical, measured from base to 3,967 foot summit.
Snowmaking: 82% of ski trails.
Facilities: Attractive base lodge, cafeteria, ski and rental shops. Last Run Lounge. New Pico Village, with shops, sport center, restaurant.
Ski School: ATM method, single lessons, two- to seven-day packages geared to all levels. Race camps.
For Children: A nursery Ski School has its own cheerful building, adjacent to the base lodge, children aged 3 and up enroll in a full day program that includes three ski lessons.
Special Programs: Adult Racing Camp available on a five-day basis.
Rates: $29 per adult, $17.50 per child under 15, also half-day and multi-day rates.

ICE SKATING   See **Cortina Inn** and **Summit Lodge** under *Lodging*: Skate rentals and sharpening at **Downdraft Sports** (411-3510), Killington Road. They may be able to direct you to other skating ponds in the area.

LODGING   Killington Lodging Bureau (800-372-2007; 773-0755), 100 Killington Road, Killington 05751, open daily 8 AM–9 PM mid-November through May, in summer, 8 AM–5 PM. The Bureau keeps a tally of vacancies and makes reservations.

    Pico Lodging Service (775-1927 and 800-225-PICO) offers a reservations service for more than 100 local lodging places during ski season.

RESORT INNS   Mountain Meadows Lodge (775-1010), 20 Thundering Brook Road, Killington 05751. The main building is an 1856 barn, nicely converted to include an informal dining room, spacious living room, a BYOB bar and game room. Geared to families year-round, catering to hikers in warm weather months and cross-country skiers in winter, this is a hospitable, thoroughly relaxing kind of lodge. There are 15 guest rooms, including 2 small bunkrooms, all but 3 with private baths. In summer there is a swimming pool, and 100-acre Kent Lake that abuts the property, good for fishing and canoeing as well as swimming; the town tennis courts are just down the road. In winter this is a major ski touring center (See *Cross-Country Skiing*). Winter rates are $42-48 per person MAP in a double room with bath; lower family rates and for longer stays; there are a variety of packages winter and summer, including a rate for those hiking Inn to Inn.

    Cortina Inn (773-3331, 800-451-6108), Killington 05751. This modern luxury lodge in Mendon is designed for the average American family willing to pamper themselves. Innkeepers Bob and Breda Harnish are enterprising hosts who offer a full summer program: tennis with pros using eight courts, a Fitness Center with whirlpools, saunas, exercise machines and indoor pool, a game room, and special hiking, fishing, and picnicking expeditions. Year-round there is candlelight dining (open to the public) in the attractive, formal dining room and Theodore's Pub. The grounds include an extensive nature trail and a touring trail connecting with both the Mountain Meadows and Mountain Top trail networks in winter. Afternoon tea is served in the unusual two-story lobby that has a round hearth in the center and exhibit space for local sculpture and art in the gallery. There are 98 rooms including 60 motel-style guest rooms each with small balconies. In winter $85–115 per person MAP, $60–100 per person without meals, less in summer.

    Mountain Top Inn (483-2311, 800-445-2100), Chittenden 05737. Closed April to Memorial Day and weekends after Columbus Day until mid-December. Set on 500 rolling acres, overlooking Chittenden Reservoir and Mountain, this is one of Vermont's few truly self-contained resorts. Nicely rebuilt in 1977 when fire destroyed the old facility, it has been owned and managed by the Wolfe family for the past 50 years. There are 40 rooms, all with private bath, also a few chalets with maid service. Facilities include a heated pool, tennis, lawn games, sauna, canoeing, horseback riding, chip'n'putt golf and, in winter, a major cross-country skiing center and trails with limited snowmaking: $65–127 per person, MAP.

Summit Lodge (422-3535, 800-635-6343), Killington Road, Killington 05751. This is one of the zaniest inns in Vermont. An antique car festooned with a variety of other unexpected "objects" is parked in the lobby. Facilities include whirlpools, saunas, tennis and racquetball courts, outdoor swimming pool, lawn games and a courtesy bus to Killington lifts. In warm weather months lunch is served in the delightful Gazebo Bar; there is also a year-round dining room and Rathskeller, a library, gift shop, and game room. $88 per person MAP, less with a variety of packages.

Grey Bonnet Inn (775-2537), Killington. A nicely designed modern lodge set off by itself on Route 100 north, just beyond the Route 4 junction. There are 42 standard rooms, each with two double beds and private bath, TV, phone, flowery curtains and spreads. Bill and Barbara Flohr have created plenty of relaxing space in two comfortable, spacious living rooms. Amenities include an indoor pool, sauna, exercise room and cross-country trails that interconnect with Mountain Meadows. In summer there is tennis, an outside pool and walking trails. The dining room is large and inviting with a menu to match. $60–74.50 per person MAP in winter; $49–64 per room in summer.

COUNTRY INNS   **The Inn at Long Trail** (775-7181, 800-325-2540), Killington 05751. This is the first building specifically built to serve as a ski lodge in New England. It began in 1938 as an annex to the splendid summer Inn (see introduction to this section) that burned in 1968. Less elaborate than the original inn, its interior was also designed to resemble the inside of the forest as much as possible and so incorporates parts of trees and boulders. The 22-foot long bar is made from a single log and a protruding toe of the back yard cliff can be seen in both the pub and dining room. The 16 rooms are small but delightful, 14 with private baths, plus 6 two-room suites with their own fireplaces. Dinner is served nightly in the winter, soup and salads during summer and fall from noon until 11 PM. Innkeepers Kyran and Rosemary McGrath have brought this old landmark back to life. There is Guinness on tap and live country and folk music on weekends in the pub, also a hot tub and ample space for relaxing near the hearth. Summer rates are $16–32 with breakfast per person, in winter $60–84 per person MAP, $249–284 per five-day ski week.

Red Clover Inn (775-2290), Woodward Road, Mendon 05701. This gracious country mansion makes an ideal get-away spot for couples. There are 15 guest rooms and an outdoor pool. Chef Bill Noel has won rave reviews for his varied menu. Owners Eliot and Mary Schwartz have refurbished the entire inn. Rates are $50–62 per person MAP, double occupancy.

Tulip Tree Inn (483-6213), Chittenden 05737. This splendid home was built by inventor William Barstow, who retired here after selling his various holdings for $40 million right before the 1929 stock market crash. There is swimming, canoeing, and fishing in the Chittenden Reservoir just down the road and in winter you can cross-country ski in town. Ed and Rosemary McDowell offer eight guest rooms, all with private bath, two with Jacuzzis. There is a big stone fireplace in the paneled den and a comfortable living room, also a hot tub to steep in before cocktails in the library/tap room and a four-course, candlelight dinner. Rates are $44 per person B&B to $60 per person, double occupancy, MAP.

Salt Ash Inn (672-3748), Plymouth 05056. This is one of the few surviving small, ski-oriented inns left. Built as an inn in the 1830s, it has 15 guest rooms, most with private baths and many with bunk space. There is a great little union pub in the former general store that retains the original grocery counter and wooden post office boxes (Calvin Coolidge picked up his mail); there are inviting places to sit around the circular hearth. The new owners are Glen and Ann Stanford; winter rates: $23–28 per person including a big breakfast, $10 per extra person in room; a weekend package is $99–109 per person MAP (two nights); $59 per extra person; dinner is available, priced $6–15; in summer rooms are priced $46–56 including breakfast.

The Vermont Inn (773-9847), Killington 05751. Set high above Route 4 with a fine view of Killington and Pico mountains, this is a nineteenth-century farmhouse with a homey feel to its public rooms and a locally popular restaurant. In summer there is a pool, tennis court and lawn games. There are 16 guest rooms, 12 with private bath; winter prices range from $42–60 per person MAP, $27–45 B&B.

Pittsfield Inn (746-8943), Pittsfield 05762. Located in the center of the village on a handsome green, this double-porched old tavern has acquired a special identity under innkeeper Tom Yennerell, whose keen interests include cooking and mountain biking (see

Bicycling). There are nine newly decorated rooms here, most with shared bath. Summer rates: $45–55 per person MAP or $29–39 including continental breakfast.

Scarborough Inn (746-8141), Stockbridge 05772. Built in 1780, this post and beam farmhouse (formerly the Durkee Farm) has been lovingly restored and is furnished throughout with antiques. There are five bright, large guest rooms, three with private baths, a lovely library and living room. A shade north of most Killington lodging and way south of the Sugarbush area, the house sits on one of the prettier, quieter stretches of Route 100. It's still a short ride back to Killington and there is cross-country skiing within walking distance at Trail Head. Ken and Jean Scarborough are warm hosts, and Ken likes to share his knowledge of the evening sky (through his telescope). Rates are $35–50 per night including breakfast. The suite is more and weekly rates are less. Smoking is not permitted in the bedrooms.

LODGES   The Cascades Lodge (422-3731), Killington Road, Killington 05751. A modern, functional lodge with an indoor pool, bar, whirlpool, exercise room, electronic games and informal dining room serving breakfast and dinner, handy to the Killington lifts. In winter $49–56 per person per night, no meals, in summer $20–40 per room per night; frequented by bus groups.

Trailside Lodge (422-3532), Coffee House Road, Killington 05751. This classic Vermont farmhouse, complete with crazy window, has grown a long way out back. A homey, old-fashioned downhill ski-oriented place with a loyal following. Meals and rooms are family style with bunk beds (sleeping up to nine) or double, all with private bath. There's a hot tub and a big, comfortable living room. The place is geared to groups but families and individuals are welcome. $42.50 per person MAP. Shuttle service is offered to the lifts.

Swiss Farm Lodge (746-8943), Pittsfield 05762. This is a working farm that can accommodate 48 people in basic rooms—14 with private bath and 3 with shared. The Begin family make their own syrup and honey and take pride in making guests welcome. The farm sits right on Route 100 north of Pittsfield, handy to cross-country skiing and not far from Killington. Summer rates are $20 per person B&B, $25–30 in winter MAP. The place is geared to groups but welcomes families.

The Mountain Inn (422-3595), Killington Road, Killington, 05751. This is a modern luxury lodge, three stories high, within walking distance of the Killington lifts. There are 50 rooms, each with private bath and color TV. Facilities include meeting rooms, saunas, game room and nightly entertainment in the lounge; $244 per person MAP for two days in winter; $140 per couple for three days in summer, no meals.

Butternut on the Mountain (422-9242), Box 306, Killington Road, Killington 05751. A large, modern ski lodge with large standard rooms, color TV, indoor pool, whirlpool, fireside library and lounge, game room, laundry facilities, Mrs. Brady's Restaurant; $30 per person with continental breakfast.

CONDOMINIUMS **Killington Village** (442-3101; from Eastern US except Vt.: 800-343-0762). There are a total of 700 condo units in 13 distinct complexes. In summer, with Snowshed Lodge offering dining and theater, this becomes a mini-resort in its own right, nicely land-scaped and filled, primarily, with Florida retirees who have dis-covered the value of long-term rentals (from $589 per month). In summer golf packages are $59 per day, including greens fees and breakfast. Amenities include pools and whirlpools for each condo cluster. In winter you can walk to the lifts, and while the village is not "slope-side" (it's a schlep of shuttle to the base lodge) you are right at the nerve center of Killington's vast lift and trail network here (other "slope-side" lodging tend to be on peripheral trails that require a constant logistics game to locate). Winter rates: $222 for a studio to $998 for a four-bedroom for two nights; inquire about special packages.

Hawk Inn and Mountain Resort (672-3811 or 800-451-4109), Plymouth 05056. Over the past 26 years hundreds of Hawk homes and condominiums have been built on three different properties in the Killington area. The largest of these is the Salt Ash complex, south of the Killington's Northeast Passage entrance on Route 100. Both the free-standing homes (salted away in the woods and on hillsides with splendid views) and the condo units are architec-turally striking and luxuriously furnished and equipped. The newly completed inn is a center piece. In summer there is horseback riding, swimming and boating on Lake Amherst, and tennis. In winter you can appreciate the indoor pool, ice skating, and sleigh rides. Hawk prices vary widely depending on the season and spe-cial packages. Rack rate rates are $130 per night for a two-bedroom condo to $380 for a four-bedroom house; in summer it's $105–260. Four-day, three-night midweek packages begin at $432 for a two-bedroom condo. Three days, two nights at the inn are $330–390 per couple MAP.

Sunrise Mountain Village (422-9293), Killington 05751. Built and managed by Hawk (see above), this dramatically designed condo cluster sits high on the shoulder of one of Killington's six moun-tains. A health center offers whirlpool, sauna, hot tub and exercise equipment. There is also a restaurant and lounge, an ice-skating

The Coolidge homestead in Plymouth reflects simple virtues

pond and cross-country trails. $356 per person for three nights includes lift tickets.

Hogge Penny Motor Inn (773-3200), P.O. Box 914, Rutland 05701. The complex represents the newest concept in resort lodging: well-constructed, attractive units that can be rented as motel rooms or as part of a one- or two-bedroom condominium suite. The buildings command a spectacular view across the Otter Valley to the Taconics and are set well back from Route 4, surrounded by grounds that include tennis courts and pool. Each bedroom has a private bath, two double beds and color TV and each building includes a laundry room. There is a separate restaurant and tavern, also an office staffed round-the-clock. Winter rates are $66–84 per couple, less in summer.

Pico Village Lodging (773-4464). In the past two years 132 slope-side units have mushroomed at the base of Pico, and they are well done: one-bedroom suites in the Village Square; two-, three- and four-bedroom units in the Village with phones, marble-faced fire-places. The sports center offers an indoor pool, Nautilus equipment, aerobics room, Jacuzzis, saunas and lounge. Winter rates: $308 per couple for a two-day weekend, $460 for a five-day ski week, from $140 per weekend in summer.

MOTELS   **Val Roc Motel** (422-3881), Killington 05751. Located on Route 4 east, handy to the Gondola. This is a modern, immaculate motel with 24 units, some kitchenettes and two-bedroom condos; facilities include in-room coffee, tennis, pool, and game room. $24–33 per person in winter, breakfast included.

Farmbrook Motel (672-3621), Route 100A, Plymouth, 05056. An unusually attractive, 12-unit motel 3 miles from Coolidge's birthplace; units include kitchenettes, and the brook-side grounds have outdoor fireplaces, picnic tables. Double: $40–46. Some rooms sleep five.

DINING OUT   **Hemingway's** (422-3886), Killington. Between Linda's eye for detail in the decor and service and Ted's concern for freshness, preparation, and presentation of the food, the Fondulas have created one of the most elegant and rewarding dining experiences in Vermont. Chandeliers, fresh flowers, floor length table linens grace the high-ceilinged main room, while a less formal atmosphere prevails in the garden room and stone-walled wine cellar. Specializing in "regional, classic cuisine" with grilled pheasant with Beaujolais wine, and fillet of beef with morels, entrées hover around $20. Prix fixe dinner at $36, and a per person $50 wine-taster's delight. Closed Tuesdays and Wednesdays.

The Countryman's Pleasure (773-7141), Mendon. Known for Austrian/German specialties: Veal Schnitzel Cordon Bleu, Sauerbraten, goulash, etc. The dining rooms occupy the first floor of a house, just off Route 4, opposite the Hogge Penny. Open 5:30–9 daily. The atmosphere is cozy, informal. Entrées ranging from $8.95–16.95, a gift shop has been added.

Alpine Country Dining (422-3485), Killington Road. Unpromising from the outside but atmospheric within, either in the oak lounge or the cozy, candlelit dining room. Specialties include rack of lamb, veal and duck; Sunday brunch is popular locally. Entrées range from $10.95–18.95.

Red Clover Inn (775-2290), Route 4, Mendon. Set way back from the road in its own grounds, a former summer estate offers a gracious candlelit dining room and nicely prepared entrées like pan-blackened Norwegian salmon and roast duckling with a glaze of port wine, ginger, and homemade sour plum preserve. The menu changes daily, usually featuring two soups, a choice of appetizers like homemade fettuccini with grilled shrimp or sesame scallop sautée, desserts like zabaglione Grand Marnier or chocolate truffle cake. Moderate/expensive.

Churchill's Restaurant (775-3219), Route 4, Mendon. Open for dinner only; closed Mondays. This is a serious steak house featuring filet mignon ($13.95), seafood like baked stuffed shrimp or broiled scampi (both $12.95). All stocks and sauces are prepared daily and entrées come with home baked breads, relish tray, and fixings. A children's menu for age 12 and under is priced $3.25–6.95.

Hawk's River Tavern (672-5300), Route 100 in Plymouth. Open daily from 3 PM. A small, intimate restaurant featuring *nouvelle* American cuisine; entrées are priced $6.95–15.95 and there is a light bar menu.

The Vermont Inn (773-9847), Route 4, Killington. Open for dinner except Mondays. A pleasant inn dining room with a fireplace and a varied menu that might include fresh rainbow trout ($10.95), shrimp fettuccini primavera ($10.95) or Vermont baked veal ($14.95); a children's menu (10 and under) is $5.25.

Grist Mill (422-3970) at the Summit Lodge, Killington Road, Killington. A new building, nicely designed to look like a grist mill that has always stood on Summit Pond (there's a 90-year old water wheel), this is the hot new place to try. The space within is airy and pleasing, dominated by a huge stone hearth. The menu ranges from steaks and veal dishes through grilled swordfish to vegetable stir fry; a child's pasta is $4.95 and entrées run $9.95–12.95.

Cortina Inn, Route 4, Killington. The attractive dining room is open to the public for dinner. The à la carte menu includes specialties like fettuccini with fresh reggianito parmesan, ham julienne and cream ($8.75) as well as grilled loin lamb chops in rosemary oil and garlic ($18.75). Popular Sunday brunch.

Inn at Long Trail (775-7181), Route 4, Killington. The dining room in this unusual inn (see *Lodging*) looks out on the spotlit face of a steep cliff. A limited choice of entrées (sampling for Sunday: roast duck L'Orange, scallops, and beef Provençal) changes every evening; all dinners include salad, bread, and vegetables and run $9.95–13.95; dinner served winter only, in summer soups and salads all day from noon until 4 PM.

EATING OUT   **Little Naples** (773-5663), Route 4, Mendon (an offshoot of the one in Rutland), serves regional Italian cuisine for dinner, except Mondays, in the $12–18.95 range.

Charity's 1887 Saloon Restaurant (422-3800), Killington Road. Open for lunch and dinner, for brunch (11:30–3) on Saturday and Sunday. Hanging plants, Tiffany shades and plenty of gleaming copper and shiny wooden booths, this place is good for a Reuben or vegetarian casserole at lunch, for steak Teriyaki or just onion soup gratinée for dinner, informal, satisfying. Entrées range from $8.95–12.95.

Back Behind Saloon (422-9907), Juntion of Routes 4 and 100 south. Basic American fare: steaks and chicken, generous portions, colorful decor. Entrées range from $9–16.

Casey's Caboose & Whistlestop Saloon (422-3795), Killington Road. Housed in an old railroad car, specializing in barbecues, chops, and "chopped sirloin."

Ripley House Restaurant and Dinner Theater (773-1581), Route 4, Mendon. Vermont's first "dinner theater" opened last year behind Sugar and Spice, the popular roadside pancake house. Skits, songs, drama, and variety acts performed by the Ripley House Troupe of waiters and waitresses punctuate the hearty, moderately priced New England dinners (chowders, Yankee pot roast, native lamb, and veal, seafood, fowl, deep dish apple pie) served around a massive fireplace and hearth where meats are roasted on spits, soup cauldrons hang from cranes, and Dutch ovens hold freshly baked breads. A "family restaurant" with a wide range of alcohol-free beverages. Open 5-10 daily.

Maple Sugar & Vermont Spice (773-7832), Route 4, Mendon. A rather unique Pancake House Restaurant housed in a large replica of a classic sugar house and surrounded by a 50-acre sugarbush. Besides dining on a variety of pancake, egg, and omelette dishes, soups and sandwiches, you can watch both maple candy and cheese being made 3-4 days a week (usually weekends). Open 7–3 daily, gift shop.

Blanche & Bill's Pancake House, Route 4, 1 mile east of junction with Route 100 south. "Serving breakfast anytime," 7 AM–2 PM, closed Monday and Tuesday. Blanche has been serving reasonably priced meals in the front rooms of her small house by the side of the road for over ten years.

Marge & John's Country Breakfast, Route 4, Mendon. Closed Tuesday, otherwise open 7 AM–3 PM. Specializing in fresh sourdough bread French toast. Another roadside house with reasonable prices.

APRÉS SKI   **The Wobbly Barn** (422-3392), Killington Road. A steakhouse (dinner: 5–11) with plenty of music, dancing, blues, rock'n'roll; ski season.

The Night Spot (422-9885), Killington Road. Live entertainment.

Pickle Barrel (422-3035), Killington Road. "Some of the finest rock'n'roll bands in the East."

SELECTIVE SHOPPING   Spread along Route 4 at the intersection of the Killington access road and Route 100 is a nice variety of shops all within walking distance of each other: **Bill's Country Store, Southworths** (a wide selection of sports clothing and ski and tennis equipment). **Lothlorien** (Vermont products and crafts, fine gifts and souvenirs, selected wines and foods), and **Mountain Wine & Cheese Shop** (State Liquor Store). Across the road is the **Ski Shack,** a discount outlet for national brand sports wear. It's open year-round, seven days a week, 8–5:30.

SPECIAL EVENTS   January, February, March: frequent alpine ski races for all ages at Killington, Pico.

May 1: **Annual May Day Fun Slalom**—limited to first 150 entrants.

Late May: **Annual Antiques Show**. A three-day event at Pico Base Lodge, Route 4.

June 1: **Annual June 1st Fun Slalom**—a three-day event at Pico.

July 4: Calvin Coolidge Birthday memorial, Plymouth.

July: **Killington Mountain Equestrian Festival**, two-week competition including North American Hunting and Jumping Championships.

July and August: **Killington Music Festival**

July–mid-October: Aerial Chairlift and gondola rides at Killington, Killington School for Tennis.

July, August: Killington Playhouse.

August: **Annual Antiques, Craft, Sportsman's Shows**, Killington.

Mid-July to mid-September: Hanson Carrol School of Photography, two-day weekends.

September: **Taste of Vermont**, Killington Resort, competing restaurants prepare a public feast.

MEDICAL EMERGENCY   773-6252. **Rutland Hospital** (775-7111), 160 Allen Street, Rutland.

Sugarbush/Mad River Valley

There were farms and mills in this magnificent valley before Mad River Glen began attracting skiers in 1948, but the unique look and lifestyle of this community has evolved in the past thirty years, spawned by the three ski areas, just as truly as earlier villages took shape around their greens. Early patrons at Mad River built themselves New England's first trail-side homes and in the early 1960s Sugarbush built the region's first bottom-of-the-lift village. By the mid-1960s new homes were being built each year—many in unconventional shapes by young architects eager to test new theories of solar heating and cluster housing. For their own enjoyment, the settlers—most of them sophisticated refugees from Megalopolis—formed polo and fox hunt groups, built an outstanding arts center, an airport and other amenities. For their livelihoods they opened some delightful inns and two unusually tasteful shopping centers full of specialty shops. The shops plus a choice of restaurants are in the village of Waitsfield at the junction of roads to the three ski areas. In the village of Warren, five miles south, life revolves around a general store featuring French bread, fine wines, and deli salads.

As for skiing, the Valley rivals all comers. Between Sugarbush, Mountain Ellen (alias Sugarbush North, Glen Ellen, before that) and Mad River Glen, there are a total of twenty lifts servicing ninety-nine trails. There are also five ski touring centers with a total of 260 km of cross-country trails. In summer and fall there is hiking on the Long Trail as it traverses some of the highest peaks in the Green Mountains (Mountain Abraham, Lincoln Peak, and Mountain Ellen are all more than 4,000 feet high). There is soaring above the seven-mile wide valley, fishing and swimming in the Mad River itself.

GUIDANCE **Sugarbush Resort Association (SRA)** (496-3409), Box 173, Waitsfield 05673. A walk-in visitors center in the Village Square Shopping Center is open year-round (closed weekends in summer), 10 AM–4 PM. Write for the SRA free guides and lodging listings.

GETTING THERE   By bus: Waterbury is the nearest Vermont Transit stop.
By air: Carriers serving Burlington (55 miles away) include US Air, Continental, and Brockway Air. Eastern Express serves Montpelier (21 miles north) from Boston.

GETTING AROUND   During ski season the Sugarbush Shuttle Bus offers free rides from the inns along its access road to lifts at Sugarbush and Sugarbush North. Many inns have their own transport to the lifts and Sugarbush Village Real Estate offers yet another free ride. None of these, however, go as far as Route 100, let alone into Waitsfield.

"Vermont with Lamont" (496-6535), PO Box 295, Waitsfield 05673. Mark Lamont arranges day, half-day or longer guided sightseeing or "adventure" tours for visiting conference or private groups to mountain tops, sugar houses, Morgan horse farms, swimming holes, and specialty shops; or on sailing cruises, canoe treks, sledding, skiing, or snowshoeing, (depending on the season). He also offers several "Adventure Vacations" abroad.

Taxis: **Mad River Transit Co**. in Waitsfield (1-800-451-4580 from outside Vermont, otherwise: 496-4279) offers car rentals and a 14-passenger van as well as taxi service. **Alpine Taxi** (244-8697).

TO SEE AND DO   **Warren Village**. The population of Warren has doubled since the development of Sugarbush within its borders. Still, it's just 950 people. And the village of Warren, set west of Route 100, is a delightful place to stroll any time of year. In addition to the store (see introduction) there is the **Parade Gallery** (original paintings, graphic art, and sculpture; open daily), **Village Pottery**, a classic little cemetery, and a library/town hall in which you can pick up used books for 10¢; library hours are Monday 1–4, Wednesday 10–8; Friday and Saturday 10–4. The river tumbles through the middle of the village on through a swimming hole and under a covered bridge.

Prickly Mountain. A very unusual cluster of homes developed by architect David Cellars in 1966.

A Covered Bridge and Round Barn. In Waitsfield, a 113-foot-long covered bridge, built in 1833, leads to the Warren Road, a scenic drive that brings you past the Joslin Round Barn—a beauty—and the last of four round barns that once graced the valley.

The Valley Players (496-3485), an amateur theater company, produces four plays a year in the Odd Fellows Hall just north of Waitsfield Village, Route 100.

Phantom Theater (496-5207) Box 341, Warren. Plays at the Odd Fellows Hall, Monday theater workshops for adults in July and August (at the Warren Town Hall) and summer classes in theater skills for children (visitors welcome).

BICYCLING   Rentals are available from **Inverness Sports** (496-3343) and mountain bikes from **Clearwater** (496-2708), Route 100, Waitsfield.

CANOEING AND WINDSURFING   **Canoe Vermont!** (496-2409), Waitsfield. Sponsors weekend, five-day and seven-day canoe trips on Otter Creek, and the Batten Kill and Connecticut River.

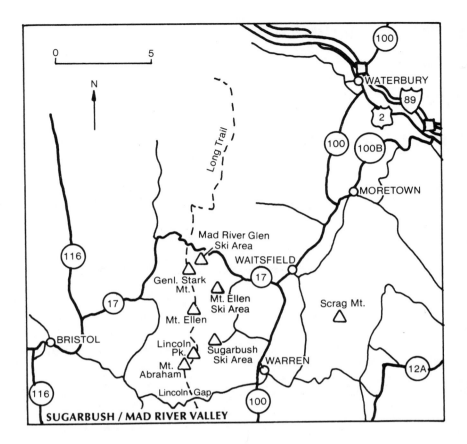

SUGARBUSH / MAD RIVER VALLEY

Clearwater Canoe (496-2708) offers windsurfing rentals and lessons, learn-to-canoe and kayak programs, also a children's day program (age 9-13) and a five-day wilderness camp program for 9-13 years old. Canoes and paddleboats are on hand at Blueberry Lake.

GOLF **Sugarbush Golf Club** (583-2722), Warren, at the Sugarbush Inn. An 18-hole, Robert Trent Jones Championship course, PGA rate 42, par 72; per person weekdays $15, weekends, $18; carts, lessons available.

HIKING **The Long Trail**. For details—which you should have before attempting an actual hike—consult the *Long Trail Guide* or *Fifty Hikes in Vermont*. **Mount Abraham** can be reached from the Warren-Lincoln Highway 4.7 miles west of Route 100; since this is one of the most popular day hikes on the entire trail, be advised to come early (parking is limited). A 5-mile round-trip trail leads to the summit (4,052 feet) with views west across Lake Champlain to the Adirondacks, south as far as Killington Peak, north as far as Belvidere Mountain.

Lincoln to Appalachian Gap. From Mount Abraham north to

Lincoln Peak to Mountain Ellen (4,135 feet); 11.1 miles, much of it above tree line; the Battell Shelter and Glen Ellen Lodge, maintained by the Green Mountain Club, offers bunkspace.

General Stark Mountain. A hike up to the 3,600-foot summit, 2.6 miles south of the Long Trail access at Route 17. In the 1940s when Mad River Glen opened, the road west from Waitsfield stopped here. There is an excellent view from Stark's Nest; the Theron Dean Shelter has bunks for four to six hikers, 1.4 miles west of Mad River Glen.

Scrag Mountain, Waitsfield (see *Day Hiker's Guide to Vermont* and *Fifty Hikes in Vermont*). From Waitsfield Village take the East Warren Road through the covered bridge but bear left at the fork, turn right onto Cross Road and across the next intersection to parking area. The 3-hour, 4.2-mile round-trip hike is wooded but the summit view of the Green Mountains across the valley is extraordinary.

HORSEBACK RIDING   **Holly Ward Barn** (496-3016) north of the four corners on the East Warren Road. English instruction, polo clinics and trail rides.

Applewood Riding Center (496-8896), Warren. Instruction, heated indoor riding area.

SOARING   **Sugarbush Airport** (496-2290), Warren. Respected as one of the East's prime spots for riding thermal and ridge waves; glider lessons, rides, food; open daily 9–5.

SWIMMING   Many condominiums and inns have their own pools. **The Sugarbush Sports Center** (see *Year-Round*) features a large, L-shaped outdoor pool with adjacent changing facilities, cafe, bar and Jacuzzi. In the vicinity of Warren, the Mad River becomes a series of dramatic falls and whirlpools cascading through a gorge. The most secluded place is by the **Bobbin Mill** (the first right off Route 100 after the Lincoln Gap Road, heading south); park by the gravel pit and follow the path through the pines to a series of pools, all icy cold. Ask locally about the best spot for skinny dipping. The best area for kids is just south of Waitsfield off Route 100: there is a public parking area, small beach, a rock for jumping off, and muddy downstream clay for children to coat themselves with. Also, **Blueberry Lake** (496-6687) in Warren.

FISHING   **Northland Trout Tours** (496-6572) is a local guide service specializing in the Mad River, Dog River, the Winooski, and Lamoille. Half-day trips available.

TENNIS   **The Bridges** (see *Lodging*) and the **Sugarbush Sports Center** (see *Year-Round*) both offer five-day clinics in conjunction with lodging; many local inns also have their own courts. **The Alpine Inn** becomes a Windridge Tennis Camp late June–early August, a summer camp for youngsters; before and after this period the inn's ten plexi-paved courts are open to the public at reasonable rates.

YEAR-ROUND Sugarbush Sports Center (583-2391), Sugarbush Village, Warren. An outstanding complex of pools, outdoor and indoor jacuzzi, whirlpool, sauna, steamroom, exercise room, indoor squash, tennis, and racquetball courts, massage room, hairstyling salon and restaurant.

CROSS-COUNTRY SKIING North Wind Touring (244-5726/496-5571), P.O. Box 46, Waitsfield 05673. Clif and Dae Todd lead inn-to-inn ski and snowshoe tours around central and northern Vermont from January to early April. Tours range in duration from weekends ($210) to five days ($525); prices include all meals, double-occupancy lodging, trail fees, taxes and gratuities. Round-trip transportation from airport, bus or train terminals is available, as are ski rentals.

Tucker Hill Ski Touring Center (496-3202), Waitsfield 05673. A network of 45 km of trails at elevations of 1,000 to 1,900 feet, radiate from the center located at the back of the Tucker Hill Inn, open daily 8:30–5. Features young peoples' rental and retail equipment.

Ole's Cross-Country Center (496-3430), Warren 05674. Sited at the airport on the East Warren plateau at altitudes of 1,200–2,450 feet: ten trails overlooking the valley, half wooded, half open, totaling 75 km, 32 km of them set. Change rooms and showers as well as food, sales, rentals, and instruction are available at the airport building; guided day tours and waxing clinics also offered.

Sugarbush Inn Rossignol Touring Center (582-2301), Sugarbush Access, Warren. Open, rolling terrain on a 10 km golf course trail is good for novices and ski racers. More demanding trails—a total of 60 km set, 40 km tracked, wind through hardwoods and high meadows at elevations of 1,300 to 1,900 feet; instruction, change rooms, showers, telemark instruction and guided tours, all available along with equipment sales and rentals.

Blueberry Lake Cross-Country Ski Center (496-6687), Plunkton Road, Warren. On the scenic, east side of the valley, a total of 75 km of trails, 44 machine tracked; instruction, rental, retail, repair, cafe, lodging, day care, change rooms, showers, guided tours.

Local trails: Puddledock in Granville Gulf State Reservation on Route 100, south of Warren: 3.5 miles of ungroomed trails marked with red, metal triangles; map available at the registration box. **The Long Trail**, 5.7 miles from the summit of Lincoln Peak to the top of Mad River Glen, should be attempted only by expert skiers using proper equipment, guided by instructors from a local touring center.

DOWNHILL SKIING Sugarbush Ski Areas (information: 583-2381; ski report: 583-SNOW; Lodging: 800-451-5030). Two separate trail systems cascade down from two big-league peaks (3,975 foot Lincoln Peak and 4,038 foot Mountain Ellen), separated by an undeveloped swatch of mountain, the Slide Brook Area. **Sugarbush** itself opened in 1958 as New England's first destination ski resort, complete with gondola, village shops, restaurants, and condominiums. It immediately acquired the following it wanted: wealthy "cafe society" New Yorkers, many of whom invested in trailside condos and still form a core clientele. Sugarbush has recently renamed its original area **South Basin**.

The second area, opened as **Glen Ellen** in 1963 and known as Sugarbush North for the decade before 1987, is now **Mountain Ellen**. Its **Glen House Restaurant** at 3,000 feet is a staging ground for easy trails off the top and is a favored spot for sunning. The two areas are not connected by any trail but a shuttle bus provides frequent transfers.

Lifts: 16 lifts, including 4 Pomas, 9 double and 3 triple chair lifts

Trails: 68 (This is down from 81 in our last edition but it adds up to the same amount of skiing.)

Vertical drop: 2,600 feet

Snowmaking: 56% of trails

Facilities: cafeterias, lounges, ski shops, rentals, restaurants, sports center, condominiums

Ski school: GLM, ATM

For children: nursery from infancy, special morning and afternoon programs

Rates: $32 per adult, basic, less for two days and for juniors.

Mad River Glen (496-3551), Waitsfield 05673. One of New England's oldest major ski areas, still retaining its enviable reputation as one of the most challenging yet friendliest places to ski. Its vertical drop puts it in the big league yet the number of lifts and trails remain consciously limited; all trails funnel into the central base lodge area, the better for families—many of whom are now third generation Mad River skiers—to meet.

Lifts: 4 chairs

Trails and slopes: 30; expert, intermediate, novice

Vertical drop: 2,000 feet

Snowmaking: 15% on novice slope and base areas

Facilities: Base lodge cafeteria and pub, also the Birdcage, halfway up the mountain, serving sandwiches, drinks; ski shop, rentals

Ski school: American Teaching Method (ATM)

For children: Cricket Club Nursery for three-months—toddlers, SKIWEE (4-12) Junior Racing Program and Junior Mogul Program.

Rates: $20 per adult, $14 junior (14 and under), special half-day, multi-day, senior citizen and student rates. $22 per adult, weekends.

ICE SKATING   **Sugarbush Inn** offers skating on flooded tennis courts at $3 per person. There is free skating on the river, inquire locally.

SLEIGH RIDES   Applewood Riding Center (496-8896), Warren. **Lareau Farm County Inn** (496-4949).

LODGING   **Sugarbush Reservations** (800-537-8427), Warren 05674, offers a ski season lodging service linked to 50 local inns and condos. Request its free *Directory* pamphlet.

Sugarbush Inn & Club Sugarbush Condominiums (800-451-4320; 583-2301), Warren 05674. A self-contained resort complex has been built around this semi-formal inn by the Young family, Bermudians who also own the Lantana Colony Club on their native island. There are comfortable accommodations at the inn and in more than 60 condo units, plus a sports center with an indoor pool, Jacuzzi, indoor and outdoor tennis courts and a conference center, as well as an 18-hole golf course. Cross-country skiing and ice skating available in winter. Special packages include golf, tennis, and ski weekends and five-day sojourns. Winter rates: $110–140 per room, $198–220 per couple including lifts and meals; $160 for one-bedroom, $310 for three-bedroom condos. Much less in summer.

Madbush Resort (495-3966; 451-4580, ext. 66), Waitsfield 05673. This lodge has an attractive dining room and sitting rooms, a game room, BYOB bar with setups and après ski snacks, a hot tub, and sauna. The 22 rooms are motel-style units with TVs and phones, 8 lofts for families; there are also one-bedroom apartments, each sleeping six. In warm weather there is swimming in the pond (good for winter skating). $60–65 per room in summer and fall.

COUNTRY INNS AND LODGES   **Millbrook Lodge** (492-2405), Route 17, Waitsfield 05673. From the road, this nineteenth-century farmhouse doesn't look particularly promising but once inside you know you have found a gem. You enter through the warming room, actually warmed by a woodstove in winter. The living rooms invite you to sit down. The heart of the ground floor is, however, the dining room, well known locally as one of the best places to dine in the valley. Each of the seven guest rooms is different enough to deserve its own name; all have stenciled walls, antique beds and bureaus. A ski lodge since 1948, Millbrook has become a true country inn under ownership by Joan and Thom Gorman. $44–60 per person MAP, $130–240 per five-day ski week, cheaper in summer. Children are welcome, special rates under age 16.

The Sugartree Inn (583-3211), Sugarbush Access Road, Warren 05674. This is an intimate, personal place with more than a touch of fantasy. It's a modern ski lodge but Howard and Janice Chapman have done their utmost to create a country inn atmosphere. The Virginia-born couple were living in the mid-West when the Vermont bug bit them, and they have created the kind of New England atmosphere that the rest of the country expects to find. All ten rooms have quilts that Janice has sewn and many have canopy beds (all have private baths). The TV and fireplace are in the living room, and there are just four tables in the adjoining dining room; the idea is to bring guests together. At breakfast your waffles may be topped with fruit and whipped cream. $35–46 per person B&B.

The Lareau Farm Country Inn (496-4949), Route 100, Waitsfield 05673. A 150-year-old farmhouse set in a wide meadow by Route 100 offers six guest rooms, all with private baths, all nicely furnished with antique beds, quilts, and rockers. Dan and Susan Easley are warm hosts and guests feel right at home, checking in via the kitchen and settling into the living room. There are three horses (sleigh rides are offered in winter), five children, four dogs, and two cats in residence and 45 acres outside, good for cross-country skiing. Dan is happy to lead a tour for four or more guests. $40–45 per person includes a full breakfast; $30–35 in summer.

Knoll Farm Country Inn (496-3939), Bragg Hill Road, Waitsfield 05673. This genuine, working farm sits high above the Valley but handy to everything, a half mile up off Route 17 near its junction with Route 100. The snug, welcoming farmhouse can accommodate just 12 guests and it's a good idea to reserve far in advance; Ann Day Heinzerling has acquired a strong following since she began taking in skiers in 1957. Abundant meals are served family-style prepared from food raised on the 150-acre property. There is a classic old barn out back and animals include Scotch Highland cattle and horses. The hosts are up early with barn chores and guests are welcome to get in a ski tour, some snowshoeing, or hiking before breakfast. In warm weather there is horseback riding and swimming in the 14-foot deep pond. Children over 6 are welcome. Conferences on social issues are scheduled for some weeks but other guests are welcome. Horseback riding is included in $84 per person MAP, double occupancy for a two-day weekend, $170 for five days, $230 for seven days. Open May–November.

Round Barn Farm (496-2276), East Warren Road, Waitsfield, is a landmark because of the remarkable round barn built in 1910, one of the few remaining. Guests have a wicker-filled solarium, stone terrace, and book-lined library, all recently decorated by Jack, Doreen and Anne Marie Simko. The six rooms range from $65 for the Jones, with a double spool bed and shower, to the Barnard with canopied queen, Jacuzzi and shower at $95, and the Joslin with a canopied king bed, Jacuzzi and shower at $110. Prices include "gourmet breakfast, game room with TV and pool table, workout room, après ski edibles, Bach, Vivaldi and goodnite [sic] chocolates." No smoking.

Mountain View Inn (496-2426), Box 69, Waitsfield 05673. A typical Vermont house by Route 17 that can accommodate 12 in nicely decorated rooms. Guests gather around the wood-burning stove in the living room and around the long harvest table for dinner. Fred and Suzy Spencer are genial hosts. Handy to Sugarbush North and Mad River Glen, the inn's ski-touring trails tie into the extensive local network. $48–60 per person MAP in winter.

Waitsfield Inn (496-3979), Waitsfield Village 05673. A Federal-era parsonage with 11 rooms upstairs over the public dining room and in the rambling posterior, also 6 new rooms in the upper levels of the attached barn and woodshed. Owned by Bill and Judy Mapp, who pride themselves on the cuisine and atmosphere. $50–75 per person MAP.

Pitcher Inn (496-3831), Warren Village 05674. This is a find, and more than for breakfast (see *Eating Out*). When this traditional-style guest house came up for sale a few years ago, a group of local people chipped in to buy and to create an authentically welcoming place. Jenny Duel is the friendly innkeeper. There are 12 bright, comfortable rooms, sleeping a total of 20 people. While breakfast is the big thing, dinner is also served on Thursdays by reservation. The location is great, right in the middle of a traditional village, handy to cross-country ski trails and summer horseback riding and swimming. $35 per person B&B in winter.

Beaver Pond Farm (583-2861), Warren 05674. This traditional Vermont farmhouse has a superb setting on a hillside overlooking a beaver pond and a rolling expanse of golf course. The Hansens have created an elegant little inn with a formal dining room and attractive living room with a BYOB bar in one corner. In summer there are tables on the large deck, and in winter you can ski right out the front door. Rates include a full breakfast. $37–40 per person per night; a minimum of two days is required in winter; 10 percent discount on five days, midweek.

The Christmas Tree Inn (583-2211), Box 23, Sugarbush Access Road, Warren 05674. This is a modern ski lodge with a nice feel and reasonable prices. There are 12 inn rooms, $60 per room in winter, $45 in summer, plus 24 new one-bedroom condominiums, each accommodating two to four people, $90 per unit in summer, $100–120 in winter.

The White Horse Inn (496-2476), Waitsfield 05673. One of the few lodging places located on German Flats Road connecting Sugarbush and Mountain Ellen, also handy to Mad River Glen. This is a modern ski lodge with 28 rooms, all with private bath, geared to groups. $25–45 per person B&B.

South Hollow Farm (496-5627), R.R.1, Box 287, Warren 05674. Off by itself on a back road this 1837 farmhouse (accommodating six guests) has been completely restored and renovated, furnished with antiques. $45 per couple, fine breakfast.

The Schultzes' Lodge (496-2366), Moretown 05660. Located on Route 100, 5 miles north of Waitsfield, this is an exceptionally friendly, homey place with six guest rooms, four bunk-style, and three doubles that can be mixed and matched as family suites. It is an ideal place for children since John and Annette Schultz have two of their own; $25 per person including breakfast in winter, $20 with breakfast in summer; cross-country skiing out the back door; available for groups of up to 20 who want to do their own cooking.

Wait Farm Motor Inn (496-2033), Waitsfield 05673. Eight motel units, four with kitchenettes, also two double rooms and one bunk-room in the main house comprise this friendly family business; $25–40 per person.

Carpenter Farm (496-3433), Box 2710, Meadow Road, Moretown 05660. Dorothy and George Carpenter have been juggling guests and farm chores for 20 years. Their working dairy farm is off by itself up a back road a few miles north of Waitsfield: nothing elegant, but unquestionably hospitable, with a range of rooms (private bath, semi and dorms) $30–40 per person per day MAP.

Tucker Hill Lodge (496-3983), RFD 1, Box 147, Waitsfield 05673. A new home built along traditional lines with a fieldstone hearth in the inviting living room and 20 nicely furnished guest rooms, 11 with private baths, and puffy quilts. Handy to both Waitsfield Village and Sugarbush North, it has an away-from-it-all feeling enhanced by an extensive cross-country ski trail network up into the woods. $41–59 per person, MAP. Being part of a chain, now, has made the place impersonal.

CONDOMINIUMS   **Sugarbush Hotel and Sugarbush Village Condominiums** (583-3000, 800-451-4326). At the base of the lifts some 400 units have been developed by a half dozen different groups. They come in a range of sizes, shapes and prices, selling for between $65,000 and $216,000 and are all managed through Sugarbush Village Real Estate. Look for special packages that include use of the adjacent Sports Center with the rental, especially in summer when the Center offers the only convenient tennis and pool for this complex. Units vary from one-bedroom units in the former Hotel Sugarbush and the adjacent, five-story Village Gate cluster to four-bedroom condominiums and townhouses in Unihab; in the three-bedroom Forum complex each unit has its own garage, three bedrooms, two living rooms—each with a fireplace—and a washer/dryer. Rates are from $115 per couple in the hotel, $140–290 in condos, less for longer stays and in summer.

The Battleground (496-2288/3034), Fayston (Waitsfield) 05673. An unusually attractive cluster of condominiums, each designed to face the brook or a piece of greenery, backing into each other, thus preserving most of the 60 acres for walking or ski touring (the area's 60 km network of trails is accessible); in summer there is a pool, tennis, paddle tennis, and a play area for children; Mad River Glen is just up Route 17; summer rates nightly (two-night minimum) for two, three, or four bedroom units are $110–160, cheaper by the week or month. Winter rentals are $170–230 per night, $660–880 weekly, also available monthly.

South Village (583-2000, 800-451-4574), RR 1, Box 300B, Warren 05674. An entirely separate development from the Sugarbush Village condo clusters, yet also just a short trudge or schuss (in the other direction) from the lifts: luxury units with fireplace, washer, dryer, summertime tennis and pool; $310 per night for a three-bedroom unit in winter.

The Bridges Resort and Racquet Club (583-2922, 800-451-4213), Sugarbush Valley, Warren 05674. A self-contained condo resort just down the access road from the Sugarbush lifts: 100 units ranging from one to three-bedroom units each with fireplaces, sundecks, TV, and phone, some with washers/dryers. Facilities include an indoor pool, indoor tennis and squash court, a game room and saunas; in summer there is also the outdoor pool, a full tennis program using outdoor courts as well, lawn games. Handy to golf course. In winter $103–204 per night, $531–1054 per seven-night ski week.

DINING OUT   Chez Henri (583-2600), Sugarbush Village. A genuine bistro. Twenty years ago, Henri Borel relinquished his position as food controller for Air France to open this snug, inviting cafe with a fireplace, a marble bar (imported from a Barre soda fountain) and terrace dining out front in summer. After dinner the back room becomes a disco, open until 2 AM (nightly in winter, Friday–Sunday in summer). Year-round you can always find something light and delicious in the cafe from noon on: onion soup, Moules à la Provençale or Coquille St. Jacques. Entrées in the more formal dining room include Les Supremes de Volaille (young chicken breast prepared differently every day); or rack of lamb broiled with thyme; specials change frequently so that lóng-time patrons can always find something new. Entrées range from $9–16.

Millbrook Restaurant (496-2405), Route 17, Waitsfield. The attractive, unpretentious dining room in this roadside inn is the right setting for satisfying dining that ranges from garden lasagne or cheese cannelloni ($7.95) to veal Roma (Vermont veal quickly sautéed with fresh sage, shallots, white wine and mushrooms). There are always a choice of Indian entrées too, including locally raised

lamb simmered in a rich curried sauce of cardamom, cumin, cor-
iander, coconut, almonds, ginger, yoghurt, and tomatoes.

Sam Rupert's Restaurant (583-2421), Sugarbush Access Road,
Warren. Open for dinner only, year-round. The core of this building is a sugar house; it has gone through several changes but has
evolved over the past decade under present ownership into a widely
respected dining place in which a choice of seafood and vegetarian
specialties, plus veal, duck and lamb is served amid greenery. A
dinner here might consist of escargots Florentine ($5.25), new pea
salad ($4.50), and linguine au fruits de mer ($15); a children's menu
is available.

The Common Man (583-2800), German Flats Road, Warren. Dinner only, closed Mondays off-season. This unusual, immensely
popular landmark, damaged by fire early in 1987, has been replaced
by an equally elegant barn. You might begin with pâté de compagne
($3.75), feast on lapin à la forestière (Valley-raised rabbit, braised
in white wine and glazed with wild boletus and white mushrooms
($9.50) or carré s'agneau à la Provençale (loin of domestic lamb
$17.50).

The Phoenix (583-2421), Sugarbush Village. Open for dinner only,
closed Wednesdays in summer. The decor is a classic combination
of brick walls, stained glass, and hanging plants with linen covered
tables and delectable dishes such as roast duckling and Veal Citron.
Their dessert tray has to be seen to be believed. Prices range from
$12.50 for spinach fettuccini with a veal and brandied sauce to
$17.50 for domestic lamb chops grilled with mustard lingonberry
sauce.

EATING OUT   **Northern Light Cafe & Deli** (496-7740), Bridge Street Marketplace, Waitsfield. Michael Flanagan smokes his own salmon and
meats, forages for mushrooms, makes his own mustards and wild
raspberry dressing. His small cafe, open daily 8–5, is a source of
imaginative eggs (Northern Lights Frittata is an open face omelet
made with ham, cheese, fresh veggies, and herbs), buttermilk pancakes or French toast topped with amaretto butter and toasted
almonds. The lunch menu includes homemade soups and a wide
choice of salads, pasta, and sandwiches. The deli items have a
strong local following. Wine and beer are served.

Odyssey (583-2001), Warren. Open for dinner nightly, 5–11. This
place is far more attractive and the food better than almost any
place we can think of that specializes in pizzas and $5.75 pasta
dishes. For families it's a life saver, also pretty handy if you arrive
late any night. There's beer on draft and wine by the glass.

Reveille at the Pitcher Inn (496-3831), Warren Village. Open
weekdays, 7–11, weekends, 8–12. This pleasant village inn enjoys
giving friends and neighbors an excuse to gather for breakfasts like

Warren's covered bridge overlooks a favorite swimmin' hole

Eggs Reveille (poached eggs with a slice of tomato and creamed spinach on an English muffin with hollandaise sauce) or corned beef hash, or French toast, pancakes, and waffles served with real Vermont maple syrup, or just about any kind of omelet you can think up.

China Jade (496-7770/7788), Route 17, Waitsfield. Formerly the China Barn and purportedly improved under its new name and ownership, a good bet for families who can dine off a $13 pu-pu platter. Dinner specials like Kung Pao chicken, boneless spareribs, and pork fried rice are $6.25; luncheon specials begin at $2.95.

Ron's Deli (583-2222/2345), Sugarbush Village. Within walking distance of the lifts, outstanding breakfasts; scrambled eggs with hot biscuits or toast, also featuring pancakes; huge sandwiches and homemade soups, salads for lunch.

Beggar's Banquet in Fiddler's Green (496-4485), Route 100, Waitsfield. Open for lunch and dinner. Lunch specials are quiche and salad, sandwich platters. Dinners include vegetable tempura, veal du jour, and Kushiqaki (skewered meat and vegetables).

APRÈS SKI   Gallaghers Pub & Steak House (496-8800), Waitsfield. A rambling old cider mill with an eclectic mix of antiques featuring après ski rock and other dancing; also open weekends in summer; good for soups, salads, steaks, chops, pizza, and other pies.

The Blue Tooth (583-2656), Sugarbush Access Road. A "mountain saloon" geared to ski season, closed in summer; après ski snacks and drinks, moderately priced dinners, live entertainment; a prime boy-meets-girl place.

SELECTIVE SHOPPING   Green Mountain Coffee Roasters, Village Square, Waitsfield. Open Monday–Saturday, 10–5:30. Jamie Balne founded this highly successful enterprise as a means of supporting himself in the Valley. The son of a Connecticut coffee importer, Jamie roasts 30 varieties of coffee on the spot; a pot of java (or whatever) is perpetually brewing and muffins, cookies, etc., are sold to go with it. House specialties include water-washed beans (coffee decaffeinated without chemicals) at $5 a pound; a full line of coffeemakers are also sold. Pastries and light lunches go with the coffee on the premises.

Tulip Tree Crafts (496-2259), Village Square, Waitsfield. Judy Dodds runs this exceptional outlet for 75 different Vermont craftspeople. Judy herself is a fibre artist, specializing in quilted pictures.

The Troll Shop (496-2171), Waitsfield Village. The Valley's leading source of ski and general sportswear; a Troll Shop II also services the Sugarbush Access Road.

The Warren Store (496-3864), Warren Village. Open daily 8–7, Sundays until 6. The bakery in the rear produces French and health breads, also croissants on Sundays; the deli specializes in eat-in (or outside on the porch) salads and sandwiches, ideal for passing bicyclists and cross-country skiers; there is also a fine collection of wines and a More Store upstairs, selling assorted clothes, toys, and housewares.

Cabin Fever Quilts (496-2287), The Old Church, Waitsfield. Closed Tuesdays, otherwise open 10–5. Machine sewn, hand-tied quilts come in a range of sizes and patterns, priced from $155–300, also pillows.

Rosie Borel's Lescalier (583-2666), Sugarbush Village. Literally a stairwell, crammed with French Provincial prints: cloth, clothes, purses, also exceptional pottery from the southern French town of Moustier.

All Things Bright and Beautiful (496-3397), Bridge Street. There are an incredible number of stuffed animals and unusual toys on two floors of this old village house.

Tempest Book Shop (496-2022), Village Square, Waitsfield. This family-run bookstore is a trove of titles in most categories, including children's books. We like their motto: "A house without books is like a room without windows. (H. Mann)".

SPECIAL EVENTS   Late February: **Sugarsap Run**—15 km cross-country race.

March: **March Madness**—special series of happenings to celebrate spring skiing. **Annual New England Telemark Festival**, Mad River Glen.

Late March: **Chamber Challenge Hill Triathlon**—canoe, kayak, bicycle, cross-country ski race.

July 4: Outstanding, long-standing parade and celebration, Warren Village.

July and August: **Mad River Playhouse** series of concerts and live entertainment staged either in the outdoor theater behind the Bridge Street Marketplace or at the Sugarbush Gatehouse. Also summer productions by the **Valley Players** and by **Phantom Theater** (see *To See and Do*).

Late July, early August: **Sugarbush Horse Shoe and Green Mountain Polo Tournament**

September: **Sugarbush Antique Car Show.**

Early October: **Fall Wave Soaring Encampment**.

MEDICAL EMERGENCY   Ambulance (496-3600). Mad River Valley Health Center (496-3838).

Barre/Montpelier Area

Montpelier is the smallest and possibly the most livable of the nation's state capitals. It is a town of less than 9,000 people with band concerts on summer Wednesdays, high school playing fields just a few blocks from the capitol, and a bus depot so small that patrons frequently wait on the sidewalk. The gold dome of the statehouse itself is appropriately crowned by a green hill rising steeply behind it and unless you follow the commercial strip along Route 302 to Barre, you are quickly out in the country—in the wooded Worcester range to the north or the wilderness to the west; East Montpelier is a crossroads village.

Any attempt to understand the character of Vermont entails a visit to Montpelier: a stroll through the Vermont Museum (an extraordinary collection of things past, housed in a replica of a steamboat Gothic-style hotel) and into the fine statehouse built of Vermont granite and marble. The surrounding nineteenth-century brick business and state office buildings harbor an increasing number of good restaurants and pleasant shops.

Why precisely this narrow floodplain of the Winooski was selected as Vermont's statehouse site in 1805 seems uncertain, or why it was named for a small city in the Languedoc region of France. The fact is, however, that Vermont's first legislators picked a town noted for its unusual number of whiskey distilleries and named it for a town best known for its wine and brandy. It's also true that Montpelier is unusually accessible, by roads both old and new, from every corner of central and northern Vermont.

A city of 9,824, surrounded by a town of 7,090, **Barre** (pronounced "berry"), is larger than Montpelier to which it is linked via the five-mile commercial strip of Route 302. Barre's Main Street is a perpetual bottleneck and motorists caught in it may ponder the conspicuous absence of granite in the facades of the commercial buildings—most of which date from the 1880-1910 period when Barre became known far and wide for granite memorials. During that era the community's population jumped tenfold, swollen by stonecutters and craftsmen from Scotland, Eastern Europe, Italy, and French Canada not to mention England, Scandinavia, Spain, Germany, and the Middle East—a volatile mix of largely underpaid

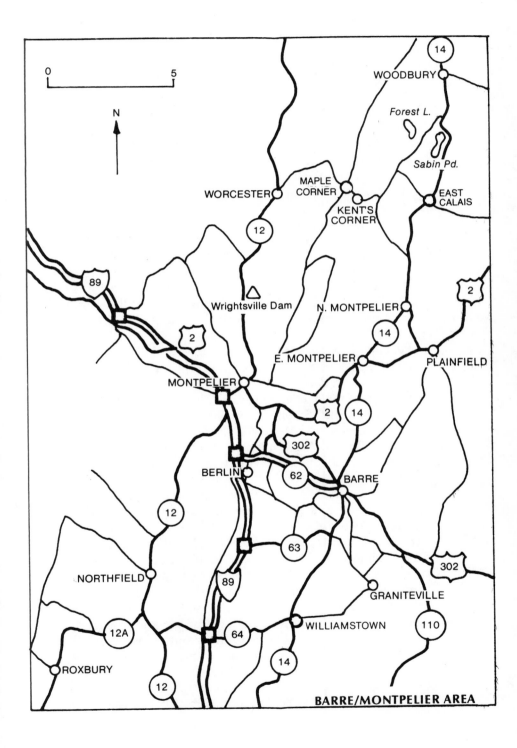

BARRE/MONTPELIER AREA

workers who elected a socialist mayor and were not afraid to strike for their rights or to shelter victims of strikes elsewhere. Around the time of World War I, the famous radical feminist, Emma Goldman, was arrested here. The quarries continue to employ some 2,000 people.

The granite quarries are southeast of town, primarily in Graniteville where Millstone Hill has been chipped and chiseled since 1812 when the bedrock was turned into millstones, doorstoops, and posts. In the 1830s, huge slabs were hauled thence by oxen to build the State House. It was only after the Civil War that the railway and a series of inventions enabled Barre to make its mark. The memorial stone business escalated after 1888 when the branch railroad finally linked the quarries to finishing sheds in the valley and outlets beyond. Today, Barre continues to produce one-third of the country's memorial stones for which its own Mt. Hope Cemetery serves as a museum. All but one of the major quarries are owned by Rock of Ages, a company which has long given its operations a showcase for visitors, who can view the unforgettable, surrealistic landscape of the quarries themselves, hear the roar of the drills and watch ant-sized men chip away at the giant pits.

GUIDANCE   Central Vermont Chamber of Commerce (229-5711), Box 336, Barre 05641.

Vermont Chamber of Commerce (223-3443), Box 37, Montpelier, is located off I-89, Exit 7 near its junction with Route 302 between Montpelier and Barre, 9–5 weekdays.

Vermont Travel Division (828-3236) has its main information center at 134 State Street, Montpelier.

Montpelier on the Move (229-4943), 64 Main Street.

GETTING THERE   By bus: An express stop for Vermont Transit buses from Boston to Montreal, connecting with New York and Connecticut service.

By air: Eastern Express to Knapp Airport, flights from Boston.

Ground transfers: **Alpine Central Cab**, Barre; **Royal Limousine Service** (479-2090).

TO SEE AND DO   Vermont State House (828-2228), State Street, Montpelier. Open Monday–Friday 8–4, closed holidays. July–October "Friends of the Vermont State House" offer tours Monday–Friday, 10–3, otherwise by appointment. In 1805 when Montpelier was chosen as the "permanent seat of the legislature for holding all their sessions," it was on condition that the town had to give land for the capital and get it built by 1808. The resulting building was ninesided, three stories with a cupola, warmed by a two-story stove. Legislators sat on plank seats at pine desks that were said to have been "whittled out of use" by the representatives' jackknives. The whole building had to be demolished in 1836 and was replaced by

Morgan horse and cutter cross the Capitol's front yard

a granite Grecian temple designed by Federal-era architect Ammi Young. After it was virtually destroyed by fire, it was rebuilt along the same but larger lines, completed in 1857. Visitors are welcome to watch the legislature in action, January to mid-April. Note that the 150 state representatives and senators talk with their constituents while standing in the Hall of Flags or seated on the black walnut sofas (which cost $60 apiece in 1859) at either end. Larkin Mead's statue of Ethan Allen on the steps is Danby marble and the handsome black and white floor of the lobby was quarried on Isle la Motte. The lobby is lined with portraits of Vermont-born heroes including Admiral George Dewey, Admiral Charles Clark (like Dewey, a hero of the Spanish-American War) and Calvin Coolidge, thirtieth president of the U.S. The cannon on the front steps was captured from Hessians at the Battle of Bennington in 1777. The Roman lady atop the gold-leafed dome is, of course, Ceres, goddess of agriculture, also sculpted by Larkin Mead.

The Vermont Museum (828-2291), 109 State Street, Montpelier. Open weekdays, year-round 8–4:30; weekends only during July, August, and Foliage Season: 10–5. Donation. This outstanding state museum is maintained by the Vermont Historical Society, housed on the ground floor of the replica of the Pavilion Hotel, which occupied this site between 1870 and 1966. You climb the steps, cross the verandah as if you were a hotel guest, enter a Victorian lobby with horsehair and elaborately carved furnishings. Children and adults alike can enjoy the displays dramatizing Vermont history and relics ranging from the state's first printing press to Ethan Allen's gun. We were particularly intrigued by the story of Merino sheep, which were first introduced in 1810 and by 1840 outnumbered people six to one. There are also changing exhibits, a small gift store, and a large, excellent library of sourcebooks.

T.W. Wood Art Gallery at the Vermont College Art Center (223-8743), open Tuesday–Sunday, noon–4 PM. The Gallery displays Civil War-era art by local artist Thomas Waterman Wood and has excellent shows of contemporary Vermont artists and craftspeople.

Mural of Vermont Life, National Life Insurance, Montpelier. This huge mural fills a wall of the lobby of the home office of National Life Insurance (founded by Admiral Dewey's father) on Memorial Drive, just off I-89, open weekdays 9–4:30. It is a monumental piece by Paul Sample, depicting the sweep of the state's present and past.

Barre Opera House (476-8188), corner of Prospect and Main streets. Built in 1899, after fire destroyed its predecessor, this elegant, acoustically outstanding, recently restored theater occupies the second and third floors of City Hall. Performances are scheduled mid-April through mid-October.

Rock of Ages Quarry and Craftsmen Center (476-3115), Graniteville. The Craftsmen Center, in which stone is polished and sculpted into memorials, is open year-round, Monday–Friday, 8:30–3:30. The Visitors Reception Center a mile up the road, open May–October, 8:30–5, has displays explaining the geology of granite; a path leads you the short way out back to the State's oldest, 27-acre wide quarry. From June through September an open-car train departs every half hour, 9:30–3:30, for the working quarries farther up the hill.

Hope Cemetery, Route 14 just north of Barre. The memorials that stone cutters have sculpted for themselves and their familes are among the most elaborate to be found anywhere in the world.

Barre Historical Society Museum (467-7550), Aldrich Library. An outstanding collection of nineteenth-century paintings, furnishings, and articles relating to Barre's stormy history are displayed upstairs in Barre's unusually fine library; by appointment.

Kent Tavern Museum (828-2291; summer 223-5660), Kents Corner. Located 11 miles north of Montpelier, marked from Maple Corner, 1 mile east on a dirt road. Open July, August daily except Monday, noon–5, also weekends in Foliage Season. Restored and maintained by the Vermont Historical Society, this tavern, adjacent country store/post office formed the centerpiece for a classic, early nineteenth-century "four corners." It demonstrates the interdependence of such rural communities; built of granite from a local quarry, brick from a family kiln, wood sawed down the road and iron made in town; buildings are well furnished and interpreted.

NORTHFIELD   The town's mid-nineteenth-century commercial blocks suggest the prosperity that it enjoyed during the term its native son Charles Paine served as governor. Paine literally railroaded the Vermont Central Railroad through his home town instead of the more logical Barre. The old depot, now a bank, stands at one end of the handsome common. Today the town's pride is Norwich University, a private, coed college of 1,000 cadets, which bills itself as "the oldest private military college in the U.S." In the Norwich University Museum in White Memorial Chapel, you learn that this institution sent more than 300 officers into the Civil War. It wasn't until 1867, however, that the college moved to Northfield from its original site in Norwich. More Northfield memorabilia as well as changing exhibits can be seen in the Northfield Historical Society museum housed in the Old Red Brick Schoolhouse, Stagecoach Road (open June–Labor Day, Sunday 2–5 PM).

East Roxbury Fish Hatchery, 2 miles south of Roxbury on Route 12A. This is a state hatchery in which salmon species are raised; children are allowed to feed the fish.

Drive from Roxbury to Warren. The road through Roxbury Gap, while not recommended in winter, is spectacular in summer and fall, commanding a breath-taking view of the Green Mountains from the crest of the Roxbury Range. Do not resist the urge to stop, get out, and enjoy this panorama. Ask locally about the hiking trail that follows the ridge line from the road's highest point.

Goddard College (454-8311), Plainfield. Founded in 1863, a progressive college with several buildings designed by students; frequent live entertainment, films, concerts.

COVERED BRIDGES   On Route 12 to Northfield Falls stand three covered bridges: "The Station Bridge" spanning 100 feet and "The Newell Bridge" are within sight of each other; further along Cox Brook Road is "The Upper Bridge" with a span of 42 feet.

GREENSPACE   **Hubbard Park**. More than 110 acres in the upper reaches of the city, primarily leafy windy roads, good for biking, jogging.

BOATING AND FISHING   **Wrightsville Dam**, just north of Montpelier; **North Montpelier Pond**, with a fishing access off Route 14; **Curtis Pond** and **Mirror Lake** in Calais. **Nelson Pond** and **Sabin Pond** in Woodbury are both accessible from Route 14, as are **Valley Lake** and **Greenwood Lake** (good for bass and pike). **Steven Branch** south of Barre offers brook trout. Also see nearby Marshfield and Groton for their facilities.

GOLF   **Montpelier Country Club** (223-2600), 9 holes. **Barre Country Club** (476-7658), 18 holes. **Northfield Country Club** 9 holes.

HORSEBACK RIDING   **East Hill Farm** (479-9258), Plainfield, year-round lessons, no trail rides. **Hillcrest Riding Center, Inc.** (454-8597), Plainfield, trail rides, lessons.

HIKING   Guidance: **The Green Mountain Club**, headquartered at 43 State St., Montpelier (223-3463) encourages general inquiries and trail description updates. See *Hiking* under *What's Where*.

Spruce Mountain, Plainfield. An unusually undeveloped state holding of 500 acres, rich in birdlife. The trail begins in Jones State Forest, 4.2 miles south of the village; the three-hour hike is described in *Fifty Hikes in Vermont* by Heather and Hugh Sadlier; also in *Day Hiker's Guide to Vermont* published by the Green Mountain Club.

Worcester Range north of Montpelier. There are several popular hikes described in the above books, notably Elmore Mountain in Elmore State Park (a 3-mile trek yielding a panorama of lakes, farms, and rolling hills), Mount Worcester (approached from the village of Worcester), and Mount Hunger.

SWIMMING   **Wrightsville Dam Recreation Area**, Route 12 north, also numerous swimming holes in the Kent Corner area; also see Marshfield and Groton for their extensive facilities.

TENNIS   Public courts on Upper Elm Street, night lights, nominal fee (223-5141).

CROSS-COUNTRY SKIING   Montpelier Elks Ski Touring Center, contact **Onion River Sports, Inc.** (229-9409), 20 Langdon Street. This facility uses gently rolling golf course terrain, offers 10 km of set trails, instruction, rentals, food.

DOWNHILL SKIING   Lybrand Ski Area (485-5011), at Norwich University, Northfield. Open to the public; a reasonably priced area with rentals, instruction, two lifts.

LODGING   The Montpelier Tavern Hotel (223-5252/6136), 100 State Street, Montpelier, has 103 guest rooms and suites plus conference and banquet rooms, fitness facilities with an indoor pool, the Justin Morgan lounge, and dining room. Legislators hang out here during their winter session of the Assembly and Senate. Rates: $55 single, $65 double during the foliage season, $49.50 and $59 otherwise.

The Hollow Motel (479-9313), 278 South Main Street, Barre 05641, looks like a conventional motel but is much more like a suburban inn than the name implies; Peg and Bill Whitehouse add a personal touch. From the south, use I-89 Exit 6 to Route 14, then ½ mile north; from Barre and the north, 1 mile south of the center of the city. The outdoor pool is surrounded by plantings, wood fences and a natural stone wall, and boasts a summer kitchen and gas grill. The indoor Swallow Relaxation Center is equipped with whirlpool, sauna, and fitness equipment. Double room rates begin at $48 (October 19 to December 11) to $62 for efficiencies; $61 to $71 (June 5 to September 17); and $68 to $78 (September 18 to October 18), including continental breakfast. Most rooms have VCRs as well as TV, and video tapes can be rented. Discounts available for stays of more than three or seven consecutive nights.

LaGue Inns (229-5766), RD 4, Box 1720, Montpelier 05602. Conveniently located on Exit 7 of I-89 near the Central Vermont Hospital and the Barre-Montpelier Airport, this 80-unit motel has pleasant rooms, an outdoor pool, convention facilities for up to 300 persons, and Suzanna's Restaurant. Rates are moderate: $36 single, $44 double.

OTHER MOTELS   Brown Derby Motel & Restaurant (223-5258), 101 Northfield Street, Montpelier; **Sir Anthony Motel & Round Table Restaurant** (476-6678), 173 South Main Street, Barre; **The Heiress** (479-3333), 573 North Maine, Barre; **Holiday Inn** (244-7822), Exit 10, I-89, Waterbury.

BED & BREAKFAST   North Branch House (229-0878), 22 North Street, Montpelier 05602. A ten-minute, half-mile walk from the Capitol, the Kitzmiller family offers three guest rooms decorated with antiques and their own quilts and silk-screen prints. Rates are from $25 single to $35 double, shared bath, with breakfast. Weekly rates available; no smoking, no pets.

DINING OUT   Tubbs Restaurant (229-9202), 24 Elm Street, Jailhouse Com-

The world's largest granite quarry, Rock of Ages, Barre

mon, Montpelier. This renovated jail is one of Vermont's outstanding places to eat. It is run by the New England Culinary Institute, whose student chefs produce delectable dishes for lunch and dinner at moderate prices (dinner entrées $12.95–14.95). The menu, changing daily, might include duck consommé with fresh ginger, hot oysters with spinach and caviar, escalope of salmon with sorrel, veal steak with peppercorns and cognac. Dessert pastries and bread are baked by **La Brioche**, on the premises, which serves Monday–Friday, 7:30–3:45, Saturday 7:30–1, indoors and on the patio. Tubbs itself is open for lunch Monday–Friday and for dinner Monday–Saturday.

Elm Street Cafe (223-3188), 38 Elm Street, Montpelier, around the corner from Tubbs and its more casual sibling, is also operated by the Culinary Institute, serving breakfast, lunch, and dinner Monday–Saturday, at reasonable prices: baked Vermont cheddar in phyllo ($2.50), Cajun barbecued shrimp ($10.75), grilled pork tenderloin ($8.75).

The White House Restaurant (229-9847), Kent's Corner, Calais, 11 miles north of Montpelier off Route 12 or 14 offers an elegant dining experience, with cocktails served in the Bird Parlor or on the front porch, dinner in the barrel-vaulted main dining room or music room, where chamber music is sometimes played. A five-course dinner costs $25 prix fixe. Open Wednesday–Saturday and for Sunday brunch in the summer. Check for winter and spring hours. Reservations required.

EATING OUT **Horn of the Moon Cafe** (223-2985), 8 Langdon Street, Montpelier. Open Monday from 7 to 3; 7–9, Tuesday through Saturday; Sunday, 10–2. Smoking and sugar are out, innovative, vegetarian dishes definitely in: herb teas, local organic products, wheat bread, pancakes, tofu, soups, and salads predominate the inexpensive menu. Beer and wine served.

Country House Restaurant (476-4282), 276 North Main Street, Barre, serves modestly priced Italian specialties at lunch and dinner Monday through Saturday.

Jack's Backyard (479-9134), 9 Maple Avenue, Barre, "an adult watering & feeding place," serves a wide selection of inexpensive sandwiches, chili, crepes, soups, quiche, salads for lunch Monday–Saturday and Sunday brunch.

Julio's (229-9348), 44 Main Street, Montpelier. Good, reasonably priced Mexican food in a second floor dining room which used to be MJ's. Entrées range from $3.25–5.75.

Vermont Dept. of Employment & Training Cafeteria (229-0311, ext. 146), open for lunch and dinner, serviced by students of the New England Culinary Institute, the best buy in town for breakfast and lunch.

Green Mountain Diner (476-6292), 240 North Main, Barre. Open 6 AM to 9 PM, our choice of eating spots in town: friendly booths, a blackboard menu with specials like stew ($2.95) or Spanish pork chops ($3.50); beer and wine served.

Sambel's on The Common (485-7777), Northfield, serves lunch, dinner and a great Sunday brunch. Closed Monday.

SELECTIVE SHOPPING   **The Artisans' Hand** (229-9492), 7 Langdon Street, Montpelier. Monday–Saturday: 10–5. An exceptional variety of quality Vermont craftwork.

Bear Pond Books (229-0774), corner of Langdon & Main Streets, Montpelier. One of the state's most inviting bookstores, heavy on literature, art and children's books.

Morse Farm (223-2740), County Road (the western extension of Main St.), Montpelier. Open daily, year-round except holidays. The farm itself has been in the same family for three generations. This is a place to come watch sugaring off in March; a large farm-stand sells Vermont crafts and cheese as well as produce in summer, fall, and Christmas greens in December. Sugar on Snow.

Knight's Spider Web Farm (433-5568), off Route 14 on Cliff Place, Williamstown Village. In season, visitors can see spider webs being collected and mounted; gifts and pine accessories. Open daily 9–6; January–March by appointment.

Great American Salvage Company (223-7711), 3 Main Street, Montpelier 05602. A treasure trove of antique architectural artifacts: doors, stained glass, columns, mantels, tubs—the motherlode for the company's Cooper Square branch in New York City.

SPECIAL EVENTS   Early June: **Vermont Dairy Celebration**, State House lawn.

June–August: **Montpelier City Band Concerts**, State House lawn.

July: **Midsummer Art and Music Festival**, Vermont College campus, sponsored by the Onion River Arts Council (229-9408), **Victorian Ice Cream Social**, State House lawn, **Vermont Fool's Fest**, two and a half days of street festival for the whole family the last weekend in July, transforms Montpelier and the statehouse grounds into a three-ring circus of mimes, clowns, comedians, musicians, vaudeville, parades, and cabarets, including Vermont's home-grown Circus Smirkus. Fool's Fest buttons are sold in various stores. For information call or write Montpelier on the Move (229-4943), Box 1085, Montpelier 05602.

Late September: **Old Time Fiddlers Contests**, Barre Auditorium—one of the oldest contests, attracting some of the East's best fiddlers.

Early October: **Vermont Apple Celebration**, State House lawn.

Late October: **Festival of Vermont Crafts**, Montpelier High School (Central Vermont Chamber of Commerce, 229-5711).

MEDICAL EMERGENCY   Barre (476-6675); Montpelier (229-4911); North-field (485-7744). **Central Vermont Hospital** (229-9121), Barre (off Route 302, Exit 7, off I-89).

Lake Champlain Valley

INTRODUCTION

Lake Champlain, one of the most beautiful inland waterways in America, flows—contrarily—north for 120 miles from Whitehall, New York, and drains into Quebec's Richelieu River. Covering 452 square miles, it is only 12 miles across at its widest point, but its historic, strategic, and commercial influence affects a broad area.

Discovered by Samuel de Champlain in 1609, the lake was controlled by the French until 1759 when Jeffrey Amherst, the legendary British officer, drove them out of Fort Carillon (renamed Ticonderoga) and Crown Point. Major Robert Rogers' Rangers were then trained at Crown Point for guerilla warfare against the French and Indian marauders, later dramatized in Kenneth Roberts' famous novel, *Northwest Passage*. Amherst ended French sovereignty in North America by capturing Montreal in 1760.

Early in the American Revolution, the British strategy to divide and conquer the northern colonies was thwarted when Ethan Allen's rambunctious Green Mountain Boys seized Fort Ticonderoga on May 10, 1775, and again when Benedict Arnold and a hastily assembled American flotilla engaged a heavier British squadron in the Battle of Valcour Island in October 1776. Arnold's outgunned navy was beaten, but this prong of the British invasion was blunted, frustrated again near Bennington, and finally brought to a halt when Burgoyne's army surrendered at Saratoga in October 1777. One of Arnold's small gunboats, the *Philadelphia*, sunk by the British off Valcour, was salvaged in 1935 and now reposes in The Smithsonian as the oldest surviving American naval vessel.

In 1814, the British again tried to use Lake Champlain as an invasion route. The vigorous, 31-year-old Commodore Thomas Macdonough moved his headquarters from Burlington south to Vergennes and a shipyard at the mouth of Otter Creek where he quickly outfitted a small fleet, which barely managed to defeat British ships at Plattsburgh Bay—a bloody but decisive engagement that helped end the War of 1812.

Before, during, and after this war, the lake was the major artery for trade with Canada, much of it illegal, which in turn spawned the great nineteenth-century decades of Champlain steamboats. When the canal from Whitehall to Troy and the Hudson River opened in 1823, ports on Lake Champlain, especially Burlington, boomed. The age of the side-wheelers lasted from the launching of *The Vermont* in 1809 to the demise of *The Ticonderoga* (1906–1953); this stately, steel-hulled steamer has been preserved for posterity at the Shelburne Museum, after a remarkable two-mile, sixty-five-day overland rail portage in the fall and winter of 1954-55.

Ferries still ply the sparkling waters of the lake, providing spectacular panoramas of both the Adirondacks and the Green Mountains and magnificent sunsets. No longer a significant commercial waterway, Champlain offers exhilarating cruising and sailing opportunities. But recreational sailors beware: the lake's moods can change quickly from serenity to tempestuous squalls!

Bass, walleyes, yellow perch, northern pike, and other warm-water fishing has always been good; a recent restoration project improves the prospect for lake trout, steelhead rainbows, and land-locked salmon, north of the Sand Bar Bridge. Ice fishing is a winter passion for many.

Anglers may even spot "Champ," the elusive serpentine creature described by those who claim to have seen (and photographed) it as resembling its cousin, the "Loch Ness Monster."

Lower Champlain Valley

RUTLAND REGION

The western portal of the lower Champlain valley from New York state is Fair Haven, where there's a relatively new State Welcome Center that has well-displayed examples of Vermont products, on Route 4, a principal artery running across the state to the New Hampshire border, through Castleton (4A) and Rutland. In this greater Rutland region, we also include Poultney, the lake district, and Proctor in the western quadrant; Clarendon Springs, Wallingford, Cuttingsville, and Shrewsbury in the east; and Pittsford to the north. (The hill towns of Mount Holly and Hortonville are included in the Ludlow Area.)

Rutland, Vermont's second largest city (18,435), is more than just a convenient commercial adjunct to the Killington-Pico ski resorts. Stolid early Victorian mansions and streets criss-crossed with railroad tracks testify to nineteenth-century prosperity—when Rutland was known as "the marble city."

Today, city fathers are trying hard to reconstitute the downtown core, buoyed by the fact that the area's largest employer, General Electric, keeps about 1,800 people working on defense contracts in two plants. It is justifiably proud of the daily *Rutland Herald*, the oldest newspaper in the state, which wins frequent journalism awards for its format and content; and of its small but rising College of St. Joseph the Provider.

Rutland's cultural resources are growing, thanks to the Cross Roads Arts Council, which, like other local groups around the state supported in part by the Vermont Council on the Arts, sponsors artists-in-residence in the schools; the city is also the home for the Central Vermont Symphony Orchestra, formed in the early 1940s and composed of about thirty graduate students, music teachers, and professional musicians who present periodic concerts.

GUIDANCE   The Rutland Region Chamber of Commerce (773-2747), 7 Court Square, Box 67 05701; visitor's center (appropriately sheeted in marble) at the junction of Routes 7 and 4 (775-0831). The Chamber supplies two new, free folders, "The Marble Valley Tour" and "The Sherburne Sojourn Tour," describing sights, sites, and accommodations in the respective locales.

Rutland Seasons, published quarterly and available locally gratis or from Prosper Publishing, Inc., Box 206, Barnard 05031.

GETTING THERE   By car: Routes 7 and 4; 103 from Bellows Falls.

By bus: Vermont Transit, from Albany and other points.

By air: Eastern Express (800-451-4221) to and from Albany, Boston, New York, Newark, Philadelphia. The Rutland Airport, off Route 103 south of the city, opened a new terminal in 1986 that has Avis and Hertz counters.

GETTING AROUND   Stretch limousine services: **Aldous** (773-6252); **Green Mountain** (800-257-LIMO, outside Vermont, 800-437-LIMO in Vermont); **Luxury Limos** (775-0516); **Michael's** (775-3419).

TO SEE AND DO   **Chaffee Art Gallery** (775-0356), 16 South Main Street, is a former private house listed on the National Register of Historic Places. It has permanent and periodic exhibits, and a youth gallery for school displays. Traditional and contemporary paintings, sculp-

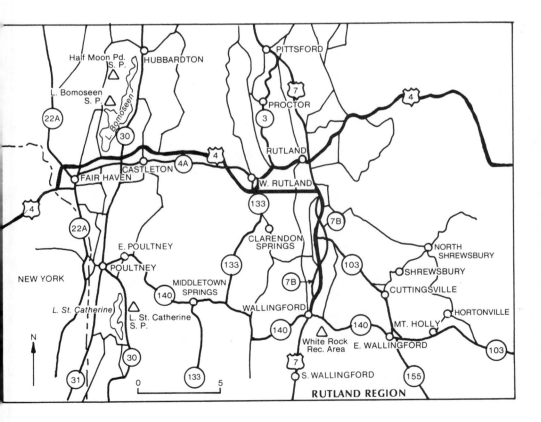

ture, crafts, graphics, and photography are included. Open Monday–Friday, 10–5, June–October; weekends by appointment.

Moon Brook. A showcase for the work of area artists, plus readings and films. Arts Union (775-9548), Center Street.

Wilson Castle (773-3284), Route 3 from West Rutland toward Proctor. This 32-room nineteenth-century stone "chateau" on a 115-acre estate, is furnished with elaborate European and Oriental pieces, stained glass, and a variety of wood panelling. Guided tours given daily, mid-May through mid-October. Admission $2.75 for adults.

Vermont Marble Exhibit (459-3311 Ext. 435), Route 3 from West Rutland, Proctor. The first commercial marble deposit was discovered and quarried in Vermont in 1784. The Vermont Marble Company, formed in 1870 when Redfield Proctor merged several quarries, has been one of the state's principal resources. Marble from Proctor and Danby was used for the U.S. Supreme Court building, the Lincoln Memorial, and the Beinecke Library at Yale, among many other notable edifices. Proctor himself served as governor, United States Senator, and Secretary of War. Several other members of the Proctor family and chief executives of the company also filled the governor's chair, forming a political dynasty that lasted nearly a century. The company has been owned by the Swiss-based Pleuss-Staufer Industries since 1976 and is currently filling an 1,800-ton, multi-million dollar contract for Saudi Arabia's Monetary Agency building in Riyadh. Nearly 100,000 people visit the marble exhibit every year, making it one of the biggest tourist attractions in New England. Featured are a special geological display, a gallery of bas-reliefs of American presidents, a movie, slide show, gift shop, replicas of the *Pieta* and *The Last Supper*, a sculptor-in-residence, and a factory viewing site to watch the various stages of transformation from rough-cut blocks to polished slabs. Open daily 9–5:30, Memorial Day to mid-October. Admission $1.50, children under 12, 50¢; under 6, free.

The New England Maple Museum (483-9414), Route 7 north of Pittsford, has an attractive display of the history, production, and consumption of maple syrup, once called "sweet water," and it's by-products. One can view the Danforth Collection of antique equipment, murals and a 10-minute slide show, and there is a tasting area and gift shop. Mail order service. Open daily, 8:30–5:30, May 23–October 31; 10–4, November 1–December 23, and March 15–May 22; closed January and February. Small admission; group rates.

Paul P. Harris Memorial. Route 7 south of Rutland, Wallingford. Paul Harris (1868–1947), founder of Rotary International while he was working in Chicago, was born in Wallingford and went to school in the small brick building on Main Street, where the local club meets Mondays at 6:30 PM.

Pittsford Fish Hatchery (483-2300), Furnace Brook Road, Pittsford, open 8–4 daily for viewing landlocked salmon.

VILLAGES **Fair Haven** 05743, located where Routes 4, 4A, and 22A intersect, is at the core of Vermont's slate industry. One of its earliest developers in the 1780s was the controversial Matthew Lyon, who started an iron works and published a newspaper called *The Scourge of Aristocracy*, in which he lambasted the Federalists. Elected to Congress in 1796, Lyon had scuffles on the floor of the House and criticized President Adams so violently that he was arrested and jailed under the Alien and Sedition Act. Lyon's case caused such a national uproar that this patently unconstitutional censorship law was soon rescinded; Lyon was reelected to Congress while still in jail, and took his seat in time to cast the tie-breaking vote that made Thomas Jefferson President instead of Aaron Burr.

Around the spacious green are three Victorian mansions (two faced with marble) built by descendants of Ira Allen.

Poultney 05764, on Route 30, the home of Green Mountain College, also has significant journalistic associations: Horace Greeley, founder of the *New York Tribune,* lived at the venerable Eagle Tavern (now a B&B) while he was learning the printing trade at the East Poultney *National Spectator* in the 1820s (and organizing a local temperance society). Working with him was George Jones, who helped to found the *New York Times* in 1851.

A few miles south of Poultney on Route 30 lies **Lake St. Catherine** with lots of summer cottages.

Castleton 05735, at Routes 4A and 30, has triple historical significance: Ethan Allen and Seth Warner planned the capture of Ticonderoga here; on a nearby hill in Hubbardton, Col. Warner's scrubby militiamen made a valiant rear-guard stand at halting the British invasion force on July 7, 1777, the only Revolutionary War battle actually fought on Vermont soil; and the town itself is a showcase of Greek Revival houses. One offshoot of the conspiratorial meeting in Remington's Tavern in 1775 was the exploit of the blacksmith Samuel Beach—Vermont's own Paul Revere—who reputedly ran some 60 miles in 24 hours to recruit more men from the countryside for the raid on Ticonderoga.

The Hubbardton Battlefield is north of the town, off Route 30; a visitors' center holds a lounge, museum, diorama, and audio-visual display.

After the Revolution, Castleton grew rapidly. Thomas Royal Dake, who arrived about 1807, has left his hallmark of design and workmanship on the pillared houses that line Main Street, including the Ransom-Rehlen mansion with 17 Ionic columns, and Dake's masterpiece, the Congregational Meeting House, now the Federated Church, with the lovely pulpit, which Dake completed with his own funds. These heirloom houses are open for tours during Castleton's Colonial Days, usually held in late July. Between 1850 and 1870, the West Castleton Railroad and Slate Company was the largest marble plant in the country. During these years a large Welsh commuity grew up in the area. The town is also the site of Castleton College, part of the Vermont State College system, which has an active arts center.

At the foot of Route 30 lies **Lake Bomoseen**, a popular local summer colony. The lake gained notoriety in the 1930s because of Alexander Woollcott's summer retreat on Neshobe Island. The portly "Town Crier" entertained such cronies as Harpo Marx, who was known to repel curious interlopers by capering along the shore naked and painted blue. The 17-passenger *Algonquin* plies the lake in summer. (For brochures and cottage rental listings in the area, write **Lakes Region**, VT, Box 77, Bomoseen 05732).

SUGAR HOUSES   "Rutland County—Heart of the Maple World" brochure (Rutland Chamber of Commerce, Box 27, Rutland 05701), lists all sugar houses in the Rutland area open to visitors.

STATE PARKS   **Bomoseen State Park** (265-4242/483-2314), Route 4 west of Rutland, Exit 3, 5 miles north on town road. Its 60 campsites and 5 lean-tos are set in a lovely wildlife refuge; beach, picnic area, nature program, and trails, boat ramp and rentals.

Half Moon Pond State Park (273-2848/483-2314), Fair Haven, off Route 4 west of Rutland, Exit 4, 7½ miles north on Route 30, 2 miles west on town road, 1½ miles south on town road. Wooded campsites around a secluded pond; rental canoes; hikes to High Pond, a remote body of water in the hills.

Lake St. Catherine State Park (287-9185/483-2314), Poultney, Route 4 west of Rutland, Exit 4, 9½ miles south on Route 30. 52 campsites, sandy beaches, fishing, boat rentals, nature trails.

RECREATION   Because of its proximity to Rutland, be sure to check the Killington-Pico area for recreational opportunties.

Brookside Health & Racquet Club (775-1971), 40 Curtis Avenue, Rutland. Indoor and outdoor tennis, enclosed pool, "Total Plus Gym," suntanning booth, health bar.

The Rutland Country Club (773-9153), a mile north of the business section on North Grove Street; 18-hole golf course on rolling terrain, restaurant. (See also **Bomoseen Golf Club** below under *Lodging*).

Proctor Pittsford Country Club (483-9379), Corn Hill Road, Pittsford. 9 holes, lounge, and restaurant.

Lake St. Catherine Country Club (287-9341), Route 30, south of Poultney. 9 holes, lounge, and restaurant.

White Rock Recreation Area, east of the side road between Wallingford and South Wallingford. Traversed by the Long Trail, the big feature here is a 2,600 foot conical white peak surrounded by quartzite boulders that retain ice and snow into the summer.

Swimming: Elfin Lake beach, off Route 140 west, 2 miles southeast of Wallingford.

Horseback riding: Pond Hill Ranch (468-2449), Castleton. Trail rides, lessons.

DOWNHILL AND CROSS-COUNTRY SKIING   (See Killington/Pico).

HUNTING   Tinmouth Hunting Preserve (446-2337), Box 556, East Road, Wallingford, has 800 acres of varied cover where individual and group pheasant, partridge, and quail shoots can be arranged from September through March (except on Sunday). For pheasant and chukar partridge, it costs $217 for one or two hunters, and 12 birds, or three hunters and 18 birds; the same price for a 20-quail hunt for one or two, 30-bird for three; mixed bags available. Clubs or groups of ten can have a continental shoot at $14 per bird.

LODGING   *Fair Haven, Poultney, and the Lakes*

Vermont Marble Inn (265-8383), on The Town Green, Fair Haven 05743. Swathed in tan marble and full of ornate marble fireplaces and lavishly furnished in high Victorian style, Turkey carpets, crystal chandeliers, and bric-a-brac, this relatively new inn has attracted a lot of notice. Its 14 lofty bedrooms, with big four-poster or canopy beds, are named for authors: among them, Shakespeare, Elizabeth Barrett Browning, Oscar Wilde (twin beds), and George Bernard Shaw (in art deco style). Rates range upward from $60 per room, including a "Vermont Breakfast Banquet." The dining room has won a host of local admirers (see *Dining Out*).

Maplewood Inn (265-8039), Route 22A South, Fair Haven 05743. An early Greek Revival farm house, decorated in period style with four-poster and brass beds. $50–65 for two, B&B.

The Stonebridge Inn (287-9849), 3 Beaman Street, Poultney 05764, was opened in 1984 by Jane Davidson and Lenore Lyons (refugees from Southern California) in a splendid 1808 Greek Revival house. Renovated with a flair are six cheerful bedrooms (one private bath, other share), two comfortable sitting rooms, where drinks are served, and an attractive wainscotted dining room. Dinner prices range from $6.75 to $15.00. Room rates $54 single to $84 double (private bath), including full breakfast.

Eagle Tavern (287-9498), Box 587, East Poultney 05741. This simply elegant, historic 1785 tavern with its hip roof and Doric columns is the centerpiece of a pristine village which once housed the Green

Mountain Boys. William and Gertrude Horridge now make guests comfortable (except from mid-October to January 1 and the month of April) in four bedrooms ($50) with a central bath and one enormous room (the barrel-vaulted ballroom) with private bath, four-poster bed, and fine antiques (at $65). Horace Greeley slept here when he was working at his first newspaper job; you can occupy his small single for $35. Children under 12 are not welcomed; no smoking on the bedroom floor. A swimming pool has been added.

Lake St. Catherine Inn (287-9347), Poultney 05764. Here's a peaceful, cheerful lakeside family retreat that might remind oldsters of happy days at a traditional summer camp. Set in a grove on the shore of this placid little spring-fed lake, and open May–October, the inn offers rooms in the main lodge or in motel-like units. Guests can use paddle boats, Sunfish, and canoes without extra charge and relax on the sun deck or dock. Rates range from $52–63 daily, per person, double occupancy, MAP (less between May 8 and June 18 and September 8–20); $328–397 weekly; and there are Early Bird, Mother's Day, Fisherman's, Mid-Week, and other specials.

Prospect House and Bomoseen Golf Club (468-5581 for information, 800-327-6869 for reservations), Box 90, Route 30, Lake Bomoseen 05732. This is a trim, well-maintained mini-resort surrounding a 9-hole golf course, with a nice beach and a variety of accommodations, open May 21–October 13. Full season rates are $50 single, $60 double occupancy. Their "Best Golf Package" is $305 for two persons, four days and three nights in deluxe rooms, including three breakfasts and dinners; $215 for three days and two nights, less in second floor rooms, without meals, which are available à la carte in the club house. Housekeeping apartments are available, June through Labor Day, from $210 to $280 weekly.

Edgewater Motor Lodge (468-5251), Route 30, Lake Bomoseen 05732 (formerly Trakenseen Hotel) has an inn, chalet, basic motel units, efficiencies, and housekeeping apartments as well as a restaurant. Rates range from $45 single to $78 double, $450 weekly, MAP; housekeeping cottages $200 weekly. Swimming, boating, fishing available; golf next door.

The Middletown Springs Inn (235-2198), Middletown Springs 05757, at the junction of Routes 140 and 133, 16 miles southwest of Rutland, is a most unusual pure Victorian mansion on the green of this quiet village, which has an interesting assortment of architectural styles. Steve and Jane Sax are the new owners. Five of the seven rooms have private baths. The carriage house has three more rooms. Lots of space to read and relax. Rates: $75 single, $120 double, MAP, $80 B&B. A five-course, single entrée, $18 dinner is served by reservation with one sitting at 7 PM.

BED & BREAKFASTS   Wallingford   The Green Mountain Tea Room (446-

2611), RR 1, Box 400, Route 7, South Wallingford 05773. Built as a stagecoach stop in 1792, this plainly inviting hostelry has five rooms and two baths at $25 single, $35 double, including breakfast. Light lunch served too.

White Rocks Inn (446-2077), RR 1, Box 297, Route 7, Wallingford. This elegantly furnished farmhouse and its spectacular, landmark barn are on the National Register of Historic Places. The four guest rooms, each with private bath, have either king or double canopy beds, queen four-posters, or tiger maple twins, and can be had for $55 to $80 double occupancy including full breakfast. Midweek and weekly rates are 10 percent less, slightly more in foliage and holiday seasons. Children over 10 and horses ($15 for stall and feed) are welcome, but smokers are not.

The Wallingford Inn (446-2849), Route 7, is a well-preserved Victorian townhouse with oak woodwork, arched marble fireplaces and embossed wallpapers, owned until 1969 by the family that built it and started the True Temper Corporation. There are six double rooms with baths at rates from $32–48 (single, $10 less) including continental breakfast.

Dunham House (446-2600), 7 South Main Street, is a pretty 1856 Victorian house with three large front rooms sharing a bath, and two smaller rooms in the back that share another bath. One larger rear bedroom has its own bath. Rates are $30–70. Don and Claudia DeMercurio, who came here from Nantucket, have also remodeled the carriage house for an exercise room, sauna, and whirlpool.

LODGING   Rutland   The Silver Fox (438-5555), Route 133, West Rutland 05777. The nattily remodeled Elija Smith farmhouse has eight comfortable guest rooms, each with private bath, plus living room and library, with VCR and plenty of games. Rates are $45 per person midweek, $50 weekends, including breakfast and dinner; $10 more during holidays and fall foliage season.

Other lodging includes the "Old Reliables": **Holiday Inn** (800-HOLIDAY; 775-1911), Routes 7 and 4 south, includes Paynter's Restaurant, indoor pool, Centre Stage lounge; **Comfort Inn at Trolley Square** (775-2200), Route 7 south; **Howard Johnson's Motor Lodge** (775-4303), Route 7 south; **Rutland Travelodge** (800-255-3050; 773-3361), Route 7 south, has three kitchenette units.

DINING OUT   Governor Williams House (773-9336), North Main Street, Rutland (formerly the Governor's Table). Refurbished and reopened by Scott Lagasse, an experienced chef, this new restaurant features New England and continental cooking, especially fresh seafood. Serves lunch ($2.95–11.95) and dinner ($8.95–16.95) daily. Sunday dinner menu from 1:00–9:00.

Ashbel's (775-3788), North Main Street, Rutland. Located in sleek, "neo-Victorian" new quarters above Royal's Market at the junction

Killington and Pico, looming over Rutland

of Routes 4 and 7, serves lunch ($3.25–6.95) and dinner ($6.95–13.95) daily plus Sunday brunch. Visual mementos of Rutland's history surround diners and appear on the menu in the names of house specialties, like Hanrahan's veal, recalling a volunteer fire company.

The Vermont Marble Inn (265-8383), West Park Place, Fair Haven. The stately dining room in this bastion of Victorian opulence holds only ten tables, and the prices are quite reasonable considering the quality of the cooking. The menu changes every two weeks or so, but starters could include chilled seafood plate with horseradish chiffonade ($4.75); entrées, boneless loin of lamb grilled and served with mustard and tarragon sauce ($13.50), prime rib of roast veal with a garlic glaze ($14.50), or an imaginative vegetarian plate ($10.95). Bountiful desserts prevail, including a rich English trifle. Nonalcoholic wines and beer available.

Fair Haven Inn (265-4907), Marble and Adams Streets, Fair Haven. Greek bouzouki music and convivial atmosphere accompany the Athenian cuisine here: chickpeas, stuffed grape leaves, egg and lemon soup, souvlakis, baklava—the works. Entrées $9.95–14.95. Open daily.

Casa Bianca (773-7401), 76 Grove Street, Rutland. Here's a friendly, homelike Italian restaurant with excellent food and a cozy atmosphere. Dinner only; entrées $10.95–16.95.

EATING OUT **Rinquist Dining Room & Lounge** (468-5172), Route 30, 2 miles north of Route 4, Lake Bomoseen. A pleasantly remodeled farm house serving moderately priced, traditional New England fare at dinner and lunch in the summer.

Captn't John's Dockside (468-3129), Route 30, 2 miles north of Route 4, Lake Bomoseen, is a popular, amiable fish house right on the lake, serving lunch and dinner Tuesday–Saturday, and open Sundays 12–9. Salmon fillet with raspberry Hollandaise is a dinner special. Entrées in the $8.95–16.95 class, plus an early bird "chef's whim" complete dinner for $7.95 on Fridays (5–7) and Saturdays (5–6).

South Station (775-1736), at the Trolley Barn, 170 South Main, Rutland, is open daily for lunch and dinner, specializing in prime ribs of beef, and such munchies as fried potato skins, zucchini sticks, stuffed mushrooms, chicken wings, hearty soups, salads, burgers, and teriyaki beef or chicken, all at moderate prices. Their Sunday clambake includes chowder, lobster or crab legs, salad, corn on the cob, dessert, and coffee for $12.95.

Little Naples (773-5663), 163 State Street, Rutland. Open Tuesday–Monday for hearty, well-prepared Italian dinners at moderate prices.

Ernie's Hearthside Grill and Bar (775-0856), 37 North Main at the rear of the Royal Court complex, Rutland. Ernie and Willa Royal, the respected Rutland restaurateurs, are again serving lunch and dinner in remodeled quarters, 11–11 Monday–Saturday, 1–9 Sunday. Moderately priced selections include seafood salad, pâté, corn chowder, mesquite-grilled chicken or sirloin, and accompanied by popovers and sweet breads.

The Pasta Depot (775-1153), Trolley Square, Rutland, makes its own linguine, fettuccini, spaghetti, angel hair, rigatoni, fussilli on the spot. You can snack there, 10–7 Tuesday–Friday, 9–5 Saturday, or order take-outs. Lunch for under $3, continental breakfast for $1.

Royal Court (773-9128), Routes 4 (East) and 7, 37 North Main, Rutland, is a new complex which includes Ashbel's and the venerable Royal's Hearthside (both above) and Royal's Market, which serves breakfast, lunch and dinner deli-style or packed to go and has a bakery, butcher shop and an array of Vermont food products.

Back Home Cafe (775-2104), 21 Center Street, Rutland, might be called Soho North, with diversified, moderately-priced food at lunch and dinner. Its downstairs Deli & Bakery also serves lunch; and the establishment now includes **The Ritz**, an art deco nightclub, with a large dance floor (capacity 400) and live bands.

Murphy's (775-3818), 31 Center Street, Rutland. Tex-Mex plus other hearty fare in a recently-renovated restaurant, open daily except Sunday for lunch and dinner, inexpensive to moderate.

Sawdi's Steak House (773-8124), Route 7 north, Rutland. Open for dinners except Monday; moderate prices.

121 West (773-7148), 121 West Street, Rutland. Substantial food at very moderate prices for lunch and dinner daily except Sunday.

SELECTIVE SHOPPING   **The Old Stone Shop**, Route 7, Wallingford. Open as a gift shop in the summer, this historic site was built in 1848 by the Batchellers, who had been making pitchforks and farm implements since 1808.

Vermont Bean Seed (265-4212), Fair Haven. This growing mail-order outfit has opened a retail store near its test garden. Call ahead for hours.

Heartstrings (287-9565), 27 College Street, Poultney, is a Victorian cottage country store with tinware, candles, potpourri, herbcrafts, teddy bears, etc.

The Vermont Shop, Trolley Square, 170 South Main, Rutland, is awkwardly located but worth browsing for its superior stock of Vermont-only products, from souvenirs and gadgets to books, toys, foods, and expensive clocks, quilts, and other gifts.

Antiques Center & Specialty Shops, 67-71 Center Street. Forty dealers, plus doll houses, miniatures, handcrafted baby items, and natural food Pet Treats.

Tennybrook Square, 230 North Main Street, Rutland, is a cluster of shops including a **Bass Shoe Outlet, Hathaway Shirt Outlet**, and **Country Quilt & Fabric**, which offers custom-made quilts and accessories, supplies and instruction books, and cotton calicos.

The Opera House, Merchants Row, downtown Rutland. Part of this old music hall has been converted into a sleek mini-mall of shops for gifts, clothes, and especially **The Book King**, a bright, well-stocked book shop.

Charles E. Tuttle Company, Main Street, Rutland, facing the park, has one of the largest stocks of used and rare books in New England. Charles Tuttle began his publishing company in Tokyo right after World War II and has built it into a major supplier of beautifully produced books on Oriental art and other Asian subjects.

Boutique International, 85 North Main Street, Rutland, has a large assortment of gifts from many countries.

The Antique Center, 67 Central Street, Rutland. Antiques and collectibles from 30 dealers.

New England Sailboard Company, Route 4 east, Rutland, calls itself the "L.L. Bean of wind surfing." Open daily 10–6, evening appointments to 10:00.

Normal Rockwell Museum, Route 4 east, Rutland, charges an admission fee to look at its collection of magazine covers, and sells prints and memorabilia to the illustrator's faithful fans.

Fred's Carpenter Shop, Route 7 north, Pittsford 05763, is a center for dollhouses and miniature furnishings, accessories, scaled lumber, hardware, electrical systems, and wallpaper plus dollhouse and furniture kits. Open Monday–Saturday, 9:30–5, Sunday 11–5 or by appointment.

ENTERTAINMENT AND SPECIAL EVENTS   East Creek Playhouse (775-0662), Belden Industrial Park, West Street, Rutland, is a new, 140-seat theater where the Actors' Repertory company performs.

Early August: **Art in the Park Summer Arts Festival**, sponsored by the **Chaffee Arts Center** (775-0356) in the Main Street Park, junction of Routes 7 and 4 east.

Early September: **Vermont State Fair** (775-5200). Midway, exhibits, rodeo, races, demolition derby, tractor pulls animate the old fairgrounds on Route 7 south of the city (which may have to find a new location, giving way to yet another shopping center).

Mid-October: **Art in the Park Fall Foliage Festival**, sponsored by the **Chaffee Arts Center** (above).

Late February: **The Great Benson Fishing Derby**, sponsored by the Fair Haven Rotary Club: many prizes in several categories, including best ice shanty. Tickets for the Derby, P.O. Box 131, Bomoseen 05732.

MEDICAL EMERGENCY   Rutland Regional Ambulance Service (773-1700); Rutland Fire Department Rescue Paramedics (773-1811).

Rescue Squads: Fair Haven/Castleton (265-8800); Poultney (287-9510); Pittsford (483-2823); Wallingford (775-5555).

Brandon, Middlebury, and Vergennes

Pleasant inns, good restaurants, restorative scenery, and agreeable diversions (skiing, hiking, boating, golfing, swimming, fishing, apple picking) conspire to make Addison County and the hills around Brandon and Middlebury a seductive, relatively uncrowded area to settle into for a few days or more of exploring and relaxation. One outstanding feature is the number of family farms that manage to thrive between Lake Champlain and the Route 7 north-south corridor. With Brandon or Middlebury as roosts, there's a lot of gently rolling, pastoral landscape to enjoy along Routes 30 and 22A west of Route 7; east of it lie the Breadloaf Ski Area (Robert Frost country), Lake Dunmore, and the highland joys of hiking and Nordic ski trails in the Green Mountain National Forest. Travelers from Crown Point on the New York side of Lake Champlain can cross over into Addison County on the Lake Champlain Bridge (toll) at Chimney Point, or farther south on "the little cable ferry that could" from Ticonderoga to Larrabees Point where Routes 73 and 74 meet.

BRANDON

Brandon, a peaceful town of some 4,000 inhabitants and a heretofore underrated appeal, has an unusual array of eclectic nineteenth-century houses in an interesting mix of Federal and Victorian styles. Sited between Otter Creek and the Neshobe River, it was the home of Thomas Davenport, who invented and patented an electric motor in 1838, and the birthplace of Stephen A. Douglas (1813-1861), "the little giant" of the famous debates with Abraham Lincoln in 1858 when Douglas was Senator from Illinois. Brandon's hospitality to travelers is growing with the addition of some interesting new places to stay.

All places listed below are in Brandon 05733, unless otherwise noted.

GREENSPACE AND WATER **Lake Dunmore**, Salisbury, north of Brandon on Route 53 off Route 7, is a tranquil, 1,000-acre lake lined with simple summer cottages at the foot of Mt. Moosalamoo and its hiking trails.

Along the west shore road are **Waterhouse Beach** (352-4433) for swimming, boating, camping; **Sunset Lodge Cottage Colony** (352-4290, April–November; 207-674-2778, November–April), West Shore Road, PO Box 30, Salisbury 05769, has 22 cottages on the lake, at $60 per night for two people ($350 per week) and $180 for six people ($550 per week); 10 percent discount April, May and September; **Lake Dunmore Lodge** (352-4444) has pleasant housekeeping cottages and duplex apartments at weekly rates ranging from $220–320 depending on the number of people in the party.

LODGING   **The Brandon Inn** (247-5766), Brandon. This cavernous historic landmark, dating back to 1786, has recently been refurbished and the number of rooms scaled down from 46 to 28 on the second and third floors (Number 217, a two-room suite is especially attractive, at $140, MAP). Other MAP rates: $90 single, $55–65 per person double, Wednesday–Sunday; Monday–Tuesday, breakfast only, $70 single, $35–$45 per person double; September 18–October 18, $100 single, $62.50–72.50 per person double, MAP, when a two-day minimum stay is required on weekends. There's a swimming pool and handy trout fishing in the Neshobe River.

Beauchamp Place (247-3905), 31 Franklin Street (Route 7). This impressive three-story Victorian mansion with a mansard roof is on the National Register of Historic Places and has been conscientiously restored by Georgia and Roy Beauchamp in high style. Each of the eight bedrooms is furnished with Victorian and Empire pieces. The common rooms are spacious, opening onto a broad verandah with wicker rockers. Breakfast features homemade breads and muffins and Vermont roasted Green Mountain coffee. Rates are $70–85, double, shared baths. (Children under 16 are discouraged; no pets.)

The Arches (247-8200), 53 East Park Street. This is the stately Georgian Revival former summer home of Albert G. Farr, a Chicago banker whose family came from Brandon. It is also on the National Register. Very recently opened as an inn and restaurant by Jack and Ellen Scheffey, The Arches features original chandeliers and carved woodwork. There are six comfortably furnished bedrooms with hand stenciling and private baths, a 50-seat dining room and a swimming pool. The vast Room #1, holding a king size bed, queen-size sofa bed, and TV rents for $95. Room Number 6, only slightly smaller with a fireplace, has a king-size bed and double sofa bed, for $85. Four other double rooms, $70–75, including full pancake or waffle breakfast. Open for lunch and dinner daily except Tuesday, plus Sunday brunch.

The Churchill House Inn (247-3300), RD 3, Brandon, is the key-

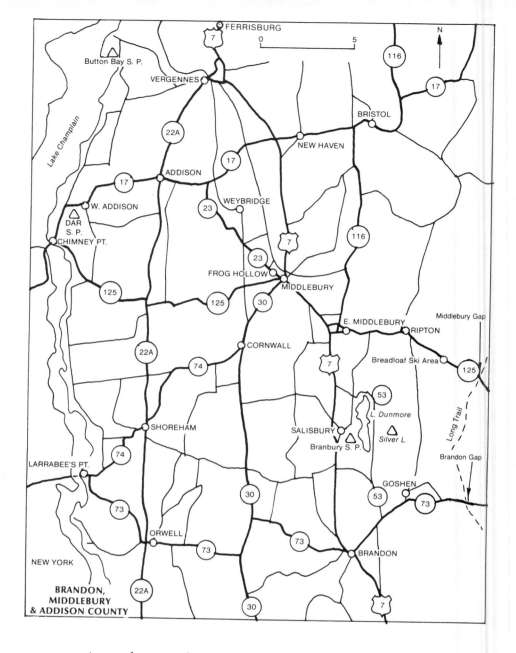

stone of seasonal inn-to-inn package tours. Located west of the Brandon Gap on Route 73, and run by Roy and Lois Jackson, this old farmhouse has eight guest rooms furnished in nineteenth-century style, serves zesty dinners and breakfasts, and offers fly-fishing and canoeing expeditions. Winter rates are $65 per person, MAP; summer $55, foliage, $59; half price for children under 13 in same room. Packages: three or four-night get-aways, summer vacation sampler, summer weekend escapes, midweek foliage specials; from $144 to $354. Write for details.

Blueberry Hill Inn (247-6735/6535), Goshen 05733, on a rough back road off Route 73 to Ripton, is another delightful, antique-filled farmhouse with good food, a craft shop, and cross-country ski center with 75 km of groomed trails. Rates are $72 per person, MAP, double occupancy, $110, single, half-price for children 14 and under in same room. BYOB. Closed November, April and May.

The Adams Motel and Restaurant (247-6644), Route 7, 1 mile south of Brandon, should really change its name, because it's not a motel, but a shady campus of 20 cozy, one-or-two-room cottages of the kind so familiar in premotel motoring days. Most of the cottages have fireplaces, TV, and there's a swimming pool, plus miniature golf across the highway. Rates range from $32 for a small cottage, $36 for a bedroom and living room, to $40 for a two-bedroom cottage (no meals), and from $72–80 with breakfast and dinner. Add $5 to all rates September 15 through October 31. Open from late spring to November.

Brandon Motor Lodge (247-9594), Route 7, 2 miles south of Brandon, is nicely situated amid acres of front lawn, with a swimming pool and two tennis courts. This old reliable is being expanded. Room rates vary with the seasons, in the $30 to $55 range, depending on size and the day of the week. Holiday weekend rates may be higher and require a two-night minimum. Polite pets welcome.

BED & BREAKFASTS   Inn at Tiffany Corners (247-6571), **Le Relais** (247-3380), **Moffett House** (247-3843), **Norlo Inn** (247-3235).

Brookside Farms (948-2727), Route 22A, Orwell 05760. This magnificent Greek Revival mansion, still another entry on the National Register, is a lovely guest house operated by the Korda family. Guests can observe the workings of a 300-acre farm, browse in a 10,000-volume library and the Kordas' antique shop, and enjoy 6 miles of cross-country ski trails. Rooms with full breakfast start at $25 per person in the nine-room annex, $50 per person in the main house. Afternoon tea, lunch, and dinner by arrangement.

DINING OUT   The Brandon Inn (247-5766), Brandon, is open to the public by reservation Thursday–Saturday, and serves a four-course $19.50 prix fixe menu, which might include chicken crêpes with mushrooms, soup or salad, chicken breast sautéed in a cream, wine, and Dijon sauce, or prime ribs, plus homemade desserts.

The Arches (247-8200), 53 East Park Street, Brandon, offers an à la carte menu: for example, baked mushroom caps stuffed with sausage ($3.95); baked Mako shark ($9.50), roast duckling with orange sauce ($12.95), or tournedoes ($14.95).

EATING OUT   Sweet Apples (247-8414), Center Street, Brandon, has an imaginative menu (with a British spin) for lunch and dinner: steamed kettle mussels cooked in English mustard and dark beer ($4.95), fish and chips ($6.95), Angels on Horseback (scallops wrapped in bacon, $11.95), Lancashire Hot Pot (beef pie with mushrooms and onions, $7.50).

Brown's of Brandon (247-3000), on the Green, has Vermont crafts, pottery, wall hangings, stenciled rugs, baskets and books.
MEDICAL EMERGENCY: 247-6828.

MIDDLEBURY

Both the town (7,574) and Middlebury College (founded in 1800 and now one of the most sought-after private colleges) owe much to the energy and vision of Gamaliel Painter, a surveyor who settled here before the Revolution. Painter accompanied Ethan Allen on the Fort Ticonderoga raid and returned to Middlebury to become the town's principal landowner, sheriff, judge, and assemblyman. The fine mansion on Court Square belonged to Painter. Another benefactor was Joseph Battell, who owned thousands of acres of forest and mountain land that he left to the college and the state when he died in 1915. He was the proprietor of the famous old summit house, Bread Loaf Inn, now the nucleus for the summer Bread Loaf School writers' conference. Battell also owned a weekly newspaper in which he fulminated against the invasion of motor cars. Emma Hart Willard, who pioneered in the education of women, was another Middlebury luminary.

All places listed below are in Middlebury 05753, unless otherwise noted.

GUIDANCE   **Addison County Chamber of Commerce Travel Bureau** (388-7951), 2 Court Street, offers brochures and referral services for accommodations.

TO SEE AND DO   **The Johnson Gallery**, Middlebury College Campus, has a distinguished permanent collection of paintings and small sculptures by Hiram Powers, Francois Rude, Auguste Rodin, Medardo Rosso, and others, as well as notable landscapes and drawings, plus transient shows. Open Monday–Friday, Sunday 12–5, Saturday 9–12, 1–5; closed during college vacations.

The Painter House, 2 Court Street recently restored to its 1801 glory by Middlebury College, is the permanent home of the **Vermont Folk Life Center** (388-4964), with its archives and exhibits. The college also has opened two parlor rooms as galleries, and there's office space for community organizations, including the Chamber of Commerce.

The Sheldon Museum (388-2117), Park Street, holds an intimate collection of furnishings, tools, household articles, clothes, books, games and other artifacts portraying Vermont folkways. A modern research ell has been added to the early Federal house. Open Monday–Saturday, 10–5, June–October 5; by appointment the rest of the year. Admission charge: 50¢–$2.00. Intriguing gift shop.

The Congregational Church (1806-09) is one of the state's most architecturally distinguished.

The Vermont State Craft Center (388-3177), Frog Hollow, on the Otter Creek falls, exhibits and sells the best work of some 250 Vermont artisans. Open daily except Sunday, 9:30–5.

The Battell House, on the park (now the community house), was built in 1816 for Horatio Seymour, Senator from Vermont from 1821–33. The end walls of this urbane mansion are capped by marble coping instead of the usual "carpenter's finish."

Morgan Horse Farm, on the edge of town toward Weybridge, is a breeding and training center operated by the University of Vermont. Guided tours of the stables and paddocks are available daily, May–October by reservation (388-2011); the farm is open Tuesday–Friday, November–April, but tours are not given. Admission: 75¢–$2.50.

Mount Independence, 8 miles west of Orwell on the shore of Lake Champlain, Route 73 off 22A, facing Fort Ticonderoga, was a key fortification defending the colonies in 1776–77, but unlike Ticonderoga the horseshoe battery was never reconstructed nor developed. This 400-acre woodlot remained neglected and almost inaccessible for 200 years until 1975 when it was opened to the public by the Vermont Division of Historic Preservation, which has been gradually restoring a sense of its importance.

John Strong Mansion, West Addison, Route 17, west of 22A, is one of several substantial brick houses and buildings made of stone taken from the ruins of Fort Crown Point and skidded across Lake Champlain by oxen. General Strong, an early settler and Green Mountain Boy, built his (third) residence here in 1796, with brick from his own claypits on the "Salt Lick" where he first hunted deer. The house is now owned by the Daughters of the American Revolution and open to the public during the summer.

The Barnes Tavern, Route 125, Chimney Point, state-owned and full of historical interest is open Wednesday–Sunday in the summer.

The Lord's Prayer Rock, on the south side of Route 17 entering Bristol from the east, is an unusual landmark: the Lord's Prayer chiseled on a flat rock, the inspiration of a physician named Joseph C. Greene, who commissioned the inscription in 1891 presumably because he was still thankful for having reached that point safely when, as a youth, he was hauling logs over steep roads.

GREENSPACE AND WATER   On the east shore road are **Wood Acres** (247-3126), another cluster of cottages; and **Branbury State Park** (247-

5925), with a sandy beach, boating, snack bar, picnic grove, museum, nature trail, and hiking to the Falls of Lana, Cascade and Silver Lakes; likely to be crowded on weekends. **Silver Lake** is accessible only on foot; campers have been spotted propelling one of the Garden Way's large-wheeled carts in and out.

BICYCLING   Country Inns Along the Trail bike tours usually begin and end at Churchill House, which has a limited number of 10- and 12-speeds for rent at $15 per day or $75 per week. Fourteen other inns are on the itinerary; the cost of an individually customized tour is approximately $55 to $75 per person per day, double occupancy, MAP, depending on which hostelries are involved. Brochure from **Churchill House** (247-3300), RD 3, Brandon 05733.

HIKING   Seven inns collaborate with Churchill House for hikers who want to explore sections along 80 miles of Vermont's **Long Trail**, from Mountain Meadows Lodge at Killington north to Camel's Hump View Farm in Moretown. The season begins Memorial Day and continues through the third week of October. Total cost for the seven inns and eight days of hiking ranges from $466 and $619, including lodging, dinner, breakfast, trail lunch, car shuttle, tax and tips. Children under 13 (up to two) sharing the same room with parents are half price. Write the **Churchill House** (above) for information and reservations.

LLAMA FARM AND TREKS   Land o'Goshen Farm (247-6015), halfway up Brandon Gap on Route 73, is where Marie and Edgar Brand raise llamas for sale and offer guided day treks with lunch and overnight camping trips by reservation. Their "nonspitting" South American llamas are drawing lots of attention. The Brands are thinking about adding camels to their farm. Meanwhile, day treks are available daily, May 15–October 20, for parties of two or more at $60 per person ($75 in foliage). Overnight treks (minimum of six people), $225/250; Churchill trek, $210/240, two nights with dinner and breakfast at the Churchill House Inn.

CROSS-COUNTRY SKI TOURING   Similar five-day inn-to-inn trekking for experienced skiers can be arranged via the **Churchill House** for $398 per person double occupancy and $448 single, including breakfast, trail lunch, dinner, lodging, tax, tip, shuttle and area use fees at Breadloaf, Blueberry Hill, and Mountain Top touring centers. Ski rentals available at Churchill House.

   High Pond Ski Area (273-2303), 15 minutes southwest of Brandon, Union Street to High Pond Road, is a pleasant, small, weekend family ski area, managed by John and Sherry Armitage of Pittsford. Five downhill trails, with a 300-foot vertical drop, are reached by a 1,450-foot T-bar. Cross-country trails adjacent to 3,800 woodland acres formerly owned by ski pioneer Douglas Burden, now under the auspices of the Nature Conservancy.

The American Ski Marathon, early February, a 25 or 50 km challenge that draws as many as 600 skiers; and the Pig Race, mid-March that winds up with a fine pork barbecue. Further information from Blueberry Hill.

The Bread Loaf Touring Center, Route 125, 12 miles from the main campus, is owned and operated by Middlebury College. It has over 50 km of trails in the area of the Robert Frost Farm and the college ski bowl. Rentals, accessories, repairs; nominal trail fee.

DOWNHILL SKIING   Middlebury College Snow Bowl (388-4356), 13 miles east on Route 125, at Bread Loaf, has three Poma lifts, double chair lift, school, rentals, restaurant. Closed December 25.

ORCHARDS TO VISIT   September and October is Apple Time in Addison County, where visitors are welcome to pick their own. A brochure from the Chamber of Commerce office has a list of orchards, among them is Patterson' Apple Acres (897-5592), Barnum Hill, 3 miles south of Shoreham, off Route 22A. Cider; plus pick-your-own sweet and sour cherries in early July and purple plums in September.

COVERED BRIDGES   The Pulpmill Covered Bridge, between Middlebury and Weybridge, near the Morgan Horse Farm, is the oldest in the state (1808-20) and the last remaining two-lane span in use.

Halpin (1824). New Haven, 2 miles east off Route 7, highest bridge above the stream bed.

PARKS AND FORESTS   D.A.R. State Park (759-2354/483-2314), 8 miles west of Addison on Route 17, has a small campground and picnic area, with steps leading down to a smooth shale beach for swimming.

Button Bay State Park (475-2377/483-2314), ½ mile south of Vergennes on Route 22A; 1 mile west on Panton Road; 5 miles northwest on Basin Harbor Road; 1 mile south of town road. Named for the unusual button-like clay bank formations, with a splendid view across the lake to the Adirondacks; campsites, picnic areas, swimming, fishing, nature museum, and trails.

Dead Creek Wildlife Management Area (759-2397), 7 miles east of the D.A.R. State Park on Route 17, is a 2,800-acre semi-wilderness tract, most of which is open to the public except for certain refuges. The information booth is not always staffed because the supervisor is generally in the field, but a self-guided tour folder is available.

The Green Mountain National Forest District Office (388-4362), Route 7, Middlebury. For information about the pick-your-own blueberry management areas, Silver Lake and the Falls of Lana, the Robert Frost Wayside and Interpretive Trail in Ripton (where quotations from his poems are posted along the way), and the Bristol Cliffs Wilderness.

GOLF   Ralph Myhre Golf Course (388-3711), just south of the Middlebury campus, is owned and operated by the college, 18 holes.

HORSEBACK RIDING   Green Mountain Pack Trips (453-4924), RD 1, Box 2535, Bristol 05443. Jessie Taylor organizes hay rides, hourly rides, lunch or supper excursions ($28 per person), and overnight treks in the National Forest ($85 per night, $150 for the weekend, including camping gear and meals).

Firefly Ranch (453-2223), Box 152, Bristol 05443 specializes in western riding, May through foliage. Rates are $70 per person per night, or $325 for five days, including lodging, three meals, horses, tack, and guides. From December 1 through March 31, Firefly turns into a ski lodge, with pick-up service in Middlebury and Burlington.

MARINAS   Le Voyageur Marina (759-2049), West Addison, boat access, pump-out station for boats under 35 feet.

Chipman Point Marina & Campground (948-2288), Route 73A, has dockage for 60 boats, grocery store, pump-out station, game room, swimming, boat rentals.

LAKE CRUISES   Champlain Lake and Canal Cruises. Operated by Champlain Gateway Cruises, Whitehall, New York (518-499-1600 or 802-453-4597, 897-5331), the M/V *Mount Independence*, a converted World War II minesweeper, treats passengers to a variety of interesting day or evening dinner cruises plus package excursions from the end of May well into the month of October. All cruises from Whitehall pass through one or more locks of the picturesque Champlain Barge Canal, and those from Shoreham focus on the strategic Revolutionary War history of Fort Ticonderoga, Mounts Independence and Defiance, Forts St. Frederick and Crown Point. On this trip, you can readily appreciate how Ethan Allen's Green Mountain Boys were able to row across the narrows at night to capture the sleeping fort.

In the July–September period, on Tuesdays and Thursdays, the "Lake Champlain Explorer" cruise offers several options from three ports, including land tours to Fort Ticonderoga or Middlebury, with round trip fares from $10 to $21 for adults, $5 to $14 for children. There are shorter trips on Wednesdays and Fridays, and longer cruises on Saturdays and Sundays, except over the July 4 weekend when special excursions from Whitehall to Burlington are scheduled. In mid-September, package trips across Shoreham to Saratoga are offered at $87 per adult. (On early and late-season trips, be sure to bring a windbreaker.) "Dinner and Dixie" ($22 per person) or "DJ" or Rhythm & Blues on Friday and Saturday nights.

HOUSEBOATS   Vermont Houseboat Vacations (401-437-1377), 90 Forbes Street, Riverside, RI 02915, provides 34- or 40-foot inboard/outboard houseboats that operate on Lake Champlain out of the Chipman Point Marina, Orwell. The boats, sleeping six or eight people, are rented for a week or weekend in late May, June, July, and August. Basic rates range from $577 to $1,179 depending on the size of the boat, length and time of cruise, and date.

BICYCLE TOURING   Vermont Bicycle Touring (453-4811), Box 711, Bristol 05443, is now the best-known and largest bike vacation organizer. The founder, John Freidin, originated the inn-to-inn concept in 1972 with a single weekend tour, and wrote the perennially popular *25 Bicycle Tours in Vermont* (published by Backcountry Publications, Box 175, Woodstock, VT 05091, $9.95 postpaid). Bill Perry, the new owner and director, offers 55 different VBT tours, including 9 new weekend trips, 11 new inn-to-inn tours, and 9 new special-interest and combination vacations, such as a Cruise & Cycle tour of Lake Champlain and another of the New England islands or Maine coast, and a two-week bicycle tour of southern England. In Vermont there are five-day Vagabonds for $495 in season; two or three-day Roundabouts or Rambles from $169–339. Or choose a Pedal & Paddle Weekend, a Performance Training Weekend, or a Brookfield Mountain Bike Ramble. All of these are spelled out in the VBT brochure; they will also loan you a 17-minute videotape.

LODGING   The Middlebury Inn (388-4961, 800-842-4666), 14 Courthouse Square, has been the town's chief hostelry since 1827. Innkeepers Frank and Jane Emanuel, who took over in 1977, have now totally renovated the 73 guest accommodations and public rooms. Rooms in the main house have private baths, cable color TV, air conditioning, and two direct-dial phones. There are ground level rooms in the contemporary motel annex (the Emma Willard and Governor Weeks Houses), and the adjacent Porter Mansion, full of handsome architectural details, has five Victorian rooms. Room rates, which vary with the size and location of the accommodations, range from $64–90 single, $70–96 double or twin, with $6 for an additional adult in the same room; no charge for children under the age of 18 sharing unless a rollaway bed is required. Pets are welcome in the motel units at $6 daily. "Seasonal Samplers" packages are available.

The Swift House Inn (388-2766), 25 Stewart Lane, was, until a few years ago, the family estate of the legendary philanthropist Jessica Stewart Swift, who lived to be over 100. Antiques, elaborately carved marble fireplaces, an elevator and other gracious amenities add to the charm of this 1814 mansion. Dinners and breakfasts are served in the cherry-panelled main dining room or in the library. There are nine guest rooms in the main house and five more in a recently acquired annex. Rates per room range from $70 to $94 (for the Governor's Suite, which has a fireplace, sitting area, whirlpool tub, and shower; and for the Swift Room, with canopied queen bed, fireplace, sitting area, terrace, and bath). Andy and John Nelson preside. Dinner is served Thursday through Sunday, May 1–November 1.

The Waybury Inn (388-4015), Route 125, East Middlebury 05740, is an inviting, historic, 15-room village inn, open all year. Bob Newhart never did sleep here, though guests sometimes ask for the "Loudons" because the exterior serves as the "Stratford Inn" on the veteran CBS series. There's no pool, but a swimmin' hole under the nearby bridge. Rates range from $88 to $110 double including a full country breakfast. Two-night minimum stay on weekends between July 1 and November 1, and holidays. Luncheon is served in the Pub during that season, dinner year-round.

The Chipman Inn (388-2390), Ripton 05766, Route 125 on the way to or from Breadloaf and the Middlebury College Snow Bowl ski area, in the heart of Robert Frost country, is an exceptionally attractive 1828 house. Most of the nine guest rooms have private baths; public rooms include a lounge/bar where guests relax before a very large Franklin stove. The dining room is lit by candles and decorated with stenciled wallpaper. Rates are $70–100 per room with breakfast. A five-course dinner is optional at $22. Closed in April and November.

The Shoreham Inn & Country Store (897-5861), Route 74 west, on The Green, Shoreham 05770. In this pleasant 1799 house, Cleo and Fred Alter welcome cyclists, canoeists, skiers, hikers, and horseback riders to their hearth and eleven guest rooms with seven baths. Rates: $35 single with breakfast, $60 double, with a winter vacation special at $25 and $40 respectively.

Bristol Commons Inn (453-2326), junction of Routes 17 and 116, Bristol 05443. An attractive A-frame style motel in a peaceful valley setting, 1 mile from the village of Bristol, with a restaurant, Rosemarie's, on premises. Room rates: $28–30 double occupancy. One large A-frame for $60 for six persons. Chip-putt green. Rosemarie's serves breakfast and northern Italian dinners in the $6–13 range. Open all year.

The Long Run Inn (453-3233), RD1, Box 114, Bristol 05443. This gabled village inn, located in Lincoln Center on the New Haven River, began life as a lumberjack's hotel soon after its construction in 1799, and offers access to hiking on Mount Abraham, horseback riding, an "ol swimmin' hole," cross-country and bike trails. Now owned by Michael and Beverly Conway. Room rates: $45 per person double occupancy MAP, $50 single; $18 per person double, $21 single, room only. Children under 10 half price. Trail lunch $4; breakfast $3.50. BYOB. Closed April and November.

BED & BREAKFASTS   Point of View (388-7206); **Robert Frost Mountain** (388-6042); **The October Pumpkin** (388-9525); **The Horn Farnsworth House** (388-2300); **Brookside Meadows** (388-6429); **Chimney Point House** (759-2632), Routes 125 and 17 at the end of the Champlain Bridge, Addison; and **Breadloaf Farm** (545-2101), Weybridge.

The ice goes out in East Clarendon

DINING OUT The Waybury Inn (388-4015), East Middlebury. Dinner in this historic hostelry could start with stuffed mushrooms ($3.25), followed by stuffed trout ($13.95), king crab legs ($15.95), or Veal Waybury ($13.95), steak, and chicken.

Swift House (388-2766), Middlebury. Between May 1 and November 1, this colonial mansion is open for dinner by reservation. Appetizers include asparagus and hollandaise crêpe ($4); entrées begin at $10 for spinach tortellini alfredo with pesto, Cajun blackened chicken ($12), rising to filet mignon with green peppercorn and brandy sauce ($17).

Otter Creek Cafe (388-7342), Frog Hollow, Middlebury. Beyond the popular bakery lies bliss in the form of ragout of wild mushrooms, breast of duck in honey and wine, or roast partridge in plum sauce. Open for lunch and dinner (expensive) except Sunday.

Woody's (388-4182), Five Bakery Lane, gives you the sense of being wined and dined on a small, three-decker art deco ship beached on the bank of Otter Creek. Open daily for lunch, dinner, and Sunday brunch, this popular spot serves up salads and quiches midday (from $4), homemade breads and desserts, and lists among dinner entrées (up to $15) spicy Cajun or Bourbon shrimp.

Mr. Up's (388-6724), on the Bakery Lane plaza, keeps up with the times and tastes in its stained-glass, oak and greenery setting and in summer in an outdoor patio. Luncheon specials could be Maryland softshell crab laced with hollandaise ($6.95) or Gulf amberjack ($5.95). Dinner entrées from $8.95 up.

The Middlebury Inn (388-4961/4666) serves a big breakfast buffet, lunch in the Country Peddler Cafe or on the front porch, and the main dining room features a "Classic Candelight Carverie," all moderately priced.

Fire & Ice (388-7166), 26 Seymour Street, Middlebury. "Good Food & Legal Vice," it says of itself; excellent lunch and dinner daily plus Sunday brunch in an informal stained-glass and mahogany setting. Entrées range from $7.45–14.95. Closed Mondays.

1796 House Restaurant (453-4699), Route 7 north of Middlebury, New Haven. This glossy, luxuriously appointed and cheerfully decorated place was opened in the summer of 1987 by chef Glenn Wendel in a renovated farmhouse with a splendid panoramic view. It's open for dinner daily except Tuesday, and serves such specialties as (the true) Bermuda Fish Chowder ($3.95), "Black" Duck Cassis ($16), and Dover Sole ($18.50), plus old standbys like steak, other fresh fish, ham, and chicken.

Mary's (453-2432), 11 Main Street, Bristol. Highly and widely regarded as one of the most delectable restaurants in Vermont, this storefront cafe serves lunch and dinner daily except Monday, and Sunday brunch, at moderate prices. Among its unusual offerings: Caribbean marinated swordfish with pineapple fritters, lobster and scallops sautéed with a lime *beurre blanc*, and grilled chicken with strawberry relish and corn cakes. Lobster clambake on Tuesdays. Call ahead to make sure you can get in.

Rosemarie's (453-2326), Routes 17 and 116, Bristol, is a superior, moderate-to-expensive Italian restaurant with specialties like fried calamari, escarole and bean soup, and conch.

EATING OUT **Rosie's** (388-7052), 1 mile south of Middlebury on Route 7, is open daily and serves a lot of good, inexpensive food. This family mecca is said to expand every eight months or so to accommodate its fans. Entrées range from $5–14.

Paisano Ristorante (388-3385), Main Street, Middlebury, features Italian pizza, pasta, and seafood; outdoor cafe in season. Entrées range from $5.95–12.95.

The Dog Team Tavern (388-7651), a jog off Route 7 4 miles north of Middlebury. Traditional New England fare (sticky buns, et al). Open for dinner daily except Monday. Open for lunch late spring through foliage. Gift shop. Opened in the 1930s by Sir Wilfred Grenfell (1865–1940), the British medical missionary who established hospitals, orphanages, schools, and cooperative stores in Labrador and near the Arctic Circle. For their benefit he collected and sold native Eskimo art, some of which remains on display.

SELECTIVE SHOPPING **Middlebury Antique Center** (388-6229), Routes 7 and 116, East Middlebury 05740, holds stock from 50 dealers.

Country Bear Gift Shop (388-6443), Route 7, 3 miles south of Middlebury, features bear stationery, mugs, ornaments, mobiles, etc., plus housewares.

Wood Ware (388-6297), Route 7 south of Middlebury, is the home of solid butternut door harps and dozens of other items. Open daily, May through October, or by appointment.

Brady Galleries (388-3350), 88 Main Street. Fine American paintings and antiques, folk art, porcelain, and other items for serious collectors can be found in the restored 1804 John Warren House, with its circular staircase and Palladian window.

Sweet Cecily (388-3353), Frog Hollow Lane. Nancy Dunn, former Frog Hollow gallery director has assembled her own selection of ceramics, folk art, hooked rugs, and other items from 100 craftspeople, including Mexican and Amish.

Vermont Bookshop (388-2061), Main Street, was opened in 1947 by Robert Dike Blair, who is one of New England's best-known booksellers and the publisher of Vermont Books, an imprint for the poems of Walter Hard.

Store Two (388-7444), 2 Park Street, next to the Sheldon Museum, is a contemporary "country" store, filled with crafts, Vermont products, and an array of comestibles and potions from all over.

Skihaus (388-4451), Battell Block, stocks sportswear of all kinds plus a ski shop for Nordic and Alpine gear.

Stardust Memories (388-4051), 10 Merchants Row. Vintage frocks and jewelry.

Frog Hollow Mill, below the state craft center in a splendidly restored stone mill, is a mini-mini shopping center as well as the site of the Otter Creek Cafe.

ENTERTAINMENT & EVENTS **Vermont Ensemble Theatre** (388-3001) performs during the summer in a tent near the Fletcher Field House on the Middlebury College campus. It's 1987 production of *La Strada* drew raves.

Point-Counterpoint Chamber Players (247-8467) give a summer concert series in various Addison County locations.

Late February: **Middlebury College Winter Carnival** (388-3711). Ice show, concerts, snow sculpture.

SPECIAL EVENTS Early July: A six-day **Festival on the Green**, featuring individual performers and groups such as the Bread & Puppet Theater.

Early August: **Addison County Field Days**, (545-2488). Livestock and produce fair, horse show, lumberjacks, demolition derby, and other events.

MEDICAL EMERGENCY   Middlebury (388-3333); Shoreham (897-7777); Bristol (453-2401).

VERGENNES

Founded by Donald McIntosh in 1764 and later named by Ethan Allen for Count de Vergenne, the French Minister of Foreign Affairs who was a strong supporter of the American Revolutionary cause, Vergennes, with 2,300 residents, is the smallest *city* in the United States. In 1811–12, Thomas McDonough used the Otter Creek basin to build, in record time, three ships including the 734-ton, 26-gun *Saratoga* and equipped nine gunboats with which he defeated the British fleet in Lake Champlain off Valcour Island in 1814.

TO SEE AND DO   **Basin Harbor Maritime Museum** (475-2317), at the entrance to the Basin Harbor Club off Panton Road. Displayed in an early nineteenth-century one-room schoolhouse are objects that reflect the 10,000-year history of Lake Champlain, with emphasis on the latest nautical archaeological explorations. Evening lectures, field trips, and demonstrations of boat-building craftsmanship are scheduled in the summer months.

Rokeby Museum (877-3406), 3 miles north of Vergennes on Route 7 in Ferrisburg 05456, is the home of Rowland E. Robinson, the nineteenth-century author, illustrator, and naturalist. The eight rooms of exhibits in this Underground Railroad station for fugitive slaves contain furnishings and personal items from four generations of the Robinson family. This under-appreciated museum is open for guided tours at 11 and 2, Saturday, Sunday, and Monday, June–October, and by appointment for groups and researchers throughout the year. Admission charge: $2 adults, $1 students, 50¢ for children under 12.

LODGING   *Lake Resort*   **Basin Harbor Club** (475-2311), Box 7, Vergennes 05491, located on Lake Champlain 5 miles west of the town off Panton Road and Route 22A, has everything, including a 3,200-foot airstrip. The attractive inn, cottages, and lodges are spread around a sheltered cove for swimming and boating and an 18-hole golf course. There are five tennis courts and a large swimming pool as well. Basin Harbor, owned and run by the Beach family, has a large and loyal following, and celebrated its centennial in 1986–87. Children and young people are more than welcome; many activities are planned for them. Special summer events include lake trips on the 40-foot tour boat, *Dynamyte II*, fishing trips, performances of the Mozart Festival orchestra, the annual Antique and Classic Boat Society Show, and July 4th festivities.

Accommodations range from rooms in the inn to suites in the 77 individualized cottages, most of which have a pantry with refrigerator and wet bar, many with fireplaces. Rates, daily, per person with a full American Plan, are $85 to $150 single, $80 to $150 double. A cottage with living room, three bedrooms, and two or three baths would be $85 or $95 per person with a six-person minimum. For less than a seven-day stay, add 10 percent. There are also Early Bird (late May, early June), Golf, Tennis, Honeymoon, and Lake Champlain Packages. Small, well-trained pets are welcome.

BED & BREAKFASTS   **The Strong House Inn** (877-3337), Route 22A, Vergennes 05491, was built in the 1830s by Samuel Paddock Strong, a local worthy, in the graceful Federal style with such fine workmanship as curly maple railings on the free-standing main staircase. Laura and Liam Murphy now offer six bedrooms, ranging from $35 for a smaller one with iron and brass double bed, shared bath, to $50 for Room 6 with its mahogany Sheraton furnishings, two double four-poster beds, and private bath, including full breakfast. (Smoking permitted only in designated areas; no pets indoors.)

Emerson's Guest House (877-3293), 82 Main Street, Vergennes, is a spacious Victorian home with four large, airy bedrooms, and gracious living areas, open porches, and extensive gardens. Rates are $30 single and $35 double, including a full breakfast.

Dunn Inn (425-2902), Route 7, North Ferrisburg. Three guest rooms, two doubles ($38) and one single ($25), with shared bath and full breakfast in an early American setting.

RESTAURANT   **Painter's Tavern** (877-3413), on the Green, Vergennes, is an attractive watering hole, open daily, serving moderately priced lunch and dinner selections specializing in seafood, Tex-Mex and Cajun dishes. Entrées $8.95–11.50, and "wickedly rich" desserts.

SHOPPING   **Kennedy Brothers** (877-2975), just off Route 7, Vergennes, an attraction for many years for its factory outlet oak and pine woodenware, has expanded its quarters to include a Factory Marketplace with three floors of Vermont products, crafts, and antiques, plus a bakery, the Owl's Basket Delicatessen for eat-in or take-out soups, sandwiches, Ben & Jerry's ice cream.

The Peddler's Wagon (877-3392), Monkton Road, off Route 7, Vergennes, stocks folk art, painted wood products, dry floral art from 30 Vermont crafters.

Bittersweet House (425-3557), Westside, old Route 7, Ferrisburg, features handpainted Vermont roof slates, wall hangings and clocks, paintings on driftwood.

Burlington Region

Now recognized by the Department of Commerce as a metropolitan area, Vermont's "Queen City" (with an area population of over 100,000) is the seat of Chittenden County, named for Thomas Chittenden, the one-eyed but foresighted first governor of the state (1777–1797). As Vermont's financial, communication, educational, and cultural center, Burlington is a junior Boston, with its colleges, excellent medical center, electronic and engineering industries (notably IBM and General Electric), and imaginative waterfront redevelopment.

Burlington was chartered in 1763, four years after the French were evicted from the Champlain Valley. Ethan Allen, his three brothers, and a cousin were awarded large grants of choice lots along the Onion (now Winooski) River. Ira Allen was responsibile for securing in 1791 the legislative charter for the University of Vermont, from which the first class, of four, was graduated in 1804. The city's prosperous growth in the 1800s is reflected in the handsome mansions arrayed in tiers that slope eastward up from the lake shore, most of them now occupied by the University of Vermont or Champlain College.

Burlington boasts many architectural landmarks. Closest to the shore, at the corner of College and Champlain Streets, stands the Greek Revival mansion built in 1840 by Timothy Follett, first president of the Rutland Railroad, designed by Ammi B. Young, architect for the state capitol. After several decades of neglect and near-destruction by fire, the house was restored and converted into offices by the principal downtown real estate developer in 1979. Earlier examples of distinguished architecture are "Grassemont," at 411 Main Street, built in 1804 and once occupied by Governor Cornelius Van Ness, now used by the university; and the Unitarian Church (1816) at the head of Church Street, which was designed by Peter Banner, one of the architects of Park Street Church in Boston, from plans by Bulfinch. Among other notable buildings are three by the renowned firm of McKim, Mead & White: the City Hall (1926), the Robert Hull Fleming Museum (1931), and the Ira Allen Chapel (1927), the latter two on the UVM campus. Next to the chapel is H. H. Richardson's last work, the romanesque Billings

Library (1885), given to the university by Frederick Billings of Woodstock to house the extraordinary collection of books assembled by George Perkins Marsh (1801–1882), the Burlington lawyer who served as Congressman and diplomat and who wrote *Man and Nature* (1864), still regarded as the ecologist's bible.

A "Who's Who" of Burlington would also include Ethan Allen Hitchcock, ambassador to Russia and Secretary of the Interior in the McKinley and Teddy Roosevelt administrations; John Godfrey Saxe, an enormously popular poet of the mid-1800s; Admiral Henry Mayo, commmander of the Atlantic Fleet in World War I; James R. Angell, longtime president of Yale University; John Dewey, the educator whose philosophy revolutionized American teaching; A. Atwater Kent, pioneering radio manufacturer; U.S. Senator Warren R. Austin, the first American ambassador to the United Nations; Philip Hoff, the first Democratic governor of the state who served three terms after 1962; and Patrick Leahy, Vermont's first Democratic Senator, who was reelected for a third term in 1986.

There's a lot of creative energy at work and play in Burlington these days, partly because of the 10,000 UVM students. The once rather stodgy city has such a yeasty atmosphere that a Socialist mayor—the only one in the United States—was elected by ten votes in 1981, by what a *New Republic* writer recently called "the 'hipboisie,' the granola-chewing exemplars of backpack chic who have come here for the university and the mountains." Mayor Sanders was reelected in 1983, 1985, and 1987, however, by a substantial plurality of voters who crossed party lines.

Yachtsmen are crowding Lake Champlain, especially Malletts Bay, where moorings are in short supply.

Within the radius of Greater Burlington are Winooski, Colchester, Essex Junction, Jericho, Bolton Valley, Richmond, Shelburne, Charlotte (pronounced sha-*lot*) and Ferrisburg, whose attractions are included in this section.

GUIDANCE   **The Lake Champlain Regional Chamber of Commerce** (863-3489), 209 Battery Street (Box 453), Burlington 05402-0453. Write for seasonal "Vacation Package" brochures.

Newspapers: The daily *Burlington Free Press*, and the weekly *Vermont Vanguard*, the latter especially for reviews, political features and entertainment notes.

GETTING THERE   By car: I-89, Routes 7 and 2.

By bus: Vermont Transit (in New York and New England, 800-451-3292).

By air: Burlington International Airport served by Bar Harbor (800-343-3210), Brockway Air (800-327-8376); Continental (863-2509); Empire Airlines (800-448-4104); PBA (800-722-3597); United Airlines (800-241-6522); U.S. Air (862-9611).

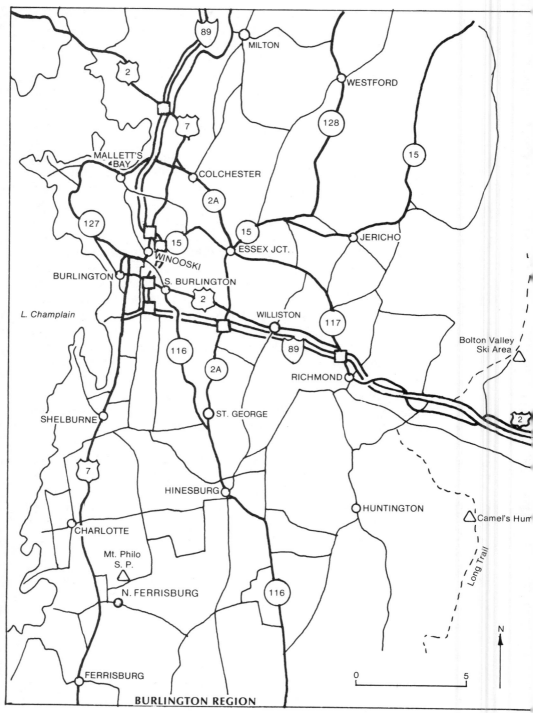

MILTON

WESTFORD

2

7

MALLETT'S BAY

COLCHESTER

2A

127

15

ESSEX JCT.

128

15

JERICHO

WINOOSKI

BURLINGTON

S. BURLINGTON

L. Champlain

2

WILLISTON

116

89

117

Bolton Valley
Ski Area

2A

RICHMOND

2

SHELBURNE

ST. GEORGE

7

HINESBURG

HUNTINGTON

Camel's Hum

CHARLOTTE

Mt. Philo
S. P.

N. FERRISBURG

116

Long Trail

N

0   5

FERRISBURG

BURLINGTON REGION

Lake Champlain Ferries (864-9804) between Burlington and Port Kent, NY; Grand Isle and Plattsburgh, NY; Charlotte and Essex, NY.

TO SEE AND DO   The Robert Hull Fleming Museum (656-2090), University of Vermont, Colchester Avenue. Open 10–5 weekdays, except Monday, 1–5 Saturday, Sunday. Closed holidays. Dedicated in 1931 as a memorial to an alumnus of the university, this expanding gallery has varied collections of art, natural history, archaeology and geology. Its holdings in ancient primitive art from several cultures and continents are especially notable. It has a well-selected retrospective collection of American portaits and landscapes, from the eighteenth century to contemporary works.

Especially for children is the **Discovery Museum,** 51 Park Street in Essex Junction about 5 miles northeast of Burlington, past Winooski, on Route 15. Summer hours: Tuesday–Saturday, 10–4:30, Sunday 1–4:30; Winter, Tuesday–Sunday 1–4:30; Saturday 10–4. Admission $1.00, children under 2, free. Call 878-8687. Nature, science, history, and art are conveyed in innovative hands-on ways with the use of permanent exhibits, including computer terminals, small animals and snakes that can be handled; rotating special exhibits and workshops.

The Shelburne Museum (985-3344) is open daily 9–5 mid-May to late October, with certain buildings open Sundays the rest of the year. This fascinating "collection of collections" portraying "the American spirit" was assembled discerningly after 1947 by the late Electra Havemeyer Webb and her husband J. Watson Webb. One can wander for a whole day or more through 35 buildings, most of them transplanted from other places in New England and Vermont. A separate guide book is needed to describe all of these extraordinary collections of Americana, but here are a few highlights: a 1915 steam locomotive and private Palace Car presented to Governor E. C. Smith in 1890 by W. Seward Webb, then president of the Rutland Railroad; paintings of North American big game in the Beach Gallery; the sidewheeler *Ticonderoga*, in her basin near the Colchester Reef Light House; the Horseshoe Barn's marvelous carriages; the Castleton Slate Jail; Shaker Horsestand Shed; Dorset House and its decoys, Audubon game bird prints, and fowling pieces; General Store; Saw Mill, and the Webb Memorial Building, in which rooms from the Webb's New York apartment have been recreated, together with their distinguished art collection. There's a museum shop and cafeteria, electric trams for the footsore, and picnic areas. Something for everyone; lots of displays geared to children, such as a model circus parade. Admission charge $6.50; 6–15, $2.50, under 6 free. Check special events.

Shelburne Farms (985-9585). Most of the grand estate belonging to Dr. and Mrs. William Seward Webb (Lila Vanderbilt) in the 1880s and 1890s is now being used as an experimental farm and educational and cultural center, under the auspices of Shelburne Farms Resources, open to the public at specified times and for certain events. Comprising 3,800 acres at its zenith, this "duchy" was landscaped by the famous Frederick Law Olmsted (who also designed Central Park) and forested by Gifford Pinchot. The Webbs' 110-room summer "cottage" on a bluff overlooking Lake Champlain, the immense five-story, 416-foot Farm Barn, and the Coach Barn, once occupied by prize Hackneys, are the nucleus of the present Webb family's nonprofit programs for continuing education in rural development, conservation, and the arts. The mansion itself has been restored as an inn and conference center. (*See Lodging*.)

For a schedule of tours and other events in this magnificent setting, write Shelburne Farms Resources, Shelburne 05482.

Historic Sites and Districts: Head of Church Street, Pearl Street, Battery Street, and the Lakeside Historic District in Burlington.

Fort Ethan Allen, Colchester on Route 15. Constructed in 1893 it was used for a variety of military purposes until 1961. Although now owned by the University of Vermont and St. Michaels College, it still retains much of its historic character.

Williston Village Historic District on Route 2 includes a concentration of Greek Revival and Federal-style buildings built during the community's agricultural prosperity in the nineteenth century.

The Champlain Shakespeare Festival, a summer repertory company, performs in the 291-seat Royall Tyler Theater on the UVM campus, named for America's first professional playwright, a Vermonter from Brattleboro (1757–1826). For information and tickets, CFS Box Office, Royall Tyler Theatre, UVM, 05405 (656-0090).

Vermont Mozart Festival Performances. Summer concerts in various settings—on ferries, at the Shelburne Museum and/or Shelburne Farms, at the Basin Harbor Club, in churches. Winter chamber series. For information, Box 512, 05402 (862-7352).

Flynn Theater for the Performing Arts (863-5966), 153 Main Street, Burlington. This cultural showcase is a refurbished art-deco movie house, now home to plays, musical comedies, jazz concerts, and lectures, many under the auspices of the George Bishop Lane Series.

St. Michael's Summer Playhouse (655-2000), St. Michael's College, Winooski.

The Vermont Symphony Orchestra (864-5741), 77 College Street, Burlington. One of the country's first statewide philharmonics, now directed by Efrain Guigui, presents a five-concert Chittenden

County Series at the Flynn; outdoor summer pops at Shelburne Farms and elsewhere.

George Bishop Lane Series (656-3085), Sponsors major musical and theatrical performances.

The Burlington Mariners, minor league AA pro baseball club. Check newspapers for schedules or call (862-6662).

Old Red Mill, off Route 117, Jericho Corners, a National Historic site, with a crafts shop. A new rolling process for flour was introduced here in 1885. The village of Jericho was the home of Wilson A. "Snowflake" Bentley, a farmer who was the first person in the world to photograph individual snowflakes and collected more than 5,000 microphotos.

Old Round Church, I-89 Exit 11, Richmond. This 16-sided building, one of the most unusual in the state, was constructed in 1812–13 as a community meeting house. It's believed that 16 men each built one side and the seventeenth man added the belfry.

SUGAR HOUSE   **Vermont Maple Orchards** (878-8384), Essex Junction. Call for directions and the best time to visit.

GREEN SPACE AND WATER   **Ethan Allen Park,** 2½ miles north on North Avenue to Ethan Allen Parkway is a good place for picnics and gazing at the two mountain ranges. A private "save the Ethan Allen Tower" group was formed to repair and reopen this monument in association with the restoration of Ethan Allen's home in the nearby intervale. The tower is now open.

Winooski Valley Park District (863-5744). Various access points to the river and Ethan Allen's restored homestead are included in the Burlington park area, and will be open as a museum.

The Green Mountain Audubon Nature Center (434-3068), Huntington. Trails wind through 230 acres of representative habitats (beaver ponds, orchards and woodlands). Interpretive classes are given. Groups welcome to watch (and help) in its wood-fired sugaring. Open all year, but call ahead to confirm. Directions: turn right at Round Church in Richmond; go 5 miles south to Sherman Hollow Road.

Mt. Philo State Park (425-2390; 372-5060), a small mountaintop picnic and campground, with spectacular views of the valley, lake, and Adirondacks. A short but steep ascent off Route 7 (not recommended for trailers or large RV's); 15 campsites; $1 per adult admission.

Kingsland Bay State Park (877-3445), Ferrisburg 05456. West from Route 7 on Little Chicago Lane about 1½ miles north onto Slang Road, 3 miles to Lake Champlain. Picnic areas, tennis courts on 130 acres.

BOAT CRUISES, CHARTERS   *The Intrepid,* America's Cup Winner (864-

Concert goers flock to Shelburne House

6800), can be chartered for day cruises from International Yacht Sales, Marble Island Road, Colchester.

Vermont Schooner Cruises (862-6918), Box 787, Burlington. Three, four, and six-day cruises on the lake can be had aboard the 76-foot, steel-hulled windjammer *Homer W. Dixon*, which holds 24 passengers in 12 double cabins. Prices range from $250–450, with a surcharge for "theme" cruises—history, geology, music weeks— or a "Sail 'n Cycle" trip.

"Spirit of Ethan Allen" (862-8300), 1 Main Street, Burlington. Daily scenic, optional dinner, brunch, and moonlight cruises on Lake Champlain on this 149-passenger replica paddlewheeler. June through October 15.

McKibben Sailing Vacations (864-7733), 176 Battery Street, Burlington. Sail and powerboat charters, crewed or bare.

Marine Explorers (864-9287), 81 Crescent Beach Drive, Burlington. Scenic cruises, scuba and snorkling, underwater historic preserve diving from a 26-foot, 12-passenger vessel.

Vermont Dive Charters (864-7766), Snipe Island Road, Jericho 05465.

Lake Champlain Transportation Company (864-9804), King Street Dock, Burlington, operates the Lake Champlain ferries for vehicles, hikers and bikers, between Burlington and Port Kent, Grand Isle and Cumberland Head, Charlotte and Essex.

FISHING CHARTERS   **Northeast Charter Agency** (864-7405), RR 1, Box 617, Huntington 05462, supplies boats and guides, April through October, for lake trout, landlocked salmon, walleyes, bass, northern pike, yellow perch. See also: **Champlain Sportfishing Charters** (862-2446), 188 Loomis Street, Burlington; **Offshore Charters** (864-1773), Lakeshore Drive, Colchester 05446; **Champlain Guide Service** (879-8931), 5 Colbert Street, Essex Junction 05452; **K. Guide Service** (862-4672), 6 Pinemeadow Drive, Colchester 05446; **Sure Strike Charters** (878-5074), 218 River Road, Essex Junction 05452.

MARINAS   **Shelburne Shipyard** (985-3326), Harbor Road, Shelburne 05482. Complete repair facilities, some transient docking, winter storage, free pump out, fuel, marine store, boat rentals and sales.

Malletts Bay Marina (862-4077), 228 Lakeshore Drive, Colchester 05446, full service, dockside and moorings, repairs.

Point Bay Marina (425-2431), Thompson's Point, Charlotte 05445.. Complete repairs, dockage for 100, mooring for 75, marine store, fuel, free pump out, restrooms, showers.

See also: **Fischer's Landing** (425-2554), McNeil's Cove, Charlotte; **The Moorings** (862-8925), Lakeshore Drive, Colchester.

SAILING   **International Sailing Club** (864-9065), 253 Lakeshore Drive, Colchester 05446, charges seasonal (May 2–October 31) membership fees ($595 or $495 weekdays), mean unrestricted use of the club's 27 foot *Olympic Solings,* free use of windsurfers, instructional workshop and clinics, sunset cruises, and club races.

GOLF   Burlington Country Club (864-9532), South Prospect Street. 18 holes.

Rocky Ridge Golf Club (482-2191), St. George. (5 miles south on Route 2A from Exit 12 off 1–89), 18 holes.

Kwiniaska (985-3672), Spear Street, Shelburne. 18 holes.

HORSEBACK RIDING   Happy Hollow Riding Stable (482-2729), Hinesburg. Trail rides, lessons.

SWIMMING   North Beach Park (864-0123), off North Avenue at Institute Road, Burlington (turn at the high school), provides tent and trailer sites plus swimming from a long, sandy beach, mid-May to October, vehicle charge. (Just before the park is the entrance to Rock Point, where the Episcopal Diocese of Vermont maintains Bishop Hopkins' Hall School, the Bishop's residence, a conference center, and an outdoor chapel.)

Other beaches: **Leddy Park,** also off North Avenue; **Oakledge Park,** off Route 7 south of the city, at the end of Flynn Avenue; **Red Rocks Park,** South Burlington's public beach on Queen City Park Road; **Bayside Beach** on Malletts Bay, Route 127 in Colchester. All have modest fees.

RACQUET SPORTS   Olympiad Health, Racquetball and Aerobic Club (863-4299), 70 Farrell Road, South Burlington. Also handball, squash, and outdoor pool available to non-members for daily fee.

Quarry Hill Tennis Club (862-5200), 360 Spear Street, South Burlington. Clubhouse, bar, seven outdoor courts, two pools and Jacuzzi. Non-members daily fee.

Twin Oaks Tennis & Swim Center (658-0001), Kennedy Drive, South Burlington.

Bolton Valley Resort, Bolton (434-2131)

BICYCLING   Ski Rack (858-3313), 81 Main Street, Burlington. Bikes, clothes, repairs, maps, rentals.

CROSS-COUNTRY SKIING   Bolton Valley (434-2131). A 100-mile network of trails ranging in elevation from 1,600 to 3,200 feet. A total of 42 km are machine groomed, meaning tracked for the most part, rolled in others. There is a wide and gently sloping 3.6-mile "Broadway," and a few short trails for beginners, but most of the terrain is backwoods, much of it splendidly high, wilderness country. You can take an alpine lift ($3) to the peak of Ricker Mountain and ski "Old Turnpike," then keep going on cross-country trails for a total of 7 miles. There are rentals in Camp Bear Paw near Bolton Valley's condominiums and experienced skiers are welcome to stay in the area's high huts by reservation. Telemarking is a specialty here, along with guided tours. $5 trail fee.

Bolton Valley to Trapp Family Lodge. This 12-mile ridge rail is one of the ultimate adventures available in New England ski touring. The trail was blazed in 1971 by Bolton Valley's Gardiner Lane and Johannes Von Trapp. It is used by a few groups every winter, recommended only for accomplished cross-country skiers. For details check either with **Bolton Valley** or **Trapp Family Lodge** (see Stowe).

Camel's Hump Nordic Center (434-2704), 10 miles south of Exit 11, I–89, Huntington. Located on the western flank of one of Vermont's most dramatic peaks, trails are challenging with some fine views: 50 km total, 30 km machine groomed. Elevations range from 1,100 to 2,300 feet; one 9 km trail drops 1,500 feet in its course. Rentals, child care, and lessons are offered.

Stark Farm Ski Touring Center (878-2282), 6.9 miles east of Essex Center on Route 128, Westford. 12 miles of groomed trails on this 400-acre farm; rentals, refreshments; lessons by reservation; $5 per day for adults, $3 ages 6 to 17; $15 family rate; open weekends and holidays.

Sherman Hollow (434-2057), Richmond. There are 40 km of one-way machine-tracked trails, 3.5 miles of them lit at night, elevation from 100 to 1,450 feet. This is the place for fitness buffs, complete with racing and training programs and an outdoor hot tub at the Main Lodge. There is also a lounge, change room and showers, rentals, instruction, and full-service dining.

Catamount Family Center (879-6001), Williston. The 40 km of trails—30 of them machine tracked, 2 km lit—are on rolling terrain, geared to all abilities. Guided tours, rentals, instruction, warming hut.

DOWNHILL SKIING   Bolton Valley (434-2131; lodging, 800-451-2131), Bolton 05477. This is a substantial ski mountain with the highest base elevation in the East and a nicely developed condominium complex hugging its hotel-base lodge. Geared to families, it is actually owned by one enterprising local family who bought the whole 6,000-acre wooded preserve in 1964. Ski trails here date back to the 1920s and 3,680 foot Bolton Mountain, which towers above its neighbors in a lonely stretch of country 20 miles east of Burlington, 20 miles west of Montpelier. Set atop a 4-mile access road that is, in turn, a long way up Route 2 from anything else, it offers a genuinely self-contained resort atmosphere guaranteed to make you want to stay put for a week.

At the base of the lifts there are a total of 108 condominium units (one-to-four-bedrooms), and 145 condo hotel rooms, most with fireplaces and/or kitchenettes. There is also a state-of-the-art sports club with indoor and outdoor pools, sauna, Jacuzzi and lounge.

LODGING   Marble Island Club (864-6800), 150 Marble Island Road, Malletts

Bay, Colchester 05446, is an attractive, year-round beach resort and conference center on a peninsula, now open to the public after a change of ownership and major renovations. Guests arriving by car should take exit 16 off I-89, follow Route 7 north for 1.9 miles, turn left on Blakely Road; continue for 3.7 miles and turn right on Marble Island Road; bear left at the fork and continue to the entrance sign. Guests have access to the 9-hole golf course, tennis courts, windsurfing, and other summer recreational facilities, plus winter hiking and cross-country ski trails.

The 12-meter yacht *Intrepid,* twice winner of America's Cup, is now making its home on Lake Champlain as Marble Island's flagship, available for charters and rides as well as informal business conferences. Half-day charters for 6 to 15 people, $40 each, which includes beverages and lunch; day charters, $60; Tuesday and Friday Sunset Cruises, $30 person. The yacht is managed by International Yacht Sales of Colchester, which also operates Marble Island's renovated marina.

Midweek summer rates at Marble Island are $69 to $89 per person per night, MAP; weekends, $105 single, $158 doubles. Additional adults are $39 per day, children from 4 to 10, $29. Pets are not welcome.

The Radisson Hotel 60 Battery Street (658-6500, 800-228-9822), Burlington, is the largest (257 rooms) and most citified hotel in the state. On the plaza level, an indoor swimming pool and whirlpool are flanked by a block of cabana rooms with balconies. For guests on the top (seventh) floor, complimentary continental breakfasts and late afternoon hot hors d'ouevres are served with cocktails by a helpful concierge. Rooms facing the lakefront have a stunning panoramic view of Champlain and the Adirondacks. You can frolic and nosh on daily "theme" munchies (German, Cajun, etc.) in Visions, its video lounge and bar, dine well amid gleaming brass railings in the Champlain Room, or patronize the coffee shop. Room rates range upward from $67–100 single and $77–120 double; various seasonal packages are available.

The Wilson Inn, (800-521-2334, 879-1515) 10 Kellogg Road, Essex Junction 05452. This handsome all-suite hotel is a "first" for Vermont, 32 units that combine bedroom, living room, and full kitchen (including Microwave oven and automatic coffee maker), designed especially for business people staying more than a day or two, and close to the IBM complex. To reach it, drive east on Route 15 from the Winooski exit on I-89, and take the first left past Fort Ethan Allen onto Wilson Road and the first left onto Kellogg Road.

Comfortably contemporary, the inn provides several welcome amenities, such as a complimentary continental breakfast in its cafe-bar, Maggie's; a grocery shopping service; direct telephone numbers; a private security system; and access to the Racquet's Edge, a fully-equipped fitness center next door. The rates are also attractive: $73 single, $83 double, daily, for one to six nights, $69 and $79 for seven or more nights. Two-bedroom suites are also available, along with nonsmoking or handicapped-fitted units.

INNS **Shelburne House** (985-8498; 985-8686, mid-October to May), Shelburne 05482. For a peerless taste of restored Edwardian grandeur, being a summer guest in this stately home is not to be missed. The 100-room Queen Anne-style mansion was built by Seward and Lila Vanderbilt Webb on a bluff overlooking Lake Champlain. Completed in 1899, the house is the centerpiece of a 100-acre estate whose grounds were designed by Frederick Law Olmsted and forested by Gifford Pinchot. The property is being maintained by the present generation of Webbs as an experimental farm.

Tours of Shelburne Farms feature visits to the immense U-shaped farm barn, carriage house, and Brown Swiss dairy. Its visitors center gift shop is stocked with farmhouse cheddar cheese, Shelburne honey, and naturally leavened bread, all produced on the farm.

For recreation, guests have access to tennis, boating, a swimming beach, carriage rides, and walking trails. A public golf course and a marina are nearby.

Turn-of-the-century furnishings predominate throughout the inn, where guests can browse in the library, and dine well in the Marble Room with a spectacular view of the lake and Adirondacks. Rates for the 24 luxurious, individualized bedrooms (Louis XVI, Empire, Colonial, Dutch Delft) are $157 to $170 single with private bath, $75 to $120 single, shared bath; $130 to $175 double, private bath; $80 to $120 double, shared bath—all depending on size, location, and time of year. Modified American Plan is available at an additional $32 a day per person. Otherwise, breakfast (a buffet with fresh fruit, luscious muffins, cold smoked ham, plus such specials as eggs Benedict with fresh basil) is $8, a box lunch $7.50, afternoon tea $3.50, and memorable dinners ($16–19 for entrees, à la carte). All of this quickly adds up to one of the most expensive stays in the state, but it's a dreamy place and worth the trip back into tranquility. No smoking is allowed in the house except in the game room, complete with heavy, carved baroque furniture, pool table, and antlered trophies. Open June to mid-October.

Lindenwood—A Country Inn (658-9211), 916 Shelburne Road, South Burlington 05401. Chuck and Jann Perkins, native Burlingtonians, run a friendly B&B and offer helpful hints about their city. Rates from $35–45, shared bath, $55 private, in the house and in the pine-paneled motel units and $75 in the chalet, out back and farther from the busy highway. $5 more in the fall.

Saxon Inn (878-4204/899-3015), Box 337, Jericho 05465. Located on South Orr Road, with panoramic views and lots of space to enjoy outdoors, swimming pond, nature trails. The inn is owned by Bernie and Anna Marie Roque, who will meet you at the airport, or bus station. Three rooms with private baths, two with shared from $25–35 per person. Corporate and other discounts available.

Shelburne Inn & Motel (985-3305), Shelburne 05482 (Route 7 near the Museum), combines an old-fashioned hostelry with modern motel units. Rooms are $57 single, $62 double in the summer; $75 in the fall. Its restaurant is reasonably good and priced accordingly.

Black Bear Inn (434-2126), Bolton Valley 05477. Innkeepers Sue and Phil McKinnis offer nicely decorated rooms (Sue makes the quilts herself), fine dining and a friendly atmosphere. The modern, ski-lodge style inn sits at 2,000 feet, adjacent to the Bolton Valley ski slopes. In summer, there is a heated pool and year-round guests have access to Bolton Valley's Sports Club (indoor tennis, pool etc.). $49–89 per couple. Special rates for children. Getaway and golf packages.

MOTELS   The Old Reliables are clustered around the I-89/Route 2 interchange. Among them: **Sheraton-Burlington** (862-6576), in a campus-like setting with indoor pool and health spas, plus Caroline's Restaurant and Baxter's Lounge nightclub, seasonal rates on request; **Ramada Inn** (658-0250), $55–70 double; **Holiday Inn** (863-6363), seasonal rates on request; **Howard Johnson's** (863-5541), rates on request; and **Econolodge** (863-1125), $51–58 double.

Along the Route 7 southern strip, a baker's dozen line Shelburne Road. Among them: a recently refurbished **Best Western Redwood** (862-6421; 800-528-1234), $60–68 double, lower in winter and spring; and **Yankee Doodle** (985-8004), $28–58.

BED & BREAKFASTS   **Dunn-Inn** (425-2902), Route 7, North Ferrisburg 05473, 10 miles south of Shelburne. Two doubles, one single $35–45 with shared bath and full breakfast in a colonial farmhouse.

Howden Cottage (864-7198), 32 North Champlain Street, Burlington. Two rooms, shared bath, no smoking.

On the Lamb (862-9626/879-1179), 60 Depot Road, Colchester 05446, has two guest rooms with a shared bath, private entrance and sitting room, $38 single, $50 double with continental breakfast. Limited smoking; no children or pets.

DINING OUT   *Downtown*   **Mather's** (658-0740), 7 Burlington Square, is a rooftop restaurant which affords a splendid view of the lake and the Adirondacks. Popular with Burlington's yuppies, Mather's exudes an aura of urbanity unusual in Vermont. Prices are on the moderate side: $3.95 to $7.95 for lunch; $11.95 for Sunday brunch; under $20 for dinner. Native lamb, veal, poultry, cheese and other local products are featured on the menu; the cuisine is not quite as *haute* as described, but satisfactory.

Déja Vu Café (864–7917), 185 Pearl Street, Burlington, has regained its reputation as one of the city's best for classic and contemporary nouvelle cuisine in a dramatic setting. Expensive entrées can escalate dinner for two to $100, but crêpes and bistro selections remain, along with such specialties as cassoulet Americaine, made with black beans and venison sausage. Open for lunch Monday–Saturday. Dinner nightly, Saturday and Sunday brunch.

Colchester   **Marble Island** (864-6800), 150 Marble Island Road, Malletts Bay, Colchester. The resort's pale blue and cream country-formal dining room is a rather small but glamorous setting for dinner, which might begin with smoked Idaho trout ($4.95) or Clams Casino ($5.95), followed by a Caesar Salad with fried oysters ($5.95), a New England shellfish stew in a lobster and saffron sauce ($18), sautéed veal rib eye with morels, cognac and cream ($16.75), or venison Marengo in pastry ($14). At Sunday brunch, try a smoked fish platter, Finnan Haddie, or shrimp curry.

Gerard's at Tradewinds (879-1000), Route 127, Malletts Bay. This new star on the gustatory horizon is the "retail" outlet, so to speak, for the company in Fairfield, Vermont, that produces vacuum-packed gourmet meals sold in Bloomingdale's and other upscale food shops. Gerard's won top awards in the annual Taste of Vermont competition in 1986 and 1987, and celebrated by serving this Grand Award menu at $34 per person: hors d'oeuvres, squab salad with a mushroom mousse and walnut dressing, lobster ravioli in sea urchin sauce, breast of duck in red wine sauce with fresh corn flan and Vermont chanterelles, ending with raspberry gratin with maple syrup, Champagne truffles. Ordinary diner entrées $12.95–18. Lunch served seasonally; call ahead to check.

Shelburne Area   **Shelburne House** (985-8498), Shelburne. Open for dinner by reservation from early June to mid-October, this turn-of-the-century manor (see *Inns*) offers imaginative cuisine in a magnificent setting—black and white marble floor, crimson flocked wallpaper, and a stunning sunset view of Lake Champlain and the Adirondacks. Canapes of Vermont smoked ham and Shelburne Farms cheddar are served with drinks. An unusual appetizer of fricassee of wild mushrooms ($6) could be followed by roast whole baby pheasant ($18), sliced leg of veal with white wine and mushroom sauce ($17) or chicken with spinach and pine kernel stuffing ($15). Vegetables come from the farm's gardens, and one can't resist a peach almond pie with blueberry sauce ($5). No smoking in the dining room, but smokers can have coffee served on the terrace or adjoining Game Room.

Pauline's (862-1081), 1834 Shelburne Road (Route 7 south), has lost some of its earlier luster, but is still worth the strip development traffic to reach it for lunch or dinner daily. In the elegant simplicity of the downstairs cafe or the more formal upstairs dining rooms (one for smokers), subtle continental and American cuisine is artfully presented in sensible portions. Cafe selections are mostly under $10, dinner entrée under $20, such as pork loin scallopini with apricot, sherry and herb sauce ($13.50), loin of Vermont rabbit with artichoke hearts and mushrooms ($15.50), or veal tenderloin with wild mushrooms ($16.50). Warm popovers are welcome dividends. A three-course dinner for two, however, with cocktails, wine, tax and tip can quickly add up to $100.

Cafe Shelburne (985-3939), Route 7, Shelburne. Conveniently located across the road from the Shelburne Museum, this chef-owned and operated, authentically French bistro has been serving uncommonly good food since 1969. It's open for lunch Tuesday through Saturday, and for dinner Monday through Saturday. Hot and cold hors d'oeuvres include escargots (or 28 grams of caviar for $22), fish soup at $3.75; and, among entrées, frog legs at $12.50, duck a l'orange at $12.75; roast pheasant ($32 for two), plus daily specials, of course, and an interesting wine list. Luncheon features lighter fare, including quiche and salads. This remains one of the better restaurants in the state.

Bolton Valley   **Lindsay's** (434-2131), Bolton Valley, a recent and enjoyable addition to the resort's charms, serves dinner daily except Monday, and features nouvelle American and continental cuisine in a romantic, formal setting with a splendid view of sunsets. Appetizers ($3–6.50) might be crabmeat Alfredo or oysters Rockefeller. Entrées ($15–19.50) include veal Aramica, steak au poivre, tournedos with Bearnais.

RESTAURANTS   *(South to North)*   **The 1810 Farmhouse Restaurant** (877-2576/658-6622), Route 7, Ferrisburg, is a pleasant place to stop for lunch or dinner in the summer, spring, and fall. Call ahead for information. Traditional New England fare at very moderate prices. Travelers can also browse around the 1824 covered bridge; the Little Red Cider Mill, in operation during apple season; the North Ferrisburg Railroad Station; and the **Old Covered Bridge Gift Shop**. They also have a 213-acre Christmas tree farm.

Village Pump House (985-3728), on the Green, Shelburne. Innovative, moderately priced American cookery, big selection of imported beers. Light suppers, three-course dinners ($12–15), Sunday brunch. Closed Tuesday and Sunday nights; check ahead for summer lunch hours.

Francesca's (985-3373), Jelly Mill Common, Route 7. Open daily for lunch, dinner, and Sunday brunch, this northern Italian restaurant in a trendy setting has a tempting selection of pastas, ravioli, veal, and shrimp; entrées from $4.95 to $13.75.

Perry's Fish House (862-1300), 1080 Shelburne Road, is a big, bustling landlocked pier with an extensive menu of moderately priced seafood that attracts large numbers of Burlingtonians. Children's menu. Open daily 5–10, 4–10 Sunday.

Chutes (864-5110), 308 Shelburne Road, is contemporary, bright, fresh, and saucy, with a 75-item moderately priced menu (bliss for grazers) and the city's most bountiful salad bar. Open daily for breakfast, lunch, and dinner.

Downtown Burlington **Sweetwater's** (864-9800), corner of Church and College Streets. A popular spot, continuous service weekdays from 11:30-midnight, Sunday 10:30–10. Relatively inexpensive, tasty entrées: mesquite broiled lime chicken, $7.50, tuna or salmon; shrimp brochette, $10.95. Lots of hearty sandwiches. Sunday brunch might include a "Texas Breakfast"—mesquite broiled ham, peppers, onion, mushrooms on English muffins with poached eggs and hollandaise, potatoes and fruit salad—and champagne for $4.95!

Swiss Mountain Cafe (658-0200), 111 St. Paul Street. In an old-world atmosphere, good, substantial fare at moderate prices: pork tenderloins with spaetzli, beef Stroganoff. Lunch and dinner daily. Reservations, please.

Five Spice Cafe (864-4045), 175 Church Street, the city's first new-style Asian restaurant. Specialities include Hunan noodles, shiitake and vegetables, and highly spiced shrimp. Moderate to expensive. Open for dinner Tuesday–Saturday, Sunday buffet 11:30–4:30.

Sakura (863-1988), 2 Church Street, Vermont's first and only Japanese restaurant, opened in 1987 and has drawn *banzais* of praise for its sashimi, sushi, tempuras, and entrées in the $9–15 class. Lunch Monday–Friday, dinner daily. Reservations please.

The Ice House (864-1808), 171 Battery Street, overlooks the Champlain ferry slip and marina in this historic renewal area. One of the pioneers in the city's upscale restaurant scene, it now serves American regional dishes, on the pricey side, including Vermont lamb and seafood, on two levels. Oyster bar. Lunch and dinner daily, Sunday brunch. Reservations recommended. (Food Discovery, the gourmet-to-go food shop is adjacent.)

Dockside Cafe (864-5266), Battery and Maple Streets, is a reasonably priced seafood and chowder house, open daily.

Henry's Diner (862-9010), 155 Bank Street, is a long-established, authentic diner around the corner from the Church Street Market Place, where you can get the meat loaf and thick gravy you've been hankering for.

Carbur's (862-4106), 115 St. Paul Street, has a 16-page menu, offering a hundred or so sandwich combos, and many entrées.

Lunch and dinner daily amid wood panels and stained-glass lamps. Inexpensive to moderate.

Grand Central (658-7415), St. Paul and College streets. Lunch, brunch, dinner daily with an international flavor, in the light-struck greenhouse or more formal dining room. Entrees $10–15.

Alfredo's (864-0854), 79 Mechanic's Lane, across from City Hall, is a zesty Italian place with a big following, open for lunch Monday–Friday, dinner daily. Tuesday is "all you can eat pasta" ($5.50), ditto Thursday for veal ($8.95), and on Friday nights, a special appetizer is added to one's lobster dinner for no extra charge.

Bove's Cafe (864-6651), 68 Pearl Street, is another excellent, moderately priced Italian restaurant with many fans.

Leunig's (863-3759), Church and College Streets, might be called SoHo North. Open daily for breakfast, lunch, snacks, dinner; outdoor cafe in the summer. Inexpensive.

The Daily Planet (862-9647), 15 Center Street, billed itself as serving "interstellar cuisine—unusually spiced entrées ($7.95–12.95)—in a trendy setting.

India House (862-7800), 207 Colchester Avenue, serves traditional curries, chicken tandoori, and the like, plus puffy poori bread, all at moderate prices. Lunch Monday–Saturday, dinner Monday–Saturday, Sunday brunch.

Winooski/Colchester   **Waterworks** (655-2044), the Champlain Mill, Winooski, overlooks the dam spillway and rapids. Lunch and dinner daily at moderate prices.

The Prime Factor (655-0300), the Champlain Mill, features, as might be expected, prime rib, as well as seafood and a 52-item soup and salad bar. Open daily for lunch and dinner, Sunday brunch. Moderate.

Stir Crazy (655-4265), 23 Main Street, Winooski, offers a fine selection of spicy Southeast Asian specialities.

Williston Road to Richmond   **Windjammer** (862-6585), 1076 Williston Road. A big, informal, relaxed, moderately priced steak and seafood house, with a glass-walled Pavillion, mezzanine for drinks, boat-shaped salad bar, open for breafkast, lunch, and dinner weekdays, Sunday brunch and dinner. Children's menu.

Silver Palace (864-0125), 1216 Williston Road. "Haute Chinese" cuisine at lunch Monday through Saturday and dinner daily.

The Checkered Restaurant (434-4203), corner of Routes 117 and 2, Richmond. This restored 1795 Georgian brick house was built by Governor Chittenden as a wedding present for his son; note the unusual brick work, one of the only surviving examples in the state. Open daily for breakfast, lunch, and dinner. Chicken, seafood, steak in various combinations, $8–14.

Daily Bread Bakery Cafe (434-3148), Richmond. People leave I-

89 south just to drop by for breakfast, lunch or Saturday and Sunday brunch, or even a slice or two of maple bread.

SELECTIVE SHOPPING *Charlotte-Shelburne Area* **Four Winds Art & Antiques Center and Tea House** (425-2101), off Route 7 on Dakin Road, Ferrisburg, shows the work of contemporary artists, serves light lunches, tea and pastries. Reservations appreciated.

The Dakin Farm (425-3971), Route 7, Ferrisburg (and the Champlain Mill, Winooski) is one of the principal purveyors of cob-smoked hams and bacon. This roadside store also stocks a variety of other Vermont food products and gifts.

African Imports (425-3137; 800-635-5009), Greenbush Road, Charlotte 05445. Lydia Clemmons specializes in authentic jewelry, soapstone carvings, batik, banana leaf prints, sisal mats and bags, masks, thorn carvings, and museum-quality items imported from Ghana, Kenya, Nigaria, Tanzania, and Zaire. Mail-order catalogue. Open Saturdays, 9–5; daily in the summer.

The Vermont Wildflower Farm (425-3500), Route 7, Charlotte. This imporant source for wildflower seeds and planting advice is open daily, May to mid-October. There are self-guided pathways through acres of wildflowers (admission charge) and a gift shop.

Harrington's, Route 7, across from the Shelburne Museum, Charlotte has been known for years by its delectable (and expensive) corncob-smoked hams, bacon, turkey, pork chops, and other goodies. The shop also displays an array of cheese, maple products, griddle cake mix, jams, fruit butters, relishes, baked goods, wine, and coffees.

The Shelburne Country Store, Route 7, encloses several gift galleries under the same roof—a sweet shop, foods, lampshades.

Jelly Mill Common, Route 7, Shelburne. An attractive, smallish country-contemporary shopping center around a village green with a variety of stores and boutiques for clothes, collectible dolls and miniatures, art, sweets, gourmet cookware, and the cheerful well-stocked **Wit & Wisdom Book Shop,** plus **Francesca's** for northern Italian meals and **Rocky Romeo's Pizza.**

Vermont's Own Products (985-2505), Tennybrook Square, Route 7, Shelburne, is a showcase for—you guessed it—all sorts of things made in Vermont: foods, pottery, jewelry, woolens, books, woodenware, quilts, crafts, toys, art.

Vermont's German Gift Shop, Route 7, Shelburne, diplays large numbers of imported items; china, crystal, linens, pewter, steins, clocks, European apparel plus a Christmas shop.

Factory Outlet Center, Route 7, Shelburne Road. More than 20 stores.

Downtown **Burlington Square Mall.** This vast indoor agora, mostly underground, has 50 stores stocking just about everything, linked to a

The Ticonderoga's last berth at Shelburne Museum

parking garage and the **Porteous Department Store.** Plenty of food stalls for grazers.

The Church Street Marketplace. More than a hundred stores, restaurants and services line several blocks of Church Street, nicely paved, landscaped, closed to traffic, and enlivened by seasonal arts and crafts shows, weekend festivals and street entertainers.

Bookshops: Chassman & Bem, which has one the largest children's book departments in New England; **Little Professor;** and the **Everyday Book Shop** are all on Church Street. **Bygone Books,** 91 College Street, is the place for old, out of print, and rare volumes. **Wit & Wisdom** has a branch in the 100 Dorset Street mini-mall, Williston Road.

Bennington Potters North, 127 College Street. Kitchenware, home furnishings, glass, woodenware, and "factory prices" on Bennington pottery.

Champlain Chocolate Company 431 Pine Street, the home of the American Truffle and other expensive candy, discounts some of its premium chocolates.

Cheese Outlet, 400 Pine Street. Sample their Vermont Velvet

Cheesecake and Quiche Puff, made on the premises; factory store for Vermont and imported cheeses.

The Millhouse Art Center, 1 Lawson Lane. Fine art and unusual clothing for men and women, from funky to formal.

The Downhill Edge Store and Sailboarding School (862-2282), 65 Main Street, features high performance sailboards, gives lessons and offers rentals at Leddy Beach and the Marble Island resort.

Sailworks (864-0111/372-6606), 176 Battery Street, has a retail store and gives private and group lessons at its Sand Bar Yacht Club, Sand Bar State Park, Route 2, where sailboards, sailboats, rowing shells, and canoes can be rented.

Winooski **The Champlain Mill,** One Main Street, Winooski, a creatively converted woolen mill, holds 30 smart shops, including the **Craft Center, Ltd.,** and the **Book Rack,** a well-stocked book shop, plus two good restaurants, bakery, and deli.

SPECIAL EVENTS   June 4-July 4: **Lake Champlain Discovery Festival** features a series of events taking place from Chimney Point north to Rouses Point—hot air balloon races; craft fairs; art shows; farm tours; ending up with a grand Fourth of July gala in Burlington.

Mid-August: **Shelburne Craft Fair,** Shelburne Farms

Late August: **Champlain Valley Exposition,** Essex Junction Fairgrounds—a big, busy, traditional county fair with livestock and produce exhibits, trotting races, midway, rides, spun sugar candy—the works.

Mid-September: **Annual Harvest Festival,** Shelburne Farms

Early December: **Christmas Weekend at the Shelburne Museum:** a nineteenth century festival. Phone 985-3344 for specific dates and details.

December 31: **First Night** (863-6005) The end-of-the-year gala—parades, fireworks, music, mimes, and other performances that transform downtown Burlington into a happy "happening."

MEDICAL EMERGENCY   Burlington: 911; Winooski/Williston (655-3212); Shelburne/South Burlington (864-4551); Charlotte (985-3233); **Medical Center Hospital of Vermont** (656-2345), Burlington. **Fanny Allen Hospital** (655-1234), 101 College Parkway, Winooski.

The Northwest Corner

Traveling between Burlington and the Canadian border, a motorist who wants more variety than I-89 has to offer can make another choice: to follow Route 7 to St. Albans and Swanton, or swing through the Islands on Route 2, rejoining Route 7 just south of the border. (With apologies to St. Albans, we can't help recommending that the wayfarer opt for the Islands, Vermont's Cape Cod.)

THE ISLANDS

Once called the Isle of the Two Heroes, this sparsely-settled chain of a peninsula and four islands extends thirty miles south from the Canadian border into Lake Champlain. Grand Isle County, embracing Isle Le Motte, North Hero, Alburg, Grand Isle, and South Hero, was homesteaded by Ebenezer Allen, Ethan's cousin, in 1783. Traveling through its fertile farms, thriving apple orchards, and simple villages and hamlets gives one a clearer picture of unspoiled Vermont than in any other region except the Northeast Kingdom. There are, to be sure, modern amenities, but one can't help the feeling of having stepped back into an uncrowded pastoral age where people lived close to the earth and water.

GUIDANCE   The Lake Champlain Islands Chamber of Commerce (372-5600), South Hero 05486, publishes a list of accommodations, restaurants, marinas, campgrounds, and trailer parks.

GETTING THERE   From Route 2 north to Rouses Point, from the Sand Bar Bridge and Routes 7 and I-89.

Plattsburgh Ferry from Cumberland Head to Grand Isle: 12 minute crossings 6:20 AM to 10:20 PM in winter, spring and fall; 6:20 AM to 11:40 PM, summer. Car and driver $5.95 one way, adult passengers $1.45, child 6–12, 50¢. Under 6 free, $10 maximum per car.

TO SEE AND DO   St. Anne Shrine, Isle La Motte, Route 129. A chapel in a pine grove on the shore marks the site of Vermont's first French settlement in 1666. There are daily outdoor masses in the summer. Near the public beach and picnic grounds is an impressive granite

THE NORTHWEST CORNER

statue of Samuel de Champlain, commissioned for Vermont's Pavilion at Montreal's 1967 Expo.

Hyde Log Cabin, Route 2, Grand Isle. Built by Jedediah Hyde in 1783, the cabin was restored by the Vermont Board of Historic Sites in 1956 and leased to the Grand Isle Historical Society, which has furnished it with appealing eighteenth-century artifacts—furniture, kitchenware, toys, tools, fabrics. Open July through Labor Day, 9:30–5:30, daily except Tuesday and Wednesday. Free admission; contributions welcome.

FISHING Lake Champlain is considered one of the finest fresh-water fisheries in America. With the right bait and a little luck, you can catch trout, salmon, smelt, walleye, bass, pike, muskellunge, and perch. Don't expect the local fishermen to give away their favorite spots, but you can find hints, maps and equipment at one of the many bait and tackle shops that dot the islands. Ask around if you would like to hire a guide.

PARKS AND FORESTS   North Hero State Park (372-8727/5060), has 117 campsites on 399 acres mostly in lowland forests with access to open fields, a beach, boat launch, and children's play area.

Grand Isle State Park (372-4300/5060), has wooded and open campsites on 226 acres, with a beach, nature trail, and recreation building. Fees for either of these two Class A parks are: tent or trailer, $7.50 per night, additional person over 4, $2.50; lean-to, $7.50 per night, extra person over 5, $1.50.

Knight Point State Park (372-8389/5060), is located on the southern tip of North Hero, where many visitors have reported seeing *Champ*, the Lake Champlain monster. The park has a nature trail, a picnic shelter, and a sandy beach, from which you can watch sailboats and yachts pass through the drawbridge between the islands.

Sand Bar State Park (372-8240/5060), fills to capacity on sunny weekends in the summer, but this arcadian oasis with its sandy beach and adjacent Waterfowl Area is a fine place to relax on weekdays. Daily admission for Knight Point and Sand Bar is $1.00 per adult, 50¢ for children 4–14, under 4 free.

LODGING   Sandbar Motor Inn and Restaurant (372-6911), Route 2, South Hero 05486 has 40 simple, pleasant lakeside units including kitchenettes and a larger cottage for six or more. Rates from $32–75, less off-season. Breakfast and dinner served.

Shore Acres Inn and Restaurant (372-8722 summer, 372-5853 winter), Route 2, North Hero 05474, has sweeping, peaceful, beautifully groomed grounds and 23 comfortable rooms facing the lake and the Green Mountains. There's a bar/lounge; breakfast and dinner served in the summer. In the winter, there are two guest rooms in the main house. In-season (June 15–late October) rates: $47.50 for a double bed; $55.50 for two twin beds; $69.50 for two double beds; $56.50–69.50 for queen size suites. Off-season: $39.50–59.50. Reserve far ahead for July and August.

Wilcox Cove Cottages & Golf Course (372-8343 summer; 862-4913 winter), Route 314, Grand Isle 05458. This homey lakeside cottage colony and 9-hole public golf course, less than a mile from the ferry, is a real find (adults preferred). Each of the 11 cottages has a living room, dining area, fully equipped kitchen, one bedroom with twin beds, bathroom with shower and one or two screened porches. They are completely furnished except for sheets, pillow cases, bath and kitchen towels, and can be rented for about $235 a week including greens fees.

North Hero House (372-8237), Route 2, North Hero 05474, has been a deservedly popular mini-summer resort for years, offering comfortable accommodations in the main house and three lakeside annexes, with a sturdy dock, sandy beach, tennis court, and sauna.

Outboards, Sunfish, canoes, sailboards, and fishing tackle can be rented. There's a good restaurant and "Lobster on the Dock" Sunday buffet. Rates range from $41–74 double in the main house; $57–95 in Cove House, Southwind, and Homestead right on the shore. Especially desirable is The Cobbler's Room ($95), which has a double and a twin bed, sitting room with fireplace, and a private screened porch.

    Charlie's Northland Lodge (372-8822), Route 2, North Hero 05474, open all year, has three bedrooms with shared bath at $30 single, $40–45 double. It's part of a nifty little complex that includes Northland Sporting and Gift Shop, tennis courts, boat and motor rentals, fishing licenses, bait and tackle.

BED & BREAKFAST **Auberge Alburg** (796-3169), South Main Street, Alburg 05440. There are three double rooms at $35 (lower for hikers and bikers) including breakfast, and $10 dormitory beds for non-motorists. It's the home also of Cafe Etcetera for espresso, capuccino, and pastries.

BOATS AND MARINAS **Anchor Island Marina** (372-5131/4763), North Hero, open daily; fishing boat and dock rentals.

    Tudhope Marine Company (372-5545), North Hero: marine sales and service, rentals, ski and fishing rigs, party boats. Open daily.

    Tudhope Sailing Center and Marina (372-5320), at the draw bridge, Grand Isle; 80-slip marina, yacht sales, charter, sailing lessons.

GOLF **Alburg Country Club** (796-3586), Route 129, 3 miles west of South Alburg. 18 holes, gentle, shady terrain, snack bar.

HORSEBACK RIDING **Contentment Farm Riding Stable** (372-4087), South Hero: trail riding, instruction, pony rides, tack shop, horse shoeing, boarding, day camp riding school.

SELECTIVE SHOPPING **Apple Farm Market,** South Hero. Open daily: apples, cider, pies, maple products, honey, preserves, cider doughnuts, eggs, cheese, and fruits in season. Their popular ice cream stand features a uniquely refreshing cider slush.

    Island Country Quilts, South Street, South Hero, (turn south off Route 2 at Apple Farm Market). Open daily except Sunday and packed with 400 bolts of calico, handcrafted quilts, pillows, tote bags, placemats, templates, hoops, kits, thread, patterns—all under the gifted hands of Irene Falby, who conducts classes and workshops and repairs antique quilts as well.

MEDICAL EMERGENCY North and South Hero: 372-4322.

ST. ALBANS

Once an important railroad center, and still the Franklin County Seat, St. Albans (8,082), on Route 7, is showing signs of revitalization. Its firm place in the history books was assured on October 19, 1864, when twenty-two armed confederate soldiers, who had infiltrated the town in mufti, held up the three banks, stole horses and escaped back to Canada with $201,000, making this the northernmost engagement of the Civil War. One of the raiders was wounded and eventually died, as did Elinus J. Morrison, a visiting builder, who was shot by the bandits. The surviving Confederates were arrested in Montreal, tried, but never extradited; their leader, Lt. Bennett H. Young, rose to the rank of General. When he visited Montreal again in 1911, a group of St. Albans dignitaries payed him a courtesy call at the Ritz-Carlton!

GUIDANCE   The St. Albans Chamber of Commerce (524-2444), 132 North Main Street, St. Albans 04578.

TO SEE AND DO   **The Franklin County Museum,** facing Taylor Park, open July and August, Tuesday through Saturday, 2–5, was established by the St. Albans Historical Society in 1971 in a three-story brick schoolhouse erected in 1861. The Beaumont Room had been fitted up as a fascinating old-time country doctor's office; one room has period costumes; and another houses Central Vermont Railroad memorabilia. Upstairs are farm tools, a maple sugaring exhibit, and other artifacts of the region. Admission is free; contributions appreciated.

Chester A. Arthur Birthplace, a replica of the little house where the 21st (and usually underrated) President was born; can be found 10 miles east on Route 36 to Fairfield (open June to mid-October, Wednesday–Sunday & holidays, 9:30–5:30).

STATE PARKS   **St. Albans Bay State Park,** 4 miles west on Route 36, is a good place for picnics, but the water is too shallow and weedy for decent swimming.

Kill Kare State Park (524-6021; 372-5060), once a fashionable summer hotel site and then, for years, a famous boy's summer camp. It can be crowded on weekends, but blissfully quiet other days.

Burton Island State Park (524-6353), a lovely, 350-acre island reached from Kill Kare by park boat or by your own. The marina has electrical hook-ups; camper's gear will be transported to the campsites by park vehicle. Fishing off this beautiful haven is usually excellent.

Lake Carmi State Park (933-8383/888-5733), Exit 19, I-89, 2 miles on Route 104; 1.5 miles north on Route 105; 3 miles north of Route 108, in Enosburg Falls. Set in rolling farmlands, the 482-acre park has wooded campsites as well as those on the beach of this sizable lake; nature trails; boat ramp and rentals.

GOLF   Champlain Country Club (524-9895), Route 7 , 3 miles north of St. Albans. 9 holes, some terraced. Snack bar.

LODGING   The Cadillac Motel (524-2191), 213 South Main Street, St. Albans 05478, is a pleasant cluster of 41 units surrounding a swimming pool, with mini-golf, badminton, and a coffee shop in the summer. Rates: $38 for double-bedded rooms, $48 for twins.

RESTAURANTS   The Blue Lion (524-3060), 71 North Main Street; **Wicker Tree** (524-4224), Lake Road.

SPECIAL EVENTS   Maple Sugar Festival: for three days in early or mid-April, the town turns into a nearly non-stop "sugarin' off" party, courtesy of the local maple producers, augmented by arts and crafts and antique show and other events.

MEDICAL EMERGENCY   527-7744.

SWANTON

Settled by the French about 1700 and later named for a British captain in the French and Indian Wars, Swanton (4,622) is growing again after a long period of relative stagnation. During the First World War the long abandoned Robin Hood-Remington Arms plant produced millions of rounds of ammunition for the Allied armies. At one end of the village green dwell a pair of Royal swans. This park is the focus for the **Swanton Summer Festival,** the last week of July, with parades, band concerts, square dancing, arts and crafts shows.

GREEN SPACE AND WATER   The Missisquoi National Wildlife Refuge, on the river's delta, lies 2 miles west of Swanton on Route 78 to East Alburg and the Islands. Habitats are about equally divided between brushland, timberland, and marsh, through which wind Black Creek and Maquam Creek Trails, adding up to about a mile and a half, or a two-hour ramble; both are appropriately marked for the flora or fauna represented. It's open most of the time, but call ahead to confirm (868-4781).

RESORT   The Tyler Place (868-3301), Route 7, Highgate Springs 05460, of which an old spa hotel was once the centerpiece, thrives on its 165-acre lakeshore spread as one of the most popular family resorts in New England. At the height of the season it is rather like a jolly, crowded cruise ship; its faithful partisans have been returning year after year for almost three generations of the Tyler family's management. They provide just about every conceivable form of recreation for all ages, and varieties of accommodations in cottages, farm houses, and a modern inn. The rate structure has many options: Dinner Plan; Spring and Fall Rates without meals; Main Season Package Rates. For example, American Plan for parents with an eight-year-old and a five-year-old in a cottage, between July 13 and August 24, daily, $192–248, less during the early and late weeks of the season. Open June 15–September 5.

LODGING   Royale Swans Country Inn & Motel (868-2010), Route 7 north, Swanton 05488. There are 6 rooms in a simple, converted farmhouse and 12 in the motel wing, all with private baths, connected to an indoor pool, spa and sauna, at $40–70 per room. Summer, winter, weekend, and midweek and five-day MAP packages. No smoking in the inn, dining room, or pool house.

RESTAURANT   The Pines (868-7893/4819), Route 7 north, Swanton. Open daily except Tuesday for lunch and dinner: big sandwiches ($4.95), steak, seafood, turkey from $6.95 for ham or roast chicken to $13.95 for the surf 'n turf crab legs and petite sirloin.

MEDICAL EMERGENCY   868-3320. **Northwestern Medical Center** (524-2161, 524-5911), St. Albans.

Northern Vermont

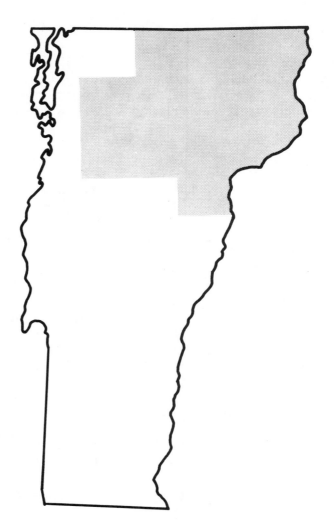

Stowe

Although it is no longer the state's biggest ski area, Stowe remains "ski capital of the East" and Vermont's premier summer resort as well.

In its path up the spine of the state, Route 100 parallels many imposing peaks but here, in the middle of this handsome village, it is joined by a road that angles off and climbs steeply right up over the shoulder of Vermont's highest mountain.

By the mid-nineteenth century, men were already taxing their imaginations and funds to entice visitors up onto the heights of Mount Mansfield, which bears an uncanny resemblance to the upturned profile of a rather jowly man. In 1858 an inn was built under the "nose," a project which entailed constructing a 100-yard log trestle above a chasm and serveral miles of corduroy road made from hemlocks. In Stowe Village at this time a hotel, the Mansfield House, accommodated 600 guests.

A number of Swedish families moved into Stowe in 1912 and began using their skis to get around. Then in 1914, the Dartmouth College librarian skied down the Toll Road. Serious skiing, however, didn't begin until 1933 when the Civilian Conservation Corps cut a four-mile-plus trail just for that purpose, and the following year the town formed its own Mt. Mansfield Ski Club, setting up basic lodging near the bottom of the ski trail in a former logging camp. By 1937 a rope tow had been rigged from the camp to the top of the trail, powered by a Cadillac engine. It cost 50¢ per day, $5 per season.

The Mt. Mansfield Company, formed in 1951 from the various small concerns that had evolved in the 1930s and 40s to serve skiers, has come a long way but is still squarely rooted in its colorful beginnings. The company itself was for many years headed by Sepp Ruschp, the "crack skier" who left his native Austria—at the request of the Mt. Mansfield Ski Club—to become its ski instructor in 1936. And innkeepers still include the Von Trapp family immortalized in the *Sound of Music*.

Although it no longer boasts the greatest number of places to stay, it still represents the state's biggest concentration of inns; condominiums, while a growing phenomena, are scattered around

Hiking the Long Trail

the edges rather than setting the tone. The Stowe Area Association has been in business since 1936, matching visitors with lodgings they can afford and enjoy.

Stowe is a genuine, year-round resort, offering excellent skiing—both downhill and cross-country—in winter, and a superb golf course, tennis, theater, hiking, and fishing in summer, plus a wide variety of lodging, dining, and shopping. It is also an excellent pivot from which to explore northern Vermont: 30 miles from Burlington, just over the Notch from the little-touristed Lamoille Valley, and a short drive from both Montpelier/Barre on one hand and the Northeast Kingdom on the other.

GUIDANCE   The Stowe Area Association (253-7321 or toll-free reservations, 800-24-STOWE), Box 1230, Stowe 05672. Open daily. From Memorial Day to mid-October, 9–6, Thanksgiving–April, 8 AM–9 PM and in the time between, 9–5. This service, housed in its own building in the middle of Stowe Village, keeps a tally of vacancies in more than 60 local lodging places and will make reservations; it also publishes seasonal guides listing most things in the area and is a walk-in source of advice about what's going on.

GETTING THERE   By bus: Vermont Transit/Greyhound stops in Waterbury with connections from Boston, New York, points south.

By train: See *Amtrak* in *What's Where,* otherwise it stops at Springfield, Massachusetts.

By plane: The Stowe-Morrisville Airport, 7 miles north, provides private plane services and charters. Burlington Airport, 34 miles away, is served by Continental from Newark, United Airlines from Chicago, USAIR from Pittsburgh, Syracuse, and Washington, DC. The Montpelier-Barre Airport, 22 miles away, is served by Eastern Express from Boston.

Shuttle: Sullivan Transportation (253-9440), Box 544, Adams Mill Road, Moscow 05662, makes daily runs between Stowe and the Burlington Airport.

GETTING AROUND   During summer and winter months, trollies shuttle up and down the 7 miles between the village and the mountain, 8–5:30. Special tours of the area are also offered.

TO SEE AND DO   Mount Mansfield. The highest point in Vermont, 4,393 feet high at The Chin, yields a truly spectacular view, accessible primarily in summer—unless you can clamber up to the summit from the Cliff House warming hut at the top of the Gondola over ice and snow. In summer there are two easy ways up: the Toll Road and a four-passenger Gondola.

The Toll Road begins 7 miles up Route 108 from the village; look for the sign on the left just before the Inn at the Mountain. Open late May to mid-October, weather permitting, 9:30–5. $6 per car, $3 per repeat trip and $4 per motorcycle; bikes, and foot traffic free. First laid in the mid-nineteenth century, this steep, windy road leads to a hotel that served the public until 1957. (It was demolished in the mid-1960s.) This also served as a ski trail until the winter of 1981–1982 when the new novice area was created at Spruce Peak. The road terminates at the Mt. Mansfield Summit Station just below The Nose (4,062 feet), a small space serving cookies and cocoa, usually crowded with hikers. A half-mile Tundra Trail follows the Long Trail (red and white blazes on the rocks) north to Drift Rock (the trek should take 20 minutes), another mile along the trail brings you to the summit of Mt. Mansfield (round trip: two hours).

The Gondola operates mid-June to mid-October, weather permitting, 9–5, $6 per adult, $3 per child round trip, $4 per adult and senior citizen, $2 per child one-way. The four-passenger, egg shaped gondola runs from the base lodge to the Cliff House, which serves light meals all day; a half-hour's trek brings you up to The Chin.

However you get there the view from the summit (The Chin) is spectacular on a clear day: to the west you see across 20 miles of farmland to Lake Champlain, east to the Worcester Range across the Stowe Valley, north to Jay Peak (35 miles distant) across the Lamoille Valley and south, back along the Green Mountains to Camel's Hump. Mt. Washington is visible to the east, Whiteface to the west.

The Alpine Slide (253-7311), Spruce Peak Base Lodge, Mountain Road. Open late June to early September, 9:30–5, $4 per adult, $3 per child, $17 and $13 for 5 rides.

Bingham Falls, Mountain Road. On Route 108 (The Mountain Road), 1½ miles beyond the Toll Road turnoff look for a widening in the shoulder and follow a well-beaten path to the right through the woods: water cascades through a flume and tumbles down through a series of chutes, falls, and pools.

Stowe Village. A classic early nineteenth-century Vermont village with a spired, white meeting house at one end of Main Street and a brick stagecoach inn at the other, a satisfying variety of stores and restaurants all within an easy stroll. The former wooden high school (one block up School Street from Main), is now the **Helen Day Memorial Library and Art Center** (open Monday–Friday, 2–5, also Wednesday 10–8, Saturday 10–12:30; closed Tuesday and Sunday; changing art exhibits). **The Bloody Brook Schoolhouse** next door is open July 4–Labor Day and during foliage season, also in early summer and in September, 1–3; small fee. A restored, one-room schoolhouse maintained by the Stowe Historical Society, which also has exhibits in the Memorial Building, Main Street. Open Monday–Friday, 2–5.

Ben & Jerry's Ice Cream Factory Tours (244-5641), Route 100, Waterbury. No American ice cream has a story, let alone a taste, to match that totally Vermont-made sweet and creamy stuff concocted by high school buddies Ben Cohen and Jerry Greenfield. Just a decade ago, they began churning out Dastardly Mash and Heath Bar Crunch in a Burlington garage, and now they have outgrown this seemingly mammoth plant that threatens to outstrip the Shelburne Museum as Vermont's number one attraction. A half-hour tour of the plant is offered all year, Monday–Saturday, 9–4. The big store, selling an amazing number of things relating to cows and Vermont, is open 9–5 and the Scoop Shop, 9–9 in summer, 9–5 in winter. The tour includes a multi-media show, a tour (from an observation platform) of the production room and a free sample of one of the 34 "euphoric flavors." The grounds include picnic facilities and some samples, black and white cows. $1 per head, children free.

COVERED BRIDGES   The Gold Brook Bridge in Stowe Hollow, also known as Emily's Bridge because Emily is said to have taken her life from it (different ways for different reasons in different stories) and is said to return to haunt it on dark occasions. There is another picturesque bridge across the Sterling Brook, off the Stagecoach Road, north of the village.

PARKS AND FORESTS   For fees and reservation rules see *Campgrounds* in *What's Where.*

Mt. Mansfield State Forest. The largest State forest—27,436 acres—much of it lies on the other (western) flank of the mountain.

Smugglers' Notch (253-4041), RFD Stowe 05472. 10 miles up the Mountain Road (Route 108) from Stowe Village, open mid-May through mid-October: 38 campsites including 14 lean-tos. A few miles beyond the camping area, just beyond the highest point in this high, windy road—open only late May through November, weather permitting—is a turnoff with parking, toilet, and an information center; for details on the trails from this area see *Hiking,* for background see the next chapter.

Little River Camping Areas (244-7103), RFD 1, Waterbury 05676. 6 miles north of Waterbury on the Waterbury Reservoir: 64 campsites including 6 lean-tos, campers' swimming, hiking, rental boats, snowmobile trails.

Elmore State Park (888-2982), Lake Elmore 05657. Open mid-May to mid-October, 14 miles north of Stowe on Route 100 then east to Morrisville, south 5 miles on Route 12; 709 acres with a beach, bathhouse, rental boats, 64 sites for tents and trailers including 5 lean-tos, picknicking, hiking trail up Elmore Mountain.

SCENIC DRIVES   Not only is Stowe pleasantly sited for touring in all directions, it is also organized to offer visitors well-researched printed tours—11 trips ranging in length from 7.6 to 112 miles. Many of the roads are dirt byways that invite parking the car and strolling off through villages, across covered bridges, down to waterfalls or whatever. Because most of the areas covered are included in other parts of the book, we omit details but strongly suggest you secure a copy of "Roads & Tours about Stowe" from the Stowe Area Association.

AIR RIDES   For hot air ballooning inquire at Stoweflake Resort (253-7355). Soaring and airplane rides are available at the Stowe/Morrisville State Airport (888-7845).

BICYCLING.   The Equipage here is a mountain bike and the rental sources are the **Mountain Bike** shop (253-7919), rear of the Depot Building, Main Street in the village, and the bike shop at **Stowe Mountain Sports** (253-4896) in the Stowe Center Complex, Mountain Road. Neophytes usually head for the **Stowe Recreation Path,** a 2.7-mile paved path through corn fields and wildflowers, paralleling the Mountain Road but at a more forgiving pitch. It begins just behind the Community Church in Stowe Village.

BOATING AND FISHING   Canoe rentals are available from the **The Fly Rod Shop** (253-7346) 2 miles south of Stowe Village on Route 100, also from **Buccaneer Country Lodge** (253-4772), 1390 Mountain Road. A printed guide to fishing, boating, and canoeing provided by the **Lamoille County Development Council** (Box 577, Morrisville 05661) and available from shops and the Stowe Area Association describes canoeing and fishing on the Lamoille River, also in Lake Elmore, Lake Eden, Wolcott Pond, and Waterbury Reservoir, among others.

GOLF   **Stowe Country Club** (253-4269), an 18-hole course with a practice range, putting green, restaurant, bar, pro shop, lessons.

WALKING   **Stowe Recreation Path** is a new 2.7 mile paved path that begins in Stowe Village behind the Community Church, winds up through corn fields, wildflowers, and raspberry patches, paralleling the Mountain Road but at a more forgiving pitch.

HIKING   **Mount Mansfield** See the introduction to this section and *To See and Do* for a general description of Vermont's highest mountain. For walkers (as opposed to hikers) it's best to take the toll road or Gondola up and follow the Tundra Trail described earlier. Serious hikers should at least purchase the weather-proof map of the Mount Mansfield Region ($1.95) and can profit from the *Guide Book of the Long Trail* ($8.50) both published by the Green Mountain Club. A naturalist is on hand May–November along the heavily traveled 2½-mile section of the Long Trail between the Forehead and the Chin; the Green Mountain Club maintains Butler Lodge, a ½ south of the Forehead and Taft Lodge, below the Chin, as shelter for hikers.

Smugglers' Notch. The Long Trail North, clearly marked, is an easy mile-plus hike to Sterling Pond, a beautiful spot at 3,000 feet, fish-stocked too. The Elephant's head can be reached from the state picnic area on Route 108; a two mile trail leads to this landmark—from which you can also continue on to Sterling Pond and thence out to Route 108 but a couple miles above the picnic area. No one should drive through Smugglers' Notch without stopping at least to see the Smuggler's Cave and to clamber around on the rocks.

Other local hikes described in the pamphlet guide to "Hiking, Camping, Bicycling" provided by the Lamoille County Development Council (Box 577, Morrisville 05661) and available from the Stowe Area Association, also detailed in *Day Hiker's Guide to Vermont* published by the Green Mountain Club: Belvidere Mountain in Eden, a 3½-hour trek yielding good views in all directions; Ritterbush Pond and Devil's Gulch, also in Eden, 2¾ hours roundtrip; and Elmore Mountain in Elmore State Park, a 2- to 3-hour hike with spectacular views.

Camel's Hump, from Waterbury. This trail is detailed in *Fifty Hikes in Vermont* and takes you from Couching Lion Farm in Duxbury, a 6½-hour round trip hike to the unspoiled summit of Vermont's third highest mountain.

Little River Trail System, Mount Mansfield State Forest, Waterbury. There are beautiful trails through the Ricker Basin and Cotton Brook area, once a settlement for 50 families who left behind cellar holes, stone fences, old cemeteries, lilacs, and apple trees.

Also see Barre/Montpelier for hiking in the Worcester Range.

HORSEBACK RIDING   Topnotch Stables (253-8585), Mountain Road. Trail rides, carriage lessons. **Edson Hill Manor** (253-8954) private lessons, trail rides.

POLO MATCHES   June through September, Sunday afternoon polo matches begin either at 1 or 3 (check weekly calendar) at the Stowe Country Club Polo Field, off Mountain Road (turn just before Stoweflake Motel).

RAILROAD EXCURSION   Lamoille Valley Railroad (888-4255), Stafford Avenue, marked off Route 100 north of Morrisville Village (10 miles north of Stowe). This is a working railroad, hauling freight to and from points between Whitefield, New Hampshire, and Cambridge Junction, Vermont (93 miles). A portion of the rail route across the roof of Vermont was for many years served by the St. J&LC, known affectionately as the "Slow, Jerky & Long Coming." On selected days in summer (late June through Labor Day) and more frequently in fall (check current schedule) the line operates excursion trains that either turn around in Greensboro Bend or continue over Walden Mountain for a picnic at Joe's Pond in West Danville. Either way, the yellow engine and its vintage 1917 cars follow the Lamoille

River, passing through one of the world's few surviving covered railroad bridges. $15 adult, $10 for the picnic trip, $12 and $8 for the shorter haul.

SWIMMING   Many lodging places have their own pools. The best swimming hole is **Forest Place** on the Notchbrook Road, marked on the Stowe Map available from the Stowe Area Association. **Salzburg Inn** (253-8541) has an indoor pool and sauna available for a fee.

TENNIS   **The Racquet Club at Topnotch** (253-9308) 4 indoor, 11 outdoor courts, pro shop, instruction, videotape, 8 AM-11 PM.

Mt. Mansfield Tennis Courts (253-7311) 6-well-maintained clay courts adjacent to the Inn at the Mountain, 8–6, available by the hour.

Free, public courts can be found at the Town Recreation area off School Street. A number of inns have courts available to the public, inquire at the Stowe Area Association (253-7321).

CROSS-COUNTRY SKIING   A 100 km network of trails adds up to some of the best ski touring in New England. The "Stowe Cross-Country Ski Map" published by Northern Cartographic clearly and meticulously covers all trails in the area, $1.95.

Mansfield Touring Center (253-7311), Mountain Road. Located near the Inn at the Mountain, this center offers 25 km of set trails at elevations from 1,200 to 2,800 feet; rentals, lessons—including telemark—and change rooms. A guided tour of the Mt. Mansfield Summit ridge is offered, lift and lunch included.

Trapp Family Lodge Cross-Country Ski Center (253-8511). Located on the Trapp Hill Road, off by itself in the upper reaches of the Valley, this is one of the oldest and most beautiful commercial trail systems, 60 km of set trails at elevations of 1,100 to 3,000 feet. Lessons, equipment rental and sales and outstanding pastries are all available, also guided tours.

Edson Hill Ski Touring Center (253-7371), Edson Hill Road. Less crowded than the other two centers, away on the uplands north of Mountain Road offering 40 miles of set trails at elevations between 1,400 and 2,100 feet; instruction, rental, sales, full lunches, and guided tours available.

Topnotch Touring Center (253-8585), Mountain Road. Novice to expert trails, a total of 20 km; instruction, rental, cafe, and restaurant available, also change rooms. $4.

Spruce Peak Alpine/Nordic Area (253-7311), Mountain Road. Cross-country is available on downhill trails with the purchase of a regular lift ticket.

DOWNHILL SKIING   **Stowe** (253-7311; snow report: 253-8521), Stowe 05672. See the introduction for the story of how the present Mt. Mansfield Company has evolved as a natural outgrowth of various enterprises serving skiers since the 1930s. There are three base lodges now, the Gondola base from which the four-passenger gondola alone hoists skiers to the Cliff House just below Mt. Mansfield's "Chin." The Mansfield base lodge serves the largest network of trails and the Spruce House, a short shuttle bus ride up Route 108, serves the novice area.Gondola, quad chairlift, triple chairlift, two double chairlifts.

Trails: 44 trails, also glade skiing; 23% expert, 58% intermediate, 19% novice.

Vertical drop: 2,350 feet on Mt. Mansfield, 1,550 feet on Spruce Peak.

Snowmaking: Covers 54% of the terrain trails served by 8 of the 9 lifts.

Facilities: Three base lodges plus the Octagon and Cliff House at the top of the busiest lifts: cafeterias, rentals, ski shops, shuttle bus.

Ski school: 50 instructors; a lift especially designed for beginners at Spruce Peak where novices learn to make the transition from easy to intermediate trails.

For children: From 3 years up children can sign on for Winnie-the-Pooh day care or a combo of care and lessons at Spruce Peak.

Rates: $33 per adult, $16 per child under 13; $19 early and late season, adult; $35 during peak holidays.

(Please note: For downhill skiing at **Smuggler's Notch,** see North of the Notch section: it is not accessible in winter from Stowe on Route 108.)

OTHER WINTER RECREATION   For ice skating, **the Village Rink,** behind the elementary school is open, weather permitting, throughout the winter; floodlit at night, $1.50. Sleigh rides are available at **Trapp Family Lodge** and at **Topnotch** (see *Lodging*). Snowmobiles can be rented at **Nichol's,** Route 100 south (see *Lodging*). Snowmobile trails have been posted across public land in the Moscow/Little River area. Snowshoes, skates, ski-racks, toboggans can all be rented at **Shaw's General Store** (see *Selective Shopping*).

HEALTH SPAS   **The Spa at Stowe** (253-9954; 800-525-5606), The Green Mountain Inn, PO Box 1198, Stowe 05672. Facilities at the spa itself, located in the rear of the Green Mountain Inn, include a whirlpool, sauna, outdoor pool, Nautilus system, massage, daily aerobics and stretch classes. This is, in fact, one of the country's more sophisticated spa programs, stressing outdoor exercise (skiing, both downhill and cross-country in winter, hiking and biking in summer), including a special menu at the inn. Participants come from throughout the country.

LODGING   Most accommodations are found either in Stowe Village and along—or just off—the 7¼-mile Mountain Road (Route 108) that connects it with the ski slopes. We have quoted the daily, winter per person prices. Rates are 5–20 percent less by the five-day ski week, as much as half price in summer. The Stowe Area Association (see *Guidance*) publishes a booklet guide listing current rates and amenities offered by its member inns, lodges, motels, resorts, and condiminium complexes. Unless otherwise noted, all places to stay are in Stowe 05672.

RESORT INNS   **Stowehof** (253-9722, 800-422-9722), Stowe, 2 miles off Route 108. A fantasy world from the moment you step through its sod-roofed porte cochere, supported by two maple trees. No two of the 47 guest rooms are alike (some suites, a few fireplace demi-suites with optional kitchenettes). The public rooms are filled with original details like the divining rod that located the water source for the building. Windows everywhere let in the magnificent view. Facilities include a Tap Room, a dining room known for nouvelle French dishes, tennis courts, a putting range, a delightful pool (with its own splendid view), sauna, and cross-country ski trails connecting with the larger network. Rates are $80-$110 per person MAP Friday and Saturday, but just $300 per person for a five-day ski package, 4 days of lifts included. In summer a five-day midweek B&B package is $189 per person.

 Topnotch at Stowe (253-8585; 800-451-8686), PO Box 1260, Mountain Road, bills itself as "Vermont's world-class resort" and its hard to quibble (though these days it would have to share the distinction with a few others). No matter: *Ski* magazine listed it as one of the world's "12 poshest ski hotels." Uncommonly comfortable rooms hold many amenities, including a runner's guide showing various routes, from an easy 1.7 miles to a challenging 5.8 miles. There are luxurious areas for lounging, the Bistro for lunch and light suppers, the convivial Buttertub Bar, and the stately, glass-sided, highly-rated main dining room. A health and fitness spa lies on the lower level; contemporary sculpture surrounds the outdoor swimming pool. A major attraction for athletic guests is the big red farm barn across the road which serves as a cross-country ski center in the winter (50 km groomed and connected with three other trails in Stowe), riding stable, indoor and outdoor tennis courts, where the August tournament is held, and a handy skating rink.

 Double room rates range from $70 to $105 off-season, $95 to $160 during ski season, when a junior suite costs $210 and a two-bed-room $460. Several package plans are offered, including what may be the only "Tenniski" vacation.

 The Trapp Family Lodge (253-8511; 800-826-7000), off the Mountain Road, remains a fabled Austrian *schloss* with spectacular views, though somewhat more impersonal than it was before the original lodge burned and the Baroness Von Trapp died. The new 73-room lodge is Alpine-modern, with a charming greenhouse sitting room.

On the slope below are tiers of condos and motel-type units. The inn's 1,700 acres constitute New England's most scenic cross-country ski terrain with 60 miles of trails, and splendid walks in the summer, plus tennis courts, and a spring-fed pool. Summer rates range from $70 per person double, MAP, in the lower lodge to a $276 suite; in winter from $74 to $288; less in the spring, more between February 13 and 21.

Edson Hill Manor (253-7371), off Mountain Road. Set in 300 culitivated acres on a high slope, this seductive place resembles the "English country" estate it once was. Many guests are drawn here because some of the amusing winter scenes of Alan Alda's *The Four Seasons* were filmed on its grounds. There are now 26 rooms, 11 in the stone manor and 15 in the remodeled carriage barns, most with private baths and some with fireplaces, plus a cheery lounge and dining room. Other attractions are a stable, outdoor pool, stocked trout pond, and 40 km of cross-country trails. Summer rates range from $59–89 per room without meals; in winter, $63–85 per person, MAP.

The Mount Mansfield Resort (800-253-4754; 253-7311), Mountain Road. The former Toll House Inn, owned by the Mt. Mansfield Company and the closest lodging to the lifts: 34 rooms in the inn itself and 53 townhouses, plus 35 "lodges" (one-, two-, and three-bedroom slopeside condominiums). Facilities include the Fireside Dining Room and Tavern, clay tennis courts, three swimming pools, the Mansfield Touring Center, and skiing on the Toll Road. $62.50 EP per person in a double room at the inn, $30 more for breakfast and dinner; five-day ski weeks from $579 per person including two meals, 4 lift tickets; children under age 12 stay and ski free midweek.

Green Mountain Inn (253-7301 and 800-445-6629), Main Street, Box 220. The brick and clapboard face of this landmark dates back to the 1830s, but it has been thoroughly and tastefully modernized. All 63 rooms, some in the inn and some in the motel annex out back, are nicely furnished in sturdy antique reproductions (including canopy beds), and Vermont watercolors. Two suites can be converted into triples. The dining room is formal and the Whip tap room is informal, overlooking the back garden and pool in summer, warmed by a hearth in winter. There are a number of inviting sitting rooms downstairs and the Spa (see *Health Spas* above) offer full facilities and special weekend, five and seven-day fitness plans. $80–110 per room, add $26 per person for breakfast and dinner; five-day packages also available.

INNS AND LODGES   **Ten Acres Lodge** (253-7638), Luce Hill Road, off the Mountain Road and near the entrance to the Von Trapp domain, this red clapboarded farmhouse radiates a luxurious, distinctive personality. It has 14 individually decorated guest rooms, 10 with baths, plus two guest cottages and two apartments, each with its own kitchen, fireplace, and private terrace from which to savor the marvelous view. There's also a pool, tennis court, and a dining room considered among the best in Stowe. Doubles range from $60–100.

The Gables Inn (253-7730), Mountain Road. A sunny, welcoming inn with a total of 17 rooms, including 15 doubles, all with private bath, some in the motel. Sol and Lynn Baumrind have created a relaxing, informal atmosphere in the public rooms; after skiing there is always a pot of soup in the ski room; dinner at 6:30 is candlelit. In summer, the sun porch is one of the most popular breakfast spots in town; there is also a pool and a hot tub. Winter rates are $32–60 per person MAP; in summer it's $45–65 per room, EP.

Foxfire Inn (253-4887), Route 100 north of Stowe Village. This early nineteenth-century farmhouse is set on 70 wooded hillside acres. The five guest rooms have wide-board floors (several have exposed beams), furnished with antiques, each with private bath. A two- or three-bedroom cabin and a four-bedroom chalet, all efficiency units with fireplaces, are also available. Downstairs there is plenty of space for guests away from the large, public dining room, well respected for its Italian fare (see *Dining Out*). $60–65 double per room includes a full breakfast.

The Yodler Motor Inn (253-4836), Box 10. Located at the corner of the Mountain Road and Route 100, the Yodler is a comfortable inn that has been in the same family for long enough to create an effortlessly friendly atmosphere. There are 53 rooms all told, some in the main house that dates from 1797, most in the motel annex in the back which includes 3 efficiencies. There is a pleasant dining room, brightened with soft pinks and greens, specializing in buffets. There is also a lounge with fireplace, and summer amenities include a pool and tennis court. $34–70 per person MAP in winter.

Scandinavia Inn and Chalets (253-8555), Mountain Road. Ed and Jan Griffiths have small children of their own and go out of their way to make other families feel welcome. Their gabled ski lodge has 18 motel-style rooms with bath and color TV; also two suites. In addition there are 3 modern, A-frame-style chalets, each with a fireplace and 3 or more bedrooms, 2 or more baths. Guests enjoy use of the hot tub, sauna, game room, and outdoor pool. Swedish pancakes with lingonberries are the breakfast speciality, from $48 per person, MAP; special children's rates.

Logwood Inn (253-7354), Edson Hill Road off Route 108. The first Stowe inn built specifically for skiers, this is a fieldstone and log lodge set back from the road amid birches and firs, its window boxes brimming with geraniums and petunias in summer. The living room is seemingly walled with books and games, warmed by an out-sized stone hearth. There are 18 guest rooms, some with private bath, also a dorm for older children, an apartment for 4 and chalet accommodating 8. Facilities include TV and game room, a ski room, the "shed" (a warming hut with rentals for cross-country skiers) and an outdoor pool. Breakfast and dinner are both buffet-style; children, when enough of them are fed separately; lunchtime bread and soup are available. In summer, $55 per room with breakfast; winter, $44–56 per person MAP.

Timberholm Inn (253-7603), Cottage Club Road, Stowe, (off Route 108). A delightful lodge off, but not far off, the beaten path, suited to couples who appreciate the beauty and peace of a gracious living room; there is a less formal game room and a total of 10 rooms with private baths, also two-bedroom suites, complimentary soup and bread after skiing. BYOB; fall/winter rates including continental breakfast range from $44–54 per room; two-bedrooms and sitting room, $78 for three persons, $84 for four. In the summer $38–48 and $72–78 respectively.

Ski Inn (253-4050), Mountain Road, Stowe. Larry and Harriette Heyer have been welcoming guests in their gracious home—one of the handiest places to the lifts—since Pearl Harbor Day. The ten guest rooms are bright, meticulously clean. There is a pine-paneled BYOB bar and attractive sitting and dining rooms, a shade too elegant for children, ideal for couples: $25 per couple with breakfast in summer, $22–$35 per person MAP in winter.

Fiddler's Green (253-8124), Mountain Road, Stowe. Less than a mile from the lifts, this pleasant, yellow 1820s farmhouse has guest rooms tucked under the eaves; guests gather around the fieldstone hearth in the living room and the long table off the sunny kitchen. BYOB. In summer B&B rates: $15.50 per person; in winter optional MAP is $29 (in a dorm) to $43 (with private bath) per person.

The Inn at Thatcher Brook Falls (244-5911), Route 100, RD 2, Box 62, Waterbury 05676. Although it sits right on Route 100, this big, handsome mansion manages to convey a real country inn atmosphere. There are 13 guest rooms, furnished comfortably and brightly. The dining room (see *Dining Out*) has established an enviable reputation in its relatively short life; there is also a tavern. No smoking allowed in guest rooms and no children under 5 years. $59-$79 per double room.

Bittersweet Inn (253-7787), Route 100 south, southern fringe of Stowe Village. This eighteenth-century brick farmhouse and converted carriage house is a find. Barbara and Paul Hansel offer seven rooms, including one suite, four with private bath. The house is right on Route 100 but there is a view and sense of space in the back. Space includes a comfortable living room, a game room with BYOB bar, a good sized swimming pool, a large lawn, and a hot tub. Rates include a substantial continental breakfast with home-made pastries, and there is afternoon tea; hot aprés-ski soup in winter. $48 double with private bath; $98 for the suite, accommodating four; 10 percent less for five days midweek, 5 percent less for a weekend.

MOTOR RESORTS   **Stoweflake Resort** (253-7355; 800-782-9009), Mountain Road. The small ski lodge that the Baraw family opened some 25 years ago has mushroomed into a full-facility, 98-unit resort, including 24 studio townhouses. There are some bright, comfortable inn-style rooms in the original lodge and many nicely furnished motel rooms (besides its own motel wing, the resort includes the former Nordic Motor Inn). All rooms have color TV, phones, and private bath. Amenities include two outdoor pools, a sports center with indoor pool, a large meeting space, Jacuzzi, steam room, and two tennis courts, also badminton, volleyball, croquet, and horse-shoes. The links at the Stowe Country Club adjoin the property. Dining options include formal Windfields and the pubby Charlie B's. $78–88 per double room, $122–132 per couple MAP; town-houses from $110 for a studio to $260 per day for a three-bedroom unit; five-day packages available both winter and summer.

Golden Eagle Resort Motor Inn (253-4811; 800-626-1010) is a combination of the original 65-unit motor inn and the 30-unit Alpine Motor Lodge that it purchased and refurbished last year. Units include 29 suites, efficiency apartments, and cottages, some with fireplaces or Franklin stoves. All rooms have color TV, radios, and phones. Amenities include a very attractive health spa with indoor pool, large whirlpool, sauna, Universal exercise equipment, mas-sage service, and exercise classes. There are also outdoor heated pools (swimming lessons are offered), a clay tennis court, fish-stocked ponds, shuffleboard, badminton, lawn games, a children's playground, and game rooms. Throughout you have a sense of a well-run resort. It's been owned by Ann and Herby Hillman for 25 years. $55–110 per room, $85–200 per night for apartments and chalets ($385–900 per week).

MOTELS   **Snowdrift Motel and Efficiencies** (253–7305), Route 108, Stowe. Besides standard motel units and some with fireplaces, there are efficiencies with full kitchens; also a lounge with fireplace, com-plimentary after-ski wine and cheese, pool and playground. $42–52 per room, summer, no meals.

Stowe Motel (253-7629), Mountain Road. This is a clean friendly place with inviting grounds. There are 16 units, all with kitchens, 2 with fireplaces, also houses: 1 with 2 bedrooms, 1 with 4; $40–50 per room in summer, $25 per person EP in winter.

Buccaneer (253-4772), Mountain Road. This is a small motel, the former home of Olympian Billy Kidd. There are just eight units, all with TV, a small fridge and coffee machine. Amenities include a hot tub, game room, a lounge with fireplace, ping-pong, and pool tables. $27.50–44.50 includes après ski soups and snacks and a full breakfast.

Die Alpenrose (253-7277), Mountain Road. A pleasant, small motel with just seven units, each with in-room coffee and fridge. It has been under the same ownership for over two decades. $20–25 per person in winter, $16–22 in summer.

EFFICIENCY UNITS AND CONDOMINIUMS   More than two dozen Stowe properties include efficiency units. Here we list just a few outstanding options that are not attached to motels or inns.

The Village Green at Stowe (253-9705; 800-451-3297). Seven nicely designed buildings set on 40 acres (surrounded by the Stowe Country Club links) contain 43 two- and three-bedroom townhouses, all nicely, brightly furnished. A recreation building houses a heated indoor pool, Jacuzzi, sauna, game and changing room; there is also an outdoor pool and two tennis courts. Summer and fall rates for a two-bedroom unit sleeping six are $300 for two nights (the minimum), $675 for seven nights, $400 for two nights, and $1,025 for seven nights in winter.

Stonybrook (253-9701), PO Box 311. Attractive condominium clusters are spread over 105 acres, with another 63 acres zoned forever as farmland. To date there are 43 units (82 are planned). Facilities include four tennis courts, a pool, pitch-n-put golf, a Scandinavian Spa (sauna and hot tub), and cross-country trails. Units have two to four bedrooms; two bedrooms begin at $800 per week in summer, $1,200 per week in winter.

Kelly's Keep (253-9427), Mountain Road. Sequestered in the pines by Notch Brook, off the Mountain Road just a mile from the lifts, this is a unique complex splendidly built in the 1930s by a lady doctor; it contains four spacious apartments, each paneled, nicely decorated, equipped with hearths and sleeping from 4 to 14 people. Rates are $120–320 in ski season; $80–140 off-season.

Notch Brook (253-4882), off Route 108, Stowe 05672. Sited in the shadow of Spruce Park, an unusually well-built (although why Vermont's premier architect, Robert Burley, designed them with flat roofs, no one seems to know) condominium complex of 150 units ranging from double rooms through three-bedroom townhouses, most available by the day and week. Facilities include daily maid service, saunas, tennis, a pool, and winter shuttle service to the lifts; there is also a complimentary, continental breakfast. In winter from $82 per night for a double to $292 for a townhouse; in summer $168–264.

STATE SKI DORM AND HOSTEL   (253-4010) on the Mountain Road. Owned by the State's Department of Forests and Parks this is the nearest lodging to the slopes, well built by the Civilian Conservation Corps in the 1930s. $24 MAP in winter, $6 per day in summer with AYH pass.

DINING OUT   Isle de France (253-7751), Mountain Road. Our spies call this consistently excellent, formal, incongruously elegant. This is a classic French restaurant in the grand manner created by chef-owner Jean Lavina from New York's French Shack. Country pâté, sweetbreads, Dover sole, frog legs, and Chateaubriand are among the nightly features, with entrées in the $12 to $20 class.

Golden Horn East (244-7855), marked from Route 100 north of Waterbury. Open for dinner, 6–10 except Sundays. Austrian chef Hubert Erhard restored an old barn as his Golden Horn East (his original Golden Horn is in Aspen) more than ten years ago. Off the beaten track, it draws devotees from all directions. The large menu includes Wiener Schnitzel, duck à l'orange, steak Tyrolean, *rehsteak* (venison), and veal kidneys Madeira. For dessert try *palatschinken*. Entrées are in the $8.50–18.50 range.

Ten Acres Lodge (253-7638/9576), 76 Corner of Luce Hill and Barrows Road. The three small dining rooms in this attractive inn are extremely popular, deservedly so—some say the best in Stowe. The menu may include roast duckling with blood oranges, red flame grapes, and orange muscat wine, scallops of veal with baby artichokes and shiitake mushrooms or sauté of gray sole, bay scallops, and lobster with asparagus and chanterelles. The wine cellar is extensive. Entrées range from $15.50–22. Reservations are a must.

Charda (253-4598), Route 100 north. Open 6-9 daily; licensed. The Hungarian food served here is rated as high as any this side of the Atlantic and the atmosphere—the interior of a nineteenth-century farmhouse with Mt. Mansfield visible from the windows—is delightful. Specialties include duckling garnished with fresh mushrooms, smoked loin of pork with sauerkraut, schnitzel style boneless breast of chicken, and an irresistible line of desserts like Black Forest cherry torte. Entrées range from $9–15.

Topnotch (253-8585), Mountain Road. Dinner here reflects top-drawer cuisine by Master Chef Anton Flory. One could begin with marinated trout with dill sauce garnished with barbecued shrimp and scallops ($5.75) or double pheasant consommé with quenelles laced with cream sherry ($3.25), proceed to Chateaubriand with Béarnaise sauce ($42 for two), or Dover Sole ($18.50), ending with an orange souffle ($3.25). Many selections are keyed to American Heart Association criteria. Distinguished wine list.

Trapp Family Lodge (253-8511), off the Mountain Road. The dining room and lounge in the new lodge are both very elegant and dinner is prix fixe: $24 per adult, $15 per child. This is a four-course event that may begin with snails in garlic and red wine sauce or fried mushrooms; soups of the day follow; and there are at least ten entrée choices, always Weiner-schnitzel, frequently quail, broiled leg of lamb, and a seafood dish as well. Desserts are elaborate. Depending on the season, a $10 luncheon buffet is served here as well.

Foxfire Inn (253-4887), Route 100 north. "There is no main course in an Italian meal. There are at a minimum, two principal courses . . . pasta 'primi' and meat, fowl, or fish 'secondi'," the menu explains. Art and Irene Segreto serve traditional fare, a wide choice of antipasti as well as pasta and veal parmigiana, marsala, piccata, paesano, saltimbocca, and rolantine. You can have chicken in numerous ways, shrimp fra diavolo, or settle for eggplant parmigiana ($7.95). Other entrées run $10.95–12.50. Try Foxfire Coffee, laced with frangelica (hazelnut liquor) and Italian brandy. The setting is an attractive dining room in one of the oldest frame houses in Stowe.

Villa Tragara (244-5288), Route 100 6 miles south of Stowe. Open for dinner except Mondays. An 1820 farmhouse with Northern Italian specialties: pasta with crab meat, broccoli and tomato, linguini with seafood, veal dishes; most entrées in the $10–14 range.

Stowehof (253-9722), Edson Hill Road, off the Mountain Road. Nouvelle cuisine prevails and the specialties are sausage-stuffed breast of duck ($17.95), planked salmon ($17.95) and sweet and sour hazelnut-thyme chicken ($15.95). The dining room is unusual as well as elegant and there is frequently piano music.

The Yodler (253-4826), junction of Route 100 and the Mountain Road. The dining room is attractive and, if you like buffets, this one is a dandy: roast beef, baked beans, maple-cured ham, turkey with dressing, soup, sea food, beef Burgundy, salads, chicken, casseroles, etc. etc. etc., all for $11.50; available every evening, 5:30–9. There's also a regular menu.

The Inn at Thatcher Brook Falls (244-5911). Route 100, Waterbury. The menu is ambitious and superbly executed. You can choose from grilled marinated lamb medallions, escallope of veal Espagnole, roast duckling, grilled Vermont quail, grilled salmon, scallop and mushroom Alfredo, shrimp Provençal, and grilled swordfish, among other things. There is also a wide choice of salads and appetizers. At this writing the inn is still new and the toast of the valley. Be sure to make reservations. Entrées run $14–17.

EATING OUT   **Restaurant Swisspot** (253-4622), Stowe Village. An old reliable, open from noon until 10 all year; soups, quiche, and fondue lovingly prepared. For lunch there are tempting burgers with swiss cheeses and a wide variety of sandwiches as well. Swiss Cheese

Mt. Mansfield towers over Stowe Village

Fondue for two is $16.95 and beef fondue Bourguignonne for two is $26.50, but most entrées are in the under $10 range.

The Austrian Tea Room (10:30–5:30 daily) is fully licensed, specializes in hot gluhwein and soups, sandwiches, and Bavarian deserts, served up by dirndl-clad fraulines. This attractive building is a part of the Trapp family complex that was untouched by the fire. The view is spectacular, especially in summer from the terrace.

Stowe-Away Lodge and Restaurant (253-8972), Mountain Road. Imaginative Mexican dishes are the specialty in this snug old Vermont house, including crabmeat enchiladas ($9.95), quesadillas ($7.95), also less expensive tortillas stuffed with cheese, meat, and vegetables.

The Shed (253-4364), Mountain Road. Open daily for lunch and dinner, the most popular dining spot on the mountain, much expanded from its core eatery with its deep wooden booths, good for a beer or prime ribs. The large menu includes salads, tacos, baked onion soup, zucchini boats, barbecued ribs and, of course, Shedburgers.

Whip Bar & Grill (253–7301), 11:30–9:30. Since recent remodeling, this space has lost a number of whips but nonetheless gained a good deal of charm. In summer it is brightened by a view of lawns and the pool, and in winter there's a fire in the hearth. There is a blackboard menu, always a choice of grilled meats or fish, a raw bar, and specials ranging from pan-blackened fish to Montreal smoked meat with hot mustard. Dinner specials include marinated oriental black tip shark, and fresh Vermont veal with fine herbs and cream. A low calorie spa menu is available at all meals, and so are seductive desserts like Chocolate Sin.

China Garden Restaurant (253-7756), Baggy Knees Shopping Center, Mountain Road. This new Cantonese and Szechuan restaurant was the talk of Stowe when we visited. It's large with plenty of pleasant atmosphere and a large, reasonably priced menu that ranges from roast pork with bean sprouts ($5.75) to Peking Duck ($30). Specialties include hot and sour soup, pepper spareribs, chicken in garlic sauce, and squid with hot peppers. Most entrées are in the $7–10 range. Service is excellent.

Hapleton's West Branch Cafe (253-4653), Main Street, Stowe Village. A posh pubby atmosphere in the middle of the village. Chicken Dijon en Croissant or a "Complete Cheesesteak" for lunch, a wide choice of moderately priced entrées for dinners. This is especially pleasant out-of-doors in the middle of the village.

McCarthy's Restaurant (253-8626), Mountain Road. This is where local people gather for breakfast and lunch; open 5:30–3 daily. There is a counter, a scattering of booths and tables, and a hefty deli section. The baking is fresh and breakfast is served all day; daily specials.

Morrisville Station Restaurant (888-3669), Morrisville (10 miles north of Stowe on Route 100). This is a great place to stop for breakfast on your way to the train (see *Railroad Excursion*), for lunch (served 11–6), or dinner on the way to a play in nearby Hyde Park. The railroad depot has included a restaurant since it was built in 1872. It remained in business until the 1930s, when it closed due to declining passenger traffic on the St. J&LCR (passenger service ceased in 1956). The dining room is pleasantly nostalgic, and there are large breakfast and lunch menus, not to mention an appetizing Sunday brunch featuring station eggs Benedict, crêpes, and quiche. The dinner menu includes a wide choice of seafood and of stir-fry dishes as well as ribeye and baked maple-glazed ham. Dinner entrées run $7.95 for fettuccine primavera to $14.95 for a baked seafood platter.

The Flying Tomato (253-4646), Mountain Road, open 11–10. Until McDonalds opened, this bright, friendly place was the cheapest bet in Stowe for families looking for a bargain-priced dinner. It's still great: pizzas, minestrone soup, all kinds of pasta, subs, beer by the pitcher and wine by the carafe.

Cafe Mozart (253-9900), Pond and Depot Streets in Stowe Village, open from 11–5 for wurst, crêpes, a variety of special omelets and tortes; also open 5–9 for delectables like stuffed cabbage ($12.50) and Transylvanian goulash ($10.95).

Trattoria La Festa (253-8480), Mountain Road. On the upper reaches of the Mountain Road with terrace dining in summer, a pleasant dining room, and a variety of pastas, chicken, veal, beef, and fish dishes in tomato and wine sauces, $5.95–12.95; also take-out.

Three South Cafe (244-8973), 3 South Street, Waterbury. Open weekdays, 11:30–midnight, Saturday: 5–9. A cafe atmosphere and nice choice of deli and hot sandwiches, soups, freshly brewed coffee, wine, and beer.

Crust'n'Cauldron (244-8995), Park Row, Waterbury. Open 6–6 except Saturday when it's 6–2, closed Sunday. This brightly lit, unpretentious place has booths, formica-topped tables, and a counter. Blackboard specials include a variety of omelets, homemade soups, deli, and vegetarian dishes. The owner-chefs make all their own breads as well as pastries and soups, serve jug wine and herb teas.

APRÉS SKI   There are reputedly 60 bars in Stowe. For after-dinner dancing there is the **Rusty Nail** (hard rock), **B.K. Clark's** (a different group each week, frequently jazz and blues), and **Sister Kate's,** good for a variety of music and dancing. Look for aprés ski action at the **Matterhorn,** in the **Butter Tub** at Topnotch, at **Charlie B's,** and at **Mr. Pickwick's Pub,** source of one of Vermont's largest selections of beers (the better to wash down its beef steak and kidney pie).

ENTERTAINMENT   **Stowe Cinema & Projection Room Lounge** (253-4678), at the Stowe Center, Route 108. Standard seats and bar viewing area for first run films.

Periodic productions by the **Lamoille County Players** at the Hyde Park Opera House.

Stowe Summer Stage (253-4325) at the Playhouse on the Mountain Road offers a series of summer musicals and Broadway favorites.

SELECTIVE SHOPPING   **Stowe Pottery,** bottom of Mountain Road. An old red mill by the covered bridge is both the studio and showroom for stoneware pottery by Jean-Paul Patnode; there is also a selection of other crafted work but Patnode's stands out. Well worth checking. Open Monday–Saturday 9–5.

Exclusively Vermont (253-8776), Mountain Road near the covered footbridge; features wreaths, baskets, candles, soaps, lamps, rugs, patchwork, wooden toys, pottery, pewter, and selected specialty foods from artisans throughout Vermont.

Old Depot Shops, Main Street, Stowe Village, is a small indoor mall with some worthwhile corners, notably **All Things Special, Bear Pond Book Shop, Purcell's Country Foods,** and **Stuffed in Stowe gifts.**

The Silver Den (253-8787), Main Street, Stowe. A small family business in a village house offers the largest selection of hand-crafted jewelry in these parts.

Lackey's Variety Store (253-7624), Main Street, Stowe Village, open 8:30–8:30 daily. This is "just a variety store," say its owners of 37 years. But it's the only one that's survived in this resort village, and it's an invaluable source of an incredible variety of essentials: nail clippers, india ink, shoe polish, scissors, not to mention patent medicine, artists supplies and soda in bottles from an old fashioned water-cooled cooler.

Moriarty's Hats & Sweaters (253-4052), Mountain Road. Many long years ago, Mrs. Moriarty began knitting caps for Stowe skiers, and her distinctive style caught on. It is now widely imitated but the originals remain a Stowe tradition.

Wool and Feather Shop, Stowe Village. Susan Bartlett and Gisela Gminder spin wool produced by their own flock. Woven goods available in the shop include sweaters, socks, mittens, and fiber art. This is a prime spot for the knitter; weaving lessons are also offered.

Samara (253-8318), West Branch Shops, Route 108. An exceptional selection of work by Vermont artisans; quilts, soft sculpture, jewelry, wooden toys, batik, stained glass, etc.

The Fly Rod Shop (253-7346), Route 100, 2 miles south of Stowe, carries such name brands as Hardy, Marryat and Cortland as well as its own Diamondback rods, which may be tried out at its casting pool. Rentals and fishing spot brochure.

The Spinning Wheel, Route 100, south. Chain saw artisans turn out an extraordinary array of wooden animals and humans: bears, a giant lobster, a charming piglet ($29). Other prices range from $75 to $750 for a larger-than-life wooden Indian.

Cold Hollow Cider Mill (254-8560), Waterbury Center. A huge red barn on Route 100 has a cider press in one corner and sells baked goods, maple, cheese, and apples and about anything anyone can think of to take home as a souvenir of Vermont.

The Hearthstone Stove Factory (888-4568), Morrisville. Located in the next town north from Stowe in the Lamoille Industrial Park off Route 100 left onto Harrell Street (just after crossing the railroad tracks). Handcrafted from soapstone and pure pig iron, these woodburning stoves are works of art. Visitors are welcome for factory tours.

The Notch Store, Route 108, at Smugglers Notch. Open in summer only, a co-op gallery specializing in painting, jewelry, hats, and sweaters.

Also see the **Johnson Woolen Mill** in the North of the Notch section, the short and scenic drive is certainly worth the effort.

ANTIQUES A score of shops cluster around Stowe, including the **Stowe Antique Center** (253-9875), and in Waterbury Center, **Sir Richard's Antiques** (244-8879), which has 14 dealers.

SPECIAL EVENTS Mid-January: **Winter Carnival:** A week of one of the oldest and most gala village winter carnivals in the country: snow sculptures, sled dog races, ski races, public feeds.

Late February: **Stowe Derby:** A 10-mile race from the summit of Mt. Mansfield to Stowe Village, usually about 300 entrants.

Easter Festivities: An Easter parade at Spruce Peak, Easter Egg hunt.

May: Lamoille County Players present musicals at the Hyde Park Opera House.

June: **Stowe Bicycle Race** through Smugglers Notch.

July 4: **Stowe Marathon.** Separate festivities in the village of Moscow, too small for its own band so they parade to the music of radios.

July and August: Green Mountain Guild's eight-week season of musicals.

Late July: **Stowe Performing Arts Summer Festival**—a week of concerts ranging from chamber to symphony, including bands and choral groups, presented in a number of places. **Lamoille County Field Days,** a weekend agricultural fair in Morrisville: tractor pulling, crafts, children's rides. **Annual Stowe Craft Show,** three days.

Early August: **Annual antique and classic car rally**—three days.

Mid-August: **Grand Prix tennis week;** top professionals from around the world.

Late August: Lamoille County Players stage a musical in the Hyde Park Opera House.

September (last weekend): **Stowe Foliage Craft Fair,** Topnotch Field.

October (first weekend): **Stowe Foliage Antique Show and Fair.**

MEDICAL EMERGENCY Stowe Rescue Squad, Police: 911; Waterbury (244-5511); **Copley Hospital** (888-4231), Morrisville.

North of the Notch

Smugglers' Notch, the 2,162 foot high pass traversed by Vermont's most dramatic road, is not in Stowe but the little-appreciated town of Cambridge. Nestled at the northern foot of Madonna Mountain (a Siamese twin of Stowe's Spruce Peak) is the village of Jeffersonville, a summer and fall gathering place for artists since the 1930s. Between the Notch and the village motorists are startled by the unlikely vision of a condominium town rising out of nowhere. This is The Village at Smugglers' Notch, a self-contained resort accommodating some 1,800 people year round, busiest in the winter when Morse Mountain, rising directly behind the complex, serves as a beginners' area for the three-mountain Smugglers' Notch Ski Area.

Although the highest reaches of Route 108 are closed (between Stowe and Smugglers' Notch Ski Area) from December to May, this area is actually less isolated than you might think, nearer to the Burlington airport than Stowe, also handy to AMTRAK at Essex Junction. Year-round, however, the feeling north of the Notch is totally different from the tourist-trod turf to the south. This is the Lamoille Valley, relatively open, gently rolling farm country beloved by fishermen, canoeists, and those who generally delight in the Vermont landscape, unembellished.

GUIDANCE   **Smugglers' Notch Area Chamber of Commerce,** Jeffersonville 05464 (644-2239), publishes an area directory.

GETTING THERE   By plane: Burlington Airport, served by Continental and United Airlines, among others. Rental cars at the airport. Given a 48-hour notice, The Village at Smugglers' Notch provides its own transfer for guests.

By train: Amtrak (if service has been restored) stops at Essex Junction, 25 miles away, enroute from Washington to Montreal. Otherwise it stops at Springfield, Massachusetts, where you can pick up a bus. See *AMTRAK* in *What's Where.*

GETTING AROUND   A car is a must. When the Notch is closed the route to Stowe via Morrisville is 26 miles, but in summer via Route 108 it is 18 miles.

TO SEE AND DO   **Smugglers' Notch.** During the War of 1812 Vermonters hid cattle and other supplies in the Notch, prior to smuggling them

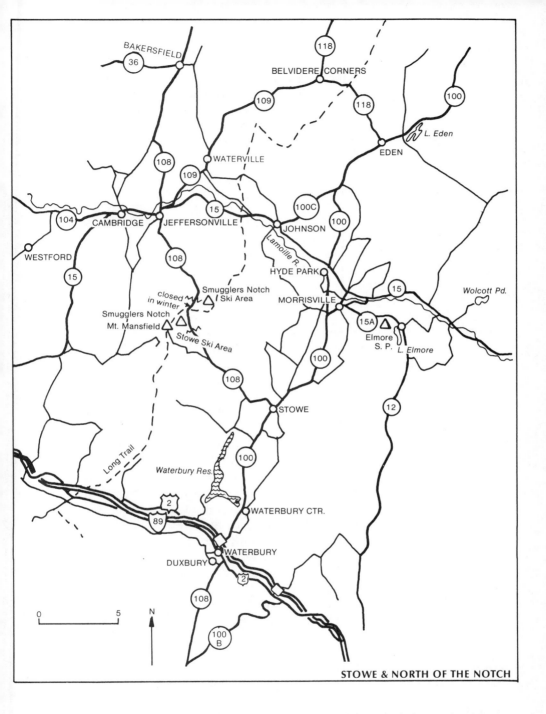

STOWE & NORTH OF THE NOTCH

into Canada to feed the British army—who were fighting the American army at the time. A path through the high pass has existed since Indian days but it wasn't until 1910 that the present road was built which, with its 18 percent grade, is as steep as many ski trails, windier than most. Realizing that drivers are too engrossed with the challenge of the road to admire the wild and wonderful scenery, the State's Forest and Parks Department has thoughtfully provided a turnoff just beyond the height of land. An information booth here is staffed in warm weather months; this is a restful spot by a mountain brook where you can picnic, even grill hot dogs. The Big Spring is here and you can ask about hiking distances to the other local landmarks: the Elephant Head, King Rock, the Hunter and His Dog (an outstanding rock formation), Singing Bird, the Smuggler's Cave, Smuggler's Face, and natural reservoir. See *Hiking* in the Stowe section for details about the easy trail to Sterling Pond, also the trail to the Elephant Head.

Mount Mansfield (see the description under Stowe). The Gondola, Alpine Slide, and Toll Road are all within a dozen miles of Jeffersonville.

SCENIC DRIVES   Three loop routes are especially appealing from Jeffersonville:

(1) Route 108 through Smugglers' Notch to Stowe Village (18 miles) and back up the old Stage Coach Road to Hyde Park (be sure to see the old Opera House) and back through Johnson (see *Selective Shopping*).

(2) From Cambridge Junction (just north of Jeffersonville) Route 109 follows the Lamoille River north by a series of five covered bridges to Belvidere Corners; here take Route 118, which soon crosses the Long Trail (see *Hiking*) and continues to the village of Eden. Lake Eden, 1 mile north on Route 100 is good for swimming and boating; return on Routes 100, 100C, and 15 via Johnson.

(3) From Jeffersonville drive west to the attractive village of Cambridge, south on Route 15 to Underhill Flats and Jericho—don't miss the photogenic Jericho gristmill, now the Old Red Mill gallery. Either continue through Essex Junction (note The Discovery Museum for Children) to Burlington or simply return on Route 128 through Westford where you can choose between the back road through the covered bridge or the paved highway via Route 104 back to Cambridge.

CANOEING   The Lamoille River from Jeffersonville to Cambridge is considered good for novices in spring, early summer; two small sets of rapids.

FISHING   See Stowe for description of Lamoille River fishing, boating guide. The stretch between Cambridge and Johnson is reputedly great fly and spin fishing for brown trout.

HIKING   Prospect Rock, Johnson. An easy hike yielding an exceptional view of the Lamoille River Valley and the high mountains to the south. Look for a steel bridge to the Ithiel Falls Camp Meeting Ground. Hike north on the white-blazed Long Trail ¾ of a mile to the summit.

Belvidere Mountain, Ritterbush Pond, and Devil's Gulch. These are basically two stretches of the Long Trail, one north (3½ hours round trip) to the summit of Belvidere Mountain, the other south (2¾ hours round trip) to a rock-filled gulch, filled with ferns. Both are described in the Green Mountain Club's *Guide Book to the Long Trail.*

PICNICKING   There are several outstanding roadside picnic areas:

(1) On Route 108, .2 mile north of the junction with Route 15 at Jeffersonville, there are picnic benches on the bank of the Lamoille.

(2) Route 108 south of Jeffersonville Village on the east side of the highway.

(3) On Route 108 in Smugglers' Notch itself; see Notch description.

(4) On Route 15, just 1.5 miles east of the Cambridge/Johnson line.

HORSEBACK RIDING   Cambridge Stables (644-2770), Jesse Taylor, Box 61, Cambridge 05444. Overnight pack trips with horse, camping gear and meals provided, also lunch and supper rides, $10 per hour (2 hour minimum), $150 per weekend. Sleigh rides in winter.

Smugglers' Notch Stables (644-5347), Smugglers' Notch, Jeffersonville. Wayne Terpstra offers winter as well as summer trail rides, western style saddles.

GOLF   Wolf Run Country Club (933-4007), Boston Post Road, Route 108, Bakersfield. Vermont's newest, and beautifully situated course opened its 9 holes in 1987.

SWIMMING   Brewster River Gorge, accessible from Route 108 south of Jeffersonville (turn off at the covered bridge).

TENNIS   Courts at Smugglers' Village, and a summer program of clinics and daily instruction.

Windridge Tennis Camp, behind the Inn, is a full program for children; courts are available to the public.

CROSS-COUNTRY SKIING   Sugarhouse Nordic Center (644-8851) Smugglers' Village. Narrow trails wind up and down through the trees then climb meadows away from the resort complex, a total of 23 miles of set trails; rentals, repairs in the warming hut where there is cocoa on the woodstove; guided and night tours, lessons available.

Smugglers' Notch. The stretch of Route 108 that is closed to traffic for snow season, is open to cross-country skiers. Guided tours are offered by the Sugarhouse Nordic Center.

Red Fox Ski Dorm (644-8888), Jeffersonville. Just 6 km of set trails but better suited for novices than the terrain right around the Smugglers' Village Sugarhouse, trails interconnect with that system; rentals, lessons, restaurant.

DOWNHILL SKIING   Smugglers' Notch (644-8851), Jeffersonville. In 1956 a group of local residents organized "Smugglers' Notch Ski Ways" on Sterling Mountain, a western shoulder of 3,610 foot high Madonna.

In 1963 a high-powered group headed by IBM board chairman Tom Watson gained a controlling interest and began developing the area as Madonna Mountain, a self-contained Aspen-style resort. Then in 1973 it was acquired by Stanley Snider, the contractor whose company (Stanmar) had been building the modular condo units in the village. Today there are almost 300 units. It is also a major public ski area, a natural snow bowl with a satisfying variety of terrain: beginners trails on Morse Mountain, 2,250 feet, some world-class trails and glade skiing on Madonna itself, along with intermediate runs that also predominate on Sterling Mountain.

The only way to the summit of Madonna, which commands one of the most spectacular views in New England, from Mount Washington to Mount Mansfield, is a 17-minute ride, one of the longest, coldest chair lifts in the East, and the way down can be via some of the region's steepest or longest runs. The ideal time to ski this mountain is early March when it's relatively warm and midweek, when its empty (on weekends the lines for the summit chair are long). Obviously this is a place you come, any time of ski season, for a five-day ski week—which automatically includes lessons for all members of the family.

Lifts: 4 double chair lifts.

Trails: 41, including a 3½ mile trail; 30% expert.

Vertical drop: 2,610 feet.

Snowmaking: 100% on Morse and Sterling, 75% on Madonna.

Facilities: Mountain Lodge, base lodge with ski shop, rentals, cafeteria, pub. The reception center/ski shop at Morse Mountain burned in March 1987 and has since been replaced with a new Village Center, source of rentals and tickets; the complex also includes a ski shop and deli. Top of the Notch warming hut at the Sterling chair terminal. (See *Lodging*.)

Ski school: ATM method, group lessons at Morse and Madonna, beginners at Morse, Star Test to rate your own level of ability.

For children: Day care from 6 months, Little Smugglers' Ski School for ages 3–6 (morning lessons at Morse Mountain), Teen Smugglers (age 7–14), all-day program.

Rates: $30 per day adults, $22 per junior (under 12). See Resorts for package rates.

ICE SKATING   **Smugglers' Village** rink (flooded tennis courts) is lighted at night.

LODGINGS   **The Village at Smugglers' Notch** (644-8851), Jeffersonville 05464. Almost 300 condominium units in a variety of shapes ranging from townhouse to multi-story can accommodate a total of 1,800 people. Geared to groups (facilities include a conference center) and to families, the resort offers a year-round combination of good things: skiing, swimming (the pool is protected by a heated bubble in winter), tennis and a varied program of summer activities including a supervised children's activity schedule of fishing, horseback rides, movies, hikes and games. Summer tennis and other packages are offered. In winter a Club Smugglers' five-day ski week includes lodging, skiing, lessons, use of tennis, pool and sauna, a dinner out and other extras at $335 per person, double occupancy; or from $995 for a family of four. In summer a comparable program, including Discovery Program for youngsters, begins at $565 for a two-child family.

Red Fox Ski Dorm (644-8888), Jeffersonville 05464. Just 2 miles down the road from Smugglers' Village there stands an old red church, now a lodge with 114 bunks geared to teenage patrons; there are also a few private rooms, peaceful in summer; facilities include ping-pong, electronic games, hot tub, cross-country ski center. $89.95 for two nights per person for non-holiday weekends, lifts and meals included, $179.95 per week for five-day ski weeks, including lifts and meals.

Three Mountain Lodge (644-8851), Jeffersonville 05464. Built beautifully of cedar logs as a ski hostel for UVM students, this exceptional lodge is now part of the Smugglers' Notch complex, offering dorm-style accommodations, a large homey living room with a fieldstone fireplace and two daily meals served family-style. Lifts, shuttle service and access to the Village resort facilities can be part of weekend and six-day packages; reasonably priced.

COUNTRY INNS   **Windridge Inn** (644-8281), Jeffersonville 05464. A very special little inn shaped by owner-artist-tennis player Alden Bryan, who discovered Jeffersonville as a place to paint 30 years ago. The inn offers just four twin-bedded guest rooms and small downstairs parlor. Guests have access to the tennis courts at the Windridge Tennis Camp, a separate but related, all-season operation for boys and girls; there is also a paddle tennis and squash court. Breakfast and lunch are available next door at the also related Windridge Dairy Kitchen. $53 per night for double room, B&B.

Smugglers' Notch Inn (644-2412), PO Box 286, Jeffersonville 05464. A 200-year-old structure built as an inn, recently refurbished by Paula and Steve DuCharme. $45 per person MAP in winter. A ski weekend, including lift tickets, two breakfasts, a dinner, shuttle to lifts and access to Smugglers' spa is less than $90 per person.

MOTEL   **Best Western Deerun Motel** (644-8866; 800-528-1234), Route 15, Jeffersonville. A 27-unit motel distinguished by its cleanliness and

Giant figures in wait for Bread and Puppet theatricals

warmth. In summer there is a pool; year-round a sauna, game room, and restaurant (Charlie's Pride). $46 double.

FAMILY FARM VACATION   Berkson Farms (933-2522), Enosburg Falls 05450. A mile north of the village on Route 108, this 600-acre dairy farm welcomes families year-round. The renovated, nicely maintained 130-year-old farmhouse, now managed by Dick and Joanne Keesler, can accommodate eight to ten persons in four crisp bedrooms, one of which has a private bath. There's a spacious living room and library as well as a comfy family and game room with TV and VCR. But the main attractions, especially for kids, are the cows, ducks, sheep, and goats and sugaring in season. Cross-country skiing can be enjoyed, along with hay rides, local swimming holes, and golf at the nearby 9-hole Enosburg Falls Country Club. Rates are $50 a day, MAP, for adults, $30 for children from 2–12, or $275 per week for adults and $130 for children, with three meals a day.

BED & BREAKFAST   B&B in Bakersfield (827-3206), Bakersfield 05441. Located in a scenic by-way village, in an old home with five rooms (four double beds, one twin) and shared bath. Audrey and Rupert Montague are hospitable hosts. $25 double, $20 single.

DINING OUT   Crown & Anchor (644-2900), Smugglers' Village. Housed in a New England-style house, one of the first structures built in the condo village, this is the most formal place to eat in town. The atmosphere is upscale English pub and entrées run $10.50–$16.

Smugglers' Notch Inn (644-2412), Jeffersonville. A large, old-fashioned, and appealing dining room, tin-roofed and decorated with paintings by patrons past, dinner nightly, locally esteemed for its Sunday noon buffet featuring Italian and American dishes.

Chez Moustache (644-5567), Route 108 between the village and Smugglers'. Open for dinner only. The atmosphere is convivial and informal and the specialties, Swiss. $6–$14.

EATING OUT   Windridge Dairy Kitchen (644-8207), Jeffersonville. A dry goods store until it became one of New England's outstanding bakeries and coffee shops; its baked goods were once distributed throughout the region but are now just available on a walk-in basis; open for breakfast at 8, serving until 4 P.M. The breads are outstanding and the pies extravagant; a standard menu is available at tables.

Jana's Cupboard (644-5454), Jeffersonville. Open from 6 A.M. through dinner at the junction of Route 15 and 109, a roadstop with surprising quality homemade soups, salads, pies, country breakfasts with fresh rolls; take-out specials.

McBaynes Brewster River Yacht Club (644-5432) Route 108 near Smugglers' Notch. The local hangout featuring a pool table, video games, pizza, soups, and subs.

SELECTIVE SHOPPING   Johnson Woolen Mills (635-2271), Johnson 05656. Open year-round except Sunday, 8–5; Saturday 9–4. Although wool is no longer manufactured in this picturesque mill, the fine line of clothing for which Johnson Woolen Mill has long been known, is made on the premises. Dill Barrows, owner of the business that has been in his family since 1905, blames Vermont's strict environmental laws for the demise of his—and other—mills. This mill's label can still be found in sports shops throughout the country and its famous heavy green wool workpants, long a uniform of Vermont farmers, are especially popular in Alaska. Although there are few discounts at the factory store, the selection of wool jackets and pants—for men, women, and children—is exceptional. The mail-order catalog is filled with sweaters, wool ties, hunters jackets, blankets, and other staples available in the shop.

    Cambridge Herbary (644-2480), Box 84B, Jeffersonville 05464. Open daily 8:30–5 except Mondays, posted from Route 15 just east of Cambridge village. Vermont native Sally Bevins minds her back-road garden and shop, selling 88 different kinds of herbs in one shape or another, some woven into unusually beautiful dried wreaths or mashed into potpourri or perfumes; teas, vinegars, books on herbs, and herb gardening also sold.

    Smugglers' Forge Craft Gallery (644-5010), Jeffersonville. Crafted items and antiques sold in a house on Route 108 between the village of Jeffersonville and the Notch.

    Brewster River Mill (644-2987), Mill Street (Route 108), Jeffersonville. Open Memorial Day through fall foliage, daily. This distinctive, three-story plus cupola grist mill has been rebuilt by local welder David Albright. Using local lumber and an old barn from his father-in-law's farm, Albright and his family pegged the post-and-beam structure together, then installed a 1922 steam engine. The wares are stone-ground flour and meal, locally made syrup, honey and jams, and things locally crafted.

    Nordic Nomad Sweaters (644-5880), Jeffersonville. Sweaters and hats, made in town with 100 percent wool imported from Norway. The tight twist wool is hand loomed and the results are thick and warm.

    Mary Bryan Memorial Gallery and Art Center (644-5100), Main Street, Jeffersonville. Open daily in summer. This new gallery in an old home houses a permanent collection of the life work of the artist for whom it was named, also features work by more than 50 New England artists, most of whom have frequented Jeffersonville.

SPECIAL EVENTS   Marchfest: Two weeks of special events in mid-March: Nordic, Alpine and dog sled races, broom ball tournaments, crafts shows, folk dances, snow sculpture, fireworks, ball—all at Smugglers' Village.

July: **"Largest little town celebration in Vermont"**: auction, frog jumping, lumberjack contest, horse pulling, fleamarket, fireworks, street dance—all in Jeffersonville. **Annual Green Mountain Summer Arts Festival** (635-2359 ext. 380), Dibden Arts Center, Johnson State College.

September: **Labor Day Festivities** in Cambridge: barbecue on the green, flea market.

October: **Arts Festival** in Jeffersonville.

MEDICAL EMERGENCY Jeffersonville, Johnson, Cambridge (635-7511); **Cambridge Regional Health Center** (644-5114).

The Northeast Kingdom

"You know, this is such beautiful country up here. It ought to be called the Northeast Kingdom of Vermont."

It was in 1949 that Senator George Aiken made this remark to a group in Lyndonville. Since then word has slowly gotten around that that's what Vermont's three northeastern counties—Orleans, Caledonia and Essex—should be calling themselves. This is, after all, a world unto itself, the state's most rural and lake-spotted corner, encompassing nearly 2,000 square miles. There are a few dramatic elevations such as Jay Peak on its northwestern fringe and Burke Mountain at its heart, but generally this is an open, glacially carved land of humped hills and rolling farmland, also some lonely lumbering country along the northern reaches of the Connecticut River. Neither of the ski areas draw patrons enough to change the look of the surrounding landscape. In the days of trains there were many more summer hotels than there are now. Yet you can still stay in an unexpected range of places—from elegant country inns and full resorts through ski lodges, condominiums and summer cottages to working farms. And all the amenities are here: golf, tennis, and horseback riding as well as hiking, fishing, canoeing and, of course, skiing. But they may take some searching out and in the process you may stumble across some people and places of memorable beauty.

ST. JOHNSBURY AND BURKE MOUNTAIN AREA

St. Johnsbury is the largest community in the Northeast Kingdom. Thanks to the Fairbanks family, who began manufacturing their world famous scale here in the 1830s, it is graced with an outstanding museum of natural and local history, and a handsome Athenaeum. The general late-nineteenth-century affluence which St.J (as it is affectionately known) enjoyed as an active rail junction and industrial center has been commemorated in ornate brick along Railroad Street and sloping Eastern Avenue, and in the fine mansions along Main Street, set high above the commercial downtown.

In the 1960s, when Fairbanks became a division of a conglomerate—which threatened to move the scaleworks south—townspeople themselves raised the money to subsidize a new plant. Which is all to say that this is a spirited town boasting the oldest town band in the country, a busy calendar of concerts, lectures, and plays, and all the shops and services needed by the inhabitants of the picturesque villages along the Connecticut River to the south, the rolling hills to the southwest, and the lonely woodlands to the east. Less than a dozen miles north, the wide main street of Lyndonville is also lined with useful shops. Burke Mountain, a short way up Route 114, is accessible by car as well as foot in summer and draws skiers from throughout the Northeast in winter.

GUIDANCE   St. Johnsbury Chamber of Commerce (748-3678), 30 Western Avenue, St. Johnsbury 05819. A seasonal information booth is maintained at the corner of Main Street and Eastern Avenue, a source for lodging, dining and general information for much of the Northeast Kingdom.

The Lyndon Area Chamber of Commerce (626-9696), PO Box 886, Lyndonville 05851, publishes a leaflet guide to its area and maintains a seasonal information booth on the Common.

GETTING THERE   By bus: Greyhound/Vermont Transit from Boston, New York, and Connecticut via White River Junction. Buses stop in Wells River, McIndoe Falls, Barnet, Lyndonville, and St. Johnsbury. There also are buses from Montpelier and St. Johnsbury to Danville, and from Montreal and Sherbrooke.

TO SEE AND DO   The Fairbanks Museum and Planetarium (748-2372), Main and Prospect Streets, St. Johnsbury. Open daily, year-round; Monday–Saturday, 10–4, Sundays, 1–5; in July and August, 10–6 on weekdays; admission: $2.50 per adult, $1.25 per child, $5.50 per family. Planetarium programs: weekends at 2:30 year-round (admission: $1), also in July and August, weekdays at 11 and 2:30.

This is still a wonderfully old-fashioned place. Its main hall, which is capped by a 30-foot high, barrel-vaulted ceiling, is filled with some 3,000 stuffed animals in old-style glass cases. Ranged along the mezzanine above are treasures collected in the nineteenth century from throughout the world.

"I wish the museum to be the people's school . . . to teach the village the meaning of nature and religion," explained Franklin Fairbanks at the museum's 1890 dedication. There are exhibits from Africa, Oceania, and South America; small jewels like a letter dated "Vailima, June 19, 1891" from Robert Louis Stevenson to Annie Ide, deeding her his birthday because hers fell on Christmas. Stevenson had met the St. Johnsbury girl in Samoa, where her father was serving as U.S consul. There are also exhibits of local flora and fauna that change with the season, and exhibits on aspects of

Vermont history. In the upstairs planetarium, which seats just 50 people, you learn about the night sky as it appears in the Northeast Kingdom. It should be noted too, that the museum is a U.S. weather observation station and daily forecasts are a popular feature on Vermont Public Radio. There is also a fine little gift shop.

St. Johnsbury Athenaeum (748-8291), Main Street. Open Monday and Wednesday, 9–8, closed Sunday, otherwise: 9:30–5.

The big attraction is the art gallery in the rear of this fascinating public library. Said to be the oldest, unaltered gallery in the country, it has a distinctly nineteenth-century feel. Smaller canvases and sculptures are grouped around the outsized painting, ''Domes of Yosemite'' by Albert Bierstadt. Natural light through an arched skylight enhances the effect of looking into the Yosemite Valley; this is the setting for chamber music concerts.

VILLAGES   Peacham. High on a ridge, overlooking the White Mountains, this is an old and proud village with a library at the four corners, a distinctive old academy building (the academy, alas, is defunct) and a fine historical collection housed in an early nineteenth-century house. Inquire at the town clerk's office about hours. It is a beautiful village, and there is fishing in its pond, cross-country skiing and horseback riding at Twin Mount Farm.

Barnet. An old Scots settlement, the village of Barnet itself is on a curve of the Connecticut River, almost lost today in a curious intertwining of I-91 and Route 5. **Pearson's General Store** marks the middle of town and there is **Goodwillie House** (633-2542), built in 1790 by a Scottish pastor, later a stop on the Underground Railroad, now housing the collections of the Barnet Historical Society. Drive east to Barnet Center to find Harvey's Lake (good for both fishing and swimming) and the **Karme-Choling Buddhist Meditation Center** (633-2384), a Tibetan Buddhist meditation center formerly known as the ''Tail of the Tiger,'' one among a number of such houses established in the U.S. and Canada by Trungpa Rinpoche. From the road this appears to be a traditional white farmhouse with red trim and a big barn, but with a bright banner billowing in the wind. Inside, the house has been dramatically altered to let in the sun and a sense of the surroundings, to create a Tibetan-style temple and housing for guests who are welcome to stay overnight, for a ''weekthun'' or a ''dathun'' (month) of learning to meditate; solitary retreats can also be arranged and drop-in visitors are welcome. Meditation aids are sold in the barn where meditation pillows are made.

Waterford Dam at Moore Reservoir. New England Power offers guided tours of the huge complex of turbines. There are also boat launch and picnic sites here. The approach is from the New Hamp-

The famous Fairbanks Museum, St. Johnsbury

shire side of the Connecticut River, just below Lower Waterford, Vermont, off Route 135.

Danville. Until 1855 Danville was the shire town of Caledonia County. It is an exceptionally beautiful town set high on a plateau around a large green complete with bandstand, Civil War monument and general store. The imposing town hall was built as the county courthouse, and the small, square Caledonia Bank is one of the safest strongholds around, thanks to devices installed when it was last held up in 1935. Danville is known primarily as headquarters for the American Society of Dowsers, who hold their annual convention here each September. In the red **Dowsers' Hall** (684-3417) open weekdays 9–4:30 (occasionally on weekends), you learn that dowsing is the knack for finding water through the use of a forked stick, a pair of angle rods, or a pendulum. Dowsing equipment and a wide selection of books are sold here. The American Society of Dowsers boasts 2,600 members in 27 countries.

West Danville is a crossroads (Routes 15 and 2) village. **Hastings Store** is a great, old-fashioned general store cum post office, and one of the world's smallest libraries sits across the road on Joe's Pond. There is a public beach with picnic and sanitary facilities here. The water from Joe's Pond (an old summer resort) is said to empty, eventually, into Long Island Sound, while that from Molly's Pond (a mile south, named for Joe's squaw) is said to wind up in the Gulf of St. Lawrence.

Cabot. Known during the War of 1812 for its distilleries (the whiskey was sold to the Canadians) this distinctly upcountry village is now famed for its cheese. **The Cabot Farmers Co-op Creamery** (563-2231), is open Monday–Saturday 8–4:30. Since 1984, when we researched the last edition of this book, the creamery has doubled its annual production from 6 to 12 million pounds of cheese, and it has opened a visitors center in which you see a great little video chronicling the history of the region and of Vermont cheesemaking as well as of the cheddaring process. A tour of the plant follows and there is, of course, a large gourmet gift shop featuring a wide variety of Cabot cheeses.

Lyndonville. A substantial old community that serves as a shopping center for smaller villages to the North. Since 1846, it's been the site of the Caledonia County Fair, and it's the home of Lyndon State College (1,000 students). It is one of the few New England towns to operate its own ski slopes (see *Downhill Skiing*) and the only one in which Bag Balm (see *Selective Shopping*) is made.

East Burke. A small village with a beautiful library and historical society building (The Old Museum; 626-9823; open June–October, Wednesday and Saturday afternoons, also by appointment), some attractive shops and restaurants geared to the ski trade (this is the nearest village to Burke Mountain). Elmer Albert Darling, a local boy who made a fortune with his Fifth Avenue Hotel in New York City, built a majestic estate, "Burklyn." There are two inns and assorted condos, rental chalets and Bed & Breakfasts.

Granby and **Victory** are two dirt road towns with a combined population of 120, off in lumbering country east of St. Johnsbury. The only visitors who usually come this way bring their canoes, to explore Victory Bog (see *Parks and Forests*). But the last weekend in September a Holiday in the Hills draws some 10,000 people (see *Special Events*).

SUGAR HOUSES **Cedric Houston** on South Walden Road in Cabot, Box 49 (563-2318); 200 taps, can accommodate up to four visitors at a time in his sugarhouse.

David and Myra Houston (223-7307), West Hill in Cabot; 250–500 taps, buckets, gathered with oxen, up to ten visitors at a time welcome during boiling off.

Maple Grove Maple Museum (748-5141), St. Johnsbury. May 30–late October; guided tours are offered daily 8–4:30 of "the world's largest maple candy factory." In business since 1904, this is an old-fashioned factory in which maple candy is made from molds. A film in the adjacent museum depicts maple production and displays tools of the trade.

Goodrich's Sugarhouse (563-9917), just off Route 2 by Molly's Pond in West Danville. A family tradition for seven generations, open to visitors March through December with a full line of award-winning maple products.

COVERED BRIDGES All five within northern Caledonia County are in Lyndonville—one 120 foot 1865 bridge across the Passumpsic, 3 miles north of town off Route 114 and one next to the Lynburke Motel, a genuine 1869 bridge moved from its original site; the others are in Lyndon Corner (one dating from 1879, the other from 1881, both west off Route 5), the fifth in Lyndon Center on Route 122.

PARKS AND FORESTS **Groton State Forest,** Marshfield 05658. A 25,623-acre preserve with four separate campgrounds, a beach area, yet another area for fly fishing and one for group camping. Access to all is from the "Marshfield-Groton Highway," Route 232.

Big Deer Campground (584-3823); 33 campsites with 22 lean-tos, beach privileges and hiking trails.

New Discovery Campground (584-3820). A total of 47 campsites, 14 of them lean-tos, beach privileges, hiking trails, primitive camping.

Stillwater Campground (584-3822). On the west side of Lake Groton, a total of 63 tentsites, 16 lean-tos. Campers' beach and boat launch; rental boats, dump station.

Ricker Pond Campground (584-3821). A total of 33 campsites,

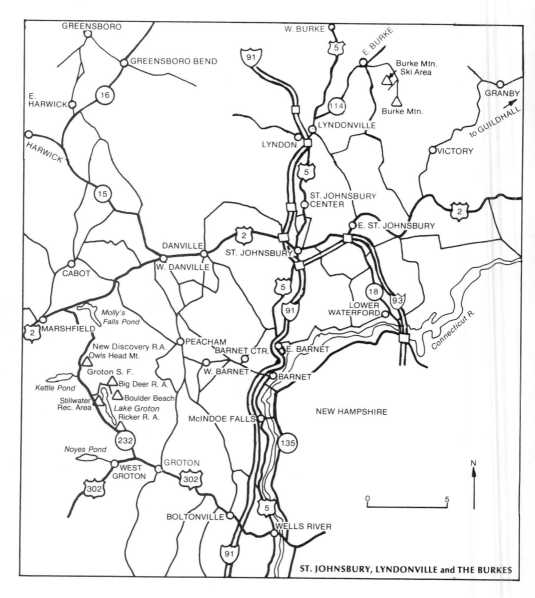

ST. JOHNSBURY, LYNDONVILLE and THE BURKES

22 lean-tos. On the south side of Ricker Pond; campers beach, rental boats, nature trail, dump station.

Owls Head Area (584-3820). Picnic area, shelter, trail to Owls Head Mountain and summit views.

Seyon Fly Fishing Area (584-3829). On Noyes Pond. Trout fishing with flies only from boats rented at the site.

Kettle Pond (584-3820). On the south side of Kettle Pond; walk-in fishing, group camping, hiking, and snowmobiling.

Boulder Beach Day Use Area (584-3820). A public beach, picnic area, snack bar, bath house.

Victory Basin, alias Victory Bog. A 4,970-acre preserve administered by the Vermont Fish and Game Department, purchased in 1969 from the New England Power Company. It includes a 25-acre boreal bog with rare plant life, a total of 1,800 acres of wetlands, 1,084 acres of hardwoods, 71 acres of clearings and old fields. The dirt road access is via Victory; there are three parking areas: Mitchell's Landing, Lee Hill, and Damons Crossing.

SCENIC DRIVE   **Burke Mountain.** A 2½-mile Auto Road to the summit of Burke Mountain (3,267 feet) commands a sweeping view of the North Country; picnic areas are provided half-way and at the summit. Formerly the 10,000-acre Darling State Forest, donated to the state in 1933, the road was constructed by the Civilian Conservation Corps. Since the 1960s it has been acquired by Burke Mountain Recreation, Inc., which charges $2, $1 per motorcycle, for the drive to the summit and maintains the campsites in the Sugar House Campground.

The **Darling Hill** road from Route 114 in East Burke, 5 miles south to Route 114 in Lyndonville follows a ridge past old homesteads, offers great views.

RAILROAD EXCURSIONS   **The St. J.& L.C. Railroad, Inc.** was originally a passenger and freight line that linked small towns all along the roof of Vermont. It was affectionately known as the "Slow, Jerky, & Long Coming." Volunteer operated, it runs foliage-season tours on the winding, scenic stretch of state-owned track between St. Johnsbury and Greensboro Bend, a 57-miles round-trip excursion. Check with the St. J Chamber (748-3678) for current schedule.

Another section is now covered by Lamoille Valley Railroad excursions that run from Morrisville to West Danville in summer and from Morrisville to Greensboro Bend during foliage season. (See Stowe.)

BOAT RENTALS   **Injunjoe Motor Court** (684-3430), West Danville; **Karl's Tent & Trailer Camp** (633-2213), West Barnet; **Village Sport Shop** (626-8448), Lyndonville.

CANOEING   This is canoeing country: down the Connecticut River itself, and along the Moose River in Victory Basin (see *Hiking*). For rentals check with the outlets listed under *Boat Rentals*. **Inwood Manor** (633-4047), in East Barnet not only rents canoes but offers shuttle service and inn-to-inn expeditions ranging from two to five days; meals, lodging, and shuttles included.

FISHING   See the pamphlet "Vermont Guide to Fishing" (available from the Vermont Fish and Game Department in Montpelier) for details about which fish are available where. Check the State Highway map for local access points.

GOLF   **St. Johnsbury Country Club** (748-9894), open daily mid-May to October, 9 holes.

HORSEBACK RIDING   **Sunny Brook Farm** (467-3380), West Burke. Year-round instruction, summer horsemanship camp for girls.

SWIMMING   **Harvey's Lake** in West Barnet; public beaches in Groton State Forest; small beach at **Ticklenaked Pond** in Boltonville, and at Joe's Pond in West Danville.

CROSS-COUNTRY SKIING   **Burke Mountain Ski Touring Center** (626-8338), East Burke. Dashney Farm serves as a center with rentals, lessons, guided tours; 40 km of tracked trails at elevations between 1,100 and 2,200 feet.

   Rabbit Hill Inn Cross-Country Ski Center (748-5168), Lower Waterford. A total of 25 km of trails with views of the Connecticut River Valley; elevation between 900 and 1,900 feet.

   Groton State Forest. Snowed-over roads, good for 20 km of cross-country skiing.

DOWNHILL SKIING   **Burke Mountain** (626-3305), East Burke 05832. The first ski trails on this majestic mountain were cut in the 1930s when it became a state park. In 1955, a Poma Lift was installed to the summit and a shelter and parking lot were opened. Long known as the "Vermonter's Mountain" it caters to local patrons, also to Canadians and Bostonians (Boston is less than four hours away via I-93). Paul Quinn, the new owner, plans improvements.
Lifts: 2 double chairlifts, 2 Poma lifts, 1 J-Bar.
Trails and Slopes: 27 trails and 3 wide-open slopes, 20% novice, 20% advanced, the remainder intermediate trials.
Vertical drop: 2,000 feet.
Snowmaking: 32 acres
Facilities: Sherburne Base Lodge is attractive, with a hearth in the glass-walled area used both for picnicking and cafeteria. Another base lodge serves the upper portion of the mountain.
Ski school: "Home of the carved turn," private and group lessons. For children; a nursery for the 4-months to 7-year-old crowd. Bear Chasers, a supervised program for children aged 7 to 14. Burke Mountain Academy, a prep school for aspiring racers, claims to have developed more competitors for the U.S. Ski Team than any other American program.
Rates: $24 per adult, $16 per child 6–14; five days: $90 per adult, $65 per Junior.

LODGING   **The St. Johnsbury Chamber of Commerce** (748-3678) is a source of advice, and in foliage season, it does an outstanding job of finding beds, many of them in private homes, for stranded leaf peepers. Plan ahead for reservations.

INNS   **The Old Cutter Inn** (626-5152), East Burke 05832. This is an 1845 farmhouse that has been an inn since 1969, with nine rooms, five with private bath, and a two-bedroom apartment next to the barn. A spotless, cozy inn with an excellent dining room, open to the public every night but Wednesday (when it still serves guests); fireside après ski in the cocktail lounge. Rates: $26–38 double occupancy, cheaper off-season. Closed April and November.

The Wildflower Inn (626-8310), Star Route, Lyndonville 05851. This is a fine old farmhouse set high on a ridge with a spectacular view, surrounded by its own 500 acres and famous for its sleigh rides. Four of the rooms are large, airy spaces upstairs in the house, sharing two baths. A dozen more have been fitted into the former Carriage Barn and some of these have lofts with bunk beds (ideal for children); two are efficiencies. Jim and Mary O'Reilly have three young boys and children are particularly welcome here. There are plenty of animals—chickens, peacocks, a donkey, pony, kittens, a dog, and 200 cows (housed in the barn and surrounding acreage). There is also a special children's corner, stocked with dress-up clothes and toys. The inn also offers some great adult spaces—an attractive parlor and library, stocked with games and the kind of books you really want to read. Breakfast is a three-course event and tea is also served. $53–58 double, higher during holidays; children under age 5 are free, to age 12 $5 in the same room with parents.

Rabbit Hill Inn (748-5168), Lower Waterford 05848. John and Maureen Magee have injected new verve into this pillared landmark, an inn since 1834. All 20 rooms have their own private bath, and all but 2 have views of the mountains and 5 have working fireplaces. Each has been painstakingly furnished, complete with a "room diary."

Inwood Manor (633-4047), East Barnet 05821. This unusual looking inn once lodged workers of "the world's largest croquet factory." To find it, you turn east in Barnet onto the Lower Waterford Road, then north onto a plateau from which the inn overlooks the Passumpsic. The inn sponsors canoeing excursions that can last for a day, a weekend, or five days. $45–55 double includes continental breakfast. Dinner, one seating, ($17.50) by reservation only.

The Peacham Inn (592-3208), Peacham 05862. A fine classical-revival mansion set in one of Vermont's most beautiful villages. There are four guest rooms, all with private bath and two with working fireplaces. They all have one or two double beds, some have down comforters. Guests have access to the large living room, warmed in winter with a woodstove. In summer, there's swimming nearby in Harvey's Lake and in winter, cross-country skiing. The small dining room is open to the public by reservation; breakfast and dinner are served daily. $36–60 per room. Dinner entrées $10–17.

The Garrison Inn (626-8329), East Burke 05832. A new house, built by Rick and Liliane McHugh to resemble an eighteenth-century garrison house. The six bedrooms have wide pine floors, private baths, antiques. The dining room has old wooden beams and the living room is warmed by a wood stove. Rates are $32 double, $27 single, a muffin breakfast included. Group rates available.

OTHER LODGING   **Burke Green Lodging** (467-9243), East Burke 05832. An 1840 farmhouse with one twin-bedded and one double-bedded (an heirloom four-poster) room, and a suite sleeping three. Guests have access to a family room with fireplace, also to a fridge and (summer) picnicking facilities. $22 single, $28–32 double.

Sherryland (684-3354), Danville 05828. A large nineteenth-century farmhouse located on a pleasant country road about a mile south of the village green. Five guest rooms are genuinely homelike. No meals; $25 double, $20 single, $5 per cot.

The Old Homestead (633-4100), Barnet 05821. A century-old home that is a family bargain: $25–46 for a big room with two double beds, a private bath and screened-in porch; large breakfast included.

Grandma's Bed & Breakfast (748-3860), St. Johnsbury 05819. A private home that offers two guest rooms, one with double, another with twins. $30 per couple per night, includes breakfast.

Danville Inn/Restaurant (684-3484), Danville 05828. Rooms in the center of the village, in a home that also houses a reasonably priced restaurant serving three squares. $40 double; includes breakfast.

Blue Wax Farm (626-5542), Pinkham Road, East Burke 05832. Kenneth and Ingrid Parr have owned this old cape home with a view of Willoughby Lake Gap for more than 30 years. The downstairs spaces are comfortably furnished, larded with books and souvenirs from the Parrs' former life overseas. Upstairs the three bedrooms share two baths. There's an outside sauna (robes are supplied) and informal cross-country skiing on the 326 acres. $27 double occupancy includes breakfast.

Twin Mount Farm Lodge (592-3579), Box 31, Peacham 05862. A fine old home with comfortable rooms, private baths; $19 per person in a double room includes breakfast.

Brick House Guests (472-5512), Box 128, East Hardwick 05836. A Victorian house with herb and perennial gardens, rooms with shared bath; $35 double, $25 single.

Broadview Farm (748-9902), 3 miles north of North Danville, has been welcoming travelers for over a hundred years. Molly Newell offers single at $28, doubles at $35. There's a family apartment— two rooms with double beds, one with single and a private sitting

Greensboro is a summer and winter resort

room and bath—for $75 (about the best buy in the state); it can be had for $350 for a winter ski week. No pets; restricted smoking.

CONDOMINIUMS   Burke Mountain Condominiums (626-3305), East Burke 05832. About 90 slopeside units in the rental pool are salted around the ski area's access roads. They range from studios to four-bedroom apartments accommodating 11 persons. All have woodstoves or fireplaces, TV, and trail access: $217–277 per weekend for four, $399–511 per ski week for four; cheaper off-season, more over holidays.

MOTELS AND CABINS   **Mountain View Cabins** (648-3814), Danville 05828. Five housekeeping cabins, one open year-round, comfortable and well-kept, picnic facilities: $29–32, less by the week.

Lynburke Motel (626-3346), Lyndonville 05851. A friendly motel with all the amenities: color TV, phones, a wax room, pool, restaurant, and lounge, 6 miles from Burke Mountain. $25 single, $30 double.

Colonnade Motor Inn and Tavern (626-9317), Lyndonville 05851. Forty rooms in a luxury motor inn just off I-91; cafe, laundry, bar; $27 single, $31–34 double, free under age 9.

DINING OUT   **Creamery Restaurant** (684-3616), Danville. Open Monday–Saturday for lunch and dinner, Sunday for brunch. A former creamery nicely converted into a gracious little restaurant that many feel is now the best in the St. J area; there is a blackboard menu featuring homemade soups and salads, pies and a choice of meat and seafood dishes. Entrees range from $8–15.

The Rabbit Hill Inn (748-5168), Route 18 in Lower Waterford. The elegant dining room holds just 11 tables. Both the food and atmosphere are carefully orchestrated here. There's candlelight and crystal, classical guitar and flute and a choice of prix fixe dinners. On the night we stopped by you could dine on steak Diane, chicken pesto, veal served with a lemon caper sauce, or swordfish with herb butter. A choice of appetizer or soup, bread, sorbet, salad, dessert, and beverage are included in the $19–20 price.

The Peacham Inn (592-3208), Peacham. A gracious, classical-revival mansion set in a classic Vermont village; a choice of three dinner entrées are served in the small, elegant dining room; wines available; by reservation only. Entrées range from $10–17.

Old Cutter Inn (625-5152), East Burke. Owner Fritz Walther prepares a few of his native specialties, like Rahmschnitzel (pork medallions, sauteed in butter with shallots, deglazed with white wine and finished with fresh mushrooms in a light cream sauce), also standard steak, chicken, and veal dishes and a choice of seafood. Entrées range from $10–15. You can also dine in the informal tavern on German Bratwurst ($5.75). Closed Wednesdays and in November and April.

Aime's (748-3194), junction of Routes 2 and 18, East St. Johnsbury. Open 7:30 AM–8:30 PM except October–May when it opens at 11 AM A dependable, dining-out kind of place in which lunch averages $5 and dinner $10; specialties include pecan pie; children's menus. Aime's styles itself "the healthy food restaurant," prides itself on using fresh certified Angus beef, fresh seafood, sea salt, minimal sugar and salt, no MSG.

EATING OUT   **Rainbow Sweets Bakery and Cafe** (426-3531), Route 2, Marshfield. Generally open for breakfast and lunch, also for dinner

Friday and Saturday. Closed Tuesday. This is a small but outstanding establishment with only five tables and a reputation that extends through much of central and northern Vermont, understandable when you sample the spanakopita (Greek spinach pies with feta cheese wrapped in filo, $11.95), the broccoli quiche, gnocchi (potato pasta with homemade sauce), outstanding pizza or sinful desserts. Imported wines and beers available, along with espresso and herb teas.

Golden City (748–5081/5082), 52 Railroad Street, St. Johnsbury. Related to the Peking Garden in Newport, a large, comfortable Chinese restaurant with more than the standard menu. Try the Pu Pu Platter for two (it's ample for three), $12.50, and the Subgum Shrimp. Most entrées are under $5.

Miss Lyndonville Diner (626-9890), Lyndonville. Open from 6:00 in the morning until supper, famed for its strawberry pancakes with whipped cream for breakfast, pie, homemade french toast, and jumbo eggs.

Miss Vermont Diner (748-9751). Memorial Drive, St. Johnsbury. Open from 6 AM through dinner weekdays, from 9 AM Saturday, 7–1 on Sunday. Under same ownership and very similar to the Miss 'ville, very popular, get there early. A BBQ half chicken is $3.15.

Danville Restaurant (684-3484), Danville Village. Housed in a village house, open 6 AM–9 PM, a family restaurant good for all three meals at reasonable prices in a friendly atmosphere; both counter and table service, from $1.25 hamburgers to full course meals, daily specials.

St. Johnsbury Country Club (748-9894), Route 5, north of St. Johnsbury. The attractive clubhouse is open to the public for lunch, a good bet.

SELECTIVE SHOPPING   Birdmen. Twin brothers Henry and Edmund Menard each maintain studios, one in Cabot (birthplace of both) on the back road from the village to Molly's Pond, the second farther down Route 2 in Marshfield. Henry (563-2501), and partner Mark Cote, specialize in exquisite, detailed bird carvings that sell from $13–150. He welcomes visitors in the house that he built, set in his commercial nursery that includes two acres of lillies (more than 100 varieties), at their best late June through August. Edmund (426-3310), who styles himself "Bird Man II," produces small impressively fantailed birds in the style taught him by the late Chester Nutting; each bird carved from one piece of green wood takes him about 20 minutes to create and costs $4; he carves some 4,000 a year.

The Craft Shop at Molly's Pond, on Route 2, west of West Danville. Open May through December, closed Sundays; otherwise

10:30–5:30; (1–5:30 in winter). One of the state's outstanding little crafts shops, here for 26 years, specializing in original metal jewelry, fine pottery, weavings, blown glass, and prints—especially those by Mary Azarian who lives nearby. Shopkeeper Martha Price knows all the craftspeople personally.

Cabot Farmers' Co-op Creamery (563-2231), Cabot (See Cabot under *"Villages"*). Cheese and other dairy products (great yogurt) sold at the Creamery.

Green Mountain Books & Prints (626-5051), 100 Broad St., Lyndonville. A book lover's heaven: new and used books; many new, discounted titles and a large stock of Vermont books; new and old prints; rare books. Open Monday–Thursday 10–4, Friday 10–6, Saturday 10–1.

Farmer's Daughter, Route 2 east, St. Johnsbury. A vast emporium of gifts, Vermont products, and others.

Jacob's Ladder, Route 302 in Boltonville near Wells River. A large, tourist-oriented shop full of New England crafts, baskets, penny candy, and general gift items.

Bailey's Country Store (626-3666), Route 114, East Burke. Open 6:30 AM–9 PM weekdays, 8–9 Sundays, close at 8 in winter. This classic old general store has been nicely fancied up by longtime local residents Jeane and Jerry Bailey. There is now a cigar store Indian on the porch and the second floor gallery has been beautifully restored and displays work by local craftsmen. Downstairs are breads, pies, cookies, and coffee cakes baked daily right here, also a gourmet deli featuring cheeses and cold cuts plus fresh fruits and vegetables and basic staples; a selection of wines, coffees, and teas, and a back room full of wicker complete the scene.

Northern Lights Bookshop (748-4463), 79 Railroad Street, St. Johnsbury. A bright, lively bookstore with a creative flair for selecting stock.

Maple Grove Maple Museum & Factory (748-5141), Route 2 east of St. Johnsbury (see *Sugar Houses*) is a source of a variety of gourmet maple-related products as well as syrup.

Bag Balm. Developed in 1908 as a cure for chapped udders, Bag Balm has enjoyed an acquired nation-wide following in recent years. Available throughout the region, it is made in an old gristmill in Lyndonville. While there is no factory store, you might check out the Lyndonville Pharmacy (the owner is Bag Balm's chemist), which sells the distinctive green tin boxes and bottom line prices. Next to the cash register there's what looks like a hot air balloon with a tiny Bag Balm tin instead of a basket. A closer look reveals the balloon is an udder.

ENTERTAINMENT   Catamount Film and Arts Company (748-2600), 60 Eastern Avenue, PO Box 324, St. Johnsbury 05819. Established in 1975 as a nonprofit cultural organization serving northern Vermont and New Hampshire, Catamount stages a variety of "showcase events" (last summer's roster included concerts by Joan Baez, Chuck Berry, and Judy Collins) at sites throughout the region, nightly film screenings at the Catamount Arts Center (the former St. Johnsbury post office) and changing shows in its gallery. Summer productions include performances of Circus Smirkus, participants in a summerlong circus workshop for area youths, aged 10–18.

St. Johnsbury Town Band concerts, weekly all summer.

SPECIAL EVENTS   February: **Snowflake Festival Winter Carnival,** Lyndonville-Burke. Events include a craft show, snow sculpture, ski races for all ages and abilities, sleigh rides, music, and art.

April: **Maple Sugar Festival** in St. J, third weekend.

May: **East Burke: Annual White-Water Canoe Race** on the Passumpsic River, May 1. **Sheep and Wool Festival** at Burklyn Barn in mid-May: weaving competitions, spinning, sheep dog trials, lamb lunch, crafts.

June: **Lumberman's Day** at Burke Mountain.

July–October: **Farmers' Market,** Saturdays, 9–noon; Wednesdays, 4–7; Western Avenue.

July: **Strawberry Festival Dinner,** second Thursday at North Congregational Church, St. J. **Burklyn Summer Festival of Vermont Arts and Crafts,** Bandstand Park, Lyndonville. **Stars and Stripes Pageant,** Lyndonville, last weekend: big auction, parade featuring Bread & Puppet Uncle Sam, barbecue.

August: **Caledonia County Fair,** Lyndonville; 4th weekend, Thursday–Sunday.

September: **Dowsers National Convention,** Danville, second week, Tuesday– Sunday. **Holiday in the Hills,** last Saturday and Sunday, Victory and Granby: the two towns with a combined population of 120 feed some 10,000 visitors who crowd up their back roads; the festival includes historical exhibits, crafts demonstrations.

September–October: **Northeast Kingdom Fall Foliage Festival,** the last week in September or first in October (following the Holiday in the Hills weekend). Six towns take turns hosting visitors; feeding them breakfast, lunch, and dinner; and guiding them to beauty spots and points of interest within their borders. In Walden, the specialty is Christmas wreath making; in Cabot, there is a tour of the cheese factory; in Plainfield, farm tours; in Peacham, sugar-on-snow parties in the hillside sugarhouse; in Barnet, there is usually a ham dinner and at the Barnet Center Church and in Groton, the wind-up **Lumberjack's Ball.** For details contact the St. J. Chamber of Commerce.

December: **Christmas Fair,** the first weekend. A major gathering of North Country craftspeople and artists in St. J. **Kirby Quilters Christmas Bazaar.**

MEDICAL EMERGENCY   748-3111. **Northeastern Vermont Regional Hospital** (748-8141), St. Johnsbury. In East Burke: 748-3111.

Craftsbury Country

Of all the high, rolling country in the Northeast Kingdom, the open farmland around Craftsbury gives you the best sense of being on top of the world. The roads follow along ridges, and the fields roll away like waves to the mountains in the distance. This area, framed by Route 14 on the west and 16 on the east, is webbed with gravel roads, spotted with small lakes and large ponds.

The resort village here is actually Greensboro, a turn-of-the-century summer compound on Caspian Lake. Craftsbury itself is a composite of scattered villages, most of which you drive through in a trice. It's Craftsbury Common that compels you to stop. So vast is the common itself that it dwarfs the surrounding white homes, academy, and church. It's so high that the countryside drops away on all sides. A number of lodging places, ranging from farms and a sports center to the Kingdom's poshest inns, are found right around here.

Hardwick is the trading center for this area. Its Victorian Main Street is the sole reminder of the town's heyday as one of the world's largest granite processing places. The granite was actually in Woodbury, five miles south, whence it arrived by rail. Thousands of skilled European craftsmen moved to town beginning in the 1870s and continuing into the 1920s; a number of French Canadians remain.

GUIDANCE   This area falls between the realms of the Kingdom's full-scale chambers of commerce. Most Craftsbury and Greensboro businesses belong to the **Hardwick Area Chamber of Commerce** (472-5906), an all-volunteer operation that maintains an information booth on Route 15 west of town in July and August. The phone number is that of the Hardwick News Center (a newsstand) owned by Velda Laird. For cottage listings on Lake Parker in Glover you can check with the **Barton Chamber of Commerce** (525-6210), Box 280, Barton 05822. If you are checking up on a particular event you can try the **Craftsbury Town Clerk** (586-2823).

GETTING THERE   From the Southeast (I-93 or 91) take the I-91 Exit 21 to Route 2 west and Route 15 to Hardwick or take I-91 all the way to Barton (Exit 25), then south on Route 16. Be sure to ask your lodging place which way works better because it can easily save a half hour.

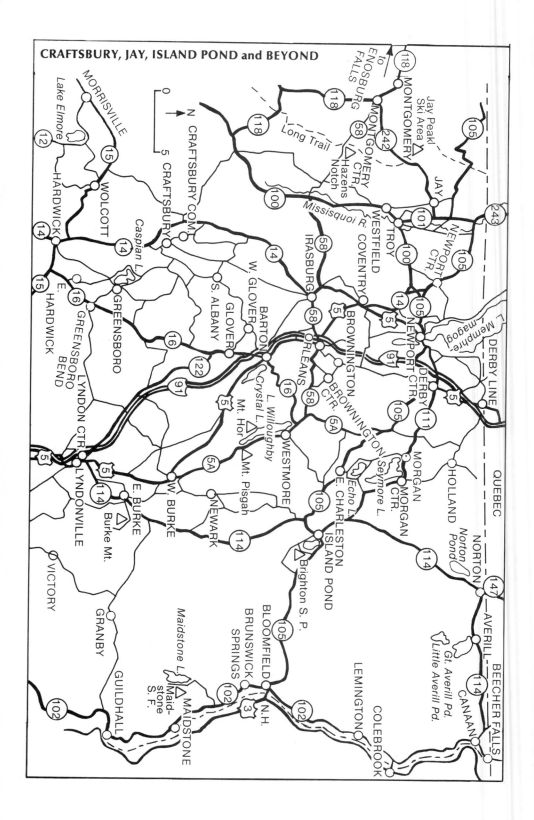

CRAFTSBURY, JAY, ISLAND POND and BEYOND

TO SEE AND DO   Bread and Puppet Theater Museum (525-3031), Glover. Open March–November on Route 122 off Route 16. The internationally-known Bread and Puppet Theater troupe lives together in a farmhouse on this back road, displaying the haunting puppet dwarfs, giants, devils, and other fantastic figures of good and evil. The puppets are the artistic expressions of Polish-born Peter Schumann, who lives with his wife Elka in a separate wooden house they built themselves. The vast meadow across the road is the scene of the annual Domestic Resurrection Circus (see *Special Events*), a free extravaganza in which the audience (of thousands) all receive free homemade bread and gibe at the expensive tickets and junkfoods that accompany most current entertainment.

Caspian Lake. Shaped like an hour glass, this is one Northeast Kingdom lake that has retained a following, summer in and summer out for more than a century. The unusual purity of its water is checked three times weekly in season by its association of cottage owners—who include noted authors, educators, and socialites, all of whom mingle in Willey's Store, center of Greensboro. There is a public beach, also a combination beach, boathouse and resort facility maintained by Highland Lodge, the only inn on the lake, now opening year-round for cross-country skiers who can take advantage of its well-groomed and extensive trails. Greensboro also claims Vermont's oldest (9-hole) golf course.

Craftsbury Common. Few places convey such a sense of tranquility and order. In summer petunias bloom in the post office window boxes and the green of the grass contrasts crisply with the white fence. In winter the general whitewash of this scene contrasts with the blue of the sky. Throughout the year there are nearby places to stay and books to check out at the desk beneath the imposing portraits of Ebenezer and Samuel Crafts in the village library.

Unlike most North Country pioneers, Ebenezer was university educated (Yale, Class of 1740). Forced to sell his tavern in Sturbridge, Massachusetts (the still-popular Public House), due to war debts, he made his way here over the Bayley-Hazen military road, eventually bringing his family and 150 of his Sturbridge neighbors this way on sleds. Ebenezer saw to it that a church and school were established soon after the saw and gristmills. His son Samuel, a Harvard graduate who served two terms as Vermont's governor, founded the Academy which still serves as public high school for the town.

Visitors can meet Craftsbury residents in a number of ways. Many farms welcome paying guests or those who enjoy watching them "sugar"; some of the state's best maple sugar is also sold at some of its lowest prices here, year-round. Two inns offer year-round lodging and **Craftsbury Center,** a former prep school campus, offers basic accommodations, an extensive cross-county ski network in winter, and a varied year-round program of workshops for all ages in everything from wild mushroom identification and tapestry weaving to sculling and rock-climbing. The extensive web of well-surfaced dirt roads meandering in all directions is also beloved by bicyclists and horse riders.

Sights to see include the **John Woodruff Memorial Library** (586-9692) in East Craftsbury, a general store built in the 1840s by the grandfather of Miss Jean Simpson (recently deceased). She converted it into one of New England's most pleasant libraries; general titles are in the room once used for bolts of cloth and general groceries (old shelves and counters remain) and there is a special backroom for youngsters with a ping-pong table amid the books. Open Wednesday and Saturday 9–9 and Sunday 1–2, except for lunch and supper.

RAIL EXCURSIONS   In foliage season, one originates in St. Johnsbury to the southeast and the other in Morrisville to the west, both turn around in Greensboro Bend. For details on both see the St. Johnsbury section.

SCENIC DRIVES   This is one of the best areas in Vermont for "back-roading." For example, Greensboro Bend to Lyndon: An old ridge road with splendid views, the 17-mile Stannard Road is unpaved, but usually well-gravelled most of the way. Check locally, though, because there are occasional washouts.

Greensboro Village to East Hardwick: the road passes through Hardwick Street (that's the name of the hamlet), a fine collection of Federal and Greek Revival houses; and from Greensboro Village to Hardwick, a bee-line through high and open farm country; and from Craftsbury Common north to Route 14 through Albany and Irasburg, following the rich farmland of the Black River Valley.

SUGAR HOUSES   In Craftsbury: **Martin Calderwood** (586-2297) South Albany Road; 1,900 taps, gathered with a tractor and sled; arranges sugar parties on request. **Harry F. Sweat** (586-2838), 3,000 taps; arranges sugar parties, on the road from the Common to Craftsbury Center. **Bruce & Elizabeth Urie** (755-6713), South Albany Road. The sugar shack is right on this picturesque back road, across from the old red dairy barn; Stillmeadow Farm has been in the Urie family since the 1920s; the syrup is outstanding and reasonably priced. **Ryan Brothers** (586-2853), on the back road from Craftsbury to South Albany; a modern, beautifully built sugarhouse down in a meadow across from the farmhouse; wood-fired evaporator, 4,000 taps.

In Greensboro: **Peter and Donald Gebbie** at Maplehurst Farm (533-2984) put out 7,000 taps, will arrange sugaring parties. Syrup sold year-round in their friendly kitchen. **Everett & George Young** (533-2964), Greensboro Bend, put out 1,100 taps and will arrange sugar parties.

BICYCLING   **Craftsbury Sports Center** (586-7767), Craftsbury Common, rents mountain bikes and offers bike tours of local roads and woods trails that are used as cross-country trails in winter.

CANOEING   **Craftsbury Sports Center** (see above) rents canoes for use on Great and Little Hosmer Ponds and on the Black River. Canoes are also made in the village by Horace Strong.

CROSS-COUNTRY SKIING   **Craftsbury Sports Center** (see above) grooms 53 km of its 100 km marked and maintained trail system, offers rentals, instruction, lodging packages, and tours in conjunction with the Inn on the Common (see *Lodging*). **Highland Lodge** (533-2647), Greensboro. A total of 40 km of trails, 30 of them well-groomed, traverse rolling fields and woods past farms and homes, though maple groves and evergreens. Instruction, rental, retail, and repair offered at the center adjacent to one of the Kingdom's best inns; ski weeks, guided tours offered.

Hilltop Cross-Country Center (888-3710) in Wolcott offers a total of 25 km of set trails through gently rolling hills, woods, and open fields.

FISHING   Caspian and other lakes in this area are good for salmon, lake and rainbow trout, and perch. There are trout in the streams, too.

GOLF   **Mountain View Country Club** (533-9294), Greensboro, 9 holes.

HORSEBACK RIDING   **Still Hill Acres** (525-6623), Glover. Open June 15– foliage escorted trail rides, English and Western lessons.

SWIMMING   In Glover, **Shadow Lake Beach,** marked from Route 16, is a delightful spot. There is also a public beach on **Caspian Lake,** near Greensboro Village.

LODGING   **The Inn on the Common** (586-9619), Craftsbury Common 05827. The most regal lodging in the Kingdom is offered by Michael and Penny Schmitt. They have 18 exquisitely decorated guest rooms, some with fireplaces, some with canopy beds, in three Federal-style buildings on and around the Common. Guests congregate in the library for cocktails at 7:00 and dine formally at long candlelit tables. Dinner might commence with a choice of pheasant soup or endive with veal pâté and the entrées might include venison and a brace of quail; a choice of fine wines is available. In summer you can take advantage of the solar-heated pool, the perennial gardens, lawn croquet, and tennis court, also of mountain bikes and canoes at the Craftsbury Sports Center, a nearby facility which teams up with the inn to offer cross-country ski tours in winter. $80–105 per person double occupancy, MAP.

Highland Lodge (533-2647), Greensboro 05841. A fine, Victorian-era summer hotel that manages to be both airy in warm weather and cozy in winter, now managed by the second generation of Smiths. A total of 60 guests can be accommodated between the lodge and ten cottages, three remaining open in winter. In summer, facilities include tennis and a pleasant beach with bathhouse and boats; in winter the draw is cross-crountry skiing on the extensive network radiating from the inn's touring center. Inside there is plenty of space to read and get away from other guests, also nice corners to socialize; plenty of books, a grand piano, and a game room for children for whom there is also organized fun when their numbers merit. In the lodge: $95–120 per couple, $10–40 per child depending on age, MAP; $120–140 per couple in a cottage, $62.50 per couple for a housekeeping cottage ($125 per night for a family of four to six).

Craftsbury Inn (586-2848), Craftsbury 05826, a village with a delightful general store, just down hill from Craftsbury Common. The handsome 1850 Greek Revival-style inn has a dignified second-story wrap-around porch and unusually attractive public rooms, dressed with interesting artwork. Dinner is taken seriously. Rates: $85–120 MAP.

The Brick House (472-5512/5104), Box 128, East Hardwick 05836. Judith Kane presides over this early nineteenth-century, two-story brick house on the edge of East Hardwick Village. There are three comfortably furnished bedrooms with shared bath (the beds have feather mattresses, feather pillows, and handmade quilts). The price includes a full breakfast served in a charming dining room and an English-style wake-up tea tray, if desired. There are books, a fireplace, and dartboard in the sitting room and amenities include woodland walks, trout fishing on the property, and a croquet court. Innkeeper Kane is British herself and serves English Cream Teas in the flower garden or gazebo Wednesday–Sunday afternoons (2:30–5), weather permitting. $35 per couple, $10 for children under 12, "well-behaved pets" welcome.

Craftsbury Bed & Breakfast (586-2206), Craftsbury Common 05827. Margaret Ramsdell welcomes guests to her farmhouse on Wylie Hill, one with views that (even by local standards) are hard to beat. Rooms are in the rear wing, sharing their own private gathering space but guests are also drawn into the big kitchen with its glowing soapstone woodstove, backed by gleaming copper. Rates include a full farm breakfast (cinnamon-apple pancakes, eggs with cheddar cheese), $55 per couple ($30 single). Dinner is also available to groups of six or more.

Carolyn's Bed & Breakfast (472-6338), 15 Church Street, Hardwick 05843. An attractive village house with five guest rooms, two suited to families. Tea and homemade English tarts served on arrival. A hearty breakfast included in $20–50 per room.

FARMS   Rodgers Dairy Farm (525-6677), Glover 05839. Jim and Nancy Rodgers take in no more than ten guests at a time, accommodating them in five guest rooms in their 1840 farmhouse. The night we stopped by guests had congregated on the porch while they waited for a generous meal that was just about to be served in the spacious kitchen-dining area. The working dairy farm encompasses 350 acres not far from Shadow Lake. $40 per adult, $25 per child includes three meals; weekly rates are $200 per adult, $125 per child.

Richard and Rachel LaFont's Dairy Farm (755-6127), Route 3, Box 90, Barton 05822. Sited 8 miles from Barton in the labyrinth of back roads west of West Glover, a working dairy farm with a comfortable atmosphere and home cooking, $30 per couple includes breakfast.

SPORTS CENTER   Craftsbury Sports Center (586-7767), Box 32, Craftsbury 05827. Accommodations are not the reason you come here. Lodging is in two large, dorm-like buildings, each with 9 large doubles and 31 smaller rooms sharing lavatory-style hall bathrooms. There are also 2 efficiency apartments, and 2 larger rooms with private bath. There are also 2 housekeeping cottages, each sleeping 4. Three meals are served, buffet-style in the dining hall. Guests come for the programs offered: running, sculling, walking, mountain biking, and cross-country skiing. Facilities include swimming at Lake Hosmer, exercise rooms, sauna, and tennis courts. Rates are best if you take advantage of weekend ($175 for lodging, meals) or six-night ($350) per person packages; a variety of rate structures are available.

DINING OUT   Alpha Warner's Restaurant (472-5470), Main Street, Hardwick. Specialties include seafood, especially scallops and salmon, fresh from Boston, and homemade soups. Chef Roger Van Sant is a graduate of the New England Culinary Institute. The dining room has a tin ceiling and stained-glass lighting fixtures, and there is a small, quiet bar area. Alpha Warner is the man responsible for naming Hardwick (he also kept a good tavern here for 60 years). Entrées range from $9.50 for pasta to $13 for filet mignon.

Craftsbury Inn (586-2484), Craftsbury. Dinner is open to the public by reservation June through August. A small dining room with just eight tables and a choice of four entrées; specialties include local lamb, pheasant, and quail, fresh fish; homebaked French baguettes and unusual soups; grapefruit sorbet before the entrée, desserts—all for $25.

Highland Lodge (533-2647), Greensboro. Open for breakfast, lunch, and dinner, served in the inn's attractive dining room. Dinner entrées might include roast sirloin Dijon, ocean catfish with tomato and wine, and chicken with peanut sauce ($10.50–12). The meal might begin with wild mushroom and apple tort and end with chocolate cheesecake or Ishkabibble (brownie and ice cream with homemade hot fudge). Breakfast includes homemade granola and lunch features interesting croissants, salads, and soups as well as the usual sandwiches, not to mention Ishkabibble.

EATING OUT **In a Pig's Eye Cafe & Deli** (472-6297), Hardwick, is a small, surprisingly cosmopolitan place located in one corner of the old hotel building on Main Street. The menu is varied, including soups, salads, and sandwiches.

Village Restaurant (472-5701), junction of Routes 14 and 15, Hardwick, offers three squares in a basic, clean, comfortable, no-frills place in the center of town.

TEA **The Brick House** (472-5512/5104), East Hardwick, serves other delicacies. A wide variety of teas are offered and served, of course, in a pot. The setting is the flower garden or gazebo, weather permitting, Wednesday–Sunday, 2:30–5. Reservations appreciated.

ENTERTAINMENT **Summer Music from Greensboro,** based at the Congregational Church, Greensboro, is a series of chamber and choral music concerts in July and August.

Craftsbury Chamber Players have brought chamber music to Northern Vermont for 23 years. The six-week summer series runs mid-July through August, Thursday evenings at the Hardwick Town House. There are also shorter, Thursday afternoon free concerts at the Town House. Most performers are faculty members at the Julliard School of Music in New York City.

SELECTIVE SHOPPING **Granite Hills Photography Gallery,** Hardwick Town House, Hardwick, an affiliate of the Craftsbury Chamber Players, open Saturday and Tuesday, 10–6 and Thursday, 1–6, features changing exhibitions of the work of distinguished local photographers.

The Old Firehouse (472-6166), downtown Hardwick, a mini-mall for antiques, yarn, crafts, and such, located in a nicely restored 1885 building, built as a church and later used as a firehouse.

Perennial Pleasures Nursery (472-5512), East Hardwick. Sited at **The Brick House** and run by Rachel Kane, this unusual nursery specializes in authentic seventeenth, eighteenth, and nineteenth-century restoration gardens. There are 2 acres of flowering perennial and herb gardens, grassy walks and arbors; more than 375 varieties of plants are available.

Brick House Shop (472-6493), Main Street, Hardwick. A sophisticated variety store operated by Judith Kane and Martina Massina, this shop is chock full of everything, including antiques, local crafts, jewelry, clothing, prints, gift items, books, cards . . . all carefully selected and very reasonably priced.

Willey's Store, Greensboro Village. One of the biggest and best general stores in the state; an extensive grocery, produce and meat section, hardware, toys, and just about everything else you should have brought but forgot for a vacation.

The Miller's Thumb (533-2960), Greensboro Village. A former gristmill with a view of the stream below through a window in the floor, open June through mid-September, a gallery with crafts. Look for the branch store on Main Street, Hardwick (open year-round). Both stores are a trove of art, crafts, and gift items, many made locally.

Craftsbury General Store, Craftsbury Village. A genuine, old-style village store, under the same ownership for many years, a source of information about the area and a full stock of everything.

SPECIAL EVENTS   March: Open sugar houses.

July: **Antiques and Uniques Fair** at Craftsbury Common.

August: **Old Home Day**, Craftsbury Common. Second weekend: **Domestic Resurrection Circus**—thousands of people converge on the meadows that form a natural amphitheater on the Bread and Puppet Theater's farm in Glover. The weekend-long happening includes a variety of events, climaxed by the pageant of giant puppets parading on stilts. The theme is always the struggle between good and evil, justice and injustice. Free, black Polish bread is offered.

September: **Banjo Contest**, last Saturday, Craftsbury Common.

MEDICAL EMERGENCY   Craftsbury (472-6666), Glover (525-4425), see also Newport and St. Johnsbury.

Newport—Lake Country

The Canadian border area around Newport is blessed with some of the most beautiful lakes in Vermont. The largest of these is Memphremagog, stretching more than thirty miles from Newport, Vermont, to Magog, Quebec.

In the heyday of railroad passenger service, large wooden hotels sprang up near the shores of these lakes. In Newport the 400-room Memphremagog House stood next to the railroad station (a site now filled by the Mobil gas station), Newport House was across the street where the Chittenden Bank now stands and the New City Hotel stood where the Mini-Mart is now. Guests came by train from Boston and Philadelphia. Lindbergh came with his "Spirit of Saint Louis," and there was a race track and a paddle wheeler.

Newport is, admittedly, a shadow of its Victorian-era photos. The brick library, courthouse, and state building remain, but surviving stores have lost their mansards and towers. The bandstand, hotels, and station are gone, and there is no place to stay on the lake.

Memphremagog (with the stress on the last syllable) has a split personality. The two-thirds of the lake north of the Canadian border is not only French-speaking (although there are English pockets like Georgeville) but more of a resort area. Montreal is just an hour's drive from the French-speaking resort town of Magog, and Sherbrooke, a Canadian metropolis of 100,000, is much nearer—in stark contrast to the American end of the lake, which is literally the end of the road (I-91) from New York and Boston. It remains a delightful refuge for frugal flatlanders, especially those who like to fish, hike, ride horseback or generally steep themselves in the beauty of this high, rolling—still pastoral—countryside.

There are a number of smaller but beautiful lakes, notably Lake Willoughby, a long narrow sheet of shimmering water between the rock walls of Mount Pisgah and Mount Hor. It is generally considered the heart of the Northeast Kingdom.

GUIDANCE Greater Newport Chamber of Commerce (334-7782), the Causeway, Newport 05855, serves much of this area but a few of the towns and lakes have their own info sources or efficient town clerks, listed with their respective lakes.

Lake Willoughby Chamber of Commerce (1-800-NEK AREA or 525-6939). The chamber operates an information center at Millbrook cottages in Westmore, publishes a brochure and advises on local lodging and other amenities.

Magog Bureau du Tourisme (819-843-2744), 1032 Principale Ouest, Magog, Quebec J1X 2B6, Canada, serves the French-speaking shoreline. It's a good source of advice on area restaurants.

GETTING THERE   By bus: Vermont Transit from Canada and most U.S. points; bus stops in Lyndonville, West Burke, Barton, Orleans and Newport. Vermont Transit Bus Depot (334-2132) Jimmy Kwik Food Store, Coventry.

By car: Really the only way to get around. Note the new link in I-93 that hooks up Lyndon Center, Barton, Orleans, Newport, and Derby Line directly with Boston: 4 hours to Derby Line.

TO SEE AND DO   **The Old Stone House Museum** (754-2022), Brownington. Open daily July–August 31; Friday–Tuesday May 15–June 30, and September–October 15; 11–5. $3.00 adults, $1.00 children. This is the Orleans County Historical Society Museum, housed in a four-story granite building dating back to 1836, built as a dormitory for a rural academy. It resembles the earliest dorms at Middlebury College from which Alexander Twilight, the school's principal and building's architect, had graduated in 1823. Although he was dark-skinned, there is some question about whether Twilight was—as Middlebury College claims—the first Black graduate of an American college. There is no question about the beauty of the building and of the historical collections: 10 rooms representing 10 of the 18 towns in Orleans County plus other eighteenth- and nineteenth-century weapons, tools, paintings, furniture, and decorative arts. Brownington Village itself is a crossroads full of outstanding early nineteenth-century buildings, the core of a once-proud hill town long since eclipsed by such valley centers as Barton, Orleans, and Newport. There are nineteenth-century gardens behind the Eaton House and a spectacular panorama from the wooden observatory set up in a meadow behind the church.

St. Benoit du Lac (819-564-0027), Austin, Quebec. Open Monday–Saturday, 9–11 and 1:15–4. This non-cloistered French Benedictine monastery, founded in 1911, is sited on the west shore of Lake Memphremagog at a fjord-like section. It's a handsome building and the 60 resident monks welcome visitors for daily mass at 11 AM and vespers at 4:30 PM, at which Gregorian chants are sung. The monastery shop sells Gregorian music records, also apple cider wine, cheese, vestments and religious articles made by the monks. The easiest route from Newport is via the North Troy border crossing; then through Mansonville, South Bolton and Austin.

Jay Peak Tramway, for a spectacular overview of this region. See Jay Peak Area.

LAKES   Lake Memphremagog A 32-mile long stringbean of a lake with only 5 miles within the United States. Memphremagog stretches north from Newport, a city of 5,500 people, a former logging and rail center, which is enjoying a renaissance thanks to enterprising small businesses like Slalom Ski Wear, Bogner of America, Sel-Bar Weaving (placemats), Newport Furniture, and American Maple Products. Main Street is a bustling shopping center, graced by some substantial gift and clothing stores as well as by its nineteenth-century Goodrich Memorial Library (334-8902) with its historical collections, a matching red brick Orleans County Courthouse and State Building. From Prospect Hill—where the spires of St. Mary, Star of the Sea, tower above everything—the city slopes to the lake, which actually seems to surround it since the downtown area separates the lake proper from South Bay. The shoreline offers access points for sailing, canoeing, fishing, and swimming; there is also an 18-hole golf course. See separate listings under these categories.

Crystal Lake Guidance: **Barton Chamber of Commerce** (525-6210), Box 280, Barton 05822. Barton was once a railroad town with six passenger trains a day stopping in summer and depositing guests to fill big hotels in town or to be transported by boat livery to their gingerbread "camps" on Crystal Lake. The hotels are now gone and the road to many of the cottages along the far shore is so rutted that outboards remain the best way of reaching them. This is a beautiful little lake with a cliff-like promontory on one side and public beaches at its northern rim. There is golf in nearby Orleans and the Interstate, Route 16 and Route 5 all cross here—making it an excellent pivot from which to explore the entire Northeast Kingdom, and an attractive summer spot in which to locate for a week or more. The town of Barton itself packs an astounding number of services into its small downtown (see *Shopping*). The *Barton Chronicle* is an excellent little weekly, covering much of Orleans and Essex Counties.

Lake Willoughby. Five-mile-long Willoughby is one of Vermont's most hauntingly beautiful lakes. Mounts Hor and Pisgah, which rise abruptly from opposite shores, create a fjord-like effect when viewed from the public beach in Westmore at the northern end, or from the southern tip. Mostly undeveloped, Willoughby is surrounded for much of its length by state forest. The view from Willoughby Cliffs is spectacular (see *Hiking*), the water is stocked with salmon and rainbow trout, and there is public boat access. It was a well-known resort area in the days of grand hotels and steamboats. Now it has a limited loyal following of sailors and windsurfers (there is always a breeze here) and year-round fishermen. Lodging is limited but ranges from campgrounds to a posh new inn, with a choice of cottages in between.

Seymour Lake Guidance: **Seymour Lake Lodge** (see *Lodging*), Morgan Center 05854, serves as an information source and will pass on inquiries about lodging to the Seymour Lake Association. This is a fair sized, pleasant lake with cottages tucked away discreetly in the woods along its shore. There is a public beach in the tiny village of Morgan Center, also the spot to rent boats for fishing for landlocked salmon. In winter, this lake is peppered with fishing shanties and there is an untracked system of local cross-country trails.

Echo Lake. Much smaller than Seymour Lake, adjoining it on the south, circled by a dirt road and by gently rolling hills. White Birch Lodge, a small cottage colony with a private beach and boat rentals, will meet guests at the bus and plane in Newport (see *Lodging*). There is also public boat access, good for trout and landlocked salmon.

DERBY LINE   This town straddles the Canadian border, the larger part actually possessing a different character and name (Rock Island, Quebec). It is worth noting on two counts: the **Haskell Free Library and Opera House** on Caswell Avenue, a yellow brick, neo-classic structure with a handsome library downstairs, has an upstairs opera house in which audiences sit in the United States watching a stage in Canada.

PARKS AND FORESTS   **Crystal Lake State Park** (525-6205), Barton. Off Route 16 at the northern rim of Crystal Lake; facilities include a swimming beach, bathhouse and picnic areas, children's swim lessons.

Willoughby State Forest, Route 5A. A 7,000-acre preserve surrounding a dramatically beautiful lake; (see *Hiking* and *Fishing*).

SCENIC DRIVES   **West Burke to Westmore.** The stretch of Route 5A along Lake Willoughby is one of the most breathtaking anywhere.

Bayley-Hazen Military Road. Begun at Wells River on the Connecticut River in 1776 by General Jacob Bayley, continued in 1778–79 by General Moses Hazen, this road was a flop as the invasion route it was intended to be, but served settlers well after the Revolution when it came time to establish towns in this area. Map still available from the Northeastern Vermont Development Association (748-5181), 44 Main Street, St. Johnsbury. The beautiful dirt stretch from Hazen's Notch to Lowell is noted in the Jay section; the next stretch to Albany is now a walking/riding trail. It continues unmarked through Craftsbury and is marked on its way through Greensboro, where a monument commemorates its story, reappearing in the St. Johnsbury area.

Route 105 west of Newport, as far as Richford, a sub-customs port and once an entry for Chinese railroad labor crews. You can return via Routes 118 and 58, but the Hazen Notch section is closed in the winter.

Hinman Settler Road from Derby Center to Brownington (mostly unpaved but good gravel). It's better to start from Derby as there are confusing forks from the other direction. The route terminates in Brownington Village historic district from which a paved road leads to Orleans and I-91. To find this route, head south on Main Street, Derby Center (Route 105). Where 105 curves sharply to the east at the lower end of the village, go straight to Brownington. You are rewarded by rolling hills and fields, sweeping vistas.

Holland-Morgan Loop. Take the paved road east from I-91 Derby Line exit. After several miles the road makes an S-curve through tiny Holland Village and continues to Seymour Lake in Morgan. Here take Route 111 to Derby Center.

AIRPLANE RIDES   The **Newport State Airport** (334-5001) in Coventry offers rides.

BOATING   Aluminum boats (14 feet) with 7½ hp motors (no canoes or sailboats) can be rented by the hour ($12.50 for the first hour, $9 for each additional hour) or the day ($45) at **Newport Marina** (334-5911), Farrants Point.

BOAT EXCURSION   *L'Aventure II* (819-843-8068), 288 St. Patrice Ouest, Magog. An excursion boat plys the northern reaches of Lake Memphremagog, twice daily in July and August, Sundays only in June and early September.

CANOEING   See the "Vermont Guide to Fishing" pamphlet for canoe access points on South Bay along the Black River, also on the Clyde and Nulhegan Rivers. Canoes may be rented at the Craftsbury Center (see Craftsbury Country) and from Vermont Voyager (see Jay Peak). They can also be rented in Newport from **Newport Aqua Sports Haven** (NASH), Farrants Point, 334-5911. This is the best way to explore the South Bay Nature area, which is more sheltered than the open lake from wind and wave conditions.

FISHING   This is fine fishing country. The catch is landlocked salmon, brown, brook, lake, and rainbow trout, and you find them in dozens of ponds with boat access as well as the lakes we describe here. The pamphlet, "Vermont Guide to Fishing" prepared by the Vermont Fish & Game Department, available locally and by writing to the Vermont Travel Division in Montpelier, tells it all. For other guides consult *Fishing* under "What's Where." There is a State Fish Hatchery in Newark; Newark Pond has an access and is good for yellow perch as well as trout. Rental boats, bait, and tackle are available for Lake Memphremagog (good for smelts, smallmouth bass, and walleyed pike as well as salmon and trout) from the

Newport Marina and Memphremagog Marina; at both Island Pond and Maidstone Lake (see *State Parks*); at Lake Willoughby from Bill & Billie's Lodge near the northern end of the lake; on Crystal Lake, Lakeview Cabins, and Crystal Lake-front Cottages, in South Barton; and on Echo Lake from White Birch Lodge. This is in no way a complete listing, just the places we have happened upon. Note that ice fishing is particularly popular on Memphremagog, Willoughby, and Seymour Lake and that many of the rivers—notably the Passumpsic, Black, and Clyde Rivers—are stocked with trout.

GOLF **Newport Country Club** (334-7715) overlooking Lake Memphremagog. Open May to mid-October, 18 holes.

Orleans Country Club (754-9392) on Willoughby Lake Road, 18 holes.

Dufferin Heights Country Club (819-876-2113), Stanstead, Quebec, just north of the border on Route 5, an excellent 9-hole course.

HIKING **Mount Pisgah and Mount Hor,** Lake Willoughby. Named respectively for the place where the Lord sent Moses to view the Promised Land and the place Moses's brother Aaron died after the Lord commanded him to go there, these twin mountains, separated by a narrow stretch of lake, form Willoughby gap. Both are within the 7,000-acre Willoughby State Forest and offer well-maintained hiking trails. Mount Pisgah (2,751 feet) on the east side of the lake (access marked from Route 5A) has fairly short climbs yielding spectacular views of the White Mountains; trails up Mount Hor (2,648 feet) begin on the Civilian Conservation Corps road, 1.8 miles west of its junction with Route 5A and also offers panoramic views of the Green Mountains to the west. For details consult *Day Hiker's Guide to Vermont* and *Fifty Hikes in Vermont*.

Wheeler Mountain. The trail begins on The Wheeler Mountain Road, which leaves the north side of Route 5, 8.3 miles north of West Burke and 5 miles south of Barton Village. From the highway, the unpaved road climbs to the trailhead, 1.9 miles.

Bald Mountain. There are excellent views from the abandoned fire tower at the summit of this the tallest peak in the Willoughby Lake area. Trails ascend to the summit from both the north (Lookout's Trail, 2.8 miles) and from the south (Long Pond Trail, 2.1 miles). From the north side of Bald Mountain, you can hike on trails and wilderness roads all the way to the summit of Mount Hor, and Haystack Mountain (a side trip) has excellent views and two trails. Details can be found in *Day Hikers Guide to Vermont* (see *Hiking* in "What's Where").

Hurricane Brook Wildlife Management Area, off Route 114, south of Norton Pond: 9,500 forested acres, also accessible via a gravel road past Holland Pond from Holland Village. A detailed map is available from the Fish & Game Department in Montpelier.

HORSEBACK RIDING   **Seldom Rest Riding Camp** (895-2868), Morgan Center. Open late June through Labor Day. Scenic trail rides, English and Western lessons, day camper and live-in programs.

LLAMA TREKS.   **Willoughby Lake Llama Farm** (525-4700), Westmore, offers organized pack trips in summer months. There are currently 40 llamas in residence and a small gift shop stocks Andean imports. These fascinating animals are well worth a visit and treks (you walk next to the llama, guiding him as he carries camping gear and food) can be rewarding. The farm is a half mile off Route 16 in Westmore on the west side of Willoughby.

SAILBOARDING   Rentals and lessons are available from **Great Outdoors Trading Company** (334-2831), 73 Main Street, Newport.

SWIMMING   In Newport at **Prouty Beach,** a public facility east of the city that also has tennis courts, picnic facilities, and campsites.

In Barton at **Crystal Lake State Beach** just east of the village on Route 15, open daily in season 10–8; lifeguard, bath house, picnic facilities; and at **Pageant Park** a mile farther east on Route 16, a town-owned park open daily until 10 PM also with a bath house and camping (primarily tenting).

Lake Willoughby has small public beaches at its northern and southern tips.

On Lake Seymour there is a public beach in Morgan Center and on Caspian Lake there is a small beach in Greensboro.

Needless to say there is also swimming at every pond and lake that offers fishing access.

CROSS-COUNTRY SKIING   **Heermansmith Farm** (754-8866), Coventry Village. A total 15 km of tracked trails, also lessons, rentals. The picturesque farm is also well known for its food (see *Restaurants*) and serves light lunches and brunch during ski season; there is also lodging. $3 trail fee.

SUGAR HOUSES   **American Maple Products** (334-6516), Bluff Road, Newport. Tours offered Monday–Friday, 8–11:30, 12:30–4, closed holidays. See a movie about maple production, sample and purchase the products that are distributed through most of the country under the Old Colony, Mrs. Appleyard, and Vermont Tea and Maple brands. A separate building housing historic maple exhibits is being planned.

Spates Maple Orchard (895-4012), Derby Line. Grant and Jeanne have 3,500 taps, use old and new methods.

Couture's Sugarhouse (744-2733), Route 100, Westfield. A modern sugarhouse with a wood-fired evaporator, open to the public whenever boiling. The maple shop at the farmhouse is open year-round.

LODGING   **Heermansmith Farm Inn** (754-8866), Coventry Village. This farm

Cyclists pause at Lake Willoughby

has been in the same family since 1807. Jack and Louise Smith offer three rooms upstairs in the snug, 1860s farmhouse that has become well-known over the past few years as one of the region's leading restaurants. Since only dinner is served to the public, guests can enjoy the lounge by day. Light lunches are also served guests during winter; the inn's extensive ski-touring network is open to the public. $35 double, $25 single including breakfast.

Valley House Inn (754-6665), 4 Memorial Square, Orleans 05860. A 112-year-old, middle-of-town wooden hotel, the likes of which you don't find anymore. It's clean but not "restored." The walls are largely pressed tin and the upstairs halls are wide and airy. The lobby still has its roll-top desk, safe, and stag heads. There are 30 rooms: from $16–23 single, $21–34 double. (Higher rate means private bath.)

Derby Village Inn (873-3604), 46 Main Street, Derby Line. Tom and Phyllis Moreau have opened their handsome village home, with five double bedrooms upstairs, each with private bath and furnished with iron bedsteads and hooked rugs. Families are welcome and dinner is served by reservation. From $35 for a former maid's room to $55 for the master bedroom, breakfast included. No smoking.

Willoughvale Inn (525-4123), Westmore (the address is: RFD # 2, Orleans 05860). There are eight upstairs rooms, one handicapped-accessible room downstairs and four, two-bedroom housekeeping cabins across the street. The large dining room is open to the public for dinner; breakfast is also available for guests. The original farmhouse here dates back to the mid-1800s and by the early 1900s it was a restaurant, its status until a few years ago when it was sold, then sat vacant. Its current owners, Frank and Joan Symcak, have replaced the old building with a new replica.

Hunt's Hideaway (895-8322), Morgan 05853. Pat Hunt welcomes guests to her modern, split-level home; facilities include lawn games, a pool, play room, and use of washing machine. The 100 acres are handy to Seymour Lake. There are two double rooms; $30 double includes breakfast.

Memphre Manor Bed & Breakfast (334-5646) or 5926), 9 Prospect Street, Newport 05455. Lawrence (called John) and Doris Hubley retired from Milford, New Hampshire, a few years ago and bought this elegant Newport mansion. There are six comfortably furnished guest rooms (one with private bath); one large alcove room sleeps three, and a first floor room is handicapped-accessible. A full breakfast is served in the formal living room or, weather permitting, on the large screened side porch. During hunting and skiing season, the aroma of soup, stew, and Doris' homemade bread will greet wayfarers. The parents of eight grown children, the Hubleys treat guests as extended family even, on occasion, taking them out in their boat to fish. Guests are welcome to make themselves at home in the large parlor with its comfortable chairs, hanging plants, fireplace, and TV. Smoking is not permitted in the guest rooms. $32 per couple includes breakfast.

Irasburg Green (754-6012), Irasburg 05845. The house is filled with handiwork by owner Steffi Huess, a silversmith who sells her jewelry, along with other local arts and crafts items, right here. Three bedrooms upstairs share a new bath; nothing fancy, but comfortable. $34 double, $28 single.

Brick House (754-2108), PO Box 33, Route 14, Irasburg 05845. Madeleine Masseau and Rita Paquette welcome you to their Victorian Brick house. The atmosphere is homey, the four guest rooms sharing two baths. $35–45 double, breakfast included.

Pauper's Manse (525-3222), R R 1, Box 96A, Barton 05822. Bill and Pat Britton offer four rooms (shared baths) in their fine old farmhouse set above meadows on the road from Willoughby Lake to Barton. $30 per night double includes breakfast.

Tester's Bed & Breakfast (525-3814), Barton, 05822. This snug old cape offers rooms at $28 double, $18 single, breakfast included; canoe available at hourly rates.

The Barton Inn (525-4721), Barton 05822. A large pleasant white house trimmed with Gothic gingerbread, set high above the street in the middle of Barton Village. $45 double includes breakfast.

Marie's Guest House (525-3649), PO 184, Barton 05822. An old-fashioned guest house right on the street in the center of Barton Village. Marie Tomlinson offers five rooms, sharing baths; $23 double (no breakfast).

Seymour Lake Lodge (895-2752), Morgan Center 05854. We are sad to see this homey little inn deteriorating, but we must report that bedrooms are plain and cramped, the bathroom smells, and the living room is cluttered. $34 per person MAP, $25 per person B&B.

Fox Hall (525-6930), RFD#1, Barton 05822. Ken and Sherry Pyden have transformed the main house at a former girl's camp into an upscale bed & breakfast. There are eight guest rooms, some round, some with fireplaces, all with antiques and porches commanding views of Lake Willoughby. There are 76 acres, including lake frontage and a dock. Guests have access to tennis courts next door and free use of bicycles. $70-90 double.

INNS BEYOND THE BORDER **Cedar Gables** (819-842-4120), 4080 Magog Road (at Cedar), Box 355, North Hatley, Quebec, Canada, JOB 2CO. Sited on Lake Massawippi (just east of Memphremagog), this large, turn-of-the-century house offers a suite (a room with king-size bed, a sitting room with woodstove, and a private bath); a canopy double bedroom with window seat, and another with shared bath. There is a secluded sundeck on the lake, good for swimming, and guests have access to a canoe. Windsurfers, paddle boats, and fishing boats are available from a nearby marina. North Hatley is an English-speaking resort village with a summer theater (see Piggery Theater under *Entertainment*). In winter there are nearby cross-country trails and alpine trails. Breakfast is included in the rate. Other meals are available by prearrangement. $60–75 B&B (note: this is in Canadian currency).

Auberge Ripplecove Inn (819-838-4296), PO Box 246, Ayer's Cliff, Quebec JOB 1CO. A small resort on Lake Massawippi offers a variety of accommodations, from antiques-furnished rooms in the inn to lakeside cottages. Facilities include tennis courts, an outdoor pool, paddle boats, and canoes, lake swimming and, in winter, sleigh rides and a choice of alpine and cross-country skiing. Food is important here and rates are $69–110 per person MAP per day, $315-495 per five-day week, Canadian currency.

MOTELS AND COTTAGES   **White Birch Lodge** (723-6271), East Charleston 05872. The term "lodge" is misleading because the central old building that once served meals is closed; this is a cluster of four, one-to three-bedroom cottages on Echo Lake. Facilities include a beach and boats (the catch is trout and salmon). $100-300 per week.

Lakeview Cabins (525-4463), Barton 05822. Eight housekeeping cottages accommodating one to five people, one or two bedrooms, also rooms in the house (from $20 per day); $37 per day for the cabins, $240 per week.

Cottages at Strawberry Acres (334-8635), PO Box 536, Newport 05455. Five well-spaced cottages on a quiet bluff overlooking Lake Memphremagog, with 650 feet of frontage including beach, are available from mid-April to mid-November from Rosemary Lalime. $200 per week for the one-bedroom to $400 for the three-bedroom.

Millers Millbrook (525-6939), RD No. 2, Orleans 05860. A cluster of housekeeping cottages on Lake Willoughby, available by the week in summer, $300–350 per week; $60 nightly per couple plus $10 per additional person; also available on a limited basis off-season.

Mountain Lake Cottages (525-3093), RFD 2, Orleans 05860. Ten log housekeeping cabins, built in two tiers along a steep slope (no beach) on the east side of Lake Willoughby, have fireplaces and two bedrooms. $75 per night, $375 per week.

Perkins Hilltop Cottages (525-6988), RFD 2, Orleans 05860. Earle and Jeanne Perkins keep these eight heated cottages nicely land-scaped. They are on the east side of Lake Willoughby, near but not on the lake with access to an adjacent boat dock and private beach. No pets. Available May–October, $230 per week for a two-bedroom, $300 for a three-bedroom.

Border Motel (766-2213), junction of Routes 5 and 105, near I-91 Exit 28, Derby 05828. A 40-room motel with a locally-liked cafe serving breakfast and dinner, bar with weekend entertainment. $36–42 double plus $6 per extra person.

DINING OUT   **Heermansmith Farm Inn** (754-8866), Coventry Village. Closed Tuesdays, otherwise open for dinner year-round. The farm itself is locally known for the quality of its produce, especially strawberries. The restaurant, opened in the summer of 1982, is the candlelit interior of the old farmhouse; a limited but quality menu specializing in fresh, poached salmon, roast duck with strawberry sauce, $12.95, shrimp Dijonaise, $13.95, and chicken saltimbocca, $10.95.

The Landing (334-6278), Lake Street, Newport. The only restaurant overlooking Lake Memphremagog and one that now boasts one of the region's best chefs (Michael of the former Derby Line restaurant, Michael's), reasonably priced lunches (homemade soup is $1.95 and hot sandwiches, $3.95, while seafood Newburg on the dinner menu is $12.95. The Quarterdeck Pub offers a sandwich and late dinner menu. Open for lunch and dinner daily, the pub remains open until 1 AM.

Forsthaus (334-7294), junction of Routes 105 and 14 in Newport Center, open for dinner only. A small, new German restaurant run by Gunter and Leoni Hartmann, which has already established an excellent reputation. Dinner entrées are in the $8–12 range.

EATING OUT   Peking Garden (334-7765), 45 Main Street, Newport. Open for lunch and dinner daily. The big polar bear in the window is a holdover from its days as Frank and Pierre's Steak House, but this is now a first-rate Mandarin and Szechuan restaurant with a large menu. Chicken with hot brown sauce and peanuts is $7.25 and a full dinner, including appetizers, is as low as $5.75.

Nichelodean Cafe (334-2777), Newport. Oak, brass, arty prints, and a generally upscale pub atmosphere make this reasonably-priced spot a find.

Rose's Deli & Cafe (334-5370), 742 East Main Street, Newport. A down-to-earth place for lunch and snacks in a converted automobile showroom, 6:30 AM to 8–9 PM daily. Roselyn Houghten is the chef-owner and specialties are basics like spaghetti, liver and onions with bacon. There are also grinders, soups, and sandwiches to go.

East Side Restaurant (334-2340), East Main Street, Newport, closed Mondays. A comfortable, conventional, recently expanded, locally popular place, open 7 AM–9 PM. The menu includes seafood, pork, poultry, beef, and homemade soups and pies, good for sandwiches (try a Mysterious Memphre for $4.99).

The Brown Cow (334-7887), 900 East Main Street, open from 6 AM–7 PM except Sunday when it's 7–1. This is a nice spot to linger over breakfast (served all day), sandwich and salad lunches, reasonably priced dinners. Homemade ice cream on homemade pie.

Country Comfort Restaurant (525-3758), Route 5A just northeast of the northern tip of Lake Willoughby. Open 7 AM–9 PM daily, 8–9 Sundays, year-round. A clean pleasant spot specializing in home cooking, fresh seafood (the haddock dinner is $6.95) and basics like BBQ beef in a bulky roll. Beer and wine served.

5–16 Pizza (525-4066) Barton Village, open daily, 11:30–9:30, from 12 on Sunday. This is a first-rate pizza place with some of the atmosphere left over from its previous life as a real Italian restaurant. There are the customary and "not so customary" pizzas, like Mexican and crab. You can also have spinach ricotta pie, calzones, grinders, and antipasto.

Dot's Restaurant, Coventry (754-6668), Irasburg. Located on U.S. Route 5, 1 mile south of Coventry Village. Dot Maxfield runs an inviting place with a varied menu. In summer you can eat on the rear deck, overlooking rolling meadows.

Candlepin (525-6513). A classic roadside restaurant, a half mile north of Barton Village on Route 5. It's locally popular and good for three squares. The menu is huge and there's a salad bar, also a small, quiet bar in the rear. The bowling lanes are in a converted barn out back.

ENTERTAINMENT **North Country Concert Association** (723-6027), Box 601 in Newport sponsors a dance, theater, and concert series in various locations throughout the area.

Piggery Theater (842-2191), North Hatley, Quebec. June through August, summer theater.

Northsong Chorus (895-2747), gives concerts at various times and places throughout the year.

The Westmore Association (525-3688) stages an entertainment series at the Community House in Westmore in July and August.

Merrill's Cinema I, II, and III (334-6830), Newport, is the local movie theater.

SELECTIVE SHOPPING **Barton Village.** An exceptional shopping center with one of the Kingdom's few supermarkets, a serious garage, a laundromat with rocking chair, barber, the Franklin Store (good for making keys), and the neighboring pharmacy complete with soda fountain, which doubles as the state liquor store.

American Maple Products (334-6516), Bluff Road, Newport. The outlet store discounts their Old Colony Brand syrup and maple sugar at an average of 10 percent below retail.

Ammex Tax-Free Shop (873-3323), Derby. At Exit 29 off I-91 this is a genuine tax-free outlet for liquor, cigarettes, cigars, tobacco, perfumes, and gifts at 20–50 percent below retail.

Walt's Corner (334-7224), Main Street, Newport. There's nobody called Walt but there are an amazing number of books, cards, games, and toys in this shop; Vermont T-shirts and locally crafted gifts are featured.

All-Seasons Factory Outlet (334-6882), Newport. Located in the lakeside shopping center on the causeway, across from the info center. This is a genuine outlet specializing in Pedigree Skiwear (made in St. Albans) and in nifty Canadian-designed clothing for women and children.

Tranquil Things, Main Street, Derby Line. Pat Wright carries an interesting selection of gifts.

Sel-Bar Weaving, off Glen Road, Newport, is a small factory store at the factory in which these distinctive cotton placemats are woven. They come in a great variety of colors.

Woodknot Books, 68 Main Street, Newport, offers a good selection of books, magazines, and VCR tapes.

Great Outdoors Trading Company, Main Street, Newport. In summer the store features an extensive array of fishing gear and sells fishing licenses; also offers guide service on the lake with an electronically equipped fishing boat. Its basement is a year-round outlet for Bogner and Slalom ski wear, both made in town. (Slalom is descended from a local 1891 overalls manufacturer and has been making ski wear since the 1920s.)

Ethan Allen Furniture (985-8028), Orleans. This is a huge factory that reluctantly offers tours to small groups (not recommended for children) and has a showroom.

SPECIAL EVENTS   February: **Newport Winterfest.** A whole week of events, including dog sled and cross-country ski races, curling championships, hockey, snow golf on the lake with artificially colored greens, pot-luck suppers, and moonlight sleigh rides.

March: Sugaring throughout the region.

July: **Memphremagog International Aquafest:** a swim race from Newport to Magog in Canada (32 miles) also, a water-ski tournament, milk carton regatta, street dance, parade, public suppers, and more. **Irasburg Church Fair** on Irasburg Green.

August: **Barton Fair:** old fashioned event at the extensive fairground. **Old Stone House Day.** Open house, picnic lunch, crafts demonstrations at the museum in Brownington Village.

September: **Banjo Contest,** last Saturday, in Craftsbury Common. **Fall Foliage Festival** on Lake Willoughby: triathalon, crafts show, fishing derby, and more.

MEDICAL EMERGENCY   Barton (525-3131); Derby, Derby Line, Morgan (873-3000); Orleans (754-6366); Newport (334-6733); **North Country Hospital & Health Center** (334-7331), Newport.

Jay Peak Area

Jay Peak towers like a sentinel above a wide valley in which the state of Vermont and the province of Quebec meet at three border crossings and mingle—not only in the waters of Lake Memphremagog but in general ambiance. The sentinel itself has fallen to the French. The face of Vermont's northernmost peak is now leased by Montreal businessmen and more than half of the patrons at Jay Peak ski area hail from across the border. Montreal is, after all, less than two hours away.

From Jay's base lodge a sixty-passenger aerial tram runs summer as well as winter to the 3,861 foot summit—which yields one of the most spectacular views in the state: a sweep from Lake Champlain on the west, off across Lake Memphremagog to the north, across the Northeast Kingdom to the east and back down the Green Mountains as far as Camel's Hump to the south.

In winter, storms sweep down from Canada or roll in from Lake Champlain, showering the clutch of mountains around Jay with truly dependable quantities of snow—a fact more pertinent to cross-country than downhill skiers in these days of snowmaking. A total 100 km of trails link the five touring centers in the area.

Aside from limited accommodations at Jay Peak itself, lodging is scattered along Route 242, which climbs steadily nine miles from Montgomery Center to the ski area, then dips as steeply the four miles down to Jay Village (named for John Jay who never saw it), which is just a crossroads inn, gas station, and general store. This remains primarily farming and logging country with a special, haunting quality conveyed in water colors by Rudi Mattesich, also famed as the "father of American ski touring," who lives in nearby Troy.

In contrast to most ski resort areas, this one does not attract transients. Its innkeepers, restauranteurs, and shopkeepers are a mix of self-sufficient natives and the interesting kind of people who tend to gather in the world's beautiful back-and-behind places.

GUIDANCE **Jay Peak Area Association** (988-4363 or, outside Vermont, 800-548-5300), Jay 05859. Open daily, 9–5 weekdays, until 7 on winter Saturdays, until 4 Sundays. Much of this area is also covered by the **Newport Area Chamber of Commerce** (334–7782).

GETTING THERE   By plane: Burlington International Airport, one and one-half hour's drive.

By train: Amtrak service to Springfield, Massachusets, bus service the rest of the way.

By bus: Greyhound and Vermont Transit service to Newport; host lodges generally pick up. From Montreal the Jay Express makes daily runs.

TO SEE AND DO   **Jay Peak Tram.** The 60-passenger tram operates daily during ski season and late June through Labor Day, again in foliage season, 10–4:30, $4 per adult, $3 under age 12, $14 per family. See the Jay Peak introduction for a description of the view. (We should note that in updating this edition of the book, these were the only prices in Vermont that came down!)

Hazen's Notch. From Montgomery Center an unpromising narrow road, Route 58, climbs steeply west, quickly changing to dirt. In winter it is open only the first 4 miles and is a popular ski touring spot (see *Cross-Country Skiing*). In summer it is a beautiful road, dappled with sunlight through the thick foliage. A fine picnic spot has been provided near the height of land, close to a clear roadside spring. An historic site plaque says the road through the high pass was built by General Moses Hazen in 1778–79, commissioned by George Washington himself. The road began in 1776, 60 miles to the southeast at Wells River on the Connecticut River and was intended to reach St. John's, Canada. It was abandoned on this spot in April 1779, when the news that British patrols might use it as an invasion route (it was meant to work the other way) reached the camp at Hazen's Notch.

Montgomery Village. The most picturesque village in this area, Montgomery is nestled among the hills that rise abruptly on all sides. It began as a lumbering center and was for a long time one of the world's major producers of timothy grass seed culture. Today it is best known for the quality wooden toys made in Montgomery Schoolhouse, a green box of a building that stands on the triangular green. The schoolhouse is open to the public; toys can be found in the ground floor shop (8 AM–4:30 PM, Monday–Friday). The town's historical collection is housed in an 1835 wooden church, open June–September at stated hours.

COVERED BRIDGES   The town of Montgomery boasts a grand total of six Town Lattice covered bridges, one right in Montgomery Village over Black Falls Creek, one south on Route 118, another nearby but three miles off Route 118 on West Hill on an abandoned side road over a waterfall, another northwest on Route 118 over the Trout River and two in Montgomery Center, both a mile west of Route 118 over the Trout River.

CANOEING   The 86-mile long Missisquoi River makes a complete loop around

Jay, passes briefly through Quebec and continues across Vermont to empty into Lake Champlain. The upper half of the River near Jay offers spring fastwater, and the lower reaches are gentle and broad, good spring and summer ground for beginners and those who enjoy traversing outstanding rural landscape. Guided canoe trips are available from **Vermont Voyageur Expeditions** (326-4789), Montgomery Center 95471.

GOLF   **The Enosburg Country Club** (933-8951) in Enosburg Falls maintains a 9-hole golf course on the north edge of the village. Greens fees are $14 on weekends, $8 weekdays.

FISHING   The Trout River deserves its name; brook trout can also be found in the Missisquoi.

Jay Peak (1-800-451-4449 or 988-4363). The ski area has stocked its sizable snow-making pond with trout and teamed up with the Orvis Company (see *Manchester*) to offer fly-fishing programs in warm weather months.

HIKING   The Long Trail terminates its 262-mile route at the Canadian border, 10 miles north of Jay Peak but the hike up Jay itself is what most hikers want. The most popular ascent is from Route 242, 1.2 miles east of the entrance to the ski area; the round trip hike takes 3 hours. For details to this and to the section of the trail between Hazen's Notch and Route 242, also for the final, fairly flat leg to the border, see the *Guide Book of the Long Trail*, published by the Green Mountain Club which maintains the Trail and four shelters in this area. Hiking weekends, designed for people who have little hiking experience, are offered by **Vermont Voyageur Expeditions;** they include guided treks along the Long Trail with dinner and lodging provided at local inns.

SWIMMING   A number of local inns have their own pools. The most popular local swimming hole is at Jay Four Corners, downstream from the Route 101 bridge.

Jay Swim and Racquetball Club (988-2880). Day membership is available to the pool, courts, and sauna at Inglenook Lodge, Jay.

CROSS-COUNTRY SKIING   **Hazen's Notch Ski Touring Center** (326-4708), Montgomery Center. Val Schadinger operates an outstanding touring center that offers meticulously tracked trails, some with fine views, also rentals, instruction, lighted practice slopes, telemark slopes, cafe, changing rooms, lodging, guided tours. A total of 53 km of marked and groomed trails are enjoyable well into March (elevation: 1,000–1,670 feet). $4.50 one day, $8.50 for two.

Vermont Voyageur Expeditions (326-4789), Montgomery Center. Rolf Anderson offers weekend and three-day midweek guided tours, including lodging and shuttle. The outfit also maintains a shop on Route 242 that serves as an informal touring center for the network of trails across the road in Alpine Haven. Rentals and instruction are available, along with the line of Goretex clothing that they produce. VVE also offers guided tours in the White Mountains and the Adirondacks.

The Snow Job (988-4464), Jay Village. Located next to the Jay Country Store, Mike Murphy rents as well as sells cross-country equipment, offers info about local touring trails.

Jay Peak Ski Touring Center (988-2611), Jay Peak. Some 25 km of trail are maintained at 1,800 to 2,915 feet, free use of the T-bar for telemark practice; rentals and instruction available.

Inn-to-Inn tours with Vermont Voyageur (326-4789), Route 242, Montgomery Center 05471. Sharon and Rolf Anderson are based at Hazen's Notch in winter months, helping Val with his outstanding touring center. But when the demand arises (actually they have a schedule worked out), you can join them on Monday to Friday, inn-to-inn tours that begin Monday evenings at the Black Lantern Inn (see *Lodging*) and take you through Hazen's Notch, down to Jay Village, and up and around Jay Peak (telemarkers are invited to ski down gradually from the summit). Two-, three-, and five-day tours are available, $325 for four nights. Backpacking tours, three-days, two nights, cost $150.

DOWNHILL SKIING **Jay Peak** (988-2611 or 800-451-4449; in Canada 800-654-5754). The original trails are stateside, on a shoulder of Jay Peak. Still considered some of the toughest runs in Vermont, they were carved 30 years ago by local residents. An enterprising Kiwanis group (it included the parish priest) convinced the Vermont legislature to reroute existing roads up over the high ridge from which Jay's access road rises—thus linking it to northwestern Vermont as well as to the Northeast Kingdom. They also imported an Austrian skimeister to create a true trail system and a ski school. Some 30,000 acres on and around Jay Peak were owned by Weyerhaeuser Corporation and in the early sixties, the mammoth lumber company—based in Tacoma, Washington—acquired the ski area, installing a Swiss-built tramway to Jay's peak, which it topped with a Sky Haus tram station, a building that emphasizes the crest of the summit, giving it a distinctly Matterhorn-like cap. Weyerhauser also built a large, sturdy Tyrolean-style base complex, which includes a 48-room hotel, and it laid out a winding access road to be lined with chalets.

And there it sat. A major mountain offering outstanding lifts, trails, and one of New England's largest vertical drops (2,100 feet). In 1978 it was acquired by the Montreal-based owners of St. Sauveur, a lucrative Laurentian ski area. The rebirth of Jay as a destination, rather than a Montreal day-tripping place, is relatively recent. But under a dynamic new operations manager, lifts have been improved and condominiums have been proliferating. This is a great place for spring skiing, but beware of weekends when it's mobbed by Montrealers.

Lifts: 60-passenger tram; double, triple, and quad chairlifts, one T-bar.

Trails and slopes: 34 trails, totaling more than 50 miles of skiing, spread over two peaks, connected by a ridgeline.

Vertical drop: 2,100 feet

Snowmaking: 75%

Facilities: Austria Haus and Tram Haus base lodges with cafeteria, pub, ski and rental shop. Sky Haus cafeteria at summit, nursery and day care facilities; no charge for childcare.

Ski school. U.S. and Canadian certified instructors, adult, and junior racing clinics. SKIWEE program for age 5 to 12-year-old group, Kinderschool for age 2–5.

Rates: $28 per adult; $52 adult, $34 junior for 2 days; $95 per adult, $70 junior for 5 days.

INNS AND LODGES   All rates quoted, unless otherwise noted are per person, double occupancy, winter MAP; all are substantially less in summer; and 10–20 percent less for ski weeks. A central reservations service is available by phoning 988-4363; 800-548-5300.

In summer, also check with the **Greater Newport Chamber of Commerce** (334-7782), Box 632, Newport 05855. Note that Jay Peak itself divides this area into two distinct regions: the Jay Village side, oriented to Canada and Newport, and the Montgomery Center side.

Hotel Jay (988-2611; from Montreal: 866-2284), Jay 05859. Located right at the lifts, an attractive lodge with 48 rooms, each with color TV and private bath, a pleasant, public dining room, a game room, outdoor pool, and use of a nearby indoor pool, also tennis courts and use of nearby racquet courts; off-season the adjacent base buildings are used as convention facilities; will pick up from Burlington Airport. $95 per person, MAP, winter including lift tickets, $399 per person for a five-day ski week, free for children under 12 in the same room (note that day care for children aged 2–12 is free for hotel guests, 9–9 daily). In summer it's $30 per person B&B (dinner is not served).

Inglenook Lodge (988-2880), Jay 05859. Located 1 mile from the lifts, this is a modern ski lodge with a sunken living room, circular fireplace, and cathedral ceiling. There are 15 rooms with private baths, 2 bunkrooms. Facilities include an indoor pool, racquet courts, game room, and public dining room and pub. $52 per person MAP.

Eagle Lodge (326-4518), Montgomery Center 05471. One of the few Vermont inns run by Vermonters—three generations of the Scott family—this 1800 farmhouse offers 16 rooms and pleasant reading and game-playing corners near woodstoves. Meals are served buffet-style in the sun-filled dining room that overlooks a backyard trout pond, good for ice skating in winter. Dinner is extra in summer, open to everyone by reservation; babysitting available on request, children are welcome. Rates: $26–35 per person MAP, $15 per person B&B in summer.

Black Lantern Inn (326-4507), Montgomery 05470. A white-pillared, brick inn built in 1803 as the Montgomery Village stage stop. The 11 bedrooms are small but nicely furnished, 9 with private baths. Downstairs there is a small reading-talking area warmed by a handsome soapstone stove, a cozy tap room and charming, seven-table dining room. Innkeepers Rita and Allan Kalsmith set an elegant table. This is not a place for children. Beyond the porch is the lovely village to explore and from the back there is a view of Hazen's Notch. Rates: from $50 per person MAP for suite with fireplace and Jacuzzi.

Jay Village Inn (988-2634), Jay Village 05859. Formerly the Jay Barn, now owned by the Angliss family. The public rooms—a large dining room and comfortable lounge with fireplace—are very pleasant. The 16 rooms upstairs are plain but comfortable, and there's an outdoor pool. $55 per person MAP in ski season, $50 per double room in summer.

Woodshed (988-4444), Jay 05859. Located on Route 242, 3 miles from Jay Peak, a warm ski-lodge atmosphere, good for both couples and families, home-cooked meals served in a candlelit dining room. $35 per person MAP.

The Inn on Trout River (326-4391), Montgomery Center 05471. Built grandly by a lumber baron, this attractive village house offers 10 guest rooms with private baths, one suite with a brass bed and fireplace. There are also hearths in the dining room, library, and foyer. The dining room is formal (see *Dining Out*), and there is also a large, informal pub. Innkeepers Terry and Ray Wheeler are breathing new life into this old place. There are touches like warm bath towels and robes for every guest. $55 per person MAP.

Slovakia Inn (326-4690), Montgomery Center 05471. Formerly the Thirsty Boot, this old village landmark is now thoroughly Czechoslovakian. Eva Arparova prides herself on the cleanliness of the ten rooms. Beds feature old country rugs instead of headboards. Rooms are all on the second floor above the large restaurant and pub. We were assured that an upstairs sitting room for guests was in the offing. $35-65 per room.

Snowline Lodge (988-2822), Jay 05859. At the base of the Jay Peak access road, these motel-style rooms are a real bargain, especially given their quality and the fireside pub and restaurant (specializing in steaks and burgers). $49 per double room weekdays, $52 weekends in winter.

Cedarwood (988-4459; in Canada: 800-338-8060), Jay 05859. This attractive modern lodge has been known under a number of names and is, once more, under new management. Sited on the fringe of Jay Village, it has 26 rooms, a trout pond, swimming pool and tennis courts, game rooms, a library, and a dining room with a covered bridge. In fall of 1987 rates were $34 for a double room; children under age 12 free in same room with parents.

North Troy Inn (988-2527), 15 Railroad Street, North Troy 05859. This handsome old home has cherry-paneled public rooms and nicely furnished guest rooms. Owners Russ and Julie Plourde are recent retirees from Westport, Massachusetts, where Russ's business was fixing cantankerous home machines like lawn mowers for grumpy owners. He finds it far more pleasant dealing with people who come to him on pleasure. $15 per person includes breakfast.

Rose Apple Acres Farm (988-4300), East Hill Road, North Troy 05859. There are four guest rooms in this comfortable house with its own 52 acres, good for cross-country skiing. Located 10 miles from Jay Peak, near a covered bridge on the Missisquoi River, good for fishing. $36 double includes breakfast.

CHALETS AND CONDOMINIUMS   Jay Peak Condominiums (800-451-4449 or 988-2611; in Canada: 800-654-5754). At this writing there are 87 condominiums at the base of Jay Peak, 52 of them slopeside. Rates are $239 per person double occupancy for two days and the price goes down (per person) as the number in the group rises; it's $129 if you are one of six. Rates include lifts. Five day packages are $489 per person (including lifts), double occupancy, $239 if you are one of six. Children aged 6 to 12 are $34, which also includes lifts. They are free under age 6 and eligible for free day care to boot. Much cheaper off-season but there tends to be on-going construction.

Alpine Haven (326-4567), Montgomery Center 05471. Eighty-two chalets, two to six bedrooms, fireplaces. Heated pool, tennis in summer, cross-country skiing on property in winter. From $125 per day.

Hazen's Notch Ski Touring Center Guest House (326-4708), Montgomery Center 05471. An old farmhouse offers a living room with woodburning stove, pleasant guest rooms and a family-style kitchen. Cross-country trails radiate from the doorstep; under the same ownership as the adjacent touring center. $132–150 per night for nine people, less by the week.

DINING OUT   Zack's on the Rocks (326-4500), Montgomery Center. "If this book takes off we plan to celebrate at Zack's. It's that kind of place" is what we wrote six years ago, and Zack (he was born "Zachadnykjon" in Blackstone, Massachusetts) tells us patrons keep asking if we've celebrated yet. The answer is no; we're still struggling; we hope this edition will be cause for the pilgrimage that Zack's patrons make from much of Northern New England and neighboring Canada. There is more than a touch of fantasy to this place. Zack frequently greets guests in purple garb. "I'm a frustrated actor" says Zack, who built this eyrie 27 years ago, using "all the things I like—marble, rocks . . ." The predominant color is purple in many shades, and it extends to the soapstone stove. Zack dislikes the word "gourmet," but the fact is that patrons come back often because the food is superb. Entrées run around $16 and might include chicken banana or roast duckling with fruit sauce. There's no set menu. Dinner is by reservation only, 6–9, and there is music in Gussie's "After the Rocks" with Tom at the keys Friday and Saturday. Closed Mondays. The adjacent fantasy cottage for two with a fireplace in the bedroom and living room runs $70–90 per night but is usually reserved on weekends a season in advance.

Slovakia Inn (326-4690), Montgomery Center. Authentic Czech, Hungarian, and Austrian dishes: goulash, Weiner Schnitzel, chicken paprika, and stuffed potato pancakes, $8.95–13.95. Live music Thursdays and weekends in the large pub adjoining the dining room.

Raymond's at The Inn on Trout River (326-4391), Main Street, Montgomery Center. The dining room in this handsome old house is fairly formal, and the menu includes dishes like veal Malagasy with green peppercorns ($15.95) and baked rainbow trout ($13.95). There is a glowing hearth and candlelight; a decent choice of wines.

Hotel Jay (988-2611) at Jay Peak. Dinner is served from 6–9 and reservations are a must in winter, the only time the restaurant serves dinner. The room itself is cheery and the menu features dishes like veal Gruyere and filet of salmon Florentine; entrées include escargots Dijonaise and coquille St. Jacques. Count on spending $20 per person plus 14% gratuity.

Black Lantern Inn (326-4507), Montgomery Village. "Continental Cuisine" is nicely served by candlelight in the low-beamed dining room of this old inn. Entrées run $13–15.

Jay Village Inn and Restaurant (988-2643), Jay Village. A large, friendly dining room specializing in steak au poivre. $9–15.

EATING OUT   **The Belfry** (326-4400), Route 242, Montgomery Center. Open 4 pm until late, nightly. An informal pub housed in an old schoolhouse with friendly wooden booths that patrons usually settle into for an hour or two. The soup is homemade and there is a blackboard menu with daily specials like pan-blackened fish, and grilled lamb chops for slightly more than the sliced London broil ($6.95) and BBQ chicken ($5.95), salads, burgers, and fried mushrooms.

The Pub at The Inn on Trout River (326-4391), Main Street, Montgomery Center. This inn offers informal as well as formal dining, with dishes like chicken in the basket, burgers, linguini, and shrimp à la chef.

SELECTIVE SHOPPING   Jay Country Store (988-4040), Jay Village. Open daily with food and wine basics, also a deli, ice cream, and a coffee shop, plus a number of gift items and a whole room—The Christmas Loft—filled year-round with Christmas trimmings, cards, and presents.

The Snow Job (988-4464), Jay Village. Adjacent to the Country Store, a year-round sports shop: clothing, sports equipment, also ski rentals.

Vermont Voyageur Equipment (326-4789), Montgomery Center, Route 242. A quality line of Goretex parkas, pants, over-mitts, and overboots is made in the VVE shop, sold primarily by commission and mail order but also available on the spot. This cross-country skier wouldn't be without the mitts and boots, which are waterproof and effective.

SPECIAL EVENTS   January, last Sunday: **Hazen's Notch ski race**

Mid-February: **Winter Festival**—varied events including a race from the summit of Jay Peak to Jay Village.

Mid-August: **Jay Day.**

Octoberfest: Art show, special events.

MEDICAL EMERGENCY   Montgomery (933-4000); **North Country Hospital & Medical Center** (334-7331), Prouty Drive, Newport.

Island Pond and Beyond

A sign in front of the city-sized, Island Pond depot reads, "Pioneer railroad planner John A. Poor's dream of an international railroad connecting Montreal, Canada, with the ice-free harbor of Portland, Maine, became a reality on July 18, 1854, when the first through trains met at this great halfway point on the Grand Trunk Railway."

During the late nineteenth century, on into the early twentieth, Island Pond hummed with the business of servicing frequent passenger and freight trains transporting logs and wood pulp. It was also a booming manufacturing center. No longer. Today it is a sleepy village on a two-mile by one-mile-long pond with a 20-acre island in its center.

For the traveler, Island Pond still looms large on the map because you must pass through it to get most places in Essex County. It also probably has more restaurants than the rest of the county put together, way stops to the empty, lake-pocked land to the northeast (there's good fishing around Averill) and to the hauntingly lonely stretch of the Connecticut between Guildhall and Canaan. Because this area is so sparsely populated, we have sketched our impressions of what lies along the obvious routes under *Scenic Drives.*

GUIDANCE **Island Pond Chamber of Commerce** (723-6222) Box 255, Island Pond 05846, maintains a seasonal information center near the depot, also a year-round information service.

North Country Chamber of Commerce (603-237-8939), Colebrook, New Hampshire 03476 also serves this upper reach of the Upper Valley, including the Canaan, Vermont, area.

TO SEE AND DO **Scenic Drive** From Island Pond head north on Route 114. The Canadian National Railway's "Grand Trunk" Line from Montreal to Portland, Maine, hugs the highway all the way to Norton. This was once Montreal's winter lifeline to Europe, since goods could not be shipped in or out of the frozen port of Montreal during the coldest months. The 16 miles between Island Pond and the border town of Norton is a lonely wilderness, much of the land owned by lumber and paper companies. About halfway to Norton, near the south end of long and slender Norton Pond, a gravel road to the left leads into the Bill Sladyk Wildlife Management Area, a vast undeveloped wilderness frequented by hunters, fishermen, and loggers. Just before reaching the tiny village of Norton (opposite slightly larger Stanhope, Quebec), the forest thins out and farmland re-appears. Norton is the site of the notorious "Earth People's Park," a 1960s-style, loosely-governed hippie commune that has survived but has dwindled from hundreds to perhaps two dozen residents. The road passes several farms, a school, and two stores, then swings abruptly eastward to avoid the imposing Canadian port-of-entry. Perhaps the most French Canadian town in Vermont, Norton is for practical purposes a satellite of nearby Coaticook, Quebec. Continuing eastward along the border, Route 114 re-enters the forest, passing a series of lakes, most of which are dotted with hunting and fishing camps. The largest of the lakes is Big Averill, which you can see by pulling off the road at Averill Village.

Shortly after passing Big Averill, you leave the St. Lawrence watershed and begin a rapid descent into the Connecticut River Valley. Halfway from Averill to Canaan, the road skirts the south shore of sizable Wallace Pond, almost entirely within the Province of Quebec.

Canaan, 14 miles east of Norton, is a pleasant pocket of civilization along the upper reaches of the Connecticut River. There are two villages. The first is Canaan itself, a village with a tiny green and a lovely little 1846 Greek Revival building that houses the Alice M. Ward Memorial Library. A left at the junction of Routes 114 and 102 will take you a couple of miles north to Beecher Falls, another port-of-entry and a factory village, dominated by a huge Ethan Allen Furniture Plant, the company's original factory site (to arrange a tour, phone 266-3355). Occasionally in winter you will hear Canaan mentioned on your weather report as the coldest spot in the United States for the day. (There is an official U.S. Weather observation station here.) Both villages hug the nascent Connecticut River, which originates in the Connecticut Lakes, a few miles to the northeast in extreme northern New Hampshire.

From Canaan you can choose driving southward on the more scenic Vermont side or the faster New Hampshire side of the river. On the Vermont side (Route 102), you travel through river bottom farmland reaching the bridge to Colebrook, New Hampshire in just under 10 miles.

Colebrook is the only big town on this northernmost end of the river. It is the terminus of Concord Trailways from Boston, and it has a golf course, a Catholic shrine, and several blocks of shops and stores, amenities that are not to be found on the Vermont side of the river.

On the Vermont side, Route 102 continues south through Lemington, past the impressively long Columbia covered bridge, to the tiny village of Bloomfield. Along the way the river valley alternately narrows and widens, and the road tunnels through forest, broken occasionally by farms, fields, and glimpses of impressive mountains. You pass the small town halls of Lemington, Brunswick, and Maidstone, but several of the townships, "gores" and "grants" are unorganized and have to be governed from Montpelier.

At Bloomfield (one store, with adjoining snack bar), the "Grand Trunk" to Portland crosses the road, bound for North Stratford, New Hampshire, on the other side of the river. Here in January 1933, the lowest Vermont temperature ever (− 50F) was recorded.

Continuing south another 16 miles to Guildhall, Route 102 winds among the bluffs and ox bows of the ever-widening river. Glimpses of the White Mountains become more frequent. The town of Brunswick was once the site of a thriving mineral spring resort. The buildings are all gone, but the springs still run pure. Nearly halfway to Guildhall, a gravel road to the right leads to beautiful and isolated Maidstone State Park.

Entering Guildhall, we are informed by a billboard-sized sign that the town was "discovered" in 1754, chartered in 1761, and settled in 1764, making it the oldest town in Northeastern Vermont (by contrast, Norton was not settled until 1860). We are further informed that the town has been the seat of Essex County since 1809. An attractive square green is flanked by a host of historically interesting buildings: a tiny courthouse, church, town hall ("the Guild Hall," 1798), and an ornate 1909 classical revival library, with stained-glass windows. An unassuming white clapboard house serves as a county lock-up. There is also an attractive inn (see *Lodging*).

Two miles downriver from Guildhall, a town road marked "Granby" runs west off Route 102, beginning as a paved road, but becoming gravel well before reaching the tiny hamlets of Granby and Gallup Mills, about 8 miles from 102. This is wild, wooded, and boggy country, good for spotting moose and bear. Lumber camps and sawmills once peppered this area and there was even a steam railway; now Granby, with neighboring Victory, are known chiefly for their late September weekend "Holiday in the Hills" (see St. Johnsbury *Special events*).

The road finally descends about 8 miles west of Granby to Route 114, joining it a couple miles north of East Burke (see St. Johnsbury). Take Route 114 12 miles north through rolling, mixed farm and forest land to its junction with Route 105, 2 miles west of Island Pond.

STATE PARKS AND FORESTS **Brighton State Park** (723-4360), Island Pond 05846. Located southeast of the village of Island Pond on the south shore of Island Pond and the west shore of Spectacle Pond. Facilities include 84 campsites of which 21 have lean-tos, also a swimming beach, dump station, snack bar, picnic area, bathhouse, rental boats, nature trail, and naturalist in residence.

Maidstone State Forest (676-3930), near Bloomfield. 5 miles south of Bloomfield on Route 102, then 5 miles on dirt road, this is a forest of maple, beech, and hemlock around a large lake with a beach, picnic area, rental boats, picnic shelter, hiking trails, and 83 campsites, including 37 lean-tos.

CANOEING   The various lakes in northern Essex county offer a variety of wilderness canoeing experiences. The Upper Connecticut River offers conditions ranging from whitewater to smooth-as-glass. Ask the Island Pond and Colebrook chambers of commerce about conditions and rental possibilities.

FISHING   **Quimby Country** (see *Lodging*) is a self-contained resort that includes 70-acre Forest Lake and is a quarter mile from 1,200-acre Big Averill, both lonely and remote but good for trout and salmon; rowboats can also be rented here by the day. Boats are also available at both Brighton and Maidstone state parks. Check the pamphlet "Vermont Guide to Fishing" for details about which fish are available where. Check the state highway map for local access points. The Connecticut Lakes in adjacent extreme northern New Hampshire offer world class trout fishing.

GOLF   There are no golf courses in Essex County. Closest in New Hampshire are the **Colebrook Country Club** (9 holes), **The Balsams** in Dixville Notch (18 holes, magnificent site), and the **Waumbec Country Club** in Jefferson (18 holes).

HIKING   **Bluff Mountain** (elevation 2,380 feet) looms over Island Pond to the north. It is a popular climb, with spectacular views. The trail starts from Route 114, north of the village. Inquire locally for directions.

Monadnock Mountain (elevation 3,140 feet) in Lemington, towers over the Connecticut River and Colebrook on the opposite shore. A trail runs west, beginning as a driveway off Route 102 near the bridge to Colebrook. An abandoned fire tower crowns the summit. Inquire at one of the houses near the trail head about the exact location of the trail.

Bill Sladyk Wildlife Management Area, off Route 114, south of Norton Pond: 9,500 forested acres, also accessible via a gravel road past Holland Pond from Holland Village. A detailed map is available from the Fish & Game Department in Montpelier.

SWIMMING   There are state facilities at Island Pond (large beach) and at Maidstone Lake (small beach); nominal entrance fee charged.

SKIING   There are apparently no developed cross-country centers in northern Essex County. With all the wild, open land, one might find having to pay to ski somewhat appalling. There is a vast network of wilderness snowmobile trails that are marked by snowmobile clubs and open to skiers.

LODGING   **Quimby Country** (822-5533), Averill 05901. About as north (less than 3 miles from Canada) and as east (10 miles from New Hampshire) as you can get in the Kingdom. This unique resort is a nineteenth-century lodge and grouping of 20 cabins overlooking 70-acre Forest Lake. It is also a quarter mile from 1,200-acre Big Averill, 4 miles from 400-acre Little Averill, and surrounded by its own woodland, in turn surrounded by forest owned by paper companies. Begun as a fishing lodge, Quimby Country evolved into a family-oriented resort under the proprietorship of Hortense Quimby, evoking a large following in the process. Fearful that the place might change when it came up for sale on Miss Quimby's death, a number of regular guests formed a corporation and bought it. We've had conflicting reports about its present condition from some people who have been going there for years. When the place is in full operation, mid-July to mid-September, the rates are $205 a day for a family of four with all three meals, less in early July and late September.

    Guildhall Inn and Restaurant (676-3720), Box 129, Guildhall 05905. Built in the early 1800s and recently restored, this is a large, elegant old farmhouse with four rooms upstairs (shared bath), furnished with an assortment of country antiques. The hosts are Annette Colson and her daughter Linda Trombley and the site is on Route 102, just south of the Guildhall town green. $30 single, $40 double, EP.

    Monadnock Bed & Breakfast (603-237-8216), One Monadnock Street, Colebrook, New Hampshire 03576. Barbara and Wendell Woodward welcome you to their large, bungalow-style house just across the bridge from Lemington. Built around the turn of the century by a local lumber baron, the house contains some magnificent woodwork. More recently it was used as a group boarding house. The upstairs is reserved for guests and contains four bedrooms, a shared bath, and kitchenette (for early risers). Rates are $25, $35 double.

    Lakefront Motel (723-6507), Cross Street, Island Pond 05846. A tidy new upscale, two-story motel right in the center of the village with sweeping views of Island Pond, which laps the edge of the property. There is no restaurant (there are enough within walking distance). A bar-lounge with fireplace, featuring low-key entertainment, is in a separate building. Four of the 20 units have built-in kitchenettes. A small dock is reserved for motel guests and just across a vacant lot is an extensive public recreation complex, including tennis courts, beach, picnic area, boat launch, lighted ice hockey rink and children's playground. Marcel and Anita Gervais charge $42 double, $10 more for efficiency units, and $5 for each additional person.

DINING OUT   Buck and Doe (723-4712), Island Pond. Open for lunch and dinner, 7 days a week. This is a chef-owned, very popular restaurant across from the old depot. The menu is huge, and so are the portions. Specialties include a choice of fresh, broiled fish with lemon butter, breaded veal cutlet, char-broiled sirloin and roast Long Island duckling. The dessert menu includes hot apple goody with ice cream. Prices range at lunch (for a complete meal) from $7.50–8.95 and, at dinner from $13.50–16.50. The restaurant operates a new storefront take-out place next door for people in a hurry.

Guildhall Inn and Restaurant (676-3720), Guildhall. Open to the public only on weekends. Dinner in this beautiful Victorian farmhouse usually includes two entrées, $8.95–14.95. Also open for breakfast and lunch, reservations strongly recommended.

Sutton Place Restaurant (603-237-8842), 152 Main Street, Colebrook, New Hampshire. Open for lunch Tuesday–Saturday and dinner every night. Don and Carmela Kelsea have created an intimate dining place in the front parlors of a Queen Anne-style house in the center of town. Dinner entrées include steak, chicken and seafood, ranging from $8.95–15.95.

Candlelight Restaurant (266-8119), Beecher Falls. A full-service restaurant in newly rebuilt, overdecorated but comfortable quarters on the edge of the Connecticut River. Dinner entrées range from $8.95–14.95.

EATING OUT   Common Sense (723-9708), Island Pond. Open 24 hours, a place for soups, salads, quiche, and homemade whole wheat bread. This pleasant place is run by "the Church," a group of some 300 born-again Christians who migrated to town from Tennessee.

Northland Restaurant and Lounge (266-9947), Canaan. A large, clean, comfortable place offering three squares, with dinner entrées in the $5–10 range. The spacious adjoining bar-lounge-dance floor hosts rock and country rock bands each Saturday evening.

MEDICAL EMERGENCY   Island Pond: 723-6262.

Index

Lodging Index

Books About New England

Explorer's Guides from the Countryman Press

Explorer's Guides are *the* alternative to the mass market guides with their homogenized listings. Explorer's Guides focus on independently-owned inns, motels and restaurants, as well as on family and cultural activities reflecting the character and unique qualities of the area.

Maine: An Explorer's Guide, Third Edition by Christina Tree and Mimi Steadman, $13.95

The Other Massachusetts; Beyond Boston and Cape Cod: An Explorer's Guide by Christina Tree, $12.95

Vermont: An Explorer's Guide, Third Edition, by Christina Tree and Peter S. Jennison, $14.95

Other Books from The Countryman Press

Vermont on $500 a Day (More or Less), by Peter S. Jennison, $10.00

New England's Special Places: A Daytripper's Guide, by Michael A. Schuman, $10.95

The Vermont Puzzle Book, Learn About Vermont the Fun Way, by Donna L. Pappe, Virginia Mueller and Carol Karle, $4.95

Vermonters, photographs by Jon Gilbert Fox, text by Donald L. Tinney, $9.95

Lake Champlain: Key to Liberty, by Ralph Nading Hill, $19.95

The Blue Cat of Castletown, A Classic Vermont Children's Tale by Catherine Cate Coblentz, $7.95

Classic Regional Humor Books by Keith Jennison:

    The Maine Idea, $7.95

    Remember Maine, $7.95

    Vermont is Where You Find It, $7.95

    "Yup...Nope" & Other Vermont Dialogues, $7.95

Home Ground: Living in the Country, by Gladys Ogden Dimock, $9.95 (paper), $14.95 (cloth)

The Story of the Shakers, by Flo Morse, $6.95

Sound Friendships, The Story of Willa and Her Hearing Ear Dog, by Elizabeth Yates, $7.95 (paper), $12.95 (cloth)

Guidebooks from Backcountry Publications

Written for people of all ages and experience, these quality softbound books feature detailed trail or tour directions, notes on points of interest, maps and photographs.

50 Hikes in Vermont, revised by the Green Mountain Club, $8.95

50 Hikes in the White Mountains, 3rd Edition, by Dan Doan, $9.95

50 Hikes in Maine, by John Gibson, $8.95

50 Hikes in Massachusetts, by John Brady and Brian White, $9.95

50 Hikes in Connecticut, by Gerry and Sue Hardy, $8.95

Walks and Rambles in Rhode Island: A Guide to the Natural and Historic Wonders of the Ocean State, by Ken Weber, $8.95

Walks and Rambles in Westchester and Fairfield Counties; A Nature Lover's Guide to Thirty Parks and Sanctuaries, by Katherine S. Anderson, $7.95

25 Bicycle Tours in Vermont, by John Freiden, $8.95

25 Bicycle Tours in New Hampshire, by Tom and Sue Heavey, $6.95

25 Bicycle Tours in Maine, by Howard Stone, $8.95

Canoe Camping Vermont and New Hampshire Rivers, 2nd Edition, by Roioli Schweiker, $6.95

Canoeing Massachusetts, Rhode Island, and Connecticut, by Ken Weber, $7.95

We also publish books about bicycling, walking, hiking, canoeing, camping, and ski touring in New York State, Pennsylvania, Maryland, Delaware, West Virginia and Virginia. Please write for our catalog.

Our titles are available in bookshops and in many sporting goods stores, or they may be ordered directly from the publisher. Please add $2.00 per order for shipping and handling. For complete descriptions of our books, write The Countryman Press, PO Box 175, Woodstock VT 05091